W9-AEW-448

CAMBRIDGE STUDIES IN EARLY MODERN HISTORY

Editors

J. H. ELLIOTT   H. G. KOENIGSBERGER

Rouen during the Wars of Religion

CAMBRIDGE STUDIES IN EARLY MODERN HISTORY

Edited by Professor J. H. Elliott, The Institute for Advanced Study, Princeton, and Professor H. G. Koenigsberger, King's College, London

The idea of an 'early modern' period of European history from the fifteenth to the late eighteenth century is now widely accepted among historians. The purpose of the Cambridge Studies in Early Modern History is to publish monographs and studies which will illuminate the character of the period as a whole, and in particular focus attention on a dominant theme within it, the interplay of continuity and change as they are represented by the continuity of medieval ideas, political and social organization, and by the impact of new ideas, new methods and new demands on the traditional structures.

The Old World and the New, 1492–1650
J. H. ELLIOTT

French Finances 1770–1795: From Business to Bureaucracy
J. F. BOSHER

The Army of Flanders and the Spanish Road, 1567–1659: The Logistics of Spanish Victory and Defeat in the Low Countries Wars
GEOFFREY PARKER

Chronicle into History: An Essay on the Interpretation of History in Florentine Fourteenth-Century Chronicles
LOUIS GREEN

France and the Estates General of 1614
J. MICHAEL HAYDEN

Gunpowder and Galleys: Changing Technology and Mediterranean Warfare at Sea in the Sixteenth Century
JOHN FRANCIS GUILMARTIN JR

Reform and Revolution in Mainz 1743–1803
T. C. W. BLANNING

The State, War and Peace: Spanish Political Thought in the Renaissance 1516–1559
J. A. FERNÁNDEZ-SANTAMARIA

Calvinist Preaching and Iconoclasm in the Netherlands 1544–1569
PHYLLIS MACK CREW

Altopascio: A Study in Tuscan Rural Society 1587–1784
FRANK MCARDLE

The Kingdom of Valencia in the Seventeenth Century
JAMES CASEY

Filippo Strozzi and the Medici: Favor and Finance in Sixteenth-Century Florence and Rome
MELISSA MERIAM BULLARD

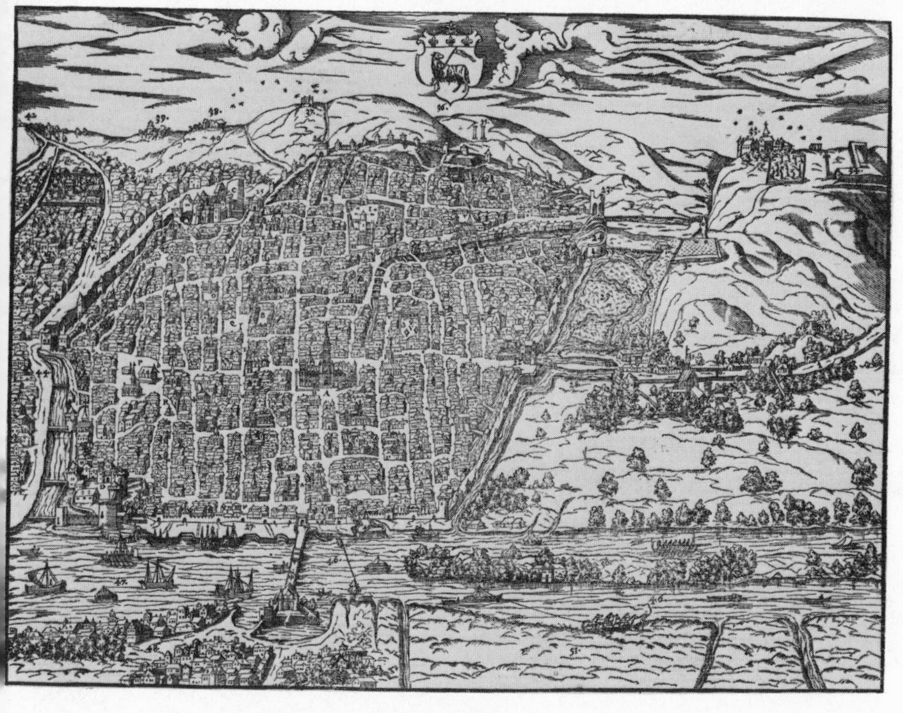

View of Rouen

Source: Sebastian Munster, *Cosmographie universelle*, rev. ed. aug. by François de Belleforest (Paris, 1575).

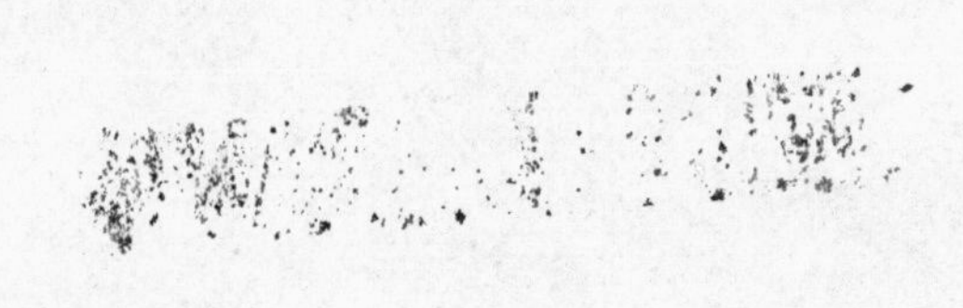

Rouen during the Wars of Religion

PHILIP BENEDICT

Assistant Professor of History
Brown University
Providence, Rhode Island

CAMBRIDGE UNIVERSITY PRESS

Cambridge
London New York New Rochelle
Melbourne Sydney

Published by the Press Syndicate of the University of Cambridge
The Pitt Building, Trumpington Street, Cambridge CB2 1RP
32 East 57th Street, New York, NY 10022, USA
296 Beaconsfield Parade, Middle Park, Melbourne 3206, Australia

First published 1981

Printed in Great Britain at the University Press, Cambridge

British Library Cataloguing in Publication Data

Benedict, Philip
Rouen during the Wars of Religion. – (Cambridge studies in early modern history).
1. Rouen – History
2. France – History – Wars of the Huguenots, 1562–1598
I. Title II. Series
944'.25 DC801.R86 79-41364

ISBN 0 521 22818 2

Contents

Illustrations

PLATES

MAPS

FIGURES

Tables

Preface

The revolution in French historiography that has occurred over the past two generations has affected our understanding of one period of French history curiously little, that of the Wars of Religion. Once, when political history was king, the later sixteenth century's wealth of dramatic events and intriguing personalities made it among the most studied eras of France's past. More recently, however, as narrative accounts of high politics have given way in popularity to detailed local studies seeking to reconstruct basic conditions of existence, nearly all French historians of *l'époque moderne* (the years from ca. 1500 to 1789) have shifted the focus of their attention to the seventeenth and eighteenth centuries. Few tumultuous events interfere with the study of persisting *structures* in these centuries, and the massive, serial source materials of the kind necessary for social history are far more abundant than they are for the sixteenth century. Over these same years, English and American historical writing about the Wars of Religion has hardly been affected at all by the newer currents stirring within the historical profession. Our view of these years of civil war has not, of course, remained entirely static since the classic histories of Lucien Romier and Henri-Jean Mariéjol were written over fifty years ago. The often brilliant work of such recent scholars as Emmanuel Le Roy Ladurie, Natalie Zemon Davis, Richard Gascon, and Janine Estèbe has opened up new vistas, and it is possible now to see the Wars of Religion not merely as the struggles for influence of rival clans of great noblemen, but a profound social and cultural crisis affecting the entire society. Still, measured against the changes in our understanding of the last two centuries of the Ancien Régime, we continue to know relatively little about the civil wars as they involved and affected the people of France. At a time when the general thrust of historical scholarship has been to understand the repercussions of national political events within the local community and to rehabilitate the role of the ordinary inhabitants of a country as actors, not merely passive spectators, in the making of their own history, the available literature about the Wars of Religion remains characterized by an overwhelming – and distorting – concern with international diplomacy and court politics. Many fine studies have chronicled the actions of the leading political figures of the day, probed the degree of foreign involvement in the events within France, and analyzed the political ideas of the time. Of few if any periods of French history do we have such a poor view of how matters looked from the perspective of a provincial town.

This book attempts to help rectify this imbalance. One overriding concern guided the research which went into its making: to re-create and to understand, in so far as the often frustratingly sparse documentation permitted, the full experience of a major provincial capital's inhabitants over nearly forty years of conflict. The story stretches from the first, highly agitated decade of the Religious Wars, when Rouen was temporarily secured by the Protestants in 1562 and serious incidents of violence occurred almost yearly thereafter, through a period of relative calm in the later 1570s and early 1580s, to the ultimate crisis, that of the Catholic League, when it was the turn of Catholic militants to revolt against the crown and seize control of the city. Why did the growth of Protestantism lead to such bitter confessional violence? How can the pattern of that violence be explained? To what extent did the conflicts also reflect social or economic tensions? Did Catholicism respond to the Protestant challenge with measures of internal reform and revitalization as well as violence? And what was the impact of over three decades of intermittent warfare on the city's economy? Did the economic disruption which ensued in turn affect political developments? These were the major questions my research sought to answer.

As the answers to these questions began to emerge, and as this study passed through its successive metamorphoses from its first drafts as a Princeton University doctoral dissertation to the version presented here, a dialectical process which seemed to be at work in the city's history also imposed itself more and more clearly on my attention. This was the reciprocal interplay between political events and religious *mentalités*.

Events and *mentalités* – even to mention them together in one sentence may seem surprising to those familiar with recent French historiography. The history of *mentalités*, usually approached in a relatively static fashion that owes a good deal to the influence of structuralism, represents the very newest of the *nouvelles vagues* that have come rolling out of the Ecole Pratique des Hautes Etudes for over thirty years now, transforming in the process our entire view of the scope of history. *Histoire événementielle* – the traditional narrative of political events – has meanwhile been a genre scorned by the French, who tend to regard it as something best left to foreigners and other fossils of an earlier epoch in the evolution of historical study. Rarely have these two sorts of history been combined.[1]

[1] Several recent articles have intimated, even proclaimed, a certain 'return of the event' in French historiography (e.g. *Communications*, 18 (1972), special number 'L'événement'; B. Barret-Kriegel,

I do not believe that events and structures can be so radically divided. In its day, the disdain shown by the partisans of 'a new form of history' toward mere events may have been a necessary weapon in the struggle to unseat a historical establishment perhaps more unrepentantly Rankean in the breadth (or, rather, narrowness) of its preoccupations than any other in Europe. Now that the insurgent partisans dominate the scene as completely as ever did their predecessors, this anti-*événementielle* ideology has surely outlived its utility. Political events indicate cleavages and solidarities within a given society; they show what values were considered sufficiently important to be worth struggling for; and they reveal the social grievances which moved people to action. For all of these reasons, their study can help illuminate a society's social structure, economic conditions, and widely shared value systems. At the same time, *l'histoire sérielle* – quantitative history based on long series of comparable data studied over time – often leads back to the *événementiel*, for it can point up certain events as crucial turning points in the demographic, economic, or religious evolution of a community. Rather than being artificially separated, events and structures are often best studied together if each is to be properly understood. This is especially true if one is examining agitated periods of conflict over fundamental values, precisely the sorts of periods (viz., the French Revolution) that Annales-school historiography has been the least successful in illuminating.

It is the basic contention of this book that the rapid religious and political changes of the later sixteenth century simply cannot be properly grasped unless events and *mentalités* are juxtaposed. The conflicts which followed Protestantism's sudden development into a mass movement around 1560 were motivated above all by two radically hostile sets of religious beliefs and attitudes which must be understood before the violence can be explained. These attitudes subsequently were themselves modified under the impact of political events, so that by the aftermath of the most traumatic episode of all in the early years of the Religious Wars, the St Bartholomew's Day Massacre of 1572, Protestantism – the minority religion – found itself so radically transformed in both size and political stance that the conditions which had produced the violence were no longer present. Tranquility returned to the city until exogenous political developments, notably the emergence of the Protestant Henry of Navarre as heir-apparent to the throne, sparked the final crisis, that of the League. The city's Catholics responded not only with militant political action but also with the first major surge toward a renewal of Roman religious life seen

'Histoire politique, ou l'histoire, science des effets', *Annales: E.S.C.*, XXVIII (1973), pp. 1437–62). Few concrete demonstrations of this trend have appeared as yet, although Michel Vovelle's *Religion et révolution: la déchristianisation de l'an II* (Paris, 1976) is a welcome recent step in this direction.

in Rouen over the entire period. Once again, the force of political events produced a change in the religious attitudes.

If this study began as a regional contribution to the understanding of the Wars of Religion, the interplay of religious attitudes and political events which it revealed thus also made it a case study in the process of religious change – to be specific, a study of how the emergence of a new religion touched off a cascade of internal conflicts and attitudinal changes that only ceased when a new equilibrium was finally reached again over thirty years later.

No genre has proliferated within French historiography more rapidly in recent years than the local study, and this proliferation has revealed both the strengths and the potential dangers of this mode of enquiry. Certain of the advantages of focussing on one community are obvious. It is often only by restricting the geographic scope of an investigation that the historian can hope to master the source material available about a given period or problem. It is also only by examining and comparing all of the material concerning a specific community – tax rolls, lists of membership in different churches or political parties, narrative sources, etc. – that one can begin to see interrelationships between different aspects of social reality – between social structure, ideological choice, and political action, for example. The multiplication of local studies has underscored the attention which must be paid to the specific configuration of economic circumstances, social relationships, and past historical experiences shaping events in any given community. By redirecting attention away from what has often been an excessive concentration on events in Paris, it has also reminded us once again of the great diversity of that remarkably heterogeneous collection of provinces and regions that was, and still is, France. At the same time, however, any local study runs the risk of leaving certain crucial questions unanswered simply because the relevant sources do not exist to answer those questions for the community under examination. Amid the recent multiplication of local studies, a disturbing tendency to treat each area as *sui generis* has also appeared. Purely local conditions are at times cited to explain developments that were in fact widespread, while broader regional or nationwide trends tend to become obscured beneath the proliferation of individual cases. On occasion the demands of research compel the historian to cast his or her net wider than the specific community under study in order to choose among several possible explanatory hypotheses suggested by the local data, yet local historians are often loath to venture into that *terra incognita*, the next town's archives.

In writing this book I have tried to keep the strengths and weaknesses of the local study in mind and to compensate for the weaknesses whenever possible. I have not felt that because I was studying Rouen I was therefore compelled to limit my vision strictly to local sources. I have used pamphlets, printed sources, and local records from other towns to clarify problems that could not be resolved solely on the basis of materials from Rouen. This has been done, however, only where the attitudes or experiences reflected in these documents seemed to be the product of conditions similar to those which prevailed in the Norman capital. I have also tried not to lose sight of the need for larger comparisons and generalizations. Where appropriate in the body of the text I have tried to point out contrasts and similarities between Rouen's experience and that of other French towns. The conclusion addresses directly the question which inevitably arises at the end of any local study: How typical was this community which has just been examined? Explicit comparisons with other regions are made here in an effort to indicate what this study of one city's history might contribute to a larger reinterpretation of the Wars of Religion.

Finally, a point of organization deserves mention. Jack P. Greene has recently commented that one of the major challenges facing today's partisans of a broader, more social scientific form of history is that of devising a literary form capable of presenting the results of complex and often arcane quantitative techniques in a fashion that appeals to a wide audience.[1] That challenge was particularly acute in this study. Because it analyzes an unfolding process of change, the basic structure of the book necessarily had to be chronological, yet much of the research which went into its making involved the quantitative exploitation of such sources as parish registers, trade statistics, and the membership rolls of churches and confraternities. Serial data normally demand a form of presentation that is profoundly anti-chronological: a lengthy preamble on the source materials and techniques used is necessary to give the reader an opportunity to assess the reliability of the findings, and these are best presented in the form of long curves stretching over many years so that their patterns of rise and fall may emerge most clearly. I have tried to reconcile these conflicting rhetorical imperatives in the following manner. The analytical sections on such topics as the social composition of the rival confessions, the numerical evolution of Protestantism, or the changes in popular Catholic religious life over the course of the period have been inserted at those points in the narrative which seemed most appropriate. In order not to overburden the narrative unnecessarily with material that was not always relevant to the theme of the interplay of religion and politics, I have chosen to eliminate from the pages which follow all of the technical discussion of the material I gathered concerning Rouen's economic and demographic evolution. Only the major findings on these questions have been included

[1] Jack P. Greene, 'The "New History": From Top to Bottom', *The New York Times*, Jan. 8, 1975, p. 37.

here, and then only when they help illuminate the political or religious climate. Fuller examinations of Rouen's demography and its foreign trade have been or will be published elsewhere.[1] The reader who is particularly interested in these subjects, or who simply wishes to see how the findings cited here were obtained and to verify their reliability, would be well advised to consult these articles directly. Appendixes 3 and 4 present in summary fashion two of the better indicators of the general movement of the city's economy: the level of baptisms and the fluctuations in house rents. These are alluded to at appropriate points in the text. Whether or not these decisions have produced a readable text is, of course, for the reader to judge.

I have accumulated many debts in the course of preparing this study. Only others who have also arrived on foreign shores, badly disoriented and not a little ill at ease, can fully understand the gratitude one feels to those who help cushion the initial shock of working in alien archives. I am especially grateful to Denis Richet, who welcomed me to his seminar at the Ecole Pratique des Hautes Etudes and counselled me about my research in France, and to Jean-Pierre Bardet, who helped guide me through the archives in Rouen and generously shared with me many ideas and some of the material he had gathered in his own research. I also realize now how unusual was the warm atmosphere of mutual assistance which prevailed at the Archives Départementales de la Seine-Maritime. I must thank collectively all those who would gather for lunch at the Champlain, and must single out for individual mention Jonathan Dewald and David Nicholls, both of whom were kind enough to pass along information from their notes. Outside Rouen, Natalie Zemon Davis and Pierre Jeannin also graciously communicated unpublished material to me. Finally, I am indebted to the many archivists and librarians for their unfailing help in the course of my research.

Others provided assistance as I wrote. By far my greatest debts here are to my teachers and advisors at Princeton, Theodore K. Rabb and Lawrence Stone. The advice, direction, and critical comment which they provided greatly improved the pages which follow, but my debt to them goes beyond the specific assistance they provided with this project. As teachers, they always encouraged me to think critically and imaginatively about historical problems. To the extent that this book succeeds in doing so, much of the credit surely goes to them, and to my undergraduate mentor, H. G. Koenigsberger. Jean-Pierre Bardet, Jonathan Dewald, Myron

[1] Philip Benedict, 'Catholics and Huguenots in Sixteenth-Century Rouen: The Demographic Effects of the Religious Wars', *French Historical Studies*, IX (1975), pp. 209–34; 'Rouen's Foreign Trade during the Era of the Religious Wars (1560–1600)', forthcoming in *The Journal of European Economic History*.

Gutmann, Robert Harding, Robert Kingdon, Herbert Rowen, and Madeline Zilfi also read and commented on some or all of the text at one stage or another in its maturation. An early draft of Chapter 8 was presented at the Ecole Pratique and to the Shelby Cullom Davis Center for Historical Studies at Princeton. I am grateful to all these readers and listeners for suggestions which helped clarify my thinking and my prose. Chapter 8 was first published in a somewhat different form as 'The Catholic Response to Protestantism: Church Activity and Popular Piety in Rouen, 1560–1600', James Obelkevich, ed., *Religion and the People, 800–1700* (Chapel Hill, N.C., 1979). I would like to thank the University of North Carolina Press for permission to reprint large parts of that article.

Material support for the making of this book came from several sources. Much of the archival work was carried out under a grant from the Fulbright Foundation, while Princeton's Shelby Cullom Davis Post-doctoral Fellowship and an award from the American Council of Learned Societies provided me with a year off from teaching duties during which I was able to write the final draft.

Finally, from start to finish my wife provided the most important assistance of all. She helped me with some of the archival research, clarified any statistical problems I encountered, and patiently edited and re-edited each successive version of the manuscript. These reasons, and others, explain why the book is dedicated to her.

PHILIP BENEDICT

Providence, R.I.
January 1979

Abbreviations

A.C.	Archives Communales
A.C.R.	Archives Communales de Rouen
A.D.	Archives Départementales
A.D.S.M.	Archives Départementales de la Seine-Maritime (Rouen)
A.N.	Archives Nationales (Paris)
Annales: E.S.C.	*Annales: Economies, Sociétés, Civilisations*
B.M.R.	Bibliothèque Municipale de Rouen
B.N.	Bibliothèque Nationale (Paris)
B.S.H.P.F.	*Bulletin de la Société de l'Histoire du Protestantisme Français*
Bull. Soc. Emul. S-I.	*Bulletin de la Société Libre d'Emulation du Commerce et de l'Industrie de la Seine-Inférieure*
Cal. S.P. For.	*Calendar of State Papers, Foreign Series, of the Reign of Elizabeth*, ed. Joseph Stevenson et al. (London, 1863–1950)
Hist. eccl.	*Histoire ecclésiastique des églises réformées au royaume de France*, ed. G. Baum, E. Cunitz, and R. Reuss (Paris, 1883–89)
Inv/Sommaire	*Inventaire-Sommaire des Archives Communales antérieures à 1790*. Vol. 1 *Délibérations*, ed. Charles de Robillard de Beaurepaire (Rouen, 1887)
L.C.M.	*Lettres de Catherine de Médicis*, ed. Hector de la Ferrière and Baguenault de Puchesse (Paris, 1880–99)
Michaud and Poujoulat	J.-F. Michaud and J.-J.-F. Poujoulat, eds. *Nouvelle collection des mémoires sur l'histoire de France* (Paris, 1836–54)
Petitot	C.-B. Petitot, ed. *Collection complète des mémoires relatifs à l'histoire de France* (Paris, 1818–29)
R.P.	Registre Paroissial

Ruiz	Archivo Simon Ruiz, Archivo Histórico Provincial y Universitario de Valladolid
S.P.Dom.	Public Record Office (London), State Papers Domestic

1

Prologue: a provincial metropolis in the sixteenth century

Veu que je suis le chef d'une duché qui passe
  Un royaume en valeur tant soit il spatieux:
  Veu qu'un grand Archevesque, un senat studieux
  Equitable et sçavant chez moy prennent leur place:

Veu qu'en trafic mon port, tout autre port surpasse:
  Veu qu'en rares esprits, grands et ingenieux,
  En subtils artisans, en guerriers furieux,
  Le renom des citez, les plus braves j'efface.

Veu qu'en foires, marchez, privileges et droits
  Franchises, libertés, en pollices et loys
  A ma gloire, une gloire immortelle est acquise.

Orguilleuse il me faut desormais devenir
  Et le rang qui m'est deu superbement tenir:
  Non! car je n'aurois plus l'aigneau pour ma devise.

'Sonnet de la ville de Rouen',
L'Histoire et Cronique de Normendie
(Rouen, 1578)

'Ritual makes explicit the social structure', E. R. Leach has written.[1] If this is so, then there is no better introduction to sixteenth-century Rouen than that which the city itself provided King Henry II when it greeted him in 1550 with a royal entry.

[1] E. R. Leach, *Political Systems of Highland Burma: A Study of Kachin Social Structure* (Boston, 1965), p. 15.

Prologue

The ceremony was a splendid one. Naked bands of Tupinamba Indians, brought from Brazil by the Norman mariners who regularly traded there, fought a mock combat on a meadow near the Seine. Neptune emerged from the river to confess to the king that, as virtue disarms Mars, so he was trembling in awe before him. Chariots 'embellished with moldings, friezes, cornices, metopes, triglyphs, consoles, and other elements of architecture' rolled past bearing tableaux vivants lauding the monarch for his attachment to the defense of the faith and assuring him of his immortal renown. Elephants, presumably of papier-mâché but in any case 'so close to nature...that those who had seen live ones in Africa would have judged them real', shambled along in front of 'captives' who represented the English soldiers recently defeated in the Boulonnais. Finally, amid the sustained paeans of praise for the vigorous and martial new king's military prowess, the organizers of the entry, who had recently seen several of their *échevins* imprisoned for failing to collect royal war taxes with sufficient alacrity, also inserted a few reminders that a monarch could obtain glory by fostering the prosperity of his subjects as well as by winning battles.[1]

Such a ceremony was a way for Rouen to show off its wealth and importance. A leading expert has called the joyous entry of 1550 the most elaborate of all French Renaissance entries,[2] and only an extremely large and prosperous town could have staged such a show. Yet the king might have expected no less from Rouen, for it was one of his largest cities and the first half of the sixteenth century had been one of its most splendid periods. At once the administrative capital of Normandy, the seat of one of the largest archbishoprics in France, and a major center of both manufacturing and trade, Rouen's importance was, in fact, such that contemporaries regularly called it the second city of the kingdom.[3] Francis I had even gone farther and told Charles V that Rouen was his largest city – adding that Paris was more than a city, it was a province.[4] Despite Lyon's spectacular growth over the first half of the sixteenth century, Rouen's claim

[1] *Cest la deduction du sumptueux ordre plaisantz spectacles et magnifiques theatres dressés et exhibés par les citoiens de Rouen...à la sacrée Majesté du Treschristian Roy de France Henry second*...(Rouen, 1551), now reprinted in a facsimile edition with an excellent introduction by Margaret M. McGowan, *L'entrée de Henry II à Rouen 1550* (Amsterdam, n.d.).

[2] Jean Chartrou, *Les entrées solennelles et triomphales à la Renaissance, 1484–1551* (Paris, 1928), p. 415.

[3] To cite just a few cases where Rouen is called the second city of the kingdom, all by authors who were not Normans and thus cannot be accused of chauvinism: M. N. Tommaseo, ed., *Relations des ambassadeurs vénitiens sur les affaires de France au XVIe siècle* (Paris, 1838), Vol. 1, p. 45; A. Chamberland, ed., 'Le commerce d'importation en France au milieu du XVIe siècle d'après un manuscrit de la Bibliothèque Nationale', *Revue de Géographie*, XXXI (1892), p. 293; François de Scépeaux, Sire de Vielleville, *Mémoires*, Michaud and Poujolat, ser. 1, Vol. 9, p. 342; *Hist. eccl.*, Vol. 2, p. 763.

[4] This story is still repeated today in Rouen, and it is through this oral tradition that I became aware of it. *See also* Fernand Braudel and Ernest Labrousse, eds., *Histoire économique et sociale de la France*, Vol. 1, part 1, *L'Etat et la Ville 1450–1660* (Paris, 1977), p. 408.

to pre-eminence among the cities of provincial France was still a strong one at mid-century. Its surviving parish registers, which begin in the middle decades of the century, suggest a total population of between 71,000 and 78,000 inhabitants.[1] By contrast, Lyon's population can be calculated from similar evidence to have been roughly 58,000 in 1550.[2] The other leading provincial cities probably all fell in the range of 20–40,000 people.[3]

But the royal entry of 1550 was more than just a major artistic event and a civic rite of conspicuous consumption; amid all the ceremonies which a committee of Rouen's most learned and cultivated clerics and 'orators' had devised, many of the city's more important inhabitants also paraded past the royal reviewing stand on the plain of Ste Catherine-de-Grandmont. A number of meticulously detailed accounts of the order of march have survived, revealing the groups into which the inhabitants of the city classified themselves and the order of precedence accorded each one. These accounts also contain an enumeration of the participating trade guilds which is the nearest thing that exists to a complete occupational census of the city.

1 Reliable parish registers have survived for 19 of the city's 36 parishes for the period 1599–1601. These record an average of 1,945 baptisms per year. In the decade 1690–99, according to Messance's *Recherches sur la population des généralités d'Auvergne, de Lyon, de Rouen et de quelques provinces et villes du royaume* (Paris, 1766), these 19 parishes accounted for 76 per cent of all baptisms celebrated in the city. Since they are scattered randomly across the city, it seems safe to assume that the percentage was not radically different in 1600. There would thus have been 2,568 baptisms celebrated in all 36 parishes. Adding to these figures, which are for Catholics only, another 156 Protestant baptisms, and assuming the birth rate of approximately 40 per thousand which demographic investigations of other Ancien Régime cities have shown to be normal for urban populations, the city's total population in 1600 can thus be estimated to have been about 68,000. Since the registers of 11 scattered parishes suggest that the number of baptisms had declined by between 5 and 15 per cent over the course of the preceding half century, the population around 1550 must therefore have been between 71,000 and 78,000 people.

On the problem of urban birth rates and the technique of estimating a total population from the level of baptisms, *see* Louis Henry, *Manuel de démographie historique* (Geneva–Paris, 1967), p. 53; Marcel Lachiver, *La population de Meulan du XVII*e *au XIX*e *siècle (vers 1600–1870): Etude de démographie historique* (Paris, 1969), chs. 8–9; Maurice Garden, *Lyon et les Lyonnais au XVIII*e *siècle* (Paris, 1970), pp. 94–105; and François Lebrun, *Les hommes et la mort en Anjou aux 17*e *et 18*e *siècles: Essai de démographie et de psychologie historiques* (Paris–The Hague, 1971), pp. 157–62, esp. p. 161n.

2 According to figures kindly supplied me by Natalie Zemon Davis, 1,910 Catholic baptisms were celebrated per year in Lyon in the 1580s. Assuming a Protestant population comparable in size to Rouen's (as seems probable) and projecting these figures backward on the basis of what we know about the general evolution of Lyon's population from the evidence of scattered parishes, one arrives at a figure of approximately 2,315 baptisms around 1550. Again using a multiplier of 25, this is equivalent to a total population of around 58,000.

3 Reliable estimates of other large urban populations in this period are rare, but it is known that Bordeaux had roughly 20,000 inhabitants at the beginning of the sixteenth century and surely more by 1550, that Amiens housed approximately 28,000 people in the 1560s, and that Angers, Nantes and Troyes all had about 25,000 inhabitants in 1600. Robert Boutruche et al., *Bordeaux de 1453 à 1715* (Bordeaux, 1966), p. 69; Edouard Maugis, *Recherches sur les transformations du régime politique et social de la ville d'Amiens des origines de la commune à la fin du XVI*e *siècle* (Paris, 1906), Appendix IV; Alain Croix, *Nantes et le Pays nantais au XVI*e *siècle: Etude démographique* (Paris, 1974), p. 208; Jean-Louis Bourgeon, *Les Colbert avant Colbert, destin d'une famille marchande* (Paris, 1973), p. 107; François Lebrun et al., *Histoire d'Angers* (Toulouse, 1975), p. 91.

By scrutinizing these accounts of the royal entry of 1550 and supplementing them with other documents, it is possible to obtain a fairly detailed view of the structure of Rouennais society around mid-century.

After the archers of the admiralty had cleared a path through the assembled crowds, the city's clergy passed in review first, as befitted the first estate.[1] At their head[2] came the members of the four mendicant orders – the Dominicans, Franciscans, Augustinians, and Carmelites – whose special purity as ratified by their vows of voluntary poverty earned them a place of honor in all processions. Next marched the secular clergy. The archbishop was absent at the time, as pre-Counter-Reformation archbishops typically were, so the dean of the archiepiscopal see led the group.[3] The canons of the cathedral chapter followed immediately behind their dean, comprising a well-to-do, highly educated group of some thirty men, many of whom also doubled as the curés of the richer city parishes. These men formed a clerical elite, drawn primarily from the leading bourgeois families which often had a tradition of membership in the cathedral chapter, passing positions on within the family from uncle to nephew. Scattered among them were also a few ex-courtiers whom the king had rewarded with rich benefices for their services, among them the erstwhile court poet Claude Chappuys, one of the chief designers of the 1550 entry. Behind the canons marched their poor relations in the cathedral, the chaplains, who came from somewhat more humble families but were nonetheless assured a comfortable living by their positions. The parish clergy came next – the single largest group within the first estate. They were a diverse lot. Several dozen well-educated and handsomely remunerated curés were accompanied by their vicars and by the numerous chaplains who formed a large clerical proletariat, living off the proceeds of the anniversary Masses that they recited each day for the souls of the dead. Bringing up the rear of the first estate came the members of the three non-mendicant – indeed, quite wealthy – religious houses located within the city walls: the Abbey of St Ouen, the Priory of St Lô, and the Hôtel-Dieu of the Madeleine.[4]

[1] The following account of the order of march is based primarily on A.C.R., A 16, fos. 110ff, supplemented by *Cest la deduction du sumptueux ordre*...

[2] The municipal authorities who laid down the order of march did not specify any order of precedence within the first estate. I am assuming here that the clergy marched in the same order they typically followed in the large clerical processions of the time, detailed accounts of which may be found in François Farin, *Histoire de la ville de Rouen* (Rouen, 1668), Vol. 2, pp. 29–32, and M. C. Oursel, 'Notes pour servir à l'histoire de la Réforme en Normandie au temps de François Ier, principalement dans le diocèse de Rouen', *Mémoires de l'Académie Nationale des Sciences, Arts et Belles-Lettres de Caen*, 1912, pp. 201–5.

[3] The archbishop of Rouen for virtually the entire second half of the century was Charles, cardinal of Bourbon. The uncle of Henry of Navarre and himself one of the leading political figures in the realm, he was usually to be found at court and visited Rouen only on rare occasions.

[4] Sources do not exist for a full-scale social portrait of the clergy. The brief comments above about the social hierarchy within the first estate are based on such bits of evidence as do exist. Liasses G

The total size of this first group in the procession was impressive. In the largest of Rouen's thirty-six parishes, forty to fifty masses were celebrated daily, supporting some twenty-five clerics per parish.[1] In all, an account of a 1534 church procession enumerates 524 parish priests and chaplains, plus another 29 canons, 197 mendicant friars, and 122 monks and nuns.[2] Allowing for those unable to participate due to infirmity or absence from the city, Rouen's first estate must have totalled approximately 900 individuals, or about 1.2 per cent of the city's population. Although imposing, such a large group of clerics was by no means exceptional for a city of the era. The percentage of clerics in the population of Frankfurt and Nuremberg had been the same or slightly higher prior to the Reformation,[3] while in more Mediterranean lands, the first estate was far larger. Madrid, for example, boasted forty-five convents housing 2,000 individuals in 1567, a date at which it was probably no larger than Rouen.[4] Sixteenth-century Bologna contained no less than 3,380 regular clerics out of a total population roughly comparable to that of the Norman capital.[5] One suspects that this far larger percentage of clerics in Spain and Italy is not unrelated to Protestantism's lack of success in these lands.

Following the clergy in the royal entry came Rouen's royal and municipal officials, who marched in reverse order of importance. At their head were the numerous minor functionaries who supervised commercial activity within the city: sixty-four *courtiers* of wine and cloth, who acted as

3424–42 and 3450–60 of the A.D.S.M. contain a large collection of wills and inventories after death of the canons and chaplains of the cathedral chapter. The extensive libraries and chests full of fine clothes they reveal indicate the education and prosperity of these men. Two studies of individual canons complement these documents and enable one to discern the ranks of society from which the chapter recruited its members: E. Le Parquier, 'Un chroniqueur rouennais à l'époque de la Réforme: Le chanoine Jean Nagerel', *Congrès du Millénaire de la Normandie (911–1911): Compte-Rendu des Travaux* (Rouen, 1912), pp. 223–44; and Louis-P. Roche, *Claude Chappuys (?–1575): Poète de la cour de François Ier* (Poitiers, 1929). A.D.S.M. 35 H, Liber Professorum des Cordeliers, reveals that the Franciscans drew their novices primarily from the surrounding rural areas; 16 of 24 new friars received from 1577 through 1585 came from rural villages. For the parish clergy one must rely on the sparse details provided by such parish histories as E. de la Querière, *Description historique, archéologique et artistique de l'église paroissiale de Saint-Vincent de Rouen* (Rouen, 1844) and L. Prévost, *Histoire de la paroisse et des curés de Saint-Maclou depuis la fondation jusqu'à nos jours* (Rouen, 1970), as well as the brief remarks in D. Julia's suggestive, 'Le prêtre au XVIIIe siècle, la théologie et les institutions', *Recherches de Sciences Religieuses*, LVIII (1970), pp. 521–34.

1 *Inv/Sommaire*, entry of Nov. 15, 1528; Prévost, *Saint-Maclou*, p. 36.

2 Farin, *Histoire de la ville de Rouen*, Vol. 2, pp. 29–32. The figures provided here appear reliable when verified against other scattered bits of data about the size of the first estate, notably A.D.S.M., G 9869; Francesco Gonzaga, *De origine seraphicae religionis Franciscanae eiusque progressibus* (Rome, 1587), pp. 577, 583; and L. de Glainville, *Histoire du Prieuré de Saint-Lô de Rouen*, Vol. 1 (Rouen, 1890), p. 128.

3 Karl Bücher, *Die Bevölkerung von Frankfurt am Main im XIV und XV Jahrhundert* (Tübingen, 1886), pp. 517–21.

4 Antonio Domínguez Ortiz, *Las clases privilegiadas en la España del Antiguo Regimen* (Madrid, 1973), p. 283.

5 K. J. Beloch, *Bevölkerungsgeschichte Italiens* (Berlin, 1940), Vol. 2, p. 94.

intermediaries for all foreign merchants dealing in such commodities, and an unspecified number of measurers of linen and grain, who watched for fraud in the sale of these goods. Then came the officials of the mint. Next were the forces of order: fifty *arbalétriers* (a special militia unit) and forty-seven sergeants of the *bailliage* and the *vicomté de l'eau*. The more important officials followed, distinguishable as such by their outfits of black satin and velours. First, side by side, were the lieutenant-general of the *bailliage* and the municipal *conseillers-échevins*. Second came the other, lesser municipal officials. A crowd of several hundred *notables bourgeois et marchands* followed, representing, in effect, the city politic – only these men voted in Rouen's municipal elections and participated in the so-called general assemblies of the city. Finally came the members of those courts whose jurisdiction extended over the entire province: the *cour des aides*, the admiralty, the jurisdiction of the waters and forests, and, most prestigious of all, the parlement.

Like the clergy, the officials formed an extremely large contingent – again some would have said too large. Constantly denounced yet inexorable, the multiplication of official positions that characterized the entire Ancien Régime had already progressed by 1550 to the point where those holding royal offices numbered at least 250. The parlement of Normandy had been founded in 1499 with 35 members; by 1554 it contained 66. The *cour des aides* had similarly grown from 8 to 15 members. Over the course of the second half of the century the proliferation of offices and officers was to continue. Three more courts were added to the already existing plethora of tribunals – the *siège présidial*, the *chambre des comptes*, and the *juridiction consulaire* – while the established courts all grew steadily.[1]

The final contingent of Rouennais to march before the king was a 627-man honor guard composed of a select group of artisans chosen from 'the elite among the great and infinite number of craftsmen of the city'. In all, seventy-two occupations were represented within this honor guard, an indication of the extremely broad range of crafts practiced in Rouen. (A comparable procession in Lille in 1565 included less than two-thirds this number of trades.)[2] No apparent logic governed the way in which the trades were arranged within the three companies into which the guard was divided, but the number of artisans from each craft represented seems to have been roughly proportional to its importance within the city. First, in red, came: 40 master weavers (*drapiers drapants*), 5 bit- and spur-makers

[1] By 1668, the *cour des aides* contained no less than 27 counsellors and the parlement well over 100. Farin, *Histoire de la ville de Rouen*, Vol. 1, p. 228; Jonathan Dewald, *The Formation of a Provincial Nobility: The Magistrates of the Parlement of Rouen, 1499–1610* (Princeton, 1980), p. 69. I would like to thank Professor Dewald for kindly showing me this work prior to publication.

[2] Robert DuPlessis, 'Urban Stability in the Netherlands Revolution: A Comparative Study of Lille and Douai' (unpub. Ph.D. dissertation, Columbia University, 1973), p. 8.

(*éperonniers*), 8 skinners, 25 innkeepers, 4 dyers, 2 furriers, 2 nail-makers, 6 saddlers, 14 tailors, 4 *pennetiers* (I was unable to identify these), 12 chandlers, 4 inkwell-makers (*corretiers*), 15 shoemakers, 8 comb-makers, 5 men who decorated and gilded swords (*fourbisseurs*),[1] 2 hook-makers (*amichonniers*), 10 joiners, 10 bakers, 2 balance-makers, 6 sheath- and wallet-makers, 15 cordwainers, 10 hatters, and 1 oar-maker. Then, in green: 30 cloth retailers (*détailleurs de draps*), 6 silk-weavers, 20 goldsmiths, 12 dyers in woad, 6 linen dyers, 12 coopers, 3 makers of trunks and chests, 8 pastry cooks, 10 *crediers*, 2 wire-pullers, 6 linen-weavers, 30 hosiers, 6 leather-dressers, 12 leadsmiths (*plombiers*), 6 plasterers, 3 makers of tennis rackets (*raquetiers*),[2] 10 roofers and slaters, 4 makers of leather clasps and brooches (*esguilletiers*), 5 rope-makers, 4 pewterers, 1 mirrorer, 7 embroiderers, 4 makers of pack-saddles, and 3 pike-makers. Finally, in white: 6 cask-makers, 4 roast-vendors (*rôtisseurs*), 5 tapestry-weavers, 1 coffer-maker (*coffretiers*),[3] 5 glaziers, 2 purse-makers, 5 knife-makers, 5 bleachers, 10 brewers, 35 butchers, 6 tinkers (*maignents*), 6 surgeons, 6 pin-makers, 2 arbalete-makers, 4 sword-makers, 15 dyers in madder, 6 cobblers, 12 playing-card-makers, 6 used-clothing vendors, 3 booksellers, 4 farriers, 2 parchment-makers, 25 tanners, 2 gold-leaf-makers, 20 apothecaries, and 10 grain merchants.

At the very end of the procession, after all the chariots, unicorns, goddesses, and elephants, a group of 70 splendidly dressed youths from the wealthiest families of the city, the children of honor, rode on horseback past the royal box. Once they had paraded past, the king stepped down and followed the procession across the bridge, past Neptune and the warring Tupinambas, and into Rouen.

Rouen's complex social structure, or at least (using Leach's words again) 'the socially approved "proper" relations between individuals and groups', could hardly have been presented more clearly than in this elaborate civic ritual.[4] First of all, the ceremony reveals that sixteenth-century Rouen was

[1] This was a classic case of guild hyperspecialization. The swords these men decorated were made by members of another guild, that of the *serruriers*.

[2] These men also often owned and operated *jeux de paume*.

[3] Precisely what differentiated these men from the *malletiers*, or makers of trunks and chests, and the *huchers*, or joiners, is unclear.

[4] In everyday life, of course, as is the case for men in any but the most primitive of societies, the inhabitants of sixteenth-century Rouen were bound by numerous and often contradictory solidarities – family, wealth, occupation, parish, and so forth. Any one of these might determine how they would behave on any given occasion. A truly complete model of Rouen's social structure would take all of these cross-cutting solidarities into account – and would be inordinately complex. But whatever the complexities of social relations in everyday life, there were certain occasions on which an explicitly hierarchical society grouped itself into the units and according to the order of precedence which it felt ought to structure it. The royal entry was such an occasion, and we will understand Rouennais society better if we examine what the ceremony can tell us. It is not suggested here that the categories into which the Rouennais divided one another were necessarily those which dominated group

highly corporate in structure. Men were regularly classified according to the guild, tribunal, or religious order to which they belonged, and this is the case not only in this entry but in all documents in which social position is indicated – contracts, court records, tax lists, and so forth. Only for the monied elite of merchants, the *notables bourgeois et marchands*, were corporate divisions insignificant. This segment of society appeared at two different points in order of march; the men marched right after the municipal authorities and their offspring appeared at the very end of the procession as children of honor. Significantly, at each of these two points they formed an undifferentiated cluster of individuals. Rouen's merchants were not divided into trading companies or other corporations as were the English merchants.[1] Wealth was the prime determinant of social status at this level of society.

The many corporations which comprised Rouennais society in turn fell into several broad categories. Within lay society, the sharpest division separated an elite which wielded formal political power from the great bulk of people from the guild members on down who were systematically excluded from normal decision-making channels. This latter group, usually referred to contemptuously with a term such as '*le menu peuple*', was by no means undifferentiated; it was divided vertically into guilds and horizontally by wealth and status. (The fact that only a select group chosen from among the artisans was allowed to participate in the royal entry reveals the existence of the horizontal divisions.) As for the elite, it too was subdivided, first into *marchands bourgeois* on the one hand and judicial officials on the other, then, in the case of this latter group, into rival corporations ranked according to a hierarchy of importance that was clearly indicated by the order of precedence followed in the entry. Finally, separate from lay society, although linked to it by ties of family, existed the parallel world of the first estate. It too was divided vertically into corporations and horizontally by wealth and status.

The royal entry of 1550 was also revealing in whom it excluded. Several segments of society were conspicuously absent, most strikingly so Rouen's lawyers, the *procureurs* and *avocats*. They had boycotted the event. After having requested permission to march with the political officials of the town, they had been ordered by the city council to take their place instead among the *corps de métier*.[2] This they found to be beneath their dignity, and so

behavior, and in fact we shall see that the religious divisions which set the city's inhabitants most bitterly against one another did not pit one distinct element of society against another. I present the following model of Rouen's social structure simply as a way of understanding the structure of groups which comprised the community.

1 Distinctions did exist within the merchant class – between linen merchants and wine merchants, for example – but these reflected merely an individual's specialization in one commodity or another.

2 A.C.R., A 16, entry of July 17, 1550.

they simply refused to march at all. Their boycott revealed their social position perfectly; it was an ambiguous one, midway between the world of officialdom and that of the guilds.

While the lawyers refused to participate in the royal entry because of their own pride, other groups were simply deemed unworthy to take part. Spectators watching the royal entry would never have known that Rouen contained a variety of sub-artisanal occupations in addition to the trades represented in the honor guard. There were, for example, the *maîtres de basses oeuvres*, whose job it was each evening to clean out the privies required by law in every house and to cart the night soil out of the city. There were the agricultural workers, primarily market gardeners, who, although not so numerous as in certain other French cities of this era, nonetheless formed a significant part of the population of the *faubourgs*. Finally, there were the domestic servants, day-laborers, and dockworkers. The members of all these sub-artisanal occupations lived on the fringes of poverty. In normal years, when employed, they could expect to scrape by, but when grain prices rose dramatically after a bad harvest, or when unemployment increased, or when (as often happened) both occurred simultaneously, these individuals, and indeed many poorer artisans too, ended up on the rolls of the *bureau des pauvres*.

With these men we touch on the final group missing from the royal entry: the poor. They had formed a substantial element within the city since the 1520s, when the classic process described by Le Roy Ladurie for Languedoc – that of rapid population growth outrunning a region's supply of arable land and breeding a growing number of dispossessed rural laborers – had produced a serious increase in the poverty problem in Upper Normandy as well. The cathedral chapter began regularly to set aside a weekly sum for the nourishment of the poor said to be flooding into the city in 1521, and ever thereafter the problem of how to provide for a sizeable group of men and women who depended upon charity for their survival was a constant source of concern for the city's authorities.[1]

The poor were not a fixed group in Ancien Régime France. They may be usefully divided between the 'structural' poor – the crippled, aged, or

[1] Emmanuel Le Roy Ladurie's classic description of the economic and demographic background to the growing concern throughout Europe with the problem of poverty in the 1520s and 1530s may be found in his *Paysans de Languedoc* (Paris, 1966), part II, esp. pp. 317–26. Guy Bois's stimulating recent *Crise du féodalisme: économie rurale et démographie en Normandie orientale du début du 14e siècle au milieu du 16e siècle* (Paris, 1976), passim, esp. pp. 67–72 and ch. 15, demonstrates that the same process was at work around Rouen. While dated, the study of Giuliano Procacci also retains considerable interest, particularly on this question of poverty: 'Strutture economiche e classi sociali in Normandia (con particolare riferimento alla regione di Rouen)', Procacci, *Classi sociali e monarchia assoluta nella Francia della prima metà del secolo XVI* (Turin, 1955). The local authorities' concern with the problem of poverty may be traced through G. Panel, ed., *Documents concernant les pauvres de Rouen* (Rouen, 1917), Vol. I.

infirm permanently dependent on charity – and the 'conjunctural' poor – those able to earn their own living most of the time but forced into mendicity whenever disaster struck, be it a personal catastrophe such as a prolonged illness or a social one such as the failure of the harvest.[1] This latter category naturally expanded or contracted in tandem with the economic situation. Two surviving censuses of those forced to rely on public charity reveal how dramatic these fluctuations could be, and how large the number of poor could become in crisis years. A year of prosperity, 1598, provides a baseline. In that year the parlement ordered the *lieutenant criminel* to assemble all beggars, vagabonds, and able-bodied poor in the city in order to choose 250 people to take part in the ill-fated attempt to establish a permanent French colony on Sable Island in Canada. The lieutenant and his men made the rounds of the city and then reported back to the court that they had found some 800 people.[2] This count does not include the aged, nor the infirm, nor, presumably, children. Furthermore, the prospect of a one-way ticket to a poorly charted, frigid wilderness may have led many among the indigent to attempt to elude the authorities. (This would not have been easy since they were inscribed on the parish rolls.) At the very most, such absentees may have quadrupled the number of the poor. The figure of 800 people thus suggests that in normal times those on relief formed a small percentage of the total population, no more than 5 to 7 per cent. The year 1586, however, was quite different. It witnessed one of the century's worst harvests, and as was common in years of famine, a combined program of public works and bread distribution was organized. The able-bodied poor were set to work on the city's fortifications in return for a daily ration of bread and a few *sous*. A list of those put to work when this program began records 917 men, 1,935 women, and 1,982 children between the ages of eight and fourteen – 4,834 people in all.[3] As the weeks passed and the crisis deepened, the number of those receiving relief grew; a record of the number of loaves of bread distributed each week between late June and early August in one of the city's four quarters indicates a 113 per cent increase.[4] If this quarter was representative of the city as a whole, the number of those dependent on relief by August would have attained 14,260, when allowance is made for children under the age of eight too

1 Jean-Pierre Gutton, *La société et les pauvres: L'exemple de la généralité de Lyon 1534–1789* (Paris, 1971), part 1, esp. p. 53.

2 A.D.S.M., B, Parlement, Registres Secrets, entries of May 20 and 23, 1598.

3 A.C.R., B 4, fos. 319–20. The far greater number of women than men should not be surprising. Single or widowed women tended to be in a more precarious economic situation than men and commonly outnumber them on lists such as this. For international comparisons, *see* J. F. Pound, 'An Elizabethan Census of the Poor', *University of Birmingham Historical Journal*, VIII (1962), p. 141, and Bartolomé Bennassar, *Valladolid au siècle d'or* (Paris–The Hague, 1967), p. 436.

4 A.C.R., Chartrier, tiroir 109.

young to be put to work.[1] While the poor made up perhaps 5 per cent of the city's population in normal times, in crisis years they could exceed 20 per cent.[2]

The royal entry of 1550 illuminates Rouen's economic foundations as well as its social structure. The large contingents of officials, artisans, and merchants participating in the ceremony reflected the city's three-fold vocation as a provincial administrative capital, a major manufacturing center, and a busy port. All three sectors made important contributions to the town's well-being.

Few if any provincial cities could claim so wide a variety of law courts as Rouen, with its parlement, its *cour des aides*, its admiralty, its *eaux et forêts*, its *bailliage*, its *vicomté*, its *vicomté de l'eau*, its *bureau des finances*, and, later on in the century, its *siège présidial* and *chambre des comptes*. Each supported not only its members and their families, but also a far larger population of *avocats*, *procureurs*, scribes, bailiffs, and their families. It is known that for every *officier* in the *bailliage* of Senlis in 1539, there were four lawyers.[3] The precise proportion of lawyers to *officiers* in Rouen is harder to calculate, but it was probably at least as high.[4]

The number of livelihoods to be earned from the judicial process was so high because sixteenth-century trials were often lingering affairs involving the services of many different individuals, every one of whom had to be paid for each service rendered. A typical case before the *bailliage* in 1582 shows how the wheels of justice were oiled. In that year, the privileged militia company of the 104 harquebusiers brought a suit against the *vicomte de l'eau* claiming that he had improperly seized certain goods from them in defiance of their privileges. In the course of the suit, the militia company paid the *huissier* of the *bailliage* to copy their charter; they paid the *greffier* on nine separate occasions for unspecified services; they paid two lawyers

[1] The figure 14,260 was obtained by doubling the number of people receiving relief on June 2, then doubling the number of children a second time on the assumption that poor children aged 1–7 were as numerous as those 8–14. Obviously, the figure is, if anything, an underestimate, since in a normal population there are more children under the age of 8 than between the ages of 8 and 14.

[2] These figures correspond with what is known about the number receiving relief in other cities of the period. *See* Richard Gascon, *Grand commerce et vie urbaine au XVIe siècle: Lyon et ses marchands (vers 1520–vers 1580)* (Paris–The Hague, 1971), pp. 403–4; Natalie Zemon Davis, 'Poor Relief, Humanism, and Heresy', *Society and Culture in Early Modern France: Eight Essays* (Stanford, 1975), pp. 62–4, and the references cited there.

[3] Bernard Guenée, *Tribunaux et gens de justice dans le bailliage de Senlis à la fin du Moyen Age (vers 1380–vers 1550)* (Paris, 1963), p. 336.

[4] The account of the 1534 procession in Farin, *Histoire de la ville de Rouen*, records 300 *avocats* and *procureurs* attached to the parlement and *bailliage* court. There were approximately 80 judges on these courts, yielding once more a proportion of 4 lawyers per court member. No indications are available about the number of lawyers in Rouen's other courts.

to plead their case; they bought gifts for (as their account book respectfully lists them) *Monsieur le Procureur de Roy*, *Monsieur le Substitut de Monsieur le Procureur de Roy*, and the servant of *Monsieur le Procureur de Roy*. Finally, when the case was over and they had won, they paid both a sergeant and his clerk for returning to them the goods that had been improperly seized in the first place.[1] In all, they spent 47 *livres* (about five months' wages for a master mason) – and this was a relatively simple case, lasting less than a year. When the parish fabric of St Vivien sued a light-fingered ex-treasurer for restitution of some silver that had found its way into his coffers, the trial dragged on for five years. The parish's record of expenditures on the case covers seventy-three full pages in its account books, with the expenses mounting to 311 *livres* and one gallon of wine.[2]

Hundreds, even thousands, of such cases were handled each year by the city's law courts, for high prices did not deter the Normans from flocking to their capital in quest of an elusive justice. Their notorious love of chicanery fueled one of the chief growth industries of the century. The number of decisions, or *arrêts*, handed down annually by the *grand'chambre* of the parlement provides the best index of that court's caseload. It reveals a remarkable expansion in the amount of legal business over the course of the century. In 1526 the parlement issued 453 *arrêts*. In 1556 the figure was 563. By 1586 it had climbed to no less than 1,346. Viewed in the light of this expanding caseload, the fantastic multiplication of judicial positions over the course of the century seems perhaps more justifiable, although in fact it was rarely justified on these grounds and was no less resented by the bulk of the population because of this growing business.

The expanding volume of judicial business provided a livelihood not only for the large numbers of legal personnel in Rouen; the presence of so many law courts was also a boon for the city's tradesmen and innkeepers. The country squire Gilles de Gouberville traveled to Rouen from his estate of Mesnil-au-Val in the distant reaches of the Cotentin peninsula three times between December 1549 and February 1551 to attend to legal matters, but only part of the time and money he spent in the city was devoted to the legal business which brought him there in the first place. He also dined out often with friends at inns such as the Saracen's Head and the Pilgrim, attended the mummeries of the *Conards* and the poetry competition of the *Puy des Palinods*, and did a great deal of shopping. For his sister, he bought a silk belt; for his uncle, leather gloves; and for himself, four coats, a sword, a pair of gloves, a sleeping cap, a copy of Marot's psalms in French, and the *livre de raison* in which – to the everlasting gratitude of later generations of historians – he recorded these and a thousand other details of everyday

[1] A.D.S.M., 5 E 120.

[2] A.D.S.M., G 7756–7.

life.[1] Gouberville noted his expenditures on two of his three visits; they amounted to 184 *livres*, of which only one-fourth went to his lawyers. The importance of the courts for the city's economy is easily overlooked, but the benefits gained from their presence were immense and widely shared. Even without its port and its manufactures, Rouen would have been a substantial city by sixteenth-century standards on the basis of its legal and administrative role alone. The town recognized as much, and when it was rumored in 1569 that the king planned to create a new parlement in Alençon and subtract the *bailliages* of Evreux and Alençon from the *ressort* of Rouen's court, the city council protested vigorously about the harm such a move would do to the city's economy.[2]

Urban economists often divide the working population of a city into two categories: those who produce goods and services which are exported from the city, and those who produce goods and services primarily for local consumption. The size of a city's export base is the chief determinant of its total size, for it brings the money into a city which can then be spent to buy the products of the local service sector. Justice, albeit a rather abstract commodity, was one of Rouen's main export bases. Cloth and stockings were other, more tangible ones.

'From all lands people insist on having stockings only from this city, and...in the fairs and towns of this kingdom there is great traffic in them', boasted Rouen's hosiers in 1526.[3] Michel Mollat declares that this industry was the city's largest in the early sixteenth century.[4] In the royal entry, however, there were 40 *drapiers drapants* and 30 *détailleurs de draps* as opposed to 30 stocking-makers, suggesting that the cloth industry was Rouen's largest. Since no complete census exists for the sixteenth century, it is impossible to be sure which of these two trades was larger around mid-century. But whichever deserved pride of place, these two stood out clearly as the most important industries in the city. One or the other ranks first on all lists of occupations which it is possible to obtain for sixteenth-century Rouen.[5]

For all of their importance, both trades were in the midst of serious crises at the time of Henry II's visit. The cause of each was the same – the tendency, so common to the late medieval and early modern periods, for industrial production to move from a city to the nearby countryside in order to escape the restrictions of the guild system and exploit cheap peasant

[1] Gilles de Gouberville, 'Journal pour les années 1549, 1550, 1551, 1552', *Mémoires de la Société des Antiquaires de Normandie*, 4th ser., II (1895), pp. 64–6, 102–6, 127–35.

[2] A.C.R., A 19, entries of Dec. 22, 1569, Jan. 23, 1570. The city raised a similar protest against a plan to move the site of the meeting of the provincial Estates to Caen every other year. A.C.R., A 19, entry of Jan. 31, 1576.

[3] *Inv/Sommaire*, entry of July 14, 1526.

[4] Mollat, *Le commerce maritime normand à la fin du Moyen Age* (Paris, 1952), p. 278.

[5] *See below*, Tables 2, 3, and 6.

labor. In the woolen industry, this tendency had been visible since the end of the fifteenth century, when weavers had begun to leave Rouen for the nearby *bourg* of Darnétal to circumvent the rules of the city's weavers' guild barring the use of the mechanical fulling mill or such new dyestuffs as brazil wood.[1] By 1550, Darnétal had grown to a cloth center of no less than 8,000 people, while the number of new masters received into Rouen's weavers' guild had suffered a steady decline for over 50 years.[2] In spite of this trend, cloth production was hardly inconsequential in Rouen itself; some 396 new masters were still received into the weavers' guild in the decade of the 1550s.[3] Since the total number of master craftsmen was probably at least twice as large as the number of masters received in any given decade, and since many of Rouen's master weavers employed over a dozen workers at their looms, the industry clearly remained one that supported several thousand people in the city.

The stocking trade had evolved according to a different pattern, but by 1550 it, too, was suffering from competition from the nearby countryside. Where the woolen industry had been a mainstay of the city's economy since the thirteenth century, stocking production on a large scale was a recent development. The trade had only blossomed into a major industry during the first decades of the sixteenth century; in the 1520s, the trade was expanding so rapidly that, to meet the need for new manpower, the hosiers' guild petitioned the municipal authorities for special permission to accept apprentice fullers who were not residents of the city.[4] But a shift from manual to mechanical fulling in the 1540s threw many of these new fullers out of work, while at the same time Rouen's mercers began to organize stocking production on a putting-out basis in the surrounding countryside. The rapid growth of the rural population over the course of the preceding three-quarters of a century had spawned a large class of impoverished peasants who needed additional employment to tide them over the slack periods of the agricultural year. The situation was therefore ripe for the development of rural industries.[5] The rapidly diminishing frequency with

1 Mollat, *Le commerce maritime*, pp. 275ff.

2 The parish registers of Darnétal's two parishes (A.D.S.M., E, Etat Civil, St Pierre-de-Carville and St Ouen-de-Longpaon) record 324 baptisms per year during the period 1549–50, equivalent to a population of at least 8,000. The number of new master weavers in Rouen is revealed by the *lettres de draperie* which each new master was required to purchase. These are noted in the parish accounts of St Nicaise, St Vivien, and St Maclou, A.D.S.M., G 6881–907, 7228–57, and 7754–94. Only St Maclou's records date back to the early part of the century. They show that while six new masters per year were entering the guild in that parish between 1520 and 1529, barely one per year was still entering it in the 1550s.In St Nicaise, where the records start in 1541, 212 new masters were received between 1541 and 1551, 161 in the following decade.

3 Records for St Vivien do not begin until 1552. Between 1552 and 1562, 212 masters were received in that parish, while 184 men living in St Nicaise became guild masters between 1550 and 1560.

4 *Inv/Sommaire*, entry of July 14, 1526.

5 Bois, *Crise du féodalisme*, pp. 108, 140–42, 340; A 13, entry of July 14, 1531; *Inv/Sommaire*, entry of Nov. 30, 1540.

which hosiers appear from 1550 onward in the parish registers of two of Rouen's parishes which had been centers of the stocking trade earlier in the century reveals how seriously the city's stocking workers were affected by the twin developments of mechanization and intensified rural competition. In the small parish of St André-de-la-Ville, whose population as a whole declined steadily from the 1530s on, the percentage of hosiers bringing children to the baptismal font dropped from 37 per cent in the 1540s to 23 per cent in the 1550s to 18 per cent in the 1560s, after which parish registers cease noting the father's occupation. In St Herbland, which also declined slightly in total size, children of hosiers represented 10 per cent of all babies baptized in the period 1546–60 but fell to 2 per cent between 1561 and 1570. By the 1580s, the stocking industry had completely disappeared from this parish.[1]

Although Rouen's two largest industries were declining in size around 1550, we must beware of leaping to the conclusion that Rouen's manufacturing sector as a whole was in decline, for perhaps more important than the size of any single trade in the city was the diversity of its manufactures. Whereas nearly half of Beauvais' population in the seventeenth century depended on the woolen industry for its livelihood,[2] no occupation dominated Rouen nearly so completely, and the 72 guilds represented in the guard of honor of 1550 failed to exhaust the full range of the city's trades. For reasons which are unclear, certain guilds did not take part in the royal entry; no masons participated, for example, yet in 1565 there were 10 masters and 60 journeymen practicing this craft.[3] While 72 guilds marched in the guard of honor, contemporaries estimated the total number of trades in the town to be between 90 and 120.[4] Quite a few of these were major export industries. Some 400 journeymen tanners were regularly employed preparing the hides which members of 6 separate guilds then turned into such leather products as shoes, saddles, and sheaths.[5] The masters of the numerous metal-working trades in the city (12 were represented in the royal entry) boasted in 1531 that their products were worthy of comparison with those of the forests of Auvergne and were sold throughout northern France, England, and Scotland.[6] The city's makers of playing cards sold their products over an even larger area; Spaniards and Englishmen alike played their games of chance with cards made in the Norman capital. Among the city's other major products were, besides cloth and stockings, hats, furniture, candles, combs and woolcards, and glassware.[7]

[1] A.C.R., R. P.'s 11 and 211.

[2] Pierre Goubert, *Beauvais et le Beauvaisis de 1600 à 1730* (Paris, 1960), p. 258.

[3] A.C.R., B 2, entry of May 17, 1565.

[4] *Inv/Sommaire*, entry of July 14, 1531.

[5] Charles Ouin-Lacroix, *Histoire des anciennes corporations d'arts et métiers et des confréries religieuses de la capitale de la Normandie* (Rouen, 1850), p. 141.

[6] *Inv/Sommaire*, entry of April 27, 1531.

[7] Mollat, *Le commerce maritime normand*, pp. 273–85; and Emile Coornaert, *Les Français et le commerce international à Anvers* (Paris, 1961), Vol. 1, pp. 218–19 both discuss Rouen's manufactures.

Because Rouen's export industries were so numerous and, in many cases, so large, the men employed in them in turn could support a large number of local service artisans such as butchers and bakers, who supplied them with the basic necessities of life. The royal entry suggests that certain of these trades in the local service sector employed almost as many people as the leading export industries. The butchers responsible for slaughtering and selling the 6,000 head of cattle and 48,000 lambs which the Rouennais consumed each year ranked as the second trade in the city in terms of the number of individuals represented in the honor guard.[1] The innkeepers who lodged the numerous visitors attracted to the city by its markets and its law courts ranked fifth. We know the total size of this latter group; it was over 300 individuals, for a census of all buildings with a supply of wine in 1597 reveals 179 taverns and inns in the city, plus another 142 *triballes* – a sort of poor man's tavern.[2] (No wonder that laws were passed, in vain, restricting the sale of wine and that popular songs of the period are full of wifely laments about husbands who drink up their income at the *triballe*.)[3] Bakers, tailors, apothecaries, goldsmiths, and building workers were other important groups of local service artisans.

English urban historians have detected a shift in the trade structure of several larger provincial cities in the sixteenth century away from relatively unskilled industrial production and toward an economy of skilled crafts and administrative and marketing functions.[4] It is tempting to argue that a similar shift was occurring in Rouen. While the woolen and hosiery trades were being lost to the countryside, it was becoming more common for inhabitants of the distant regions of the province to come to the city on legal business. Combined with the steady growth in size of the *officier* class, this probably stimulated expansion in both the hotel and provisioning trades and in the luxury crafts which catered both to the *officiers* and to those who came to the city to seek justice from them. Long-distance trade was also prospering, reinforcing the city's position as an entrepôt and market.

[1] The figures on meat consumption come from *Inv/Sommaire*, entry of March 21, 1521.

[2] A.C.R., Chartrier, tiroir 137.

[3] *See here* A.C.R., A 17, entry of Jan. 18, 1556; Anatole de Montaiglon and James de Rothschild, eds., *Recueil de poésies françoises des XVe et XVIe siècles* (Paris, 1855–78), Vol. 11, pp. 34–46, 71–86. The law of 1556 restricting the sale of wine at taverns to travellers refers to the 'effrenée et insatiable gulosité' of the city's native artisans, 'lesquelz, en lieu d'employer les bonnes heures a vacquer a leurs meneuvres employent la pluspart du temps aux compotations, tavernes et jeux prohibez, en quoy faisant commectent plusieurs blasphemes, violences les ungs aux aultres, deffraudens leurs femmes, enffans et famille jusques a leur denyer la vivre, de sort qu'ilz sont contrainctz mendyer de huys en huys.' Bourgeois alarm at the drinking problem and the role of the tavern in working-class culture was clearly not just a phenomenon of the late eighteenth and nineteenth centuries. A fascinating study remains to be done on attitudes toward drink in this period.

[4] J. F. Pound, 'The Social and Trade Structure of Norwich 1525–1575', *Past and Present*, 34 (1966), pp. 49–69; Peter Clark and Paul Slack, *English Towns in Transition 1500–1700* (Oxford, 1976), pp. 48–54, 102.

Unfortunately, few surviving documents shed any light on the evolution of the bulk of Rouen's industries, making it impossible to confirm this hypothesis of a shift in the city's trade structure. It does seem noteworthy, however, that the decline in population visible between the 1530s and 1560s in the stocking-making parishes of St Herbland and St André-de-la-Ville was not matched in the other four parishes whose registers of baptisms begin prior to the outbreak of the civil wars.[1] This suggests stability or even expansion of the other sectors of the economy, but it is slender evidence on which to base any firm assertions about the city's changing trade structure.

The organization of Rouen's numerous industries is fortunately somewhat clearer than their evolution. All but the smallest or newest trades were formally organized into guilds; Rouen, like Paris but unlike Lyon, eschewed the free labor system of craft organization. Most of the trades appear still to have operated along the traditional lines of the guild system. Independent master artisans who owned their own tools produced and sold their wares in their *boutique* with the assistance of a few skilled journeymen or young apprentices. In a number of industries the penetration of capital was beginning to create bonds of dependence beneath the surface of traditional guild organization. English merchants, for example, regularly advanced money to Rouen's makers of playing cards in return for the exclusive right to their production for a specified period of time.[2] In the woolen industry, the penetration of capital and the division of labor had advanced quite far. Just as in Beauvais, so in Rouen's eastern parishes the leading *drapiers drapants* owned large workplaces in which they employed anywhere from 2 to 20 wage-laborers – men, women, and children significantly called by contemporary documents '*ouvriers*', not '*compagnons*'.[3]

[1] These four parishes are St Eloi (number of baptisms roughly stable between 1539 and 1550 at a level 13 per cent higher than in the 1570s); St Gervais (number of baptisms modestly increasing 1537–61 – information very fragmentary); St Lô (number of baptisms roughly stable 1550–57 at a level 10 per cent above that of 1570s); and St Laurent (number of baptisms increasing modestly between 1553 and the 1560s). The case of St Gervais is especially noteworthy, since it was a *faubourg* parish. It is on the edges of the city that one would expect to see changes in its overall size reflected most dramatically. That this parish grew by less than 10 per cent between 1537–8 and 1559–61 indicates that the western portions of the city were expanding very slowly. Since the cloth-working parishes on the opposite edge of the city were probably shrinking in size, as were St André and St Herbland in the center of town, the city's overall population was in all likelihood declining ever so slightly over the middle decades of the century. *See* Appendix 3 and, for complete tables of demographic information, my Princeton University Ph.D. dissertation, 'Rouen during the Wars of Religion: Popular Disorder, Public Order, and the Confessional Struggle' (1975), Appendix IV.

[2] Pierre Jeannin, *Les marchands au XVIe siècle* (Paris, 1957), p. 93.

[3] The structure of the woolen industry in seventeenth-century Beauvais is described in detail in Goubert, *Beauvais*, ch. 9. The same author's 'Une fortune bourgeoise au XVIe siècle: Jehan Pocquelin, bisaïeul probable de Molière', *Revue d'Histoire Moderne et Contemporaine*, I (1954), pp. 8–24, shows that the same structure prevailed in the sixteenth century. Collections taken in the parish of St Vivien (A.D.S.M., G 7759, for example) prove that Rouen's cloth industry was organized along

Division of labor carried over to the retail side of the industry as well. The *drapiers drapants* specialized entirely in the production of cloth, while a different group, the *détailleurs de draps*, handled all commercial matters.

Commerce was the third pillar of Rouen's economy, and the city was, according to Emile Coornaert, nothing less than France's busiest port in the sixteenth century.[1] It owed this distinction above all to its favorable geographic location midway between Paris and the English Channel at the hub of what was probably the most highly developed region of rural industry in the country. Smaller ocean-going ships could sail up the Seine as far as Rouen, at which point cargoes destined for Paris or its region had to be transferred to river barges or pack wagons. Despite being situated forty miles inland, the city was therefore the major seaport for the entire Parisian basin. The surrounding countryside produced not only ever-increasing amounts of woolens and hose, but also sizeable quantities of linen and paper. Linen was France's single largest source of foreign exchange in this period, and the linen industry of the nearby Roumois and Lieuvin regions was in all probability France's most important.[2] Thousands of pieces of cloth were put on sale annually in Rouen's *Halle aux Toiles*. The paper industry could hardly compare in scale, but it too was of considerable significance. Centered in Déville and Notre-Dame-de-Bondeville, it produced enough paper to supply not only local needs but also much of the English market.[3]

As the chief market for these products of the surrounding countryside, as well as the wares of its own artisans, Rouen attracted merchants from the Baltic to the Mediterranean. The most active sectors of the city's foreign trade were those with the other ports of Europe's Atlantic facade. The Spanish had been sending large quantities of wool, tropical fruits, leather, olive oil, wine, and alum to the Norman capital since the later fifteenth century. In return, they purchased a wide variety of Rouen's manufactured goods – above all linen, for which the recent colonization of the Indies had produced a great upsurge in demand. 'Tela de Roan', as it was called

the same lines as Beauvais', but these are disappointingly vague about the precise number of workers per establishment. Thus, six men and 'plusieurs femmes' are recorded working in the 'maison des ouvriers' of Guillaume Lonictre, 6 men and 'plusieurs enfants' in that of Jehan de Rouen, etc.

[1] Coornaert, *Les Français et Anvers*, Vol. 1, p. 23.

[2] A.N., AD ix 473; Albert Girard, *Le commerce français à Séville et Cadix au temps des Habsbourg: Contribution à l'étude du commerce étranger en Espagne aux XVIe et XVIIe siècles* (Paris–Bordeaux, 1932), p. 350. Comparative figures about linen production in the different regions of France are not available until the later seventeenth century. At that time Rouen was the leading source of French linen exported to Cadiz.

[3] Edward Heawood, 'Sources of Early English Paper Supply, II – The Sixteenth Century', *The Library*, x (1929–30), p. 454, declares that the pot is the most frequently encountered watermark in English books and manuscripts of the period. This was the mark used to identify all paper sold in Rouen, as A.C.R., A 21, entry of Feb. 3, 1600 makes clear.

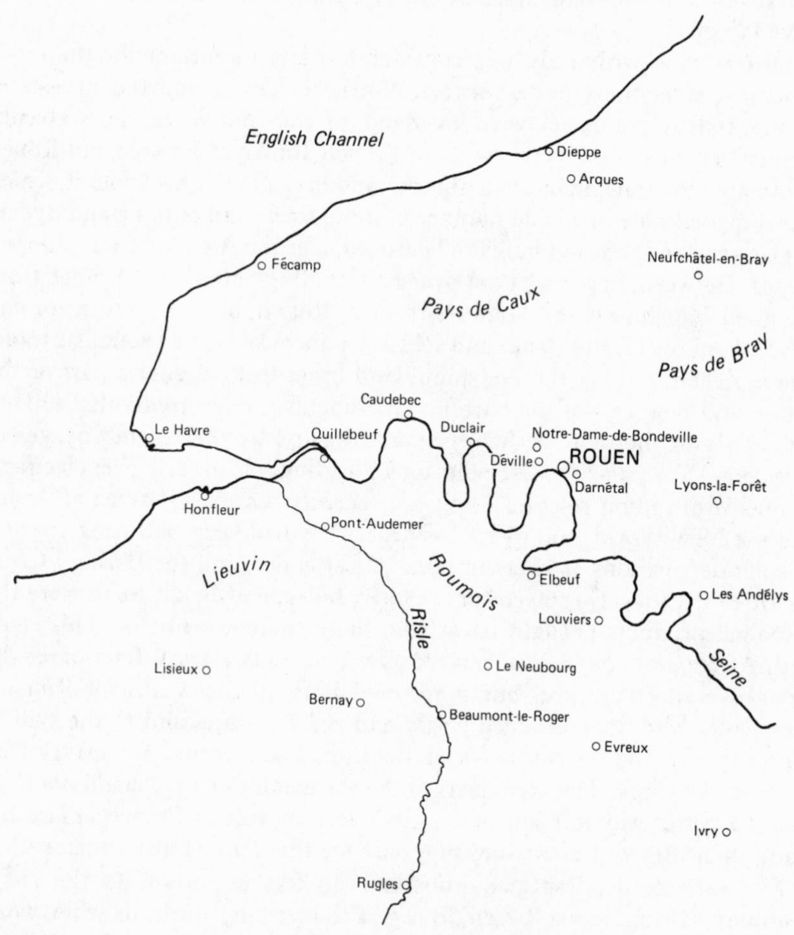

Map 1. Upper Normandy

throughout the Spanish dominions, was considered ideal for conditions in the New World, and through the linen trade Rouen's economy became intimately tied to the rhythms of the *carrera de Indias*. Trade across the English Channel was also very active, with large numbers of merchants coming to Rouen each year from both London and such southwestern outports as Poole, Totnes, and Southampton to sell the tin and lead of Devonshire and Cornwall and buy such manufactured goods as paper, hardwares, and linen. Rouen also sent its manufactures to Antwerp in sizeable amounts, receiving in return Portuguese spices, sugar, jewelry, tapestries, and the many varieties of cloth for which the Low Countries were famous.[1]

Direct trade with Italy was considerably less important for the city's economy, since most trade between Northern Europe and the city-states of the Italian peninsula went overland in the middle of the sixteenth century. Lyon was the great center of Franco-Italian commerce, but Rouen dominated the trade in one valuable commodity, alum. This mineral, which was indispensable in a wide number of industries from tanning and dyeing to glass-making, was too bulky to be carted over the Alps, so it was shipped by sea. Between 1531 and 1553 over half of all the alum sent France from the great Papal mines at Tolfa was sent to Rouen, often in return for cod fished from the Grand Banks and sold at Civitavecchia in a triangular trade. These fisheries along the Newfoundland coast formed only a part of the fifth – and newest – of the currents in Rouen's foreign trade, that linking the city with the new worlds overseas revealed by the recent voyages of discovery. Normandy's merchants took a leading role in early French efforts to open up trading relations with the recently discovered areas of Africa and the New World, and by mid-century they had been outfitting voyages to such destinations as 'Pernambouc', 'Cerleone', and the Barbary Coast for three decades. Sugar, cotton, pepper, hides, and brazil wood were the principal products brought back from these trading ventures. This trade with Africa and America accounted as yet for only a small fraction of the city's overall commerce, but it testified both to the wealth of Rouen's merchants who financed such costly and risky voyages and to the skill of the sailors of the nearby ports of Fécamp, Dieppe, and Le Havre who manned the ships. The organizers of the royal entry of 1550 could not have found a better way to boast of the city's leading role in France's maritime trade than they did in writing in a part for the Tupinamba Indians.

Domestic trade, less glamorous but no less important to the city's economy, also animated Rouen's quays. Brouage salt, Bordeaux wine, woad from Toulouse and Albi, and boxwood (used in making combs) from Oloron in Bearn all arrived in large quantities by sea from France's west coast ports. Much of this was then distributed from the Norman capital throughout northeastern France, as was much of the tin, alum, and tropical fruit imported from abroad. On their return voyages down the Seine, the river barges which carried these goods inland brought the city wine from Burgundy and Orleans, silk from Tours, Italian cloth imported via Lyon, and paper from Auvergne, much of which was then sent on overseas along with the products of Rouen's own industries.[2] Finally, closer to home, trade

[1] A fuller discussion of the main lines of Rouen's overseas commerce, together with references to the abundant bibliography on the subject, may be found in my 'Rouen's Foreign Trade', forthcoming.

[2] Mollat, *Le commerce maritime*, pp. 200–14, 304–29. Numerous acts in the *tabellionage* between 1576 and 1578 also testify to these patterns.

in such items as grain, wood, and meat fueled an active, purely local network of exchanges. The nearby market towns of Caudebec, Les Andélys, Duclair, and Elbeuf provided Rouen with its grain, while Le Neubourg was the chief market for its meat. The richness of the surrounding Norman countryside insured that in nine years out of ten these markets were able to supply the city with all of its needs, although in years of severe harvest failure grain was imported from nearby provinces or the Low Countries.[1]

A cosmopolitan atmosphere characterized Rouen as a result of its far-flung trade. The Tupinambas who battled for Henry II were by no means the city's only exotic visitors. Within a four-month span in 1588, the register of baptisms of the quayside parish of St Denis records ceremonies involving first 'Franceoys Doy, age seventeen years or thereabouts, son of Moussé Doy and of Daro Gay of the kingdom or Cadriet, village of Pordal, seaport near to Portugal and distant from this country by six hundred leagues', then 'Jehan Nego, age twenty years or thereabouts, son of Gola Ouilonengo of the kingdom of Congo, county of Aleysso'.[2] Pilgrims passed through the city from as far away as St Catherine's Monastery of Mount Sinai.[3] And merchants from several European countries settled more or less permanently in the city.

The most important foreign merchant colony was that of the Spaniards. The vigorous trade in Castilian wool had been bringing Spanish merchants to Normandy in larger numbers than any other group of foreigners ever since the late fifteenth century. A significant number settled permanently, marrying and assimilating into the native mercantile elite with a rapidity that contrasted sharply with the standoffish attitude of other groups of foreign merchants, both in Rouen and elsewhere in France.[4] While Spain

[1] On the location of the city's markets: A.C.R., A 16, entry of May 12, 1551; Farin, *Histoire de la ville de Rouen*, Vol. 1, pp. 38–9. In normal years Rouen was sufficiently well-approvisioned to be able to export grain. (There is a good discussion of its grain trade in Henri Lapeyre, *Une famille de marchands, les Ruiz: Contribution à l'étude du commerce entre la France et l'Espagne au temps de Philippe II* (Paris, 1955), pp. 537–42.) The records of the municipal government, which subsidized grain imports in time of scarcity, show that the local supply was insufficient in 1529, 1565, 1573, and 1587. In these years, grain was imported variously from Lille, Amsterdam, Brittany, Lower Normandy, Picardy, and Champagne – in other words, from the Baltic and from all the surrounding French provinces except the Ile-de-France, which Paris monopolized as its exclusive granary.

[2] A.D.S.M., E, St Denis, Baptêmes, entries of June 29 and Sept. 1, 1588. I have not been able to identify the precise location of the mysterious kingdom of Cadriet.

[3] The records of the cathedral chapter (A.D.S.M., G 2270, 2273, 2277–9, and 2464) reveal a steady stream of gifts to pilgrims. Irishmen, Orthodox Greeks claiming to need money to ransom compatriots from the Turk, and French priests chased from their homes by the Protestants during the Religious Wars were the favorite objects of their charity.

[4] Sixty per cent of all letters of naturalization granted foreign residents of Rouen went to Spaniards between 1480 and 1560, according to Christiane Douyère, 'Les marchands étrangers à Rouen au 16e siècle: Assimilation ou ségrégation?' (unpub. thesis, Ecole Nationale des Chartes, 1973), p. 159. On the assimilation of these men into the city, *see ibid.*, passim; Mollat, *Le commerce maritime*, pp. 507–22. Cf. the situation in Lyon described by Gascon, *Grand commerce*, pp. 364–9.

was less developed industrially than France, its merchants had long been masters of many of the more sophisticated commercial techniques of the day such as the use of the letter of exchange and the underwriting of maritime insurance contracts – techniques which the relatively backward French had yet to learn by the sixteenth century. The Castilians were consequently able to assume a prominent position in Rouen's merchant community. The assessment list of a tax levied in 1565 on all resident merchants to construct a building to house the new merchants' court of the *juridiction consulaire* shows that 8 of the 46 wealthiest merchants in the city were Spaniards.[1] Through the influence of this group, the sophisticated techniques of the Mediterranean traders slowly permeated Normandy's mercantile community. The first book on maritime insurance written in France was published in Rouen around mid-century, its anonymous author in all probability the transplanted Spaniard Antoine Massias.[2] The important Iberian colony also furnished a conduit for Spanish cultural influences, as the history of the Counter-Reformation would show.

Smaller groups of merchants from Italy, England, and the Low Countries also lived in Rouen. The Italians were the wealthiest and most skilled of Europe's merchants, and while they were not numerically very important in the city, accounting for just 15 per cent of all letters of naturalization granted in Rouen between 1480 and 1560, their role in its commerce was still far from negligible.[3] Their banking skills helped make Rouen a financial center of some importance, and, characteristically, the one Italian who was a permanent resident in 1565 and who therefore paid the tax for the construction of the *juridiction consulaire*, the Genoese merchant–banker Augustino Salvago, was placed in the very highest tax bracket of all. 'Flemings', as all denizens of the Low Countries were called, were slightly more numerous than the Italians but decidedly less wealthy. The three who appear on the 1565 tax list were assessed at an average rate of just 20 *livres* apiece. (Salvago had been assessed 250 *livres*.) As for the English merchants trading with Rouen, very few settled for any length of time. Most simply visited the city for a few weeks at a stretch while selling the merchandise they had transported across the Channel, staying during their visit at one of the English-run inns which formed the true centers of the local English colony.[4]

The place of these foreign merchants in Rouen's trade was hardly negligible, but foreign capital nonetheless did not play the dominant role in Rouen which it did in such rival trading centers as Lyon. Where an opulent, Italian-dominated foreign colony controlled virtually all of the

[1] A.D.S.M., C 216

[2] Mollat, *Le commerce maritime*, p. 393.

[3] *Ibid.*, pp. 401–4; Douyère, 'Les marchands étrangers', p. 159.

[4] Douyère, 'Les marchands étrangers', pp. 61–7.

Table 1. *Average tax assessment of major categories of merchants, 1565*

	Number	Assessment in *livres*
Grain merchants	18	4.2
Mercers	84	6.8
Wood merchants	17	9.4
Wine merchants	105	18.2
Wool merchants	18	19.7
Linen merchants	36	31.1
Merchants (no specialty)	125	43.3

most lucrative sectors of Lyon's long-distance trade and paid fully 28.5 per cent of a tax levied on *all* the city's inhabitants in 1571,[1] foreigners paid just 7.8 per cent of the tax assessed merchants alone in Rouen in 1565. Native merchants were thus responsible for most of Rouen's commerce. They may have been less skilled in intricate financial maneuvers than the resident Italians or Spaniards, but Rouen's leading merchant families such as the Halleys, the Puchots, and the Le Seigneurs nonetheless took part in all of the most ambitious and expensive trading expeditions which set out from the city. We find them financing voyages to Andalusia, the Barbary Coast, and Brazil, providing much of the capital for maritime insurance contracts by the 1570s, and even invading that erstwhile preserve of the Genoese, the alum trade with Tolfa.[2] Their hold over domestic trade was naturally greater still.

The list of those assessed in 1565 to finance construction of the *juridiction consulaire* provides a statistical profile of the native merchant community. It was a large and variegated group, running from several hundred small merchants specializing in the purely local trade of one or two items, assessed about 3 *livres* each, through a hierarchy of wealth to the elite of some 101 *grands marchands* assessed from 50 to 250 *livres*. In all, 1,172 merchants appear on this tax roll.[3] Table 1 sets forth the average tax assessment of

[1] Gascon, *Grand commerce*, p. 358.

[2] A sense of the range of activities of Rouen's leading merchants can be obtained from the documents printed by E. Gosselin, *Documents authentiques et inédits pour servir à l'histoire de la marine normande et du commerce rouennais pendant les XVIe et XVIIe siècles* (Rouen, 1876). The accounts of the local receiver of the tax on alum (A.D.S.M., Chartrier de Belbeuf, Papiers Ygou, 16 J 185) show the penetration of Rouen's native merchants into this previously Italian-dominated trade. Between 1572 and 1577, Rouennais merchants imported 17 per cent of the city's alum; by 1578–83, this figure had risen to 45 per cent.

[3] Like all social classifications, the rubric 'merchant' is imprecise. Many of the men on this list are *marchands cloutiers*, *marchands tonneliers*, *marchands savetiers*, and so forth – master artisans in one trade or another who had accumulated some modest wealth and come to specialize primarily in

the larger categories of merchants (those with ten or more individuals on the list). As the table makes clear, those men involved in long distance circuits of exchange were decidedly wealthier than those involved simply in retail trade or local commerce. The most successful individuals were those who did not specialize in any one product and were classified simply as 'merchant'. They were the giants of commerce, dealing in a broad range of commodities on an international scale. Among the more specialized merchants, those who traded in linen stand out for their prosperity. They were unusual in another way too. The majority (20 of the 36) were women – not all widows carrying on their husband's trade, as one might expect, but for the most part single women or working wives whose spouses ran the gamut from barber–surgeons to an *avocat au parlement*.[1] This feminine domination of the lucrative linen trade was probably tied to the fact that the spinning, weaving, and embroidering of household linens were all occupations that were the exclusive preserve of women.[2]

By virtue of its plethora of law courts, its varied industries, and its large merchant community, Rouen stood out among France's provincial cities. What sort of impression did it make on visitors? How was its variegated population distributed across its 36 parishes?

Today Rouen's industrial areas sprawl off into the smog on the left bank of the Seine, but all except a few of the 75,000 or so Rouennais who greeted Henry II in 1550 lived on the right bank. Steep hills ring the city on this side of the river. In the sixteenth century they were dotted with structures that provided both reassurance and warning to its inhabitants. Atop Mont Ste Catherine, to the east, stood both the abbey and the fortress of the same name, the latter the key to the city's defense. Atop Mont de Justice, to the north, the *fourches patibulaires*, or gallows, were etched against the skyline. At the foot of the hills, the *faubourgs* spilled out beyond the city's walls

retailing their wares and those of their fellow guild members. Such men obviously straddled the line between merchant and artisan. It is therefore potentially misleading to compare the number of merchants in Rouen as revealed by this list with estimates of the size of the merchant community of other cities. The criteria used in classifying individuals as merchants would not necessarily be the same. One would like to know just how many of these 1,172 merchants were involved in international commerce, but the tax roll unfortunately does not permit one to ascertain this.

1 Natalie Davis also finds a case of a female linen merchant in Lyon, married to, and outearning, a merchant-shoemaker. Davis, 'City Women and Religious Change', *Society and Culture in Early Modern France*, p. 70. While widows who continued their husband's business after his death were common (3 of Rouen's 46 wealthiest merchants were women who fall into this category), and while women also dominated certain manual trades, I am not aware of any other group of merchants in which working wives or single women played so important a role. On the broader place of women in the sixteenth-century workforce, *see* Davis, pp. 70–71, and Henri Hauser, *Ouvriers du temps passé* (Paris, 1909), ch. 8. Tellingly, despite the wealth and economic independence of the female linen merchants, those whose husbands were still alive appear in the tax roll under their husbands' names. Thus, for example, 'maître Gilles Delamare, notary, his wife linen merchant' is assessed 100 *sous*.

2 Four guilds were exclusively feminine in Rouen, those of the *lingères*, *brodeuses*, *rubannières*, and *fillacières*.

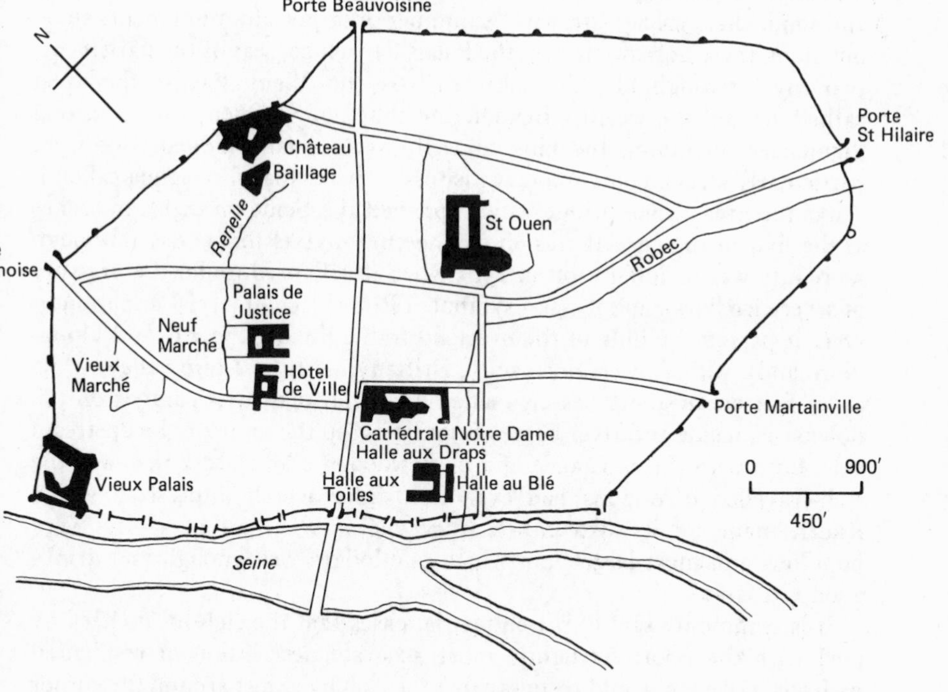

Map 2. Rouen in the sixteenth century

in a few areas, particularly to the west of the city, where the *faubourg* St Gervais housed several thousand inhabitants. The dwellings stood among small garden plots here, and the residents, many of whom were recent immigrants to the city, still had close ties to the countryside.[1] But most of Rouen's inhabitants lived within the protective girdle of the fourteenth-century ramparts, where the country seemed distant amid the closely packed single-family, two-story, half-timbered houses characteristic of the city. These houses typically contained a workshop and a kitchen downstairs, living and sleeping quarters upstairs,[2] and they impressed the visiting Italian cardinal Luigi d'Aragona in 1517 as 'large and most commodious'.[3]

[1] The rural quality of the *faubourgs* can be deduced from extant views of the city, while the frequency with which the residents of these areas married people from the surrounding countryside suggests that their ties to the country were far closer than those of the residents of the intramural parishes. Figures for marriage patterns in three parishes are provided below, p. 143.

[2] An excellent study of the city's housing is provided by Raymond Quenedey, *L'habitation rouennaise: Etude d'histoire, de géographie, et d'archéologie urbaines* (Rouen, 1926).

[3] D'Aragona's remarks on Rouen – or, to be more precise, those of his secretary – are to be found in Ludwig Pastor, ed., 'Die Reise des Kardinals Luigi d'Aragona durch Deutschland, die Niederlande, Frankreich und Oberitalien, 1517–1518', *Erläuterungen und Ergänzungen zu Janssens Geschichte des deutschen Volkes* (Freiburg-im-Breisgau, 1905), Vol. IV, 4, 3, p. 126.

The city's streets impressed him less; d'Aragona found them 'not very wide and somewhat garbage-strewn'. A number of important monuments stood out along these narrow streets: the Palais de Justice, seat of the parlement; two royal strongholds, the Château and the Vieux Palais; the great cathedral; and the wealthy Benedictine abbey of St Ouen, where visiting dignitaries, including the king himself, were usually lodged. But what particularly struck contemporary visitors – 'bellisima' d'Aragona called it – was the great stone bridge which spanned the Seine on eighteen arches at the foot of the city. It was an engineering marvel for its day (although its repute was to suffer a bit in 1565 when it collapsed under the pressure of severe ice floes), and it was a symbol of Rouen's commercial importance. Over it passed the bulk of the overland traffic linking Picardy and Upper Normandy with Lower Normandy, Brittany, and the Loire valley, while at its feet ocean-going vessels loaded and unloaded their cargoes on the downstream side and river barges from Paris did the same on the upstream side, both with the assistance of a huge wooden crane larger than any the well-travelled d'Aragona had ever seen. The overall impression which Rouen made on its sixteenth-century visitor was that of a city 'very populous and most large...in which one lodges well enough and drinks good red wine'.

It is commonly said of pre-industrial cities that the rich lived cheek by jowl with the poor. A slightly more accurate description of residential patterns in Rouen would be to say that the rich lived just around the corner from the poor. In most sections, the wealthier inhabitants tended to live on the main streets and the less well-to-do on the numerous back streets and alleys which interlaced the city. In the elite robe parishes of the north of the city, this pattern was reversed. The wealthy *officiers* built their houses along the quiet back streets, leaving the main thoroughfares to shopkeepers and artisans.[1] Whichever pattern obtained, residential segregation was far less marked than it is in a modern city. In a walking city such as sixteenth-century Rouen, few people could live far from their places of work and shopping, so every quarter needed a range of merchants, artisans, and laborers to function smoothly. Every parish therefore housed members of each group, and nearly all also sheltered at least a few lawyers or *officiers*.

While the range of occupations in any given section of town was greater in sixteenth-century Rouen than in a typical modern city, clear differences

[1] For indications of residential patterns at the level of individual parishes and streets, *see* Bourienne-Savoye, 'Saint-Vincent de Rouen: Une paroisse de marchands au XVe siècle', *Bulletin des Amis des Monuments Rouennais*, 1958–70, pp. 128–38; and Jean-Pierre Bardet, 'Enfants abandonnés et enfants trouvés à Rouen dans la seconde moitié du XVIIIe siècle', *Sur la population française au XVIIIe et XIXe siècles: Hommage à Marcel Reinhard* (Paris, 1973), p. 35. While one of these studies concerns the fifteenth century and the other the eighteenth, it seems highly improbable that the patterns which obtained in the sixteenth century were much different from those revealed here.

in tone and social composition nevertheless were evident as one moved from quarter to quarter. Many of these differences can still be noticed in a somewhat attenuated form by the visitor to Rouen today, for despite some Haussmannization in the nineteenth century and the bombardments of the twentieth, the old, intramural areas of the city have resisted change with remarkable tenacity.

The residential patterns which characterized the city in the sixteenth century can be determined from a number of documents. The parish of residence of the city's merchants is revealed by the rolls of the tax levied for the construction of the *juridiction consulaire*. The geographic distribution of the city's poor is shown by the 1586 enumeration of those employed on the public works. That of the city's *officiers* and lawyers can be determined from a survey made in 1597 when a new tax was imposed on wine and the tax collectors went from door to door gathering the impost from all individuals with private supplies of the beverage in their cellar.[1] While this last document is far from being a complete census (not all individuals could afford, even cared, to maintain a wine cellar), it does record the parish of residence of many of the well-to-do, providing a good indication of where the city's *robins* lived. Maps 3 through 5 set forth the information contained in these documents about the city's residential patterns.

Rouen's merchants, Map 3 shows, tended to cluster in the central parishes of town, along the river and just inland. Here they were near the city's quays and its major markets. The rue Grosse Horloge, running from the front of the cathedral to the Vieux Marché, was, as it remains today, the main axis of this area.

Farther away from the river stood the houses of most of the *gens de loi*. (See Map 4.) These were centered in a band of parishes stretching from St Lô, where the Palais de Justice was located, to St Patrice, seat of the Bailliage. The great *hôtels* which dominate this last parish today date not from the sixteenth but from the seventeenth century, the golden age of *parlementaire* ostentation. Traces of the earlier robe domination of these parishes can nonetheless still be found in the early sixteenth-century stained glass windows which decorate the parish church – each with a grave, black-robed donor kneeling piously in the lower corner.

Rouen's poor clustered in two regions. (See Map 5.) One was on the west side of the city, just inside and outside the Porte Cauchoise. This was an area dominated by a variety of small crafts. The other, far larger concentration of the poor was formed across town in the easternmost parishes of St Maclou, St Vivien, and St Nicaise. This last parish was particularly disfavored; not one lawyer or *officier* inhabited it, and its only 3 merchants taxed at 10 *livres* or more were wine-sellers, living off the

[1] A.C.R., Chartrier, tiroir 137.

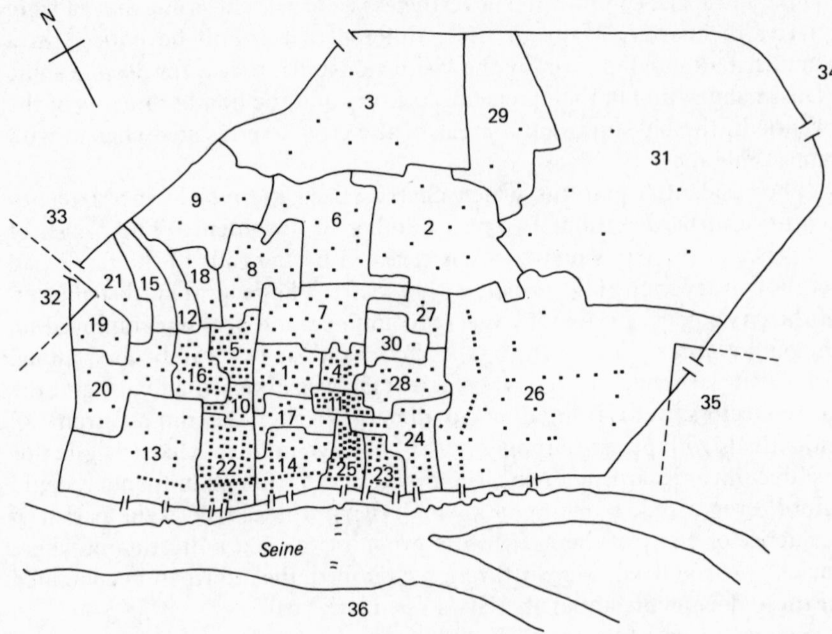

Map 3. Residential patterns: the well-to-do merchants

Quartier Beauvoisine
1. Notre-Dame-de-la-Ronde
2. Ste Croix–St Ouen
3. St Godard
4. St Herbland
5. St Jehan
6. St Laurent
7. St Lô
8. St Martin-sur-Renelle
9. St Patrice

Quartier Cauchoise
10. St André
11. St Cande-le-Jeune
12. Ste Croix-des-Pelletiers
13. St Eloi
14. St Etienne-des-Tonneliers
15. Ste Marie-la-Petite
16. St Michel
17. St Pierre-du-Chastel
18. St Pierre-l'Honoré
19. St Pierre-le-Portier
20. St Sauveur
21. St Vigor
22. St Vincent

Quartier Martainville
23. St Cande-le-Vieil
24. St Denis
25. St Martin-du-Pont
26. St Maclou

Quartier St Hilaire
27. St Amand
28. St Etienne-la-Grande-Eglise
29. St Nicaise
30. St Nicolas
31. St Vivien

Faubourgs
32. St André-hors-Ville
33. St Gervais
34. St Hilaire
35. St Paul
36. St Sever

(Each dot represents 1 individual taxed 10 *livres* or more in 1565 for the construction of the *juridiction consulaire*.)
Source: A.D.S.M., C 216.

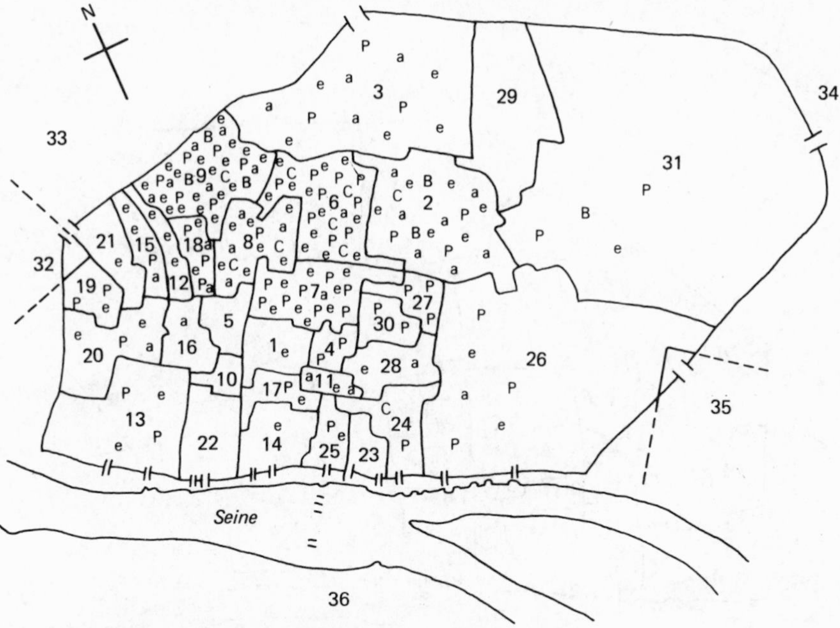

Map 4. Residential patterns: the *gens de loi*

Officiers
P = member of parlement
C = member *cour des aides*
B = member *bailliage* court

Lawyers
a = *avocat*
e = *procureur*

Quartier Beauvoisine
1. Notre-Dame-de-la-Ronde
2. Ste Croix–St Ouen
3. St Godard
4. St Herbland
5. St Jehan
6. St Laurent
7. St Lô
8. St Martin-sur-Renelle
9. St Patrice

Quartier Cauchoise
10. St André
11. St Cande-le-Jeune
12. Ste Croix-des-Pelletiers
13. St Eloi
14. St Etienne-des-Tonneliers
15. Ste Marie-la-Petite
16. St Michel
17. St Pierre-du-Chastel
18. St Pierre-l'Honoré
19. St Pierre-le-Portier
20. St Sauveur
21. St Vigor
22. St Vincent

Quartier Martainville
23. St Cande-le-Vieil
24. St Denis
25. St Martin-du-Pont
26. St Maclou

Quartier St Hilaire
27. St Amand
28. St Etienne-la-Grande-Eglise
29. St Nicaise
30. St Nicolas
31. St Vivien

Faubourgs
32. St André-hors-Ville
33. St Gervais
34. St Hilaire
35. St Paul
36. St Sever

Source: A.C.R., Chartrier, tiroir 137.

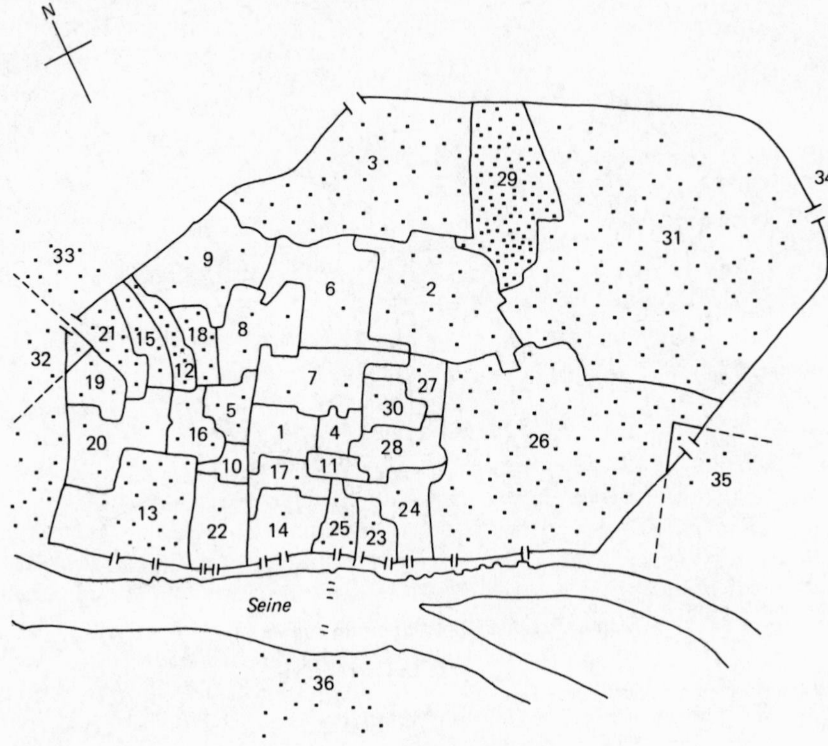

Map 5. Residential patterns: the poor

Quartier Beauvoisine
1. Notre-Dame-de-la-Ronde
2. Ste Croix–St Ouen
3. St Godard
4. St Herbland
5. St Jehan
6. St Laurent
7. St Lô
8. St Martin-sur-Renelle
9. St Patrice

Quartier Cauchoise
10. St André
11. St Cande-le-Jeune
12. Ste Croix-des-Pelletiers
13. St Eloi
14. St Etienne-des-Tonneliers
15. Ste Marie-la-Petite
16. St Michel
17. St Pierre-du-Chastel
18. St Pierre-l'Honoré
19. St Pierre-le-Portier
20. St Sauveur
21. St Vigor
22. St Vincent

Quartier Martainville
23. St Cande-le-Vieil
24. St Denis
25. St Martin-du-Pont
26. St Maclou

Quartier St Hilaire
27. St Amand
28. St Etienne-la-Grande-Eglise
29. St Nicaise
30. St Nicolas
31. St Vivien

Faubourgs
32. St André-hors-Ville
33. St Gervais
34. St Hilaire
35. St Paul
36. St Sever

(Each dot represents 10 individuals employed on the public works, 1586.)

Source: A.C.R., B4, fos. 319–20.

inhabitants' need to escape from an environment which remains today the most depressing in the city. These eastern parishes were the center of the cloth industry, and the bulk of the poor here was composed of the large proletarian population employed by that industry.

Rouen was a large city by the standards of the day, and there are times when it appears to the historian as though the number of those with a hand in governing it was almost as large as the city itself. Its system of political authority was the very antithesis of a rationalized administrative structure. Power was divided among a variety of men and institutions: the multi-tiered municipal government, the royal governor or his lieutenant-general, the *bailli*, the members of the *bailliage* court, and the parlement, to name only the most important. Each one's sphere of responsibility was vague and often the powers of the different groups overlapped, so that certain tasks came to be shared by city council, parlement, and governor alike.[1]

The complexity of Rouen's political structure was common to French cities at the time. It was the product of the monarchy's general institutional development over the course of the later middle ages and early modern period, in which growth by accretion was the fundamental rule. Occasionally old institutions might be abolished, most commonly when the monarch stepped in to punish a locality after a major revolt. At such a point a city's constitution might be fixed by royal decree, but it rarely remained fixed for long. New administrative structures were regularly being created in the provinces as the central government struggled to strengthen its hold over the localities or found itself forced to supplant earlier *missi dominici* who had drifted out of the control of the crown, become rooted in local society, and developed into defenders of local privileges rather than agents of royal centralization. These older institutions, once supplanted, were left to decay, but they were rarely abolished outright. They lingered on, geological deposits from an earlier era, claiming theoretical powers no longer exercised in practice.

In Rouen's case, the structure of political authority had been theoretically fixed in 1382, when Charles VI had imposed a new constitution on the city

[1] Because the structure of authority was ill-defined and the theoretical power of any institution rarely coincided with the power it actually exercised, the only reliable way to determine who governed an Ancien Régime city is to watch the government in operation over a long period of time. The following description of Rouen's government is therefore based primarily on a thorough reading of Rouen's municipal deliberations, the *registres secrets* of its parlement, and the surviving correspondence between the city and the court for the period 1550–1600, supplemented by the summaries of the municipal deliberations made by Robillard de Beaurepaire (*Inv/Sommaire*) for the period 1500–50 and 1600–50. Also of use were J. Félix, ed., *Comptes-Rendus des Echevins de Rouen* (Rouen, 1890) and the two brief studies of E. Le Parquier, *Contribution à l'histoire de Rouen: Une année de l'administration municipale* (*l'année 1515*) (Rouen, 1895) and *Les élections municipales à Rouen au XVIe siècle* (Rouen, 1925).

in the wake of the revolt of the Harelle. Coming as it did after a century of struggles within the city over the precise form which municipal government ought to take, this revolt had been the last straw which convinced Charles VI to suppress Rouen's status as a self-governing commune. He transferred to the royal *bailli* all of the judicial and military powers which the mayor of the city had previously exercised, suppressed the office of mayor, and left a restructured municipal government in charge of questions of city finance, public health, sanitation, and the regulation of commerce and industry.[1]

The theoretically clear-cut division of power between the municipality and the *bailli* mandated by this constitution no longer governed actual administrative practice by the sixteenth century. Over the course of the intervening years, a series of institutional changes had multiplied the number of royal officials with a say in city government.

The first important change was a metamorphosis in the office of *bailli*. By 1550, the judicial functions which the *bailli* himself had once exercised had been assumed by legal professionals, the long robe counsellors of the *bailliage* court. The *bailli* himself had been superseded by the governor as the chief local representative of the monarchy. The *bailliage* court was still the local court of first instance in the city, and the title of *bailli* still conferred a degree of authority and prestige on its holder, but it had become a superfluous position since its chief functions could all be carried out by other officials. It was left vacant for periods of up to seven years at a time during the second half of the century.[2]

If the governor was now the chief local representative of the monarchy, his primary responsibility was to ensure the military security of the city and the surrounding region, a function symbolized by his control of the keys to the city gates. He was also expected to provide leadership in maintaining order within the city, and thus he had the primary responsibility for putting down popular disturbances. Finally, it was the governor who transmitted royal commands to the municipal government, and it was therefore his responsibility to see that these commands were carried out.

But again complications arose. The governors of important provinces such as Normandy were as likely to be absentee figures as the bishops of major sees. Throughout the middle decades of the century Normandy's governors were either younger sons of the royal line or such scions of

1 The Harelle and its consequences for the city constitution are discussed in Charles Petit-Dutaillis, *Les communes françaises: Caractères et évolution des origines au XVIIIe siècle* (2nd ed., Paris, 1960), pp. 163–5, and Le Parquier, *Une année de l'administration municipale*, p. 6.

2 The list of the city's *baillis* in Maurice Veyrat, *Essai chronologique et biographique sur les baillis de Rouen* (Rouen, 1953), shows that the position was vacant from 1565 to 1570 and from 1595 to 1602. For a general discussion of the evolution of this position, *see* Gaston Zeller, *Les institutions de la France au XVIe siècle* (Paris, 1948), pp. 168–71.

leading courtier families as Robert and Henri-Robert de La Marck, dukes of Bouillon.[1] Too important to reside in their governorships, such men spent most of their time following the king. Until the governorship of Normandy was divided into three parts in 1574 and given to men of lesser prestige, no sixteenth-century governor appears to have spent more than a few months at a stretch in Rouen. Furthermore, none of Normandy's governors ever possessed either sufficient land in Normandy or sufficient influence at court to build up an important clientage network in the province. None could control Normandy from Paris to anything approaching the degree to which the Guises controlled Champagne. Indeed, the office of governor appears to have been barely more than honorific in character, and the actual administration of the province tended to devolve on its lieutenants-general. These were the men whose names appear most frequently in the local documents. They were the men who had to see to it that the king's orders were obeyed. Their extant correspondence suggests that they acted essentially as autonomous royal servants, not merely as dutiful clients of the absent governors.[2]

Responsibility for keeping order and carrying out royal edicts was not the governor's or his lieutenant-general's alone. The municipal authorities also shared the task, and by the sixteenth century a new body had also appeared on the scene, the parlement. Whenever a serious disturbance broke out within the city, both the city council and the parlement would assemble hastily and, after consulting with the governor if possible, take whatever measures they deemed necessary to suppress the disorder. This was not a responsibility which either body particularly relished, for in the event of a serious revolt against royal authority they might be harshly reprimanded by the king for their inability to maintain order. Each therefore tried to shift this responsibility onto the other's shoulders in times of potential unrest, as happened when the lieutenant-general had to leave Rouen for a few weeks in 1571 during a period of extreme tension between Catholics and Protestants. The city council and the parlement passed the

[1] For a list of Normandy's sixteenth-century governors, *see* the recent work of Robert R. Harding, *Anatomy of a Power Elite: The Provincial Governors of Early Modern France* (New Haven, 1978), pp. 225–6, a study which supersedes all previous work on this institution. The provincial governorship was held by the dukes of Bouillon for most of the first half of our period (1552–74). In 1574 the position was divided among three men, and Taneguy Le Veneur, seigneur de Carrouges, a man we will meet often in the pages which follow, was named governor for the region of Upper Normandy. In 1583 the province was reunited again under a single governor, Henry III's favorite Anne de Joyeuse. On his death in 1587 the position passed to another of Henry's *mignons*, Epernon.

[2] Among the many letters of the royal lieutenants-general which I found in the manuscript collection of the Bibliothèque Nationale, only one was directed to the governor rather than the king. Although theoretically the governor's lieutenant, the lieutenants-general of Normandy took orders directly from the crown. It is also a significant reflection of Normandy's governors' lack of power as brokers at court that the city council almost never passed through the governor when petitioning the king for some favor.

keys to the gates back and forth to each other hurriedly, each protesting its desire not to meddle in the other's affairs.[1]

While Rouen's parlement was not always eager to claim the power of keeping order in the city, it was far less modest about extending its control over other aspects of city government. The growing role played by the parlement in local affairs was perhaps the most important of all the changes taking place in municipal government in the sixteenth century. The key to the extension of its power was its ability to issue what were known as *arrêts de règlement*, administrative edicts which could set policy over all matters of government not otherwise covered by custom or royal statute.[2] Within fifteen years of its creation in 1499, the court was issuing such *arrêts* to combat a plague epidemic, and as the century progressed it steadily increased the scope and boldness of its orders. By the second half of the century, it was for all intents and purposes the chief decision-making authority on all of the matters of municipal administration which contemporaries lumped together under the general heading of *la police*, i.e. the regulation of public health, sanitation, poor relief, wages, prices, and so forth.[3] This steady increase in the role of the court in local government characterized all cities which housed provincial parlements in this period.[4]

As the parlement extended its authority over city affairs, the power of the municipal government naturally decreased. The city council assembled less and less often over the course of the century; from an average of thirty-five meetings yearly in the 1550s, the frequency of its reunions dropped to twenty-seven per year between 1575 and 1584 and to twenty-three in the 1590s. The range of affairs debated at these assemblies also shrank. Where, early in the sixteenth century, long debates had been held over measures needed to combat plague epidemics or regulate the city's industries, by the end of the century the council had to be content simply to administer those measures mandated by the parlement. As policy-making functions were lost, citizen interest in municipal government also dwindled.

[1] A.D.S.M., B, Parlement, Registres Secrets, entry of June 14, 1571.

[2] The power to issue these *arrêts de règlement* was probably every bit as important a basis of the parlements' political role as their far more famous (and less often used) right of remonstrance against royal edicts they considered ill-advised. For descriptions of this power, *see* A. Esmein, *Cours élémentaire d'histoire du droit français* (Paris, 1921), pp. 514–15, and F. Olivier-Martin, *Histoire du droit français des origines à la Révolution* (Paris, 1948), pp. 538–41. There is also a good brief discussion of *arrêts de règlement* in Steven L. Kaplan, *Bread, Politics and Political Economy in the Reign of Louis XV* (The Hague, 1976), p. 22, to which I am indebted for the above references.

[3] The court's extension of its authority over *police* matters may be traced easily from the published *Ordonnances contre la peste faictes par la court de l'eschiquier* (Rouen, 1513) and *Arrests de la Court de Parlement et ordonnances faictes sur la police en ceste ville de Rouen* (Rouen, 1587). (Until 1514 the parlement bore the title of *échiquier*.) Jonathan Dewald provides a dissenting view in 'The "Perfect Magistrate": Parlementaires and Crime in Sixteenth-Century Rouen', *Archiv für Reformationsgeschichte*, LXVII (1976), p. 293.

[4] Gaston Zeller, 'L'administration monarchique avant les intendants: parlements et gouverneurs', *Revue Historique*, CXCVII (1947), pp. 186–201.

Individuals elected to public office began to attempt to evade the honor, and elections had to be postponed on several occasions because of poor turnout.[1] Yet if municipal authority was on the wane throughout the century, it still was by no means impotent. The role of the city council in keeping order remained far from negligible in 1550; it had to administer many of the city's rather impressive range of social welfare services; and most importantly, it controlled the municipal finances. This included supervising the repartition of all taxes levied on the city, as well as negotiating the level of these taxes with the king.

The structure of the city government had been established by the same edict of 1382 which had specified the division of responsibilities between the city and the *bailli*. The structure which Charles VI had imposed involved several tiers. It was highly oligarchic. Day-to-day administrative matters were the responsibility of six *conseillers-échevins*, chosen through a combination of election and co-optation. Deliberations about questions of policy were the province of a larger body, the Council of Twenty-Four. Despite its name, this body did not have twenty-four members; it was fluid in size, being composed of the six *conseillers-échevins*, all living ex-*conseillers-échevins*, one *quartenier* from each of the city's four quarters, six *pensionnaires*, the *bailli*, and the *gens du roi au bailliage*. When dealing with particularly important questions, the Council of Twenty-Four often invited a limited number of leading residents from each quarter to join in its deliberations. Matters of truly exceptional gravity were referred to a General Assembly. This institution too was not quite what its name might imply, for far from being general, attendance at these assemblies was limited to the city's most notable inhabitants, a group numbering between one and two hundred individuals. Just what qualified somebody to participate is unclear. Wealth alone was not enough, for comparison of the lists of those who took part in the general assemblies of 1566 with the 1565 tax roll for the construction of the *juridiction consulaire* reveals that certain of the wealthiest merchants in the city did not participate, while a few individuals assessed far less than they did. A combination of wealth, personal prestige, and length of family residence in the city probably was involved, for it was a fundamental tenet of the system that only those whose fortunes were both large and long-established could be expected to put their own interests aside and govern the city with a view to the general welfare. As an outgoing *conseiller-échevin* explained in 1617, listing the qualities needed for membership in the Council of Twenty-Four:

> [Those chosen] must be natives of the city, of good and ancient family, and men of substance (*gens de bien*). When I say men of substance, I do not speak of those builders of fortunes, those harpies, those misers who never have enough and would

[1] A.C.R., A 16, entry of July 4, 1550; A 20, entries of July 10 and 12, 1578, July 4, 1581.

take the position of *conseiller-échevin* to further their own affairs and abandon the public, but I mean true men of substance, that is people content with their wealth who will abandon their own affairs to serve the public.[1]

The oligarchic nature of city politics carried over to the municipal elections as well. Only the 'best and most substantial' inhabitants could vote. They would assemble every three years in their respective quarters to nominate twelve men for the six positions of *conseiller-échevin* and four for each post of *quartenier*. The outgoing Council of Twenty-Four then chose its successors from among these nominees. The four new *conseillers modernes* (those holding the office for the first time) were always the four outgoing *quarteniers*, and the four new *quarteniers* were chosen from among the auditors of the city's accounts. That this *cursus honorarum* was rarely violated suggests that the elections were generally not the focus of bitter struggles over the political control of the city, but were instead perfunctory assemblies of a small elite which knew one another's strengths and weaknesses well and could easily agree on the proper individuals for each position. Only in 1566, at the height of the religious struggles, is there evidence that an election was strongly contested.[2] Members of a few leading families turn up time and again in the Council of Twenty-Four. But although marked, the tendency toward oligarchy in Rouen's Council of Twenty-Four never reached the point attained in other French cities of the period, where municipal offices became permanent, venal, or heritable.[3]

The city government also included a number of other officials beside the members of the Council of Twenty-Four. Each parish had its *centenier* and *cinquantenier*, ward officials chosen by the council for flexible terms of office. These men were usually simple artisans, and they fulfilled such tasks as keeping track of all non-residents lodged in their neighborhood and notifying the higher authorities if any trouble broke out.[4] Their services

[1] *Inv/Sommaire*, entry of July 4, 1617.

[2] Bibliothèque Publique et Universitaire de Genève, Archives Tronchin, Vol. 8, fos. 76–9. The appearance of harmony within the city government may be exaggerated by the sources. The accounts of the deliberations of the Council of Twenty-Four do not divulge the breakdown of votes on different issues or for rival candidates and may therefore convey a false impression of relative concord. The fact that the struggles of 1566 are known to us today only through the chance survival in Geneva of a copy of a complaint by the city's Protestant voters suggests that other elections may have been bitterly contested as well but left no record. On the other hand, all surviving Rouennais journals and memoirs are also mute about the elections. They contain nothing that would suggest that these were the focus of bitter political rivalries.

[3] Paris is the most notable example of such a city. *See* Georges Picot, 'Recherches sur les quarteniers, cinquanteniers et dixainiers de la ville de Paris', *Mémoires de la Société de l'Histoire de Paris et de l'Ile-de-France*, I (1875), pp. 151–3. Municipal offices were permanent and heritable in Poitiers as well by the end of the sixteenth century. Henri Ouvré, 'Essai sur l'histoire de la Ligue à Poitiers', *Mémoires de la Société des Antiquaires de l'Ouest* (1854), pp. 90–91.

[4] A list of the *centeniers* and *cinquanteniers* of the *quartier Beauvoisine* in 1578 reveals that fourteen of these men were artisans and one a bourgeois *vivant de ses rentes*. A.C.R., B 4, entry of Sept. 16, 1578. Their functions are evident from the municipal registers of deliberations.

were not called upon as often as those of the parish treasurers, who tended to be drawn from the leading families of each parish and may have been considered more reliable for that reason.[1] De facto city officials as well as supervisors of parochial finances, these men were responsible for drawing up the lists of those eligible for poor relief in the parish, collecting the funds destined for this purpose, and announcing newly enacted municipal legislation to the parish after Sunday Mass.

A final group of city officials was composed of specialized administrators such as the city treasurer, the scribe, the *maître des ouvrages* (roughly the public works commissioner), the auditors of the municipal accounts, and the city *procureur*. All of these were appointed to their positions with the exception of the *procureur*, who was elected for life. His position was especially important, for it was the *procureur* who had to handle the ticklish and interminable negotiations between the city and the central government that were still an important part of urban political life.

These negotiations between the city and the central government were the basic element in town–crown relations. If the king was felt to be pliable, virtually every set of royal letters-patent decreeing new taxes, and occasionally other unpopular actions taken by him or his governor as well, might provoke the city to dispatch to court a delegation led by the *procureur* to plead with the monarch and his counsellors for a reduction in the sums demanded or a change in the royal policy being implemented. Oratorical gifts were the chief requirement for the office of *procureur*, and it was on these missions that his rhetorical skills were called into play, for eloquent lamentations, it was firmly believed, could produce a royal change of heart. When Henry III decided to have the feared *reiters* pass the winter of 1574 in Normandy rather than Picardy, the Council of Twenty-Four attributed this decision to the 'beautiful remonstrances' of the Picards. The *procureur* was immediately dispatched to court in the hope that his even more eloquent tongue might convince the king to send the troops yet elsewhere.[2] If oratory failed, gifts might be tried. In 1555, no less than 3,000 *livres* were allocated for presents to be offered *les grands* at court in hopes that the city's taxes might be reduced. The investment turned out to be an excellent one, for the king modified his demands by 60,000 *livres*.[3] Not all missions to court were so successful, but it frequently was possible to obtain at least a modest reduction in the level of taxation, particularly once the Wars of Religion began to weaken the crown and make it more susceptible to

[1] The parish treasurers of St Godard, St Martin-sur-Renelle, and St Laurent, all in the *quartier Beauvoisine*, included 51 *gens de loi*, 8 merchants, and 8 artisans between 1550 and 1600. A.C.R., R.P. 445; A.D.S.M., G 6616–18, 6800–2.

[2] A.C.R., A 19, entry of Nov. 3, 1574.

[3] A.C.R., A 17, entries of Sept. 9 and Nov. 23, 1555.

pressure. As a result, such missions were repeated time and again. In times of extremely unpopular royal measures or exceptionally high tax demands, delegations could follow one another to court with such rapidity that often one had not returned before another set out. In 1564, the city even proposed that it be permitted to keep a permanent envoy at court in order to save itself the expense of frequent excursions.[1] The king angrily rejected the suggestion, but the idea of a city ambassador was simply the logical extension of the prevailing system of town–crown relations, which had almost the flavor of international diplomacy to it. The monarch's orders were regularly subjected to negotiation until either a compromise was reached or the king proved his determination to have his way through a show of either force or anger. The time had not yet come when the monarch could expect his orders to be immediately obeyed in a major provincial city.

Historians of early modern cities often lavish attention on the formal institutional structure of urban government. Less often do they address themselves to what is a surely more important topic: that of determining the actual power of city government. If the king could not expect Rouen's municipal authorities to carry out his orders at once, what about these authorities? How effective were they in ensuring that the edicts they issued were in fact obeyed?

If historians have tended to neglect this question, one reason lies with documents that rarely allow them to determine how well a given law was actually enforced. Rouen's authorities certainly tried to regulate nearly every aspect of urban life. At one time or another in the sixteenth century, edicts were promulgated ordering all householders to keep the streets in front of their house lit by lanterns in their window at night, instructing all inn-keepers to provide the authorities every two days with lists of all guests, barring people from going about masked, and forbidding the roving peddlers who sold firewood from using their customary 'declamations, swearing, and blasphemy' in hawking their wares.[2] Wages were fixed in many industries; an exceptionally detailed set of regulations running to thirteen pages governed the baking and selling of bread; and a system of public charity modelled on those of Lyon and Paris sought from 1535 onward to ensure that all the city's inhabitants had at least a minimal sustenance.[3] That many of the edicts had to be reissued periodically

1 A.C.R., A 18, entries of April 19 and July 19, 1564; B.N., MS Français 17832, fo. 82, Charles IX to *échevins* of Rouen.

2 A.C.R., A 16, entry of July 30, 1553; A 17, entry of Oct. 15, 1558; B.M.R., MS Y 214 (4), fo. 413; A.D.S.M., B, Parlement, Arrêts, Novembre 1567–Février 1568, arrêt of Jan. 30, 1568, Décembre 1568–Juin 1569, arrêt of Feb. 21, 1569.

3 Decisions fixing wages may be found scattered through the *arrêts* of the parlement and the measures of the *Chambre de la Police*. A printed copy of the 'Ordonnances du metier de boullenger en la ville de Rouen' is in A.C.R., Chartrier, tiroir 262. On the city's poor relief measures, *see* Panel, ed., *Documents concernant les pauvres*, Vol. 1, passim, esp. pp. 16–28.

suggests that they were not always obeyed. Attempts to restrict the quantities of wine sold in the taverns, to prevent disorders at carnival time, and to outlaw begging in public seem to have been particularly unsuccessful, for the authorities were constantly reissuing warnings on these scores. But one can jump too easily from such examples to the conclusion that most of the authorities' edicts were honored more in the breach than in the observance. While documents are rare which enable one to see how most edicts were actually enforced, the few which have survived suggest a municipal government conscientious about its duties.

A stray sheet among the papers in the municipal *chartrier* is typical of the ambiguities encountered in trying to determine the efficiency of the city government. It contains a report from the *enquesteur du roi* of the *bailliage* that, while making his rounds of the city inspecting its sanitation, he discovered that the inhabitants of St Patrice had been dumping their garbage at the end of the rue Etoupée, a small side street near the walls. The pile had grown so large that it blocked the street entirely.[1] Such a document obviously shows that laws against dumping were not always obeyed, but it also reveals that the authorities tried to monitor the problem. While one might assume from the frequently repeated injunctions against dumping trash in one location or another that Rouen matched Goubert's image of '*la ville puante*', other documents in the municipal archives show that the city frequently set large numbers of the unemployed to work cleaning the streets, that inspectors could and did tell tenants that they did not have to pay their rent if their landlord was not providing them with the required toilet facilities, and that even when the guard of the gate was stepped up in wartime, arrangements were always made so that the night soil could be carted out of the city.[2] Sanitation may not have been so primitive. Particularly impressive testimony to the authorities' success in enforcing public welfare measures comes from a register of the deliberations of the *Chambre de la Police*, a special commission – composed of members of the parlement, the *chambre des comptes*, the *bailliage* court, and the Council of Twenty-Four – which a royal edict of 1572 had created to coordinate enforcement between all those responsible for aspects of *la police*.[3] The volume reveals a commission that was both conscientious and effective in setting and enforcing standards for prices and wages, supervising the operations of the city's markets, and regulating the import and export of grain. The chamber engaged in long interrogations of all interested parties before setting prices or determining standards of quality for the city's

1 A.C.R., Chartrier, tiroir 75, piece of Aug 20, 1558.

2 A.C.R., Chartrier, tiroir 75, pieces of March 18, 1563, Aug. 16, 1582; tiroir 154, pieces of April 30 and May 1, 1563; A 18, entry of Nov. 19, 1562; B 4, entry of Nov. 29, 1583. Goubert's remarks on Beauvais's odoriferousness are to be found in *Beauvais et le Beauvaisis*, pp. 229–33.

3 A.D.S.M., Chartrier de Belbeuf, Papiers Ygou, 16 J 188.

industries. It regularly fined those who sold goods above the fixed prices. And it required merchants wishing to export grain in times of local surplus not only to obtain permission from the commission but also to return within a fixed period with a certificate of confirmation from the *Chambre de la Police* of the city to which they had declared they would be taking the grain attesting that they had done so.

Any final judgment about the effectiveness with which Rouen's authorities enforced their will must be a cautious one. Documents such as the ones cited above indicate that it is just as misleading to interpret the manifest failure of certain edicts to achieve their stated aim as a sign of the general impotence of the authorities as it is to assume, as certain particularly naive historians still do, that all laws enacted were in fact obeyed. Contemporary cities remind us in any case that in all eras major urban areas develop problems which even large and committed bureaucracies seem unable to solve, just as modern vice laws outlawing gambling or prostitution suggest that societies often enact legislation condemning practices which they in fact are not committed to eradicating. This is probably how the apparently unsuccessful edicts restricting drinking and carnival riotousness ought to be seen – as the homage officially paid to virtue.

However uncertain the verdict about the overall efficiency of city government, there was one area where sixteenth-century authorities were undeniably less successful than modern governments – in maintaining order. Given the unreliability of any crime statistics one might concoct from sixteenth-century judicial records, it is impossible to make precise comparisons between levels of violent crime then and now. Still, most historians seem to agree that interpersonal violence existed in early modern cities on a scale that would frighten any but the most street-hardened New Yorker today.[1] Impulsiveness reigned among rich and poor alike, and petty quarrels could escalate into violent affrays with alarming speed.[2] Certain private journals of the time are little more than lists of spectacular crimes and spectacular public executions.[3] Furthermore, it was not only individual

1 The finest description of the violence of sixteenth-century life is to be found in Lawrence Stone, *The Crisis of the Aristocracy, 1558–1641* (Oxford, 1965), pp. 223–34. *See also* the comments of Robert Mandrou, *Introduction à la France moderne 1500–1640* (2nd ed., Paris, 1974), pp. 86ff; J. R. Hale, *Renaissance Europe 1480–1520* (London, 1971), pp. 25–9; Bennassar, *Valladolid*, pp. 539–40; and Leon Bernard, *The Emerging City: Paris in the Age of Louis XIV* (Durham, N.C., 1970), p. 157, who provides at least one crime statistic – 372 murders in one year in mid-seventeenth-century Paris.

2 *See* the confessions of pardoned criminals in Amable Floquet, *Histoire du privilège de Saint-Romain* (Rouen, 1833), passim.

3 A local example of such a journal is the *Journal d'un bourgeois de Rouen, mentionnant quelques événemens arrivés dans cette ville depuis l'an 1545 jusqu'à l'an 1564*, publication of *La Revue de Rouen et de la Normandie* (Rouen, 1837). Crimes and executions were not quite all that this chronicler thought worthy of note. Along with a brief account of the early years of the religious struggles, he also records

crime that was widespread; the danger of crowd violence always lurked just beneath the surface. Even if the number of actual 'emotions' was small in the half-century prior to the Wars of Religion, a strong undercurrent of fear of popular violence nonetheless can be detected throughout this period in the deliberations of Rouen's governing bodies. The populace represented a 'hard-to-restrain beast' (*une mauvaise beste a maintenir*), the members of the parlement and the Council of Twenty-Four often reminded one another, and those pleading for a certain measure frequently invoked what might be dubbed the argument from fear of popular sedition – the argument that the measure they were proposing had better be enacted or else people will riot.[1] Christian charity may have had something to do with the cathedral chapter's decision to buy grain and distribute it to the poor in 1525, but the canons themselves declared this was done to allay the danger of '*sediciones et commociones*'.[2] This fear of sedition was by no means irrational. Any delay in imposing price controls or supplying subsidized bread in times of *disette* could lead a muttering, angry crowd to assemble,[3] and as the representatives of a small social elite, the authorities knew that any outburst of popular violence was a potential threat to their property and position. They were also aware that if they lost control of the city completely, the king would send in the one force capable of keeping order

such *faits divers* as the poisoning of a man on his wedding day and the Rabelaisian drowning of an officer of the cavalry and his servant, underneath whom the floorboards of the outhouse had given way.

1 The metaphor of the populace as a many-headed monster was used so often it would be tedious to cite all the cases. The specific phrase cited comes from the A.D.S.M., B, Parlement, Registres Secrets, entry of March 20, 1571. The argument from fear of popular sedition appears almost as often. For some cases: B.M.R., MS Y 214 (5), fos. 236, 267; A.D.S.M., B, Parlement, Registres Secrets, entry of Nov. 7, 1581; Floquet, *Privilège Saint-Romain*, Vol. 1, pp. 303–7, where the argument is used to support both sides of an issue.

2 Procacci, 'Strutture economiche', p. 25; David J. Nicholls, 'The Origins of Protestantism in Normandy: A Social Study' (unpub. Ph.D. dissertation, Birmingham University, 1977), p. 36.

3 The mild incidents which occurred in 1573 and 1587 show as much. In May 1573, as grain prices mounted rapidly in a period of *disette*, 'disorder' reported at the Halle aux Blés led the parlement to order the city councillors to organize the distribution of free bread quickly. The mobs which gathered on the first day the bread was being handed out grew so great that several people were apparently crushed to death. There was not enough bread to go around; those left out swore bitterly; and an '*émotion populaire*' seemed imminent to the parlement. The quantity of bread being distributed daily was immediately ordered increased, public works were set up to employ the able-bodied poor, and the actual task of distributing the bread was handed over to the parish treasurers so that all those on the parish rolls would all be assured of receiving their allotment of bread and no crowds could assemble at a single distribution point. A.D.S.M., B, Parlement, Registres Secrets, entries of May 20, 27, 1573; A.C.R., A 19, entry of May 28, 1573. In 1586, a year of even more serious shortage, an angry crowd turned against a merchant who had recently arranged the importation of large quantities of grain from Brittany and had apparently told the shipmasters putting the grain on sale at the docks to be firm about demanding a higher price than that set by law. The crowd threatened to hurl the man into the Seine, but he was saved through quick action on the part of a *servant de la ville*. Lest the mob think that such activity was in any way condoned, the authorities sentenced the merchant to be whipped publicly, stripped of a minor office he held, fined, and banished from the city. Albert Sarrazin, ed., *Abrégé d'un journal historique de Rouen* (Rouen, 1872), pp. 26–7.

in any city, a large royal garrison, and feeding and housing a company of chronically ill-paid and decidedly unmannerly soldiers were burdens which all sixteenth-century cities dreaded. The authorities thus usually hastened to appease the mob. Given the oligarchic nature of Rouen's government, the threat of popular violence could be seen as the one way the great mass of the population exercised any influence over the decisions of the city authorities. It might be considered almost a normal part of the operation of the political system.

If the city fathers were so vulnerable to the threat of popular disorder, their vulnerability must be attributed in large measure to the absence of a large class of full-time, professional peace officers who could be depended upon to put down a mob. It was not that the authorities lacked men they could call upon. On the contrary, maintaining order was a task which many inhabitants shared. The *bailli* had 40 full-time sergeants under his command. There were 2 privileged militia companies composed of citizens who met regularly to drill: the 50 *arbalétriers* (or *cinquantaine*), whose origins dated well back into the Middle Ages, and the 104 harquebusiers, formed in the 1520s during the wars against the emperor both to defend the city against possible attack and to rid the surrounding countryside of 'Gros Dos' and his fellow *aventuriers*. As the origins of this latter company suggest, these groups were expected both to participate in any military campaigns which might be carried out in the area and to assist in maintaining order within the city and its environs.[1] Four guards were also stationed daily at each of the town gates, with all citizens taking their turn fulfilling this duty. Finally, when special precautions were felt necessary to keep order, night watches or town militias ranging in size from 400 to 4,000 men were created.

The problem was that all of these groups were fundamentally unreliable. Modern police forces generally share a strong occupational identity; policemen have their own subculture and a strong commitment to maintaining the peace. This is precisely what was absent in the sixteenth century. The sergeants of the *bailliage* seem to have been a collection of French Dogberries: 'for the greatest part useless men of no worth', the *avocat du roi* Bigot called them in 1560.[2] They regularly panicked at the sight of a mob and could not even be counted on to fulfill their most basic

[1] In return for their services, the members of these companies received a modest salary, exemption from all taxes and subsidies designed to raise money to support soldiers, a *mine* of free salt per year, and the right to sell up to ten *queues* of wine per year tax-free. The history of the *Cinquantaine* has been written by Charles Robillard de Beaurepaire, *Notice sur la compagnie des Arbalétriers autrement dite la Cinquantaine de Rouen* (Rouen, 1885). The creation and privileges of the 104 Harquebusiers can be followed on the basis of A.D.S.M., 5 E 116–18. An excellent discussion of these two bodies at a somewhat later date may be found in André Corvisier, 'Quelques aspects sociaux des milices bourgeoises au XVIIIe siècle', *Annales de la Faculté des Lettres et Sciences Humaines de Nice*, 9–10 (1969), pp. 241–77.

[2] B.M.R., MS Y 214 (5), fo. 338.

duty, that of guarding the *conciergerie* (the town prison).[1] The members of the privileged militia companies seem to have been more courageous. They could still be called upon to play an active role in warfare, and when they were they responded bravely. During the wars of the League, they marched off to battles before Dieppe, Pontaudemer, and Caudebec, and 11 of the 104 harquebusiers died in the course of these actions.[2] But the members of these units were ordinary townsmen. An analysis of the social composition of the 104 harquebusiers around 1560 reveals a sort of sixteenth-century Elks Club, an association of average solid citizens. The militia members came from 29 different parishes and included 64 artisans from nearly 40 different trades, plus a handful each of small merchants, factors, minor officials, and surgeons and apothecaries.[3] Such men were little different from their neighbors, and when they happened to sympathize with the aims of a rioting crowd composed of their neighbors, they were prone to ignore the summons to assemble. In 1571, the company had to be purged of 67 members after a particularly flagrant case of dereliction of duty, while seven years earlier the lieutenant-general had had to look into reports that the harquebusiers were harrassing the Protestants in violation of the terms of the edict of pacification.[4] Clearly, the privileged militia companies were often as much a part of the problem of disorder as they were of its solution.

The same held true *a fortiori* for the larger night watches and town militia units set up on various occasions throughout the period. These groups lacked even the *esprit de corps* of the special militia units, so it is hardly surprising that in 1560 the parlement argued that creating a night watch was more likely to provoke trouble than it was to calm the city.[5] Throughout the Wars of Religion, night watches and town militias were constantly being created, abolished, and created anew as the authorities

[1] One of the most frequent scenes in the religious rioting of the civil wars was to be the invasion of the city's prison by a mob seeking either to set free or to set upon those being held in the *conciergerie*.

[2] For the campaigns of the militia companies: A.D.S.M., 5 E 406, petition of July 4, 1592. The casualty rate can be calculated from the list of the company's members, 5 E 117.

[3] The precise breakdown of the company is as follows:

artisans: 64 (leading trades – inn- and tavern-keepers 5; cutlers 5; hosiers 4; shoemakers 3; tailors 3; goldsmiths 3)
merchants: 8 (mercers 3; grain merchants 2; fish merchants 2)
factors or transport trades: 9
officials or lawyers: 8 (clerks 3; *auneurs* of cloth 2)
apothecaries and surgeons: 2
soldiers: 1
no occupation listed: 12

A.C.R., Chartrier, tiroir 123. The document is undated, but it can be determined that it comes from around 1560 by comparing it with other extant lists of the company's members which are dated.

[4] A.C.R., B 3, entry of May 16, 1571; B.N., MS Français 17832, fo. 74.

[5] B.M.R., MS Y 214 (5), fos. 315–18. For proof of the unreliability of the militia companies, *see* A.C.R., B 3, entries of April 5 and 6, 1571.

sought for the magic formula that would guarantee them a guard large enough to defend the city against external enemies and put down any internal disorders, yet loyal enough so that its own members would not themselves contribute to the disorders.[1] A series of measures were gradually worked out to increase the reliability of these units. Their officers came to be recruited entirely from among members of the city's governing elite; those considered '*notoirement mutin*' were regularly stricken from the militia rolls; and all members of the companies were required to swear a solemn oath to obey the king and his officers.[2] But despite such measures Catherine de Medici was still hectoring the city to tighten up discipline within the militia in the later 1580s, and on the eve of the League Henry III felt that to guarantee the loyalty of the group it was necessary to ennoble all twelve of its officers.[3] The gambit failed. As we shall see, the militia played a major role in the League takeover of the city, proving once again

[1] It is not possible to reconstruct the full history of the city's militia units and night watches from the records of the parlement and the Council of Twenty-Four, but these sources reveal the main outlines of the story over the second half of the sixteenth century. The first night watch created in this period was one composed of 30 bourgeois and 10 '*ministres de justice*' established in January 1553 in one of a series of measures spelled out in an ambitious *arrêt* of the parlement concerning public safety. The *arrêt* also forbade people to carry swords, daggers, or other '*bastons offensifs*' on the street after dark, ordered householders to keep the streets in front of their houses well lit, and expelled all vagabonds from the city. How well this *arrêt* was enforced is unclear; what is clear is that in 1560, as the religious conflicts began to heat up, a new 120-man watch and 400-man militia had to be created. They apparently remained in existence until 1563, when they were disbanded after the close of the First Civil War. Between 1563 and 1567 the crown and the local authorities tried to keep the city peaceful by keeping everybody disarmed; even the 104 harquebusiers could not carry their harquebuses or pistols when on patrol, only halberds. In 1564 a Catholic mob, fearing a Protestant coup, demanded the re-establishment of a militia, but the demand was not met until the outbreak of the Second Civil War in 1567 made the authorities feel a new militia was needed to defend the city. A group of undetermined size was created. It may then have been disbanded with the return of peace in 1570, but this again is unclear. It is known that a new guard of 150 '*bons bourgeois*' was hastily assembled in the days immediately following the major disturbance of 1571 known as the Massacre of Bondeville. Following the refusal of many of these men to turn out, a larger 400-man militia was established. It, however, was not to prove large enough to prevent the St Bartholomew's Massacre the following year, and in the wake of that event the company was increased in size to 4,000 men. Commanded by 12 captains, this 4,000-man militia managed to become a permanent fixture – not so much because it was more effective or reliable than earlier militia units, one suspects, as because popular violence died down in the city after 1572 for reasons which will be analyzed in later chapters, giving the authorities no cause to alter the structure of this unit. The militia remained in existence into the eighteenth century.

[2] A.C.R., A 19, entries of March 4, 1574, Jan. 4, 1575; A 20, entry of June 3, 1580; B.M.R., MS Y 214 (6), fos. 256–8. In the eighteenth century, according to Corvisier, the positions of captain in the militia were divided up according to a strict formula, with two coming from the parlement, two from the *chambre des comptes*, and so forth. This does not yet appear to have been the case in the sixteenth century. Measures were also taken in this period to tighten the city's control over the 104 harquebusiers. The city council started to supervise their annual election of their captain in 1575 and to require all members to sign a loyalty oath.

[3] *L.C.M.*, IX, pp. 298–9, 303–4; A.D.S.M., B, Cour des Aides, Memorial 9, fos. 94–5; P.-F. Lebeurier, *Etat des anoblis en Normandie de 1545 à 1661* (Evreux–Paris–Rouen, 1866), pp. xiv, 116. The king also granted a raise in salary to the members of the city's privileged militia companies.

that those whose responsibility it was to keep order were citizens, sharing the passions of their fellow townsmen and hardly to be counted on to do the bidding of the city authorities at critical moments.

In this large city with its highly diverse economic and social structure, the local authorities thus never had a power at their command capable of keeping the city quiet through sheer repressive force. If Rouen was to remain peaceful, its residents had to share a basic consensus of values on at least the most fundamental questions of social organization and religious belief. Such consensus is precisely what was to disappear in the second half of the sixteenth century. One of the tableaux vivants drawn before Henry II in 1550 depicted Union of Christianity as the mother of Royal Majesty. It was, in a way, prophetic. Protestant ideas had already been circulating surreptitiously in Rouen for three decades, but as yet the city's peace had not been seriously troubled by the passions which religious differences could arouse. Within a decade of Henry's triumphal entry, the Union of Christianity would be shattered by the dramatic growth of Protestantism, and for nearly thirty-five years thereafter, the men who marched in so orderly a fashion before their king would be caught up in a violent struggle with one another. In the process Royal Majesty would suffer some damaging blows.

PART I

A city divided, 1560–1571

Il ne faut pas avoir beaucoup d'experience
Pour estre exactement docte en vostre science:
Les barbiers, les maçons en un jour y sont clers,
Tant vos mysteres saints sont cachez et couvers!
Il faut tant seulement avecques hardiesse
Detester le Papat, parler contre la Messe,
Estre sobre en propos, barbe longue, et le front
De rides labouré, l'oeil farouche et profond,
Les cheveux mal peignez, le sourcy qui s'avale,
Le maintien renfrongné, le visage tout palle,
Se monstrer rarement, composer maint escrit,
Parler de l'Eternel, du Seigneur et de Christ,
Avoir d'un reistre long les espaules couvertes,
Bref, estre bon brigand et ne jurer que certes.
Il faut, pour rendre aussi les peuples estonnez,
Discourir de Jacob et des predestinez,
Avoir saint Paul en bouche et le prendre à la lettre,
Aux femmes, aux enfans l'Evangile permettre,
Les oeuvres mespriser, et haut louër la foy:
Voilà tout le sçavoir de vostre belle loy.

Vous ne pipez sinon le vulgaire innocent,
Grosse masse de plomb qui ne voit ny ne sent,
Ou le jeune marchant, le bragard gentilhomme,
L'escolier debauché, la simple femme; et somme
Ceux qui sçavent un peu, non les hommes qui sont
D'un jugement rassis, et d'un sçavoir profond.

Ronsard, 'Remonstrance au peuple de France' (1562), *Oeuvres complètes* (Bibl. de la Pléiade, Paris, 1950), II, 577–8

2

The rise of Protestantism and the outbreak of religious violence

Simply on the basis of the picture of Rouennais society sketched in the preceding chapter, much of the early development and eventual fate of Protestantism in Rouen seems almost predictable. As a large port animated by the comings and going of ships and merchants of all nations, it was to be expected that Rouen would quickly get wind of the new religious currents stirring elsewhere in Europe. Just as port cities were prone to infection by plague, so too (to use a favorite metaphor of the Catholic authorities) were they prone to infection by heresy. Furthermore, as a city boasting a wide range of skilled artisans, it was also to be expected that Protestant ideas would strike deep roots in the city, for if there is one generalization about the sociology of French Protestantism that seems to be beyond question, it is that the artisan classes, and especially the more skilled artisans, provided the bulk of the movement's early recruits. But Rouen was also a major administrative center, the seat of a parlement, and such cities proved in general less receptive to the new religion than those cities where the authorities were a comfortable distance away. Most of the greatest Huguenot strongholds – La Rochelle, Montauban, Nimes – were situated far from the watchful eyes of the local parlement, while those cities which housed high courts proved almost uniformly to be less heavily Protestant than other major towns in their *ressort*. Often, as in the case of Paris and Toulouse, they became the great bastions of Catholicism. However creaky the machinery of judicial repression might be, its presence within a city nonetheless seems to have acted as a brake on the development of Protestantism. And so it is not surprising that, no matter what success the movement might attain within Rouen and how menacing it might appear at times, Protestantism never would attain majority status. After a period of dramatic growth, the new faith was to level off in the position of an imposing but decidedly outnumbered minority. Even the conflicts which Protestantism's growth touched off seem almost foreordained. With a population ranging from the university-educated *parlementaires* in St Patrice to the illiterate *laboureurs* of the *faubourgs*, from the most opulent of international merchants on the rue de la Grosse Horloge to the proletarianized *ouvriers en draperie* in St Nicaise, Rouen housed a gamut of social groups that few French cities could match for diversity. Such a community was one with a great potential for confessional violence, not because religion necessarily served in any mechanical way as a mask for economic and social conflict, but because, with so wide a range of social types, it was particularly likely that both Protestantism and Catholicism would have their passionately committed defenders in Rouen.

Protestant ideas came early to the city and fell quickly on receptive ears. The first evidence of Lutheran 'contamination' turned up as early as 1524, when a routine inventory of the estate of a deceased canon of the cathedral chapter revealed several works by the Wittenberg theologian.[1] Within six years Protestantism had spread so widely in the region that, according to Bucer, Normandy was being called a 'little Germany'. Zwinglian ideas were already beginning to supplant those of Luther.[2]

During this and the subsequent two decades, Protestantism remained an unstructured movement in Rouen. Scattered individuals were touched and convinced by the new ideas carried by surreptitiously distributed books or proclaimed by itinerant preachers who attracted crowds in an area for a day or a week and then moved on. Condemned as heresy, these new ideas were the object of surveillance by both ecclesiastical and lay tribunals, but intermittent crackdowns and executions could not stop their circulation. The secret distribution of placards during the night of January 27, 1535, attacking the Mass and the veneration of saints, the iconoclastic attacks on roadside crosses and statues in 1541, 1545, and 1551, and the frequent heresy trials throughout this period all testify to the continued presence of Protestant opinions in Rouen throughout the 1530s, 1540s and 1550s.[3] But while the parlement and the ecclesiastical courts could not prevent the dissemination of Protestant ideas, they could and did thwart attempts to give strength and direction to the amorphous movement by forming a community with regular meetings. In 1546, Geuffroy Rivière, a doctor,

[1] The canon asked to be buried without pomp and without Masses for his soul in purgatory, which suggests that he had not simply read these works out of curiosity but had been influenced by them. David J. Nicholls, 'The Origins of Protestantism in Normandy: A Social Study' (unpub. Ph.D. dissertation, University of Birmingham, 1977), p. 49. Because this work provides a good recent account of Protestantism's early history in Normandy, I have not felt it necessary to trace the movement's early history in great detail in these pages.

[2] M. C. Oursel, 'Notes pour servir à l'histoire de la Réforme en Normandie au temps de François Ier, principalement dans le diocèse de Rouen', *Mémoires de l'Académie Nationale des Sciences, Arts et Belles-Lettres de Caen* (1912), pp. 139, 151.

[3] *Ibid.*, pp. 159–60; *Relation des troubles excités par les calvinistes dans la ville de Rouen depuis l'an 1537 jusqu'en l'an 1582*, Publication of *La Revue de Rouen et de la Normandie* (Rouen, 1837), p. 8; B.M.R., MS Y 102 (1), entry of Oct. 30, 1551.

invited a preacher with Protestant leanings to the city and lodged him in his house. The weekly sermons which the minister delivered in a field outside the city could not be kept secret, and Rivière was quickly arrested and banished from the kingdom. The unnamed preacher fled. Protestantism remained as it had been for the preceding twenty years – less an organized movement than an amorphous group of people sharing heterodox ideas of varying authorship.[1]

The arrival in Rouen in 1557 of the Calvinist minister de la Jonchée changed this situation permanently. The gradual underground percolation of Protestant ideas throughout the decades from 1524 onward had prepared the soil. The movement now entered a phase of institutional consolidation and rapid numerical growth. Through his sermons and religious instruction de la Jonchée managed to impose an orthodox Calvinist cast upon the previously ill-defined movement and to organize a formal Reformed church with regular services and the full panoply of church officials as set forth in Calvin's Institutes.[2] Henceforward, Protestantism and Calvinism were to be for all intents and purposes synonymous.[3]

The parlement tried to stem the growth of the new church. An *arrêt* ordered the prompt execution of any Reformed ministers arrested and the confiscation of any house in which a Calvinist assembly was discovered.[4] The congregation had to remain an underground body for its first few years, moving its meetings from house to house to avoid detection. Many converts chose to emigrate in this period; between 1557 and 1559, 86 refugees from Rouen inscribed their names in Geneva's *livre des habitants*, joining 53 other Rouennais who had already moved there between 1549 and 1556.[5] (The total of 139 refugees from Rouen was higher than that from any other

[1] N. Weiss, 'Note sommaire sur les débuts de la Réforme en Normandie (1523–1547)', *Congrès du Millénaire de la Normandie (911–1911): Compte-Rendu des Travaux* (Rouen, 1912), p. 213.

[2] *Hist. eccl.*, Vol. 1, p. 112.

[3] There is just one exception to this statement of which I am aware. In 1560 a minister who had fled Geneva to escape heresy charges there gave a series of sermons in a wood outside Rouen. The exact beliefs of this man are unclear, but he was certainly no Calvinist. Some sources refer to him as an Anabaptist, others as a *libertin*, and one source even claims that he denied the existence of God. Whatever his exact beliefs, they seem to have evoked a certain popular response; 2,000 auditors are estimated to have attended his sermons, which he punctuated with wild shaking and rolling of his head. After he had finished speaking, the crowd marched into Rouen, their faces covered, singing psalms. This alarmed both Catholics and Calvinists, and the preacher was quickly arrested and burned at the stake. *Cal. S.P. For.* 1560/930; 'Discours abbregé et memoires d'aulcunes choses advenues tant en Normandye que en France depuis le commencement de l'an 1559, et principalement en la ville de Rouen', A. Héron, ed., *Deux chroniques de Rouen* (Rouen, 1900), p. 189; *Journal d'un bourgeois de Rouen, mentionnant quelques événemens arrivés dans cette ville depuis l'an 1545 jusqu'à l'an 1564*. Publication of *La Revue de Rouen et de la Normandie* (Rouen, 1837), p. 6; *Hist. eccl.*, Vol. 1, p. 112; Jacques-Auguste de Thou, *Histoire universelle* (The Hague, 1740), Vol. 2, pp. 810–21.

[4] *Hist. eccl.*, Vol. 1, p. 229.

[5] *Livre des habitants de Genève* (Geneva, 1957), Vol. 1 (1549–1560), ed. Paul-F. Geisendorf, passim, esp. p. xvi.

French city, a reflection of the strength of early Protestantism in the Norman capital.) In spite of the persecution and consequent emigration, the new congregation nonetheless grew. A new pastor soon had to be summoned from Geneva to assist de la Jonchée.[1]

The pace of Protestant expansion quickened perceptibly in the years 1560–61. According to a Catholic chronicler, the Huguenots 'began to rear their head more than previously' in 1560.[2] The diary of a Calvinist records the same development in a somewhat different light: 'the Gospel began to be strong in 1560'.[3] However the development was interpreted, 1560 clearly marked a new stage both in the rise of Protestant numerical strength and in the openness with which the Calvinists held their assemblies. In February and March the Huguenots dared for the first time to hold public gatherings.[4] In May groups of people singing psalms nightly in the streets were reported.[5] When the Spanish ambassador happened to visit the city in July, he was dismayed to find 3–4,000 Protestants assembling regularly in front of the cathedral to hear their preachers.[6] This growth was not confined to Rouen; the Protestant cause was progressing at such a rapid rate throughout France that in April 1561 Catherine de Medici realized her new regency government was too weak to continue its attempt to suppress the faith. An edict of April 19 attempted to calm the growing religious agitation by forbidding magistrates to search houses suspected of holding Huguenot assemblies, ordering the release of all prisoners held on religious grounds, and outlawing the use of the insulting terms 'papist' and 'huguenot'. For the first time it appeared that the crown was moving toward an acceptance of Protestantism, and this served further to augment the growth of the Calvinists' ranks.[7] By November 1561, Rouen's Protestants felt sufficiently strong to begin holding their *prêche* publicly in the Halles. This continued until the first explicit edict of toleration, the edict of January, granted them the right to hold their assemblies legally in the *faubourgs*.[8]

How large was Rouen's Reformed church by this time? According to that vast compilation of histories of the individual congregations written by their members and sent to Geneva, the *Histoire ecclésiastique des églises réformées au royaume de France*, the church had 'not less than 10,000' members. It required 4 pastors and 27 elders.[9] If anything, the estimate

[1] *Hist. eccl.*, Vol. 1, p. 229.

[2] *Relation des troubles*, p. 8.

[3] *Journal d'un bourgeois*, p. 6.

[4] A.D.S.M., B, Parlement, Arrêts, Août–Octobre 1562, arrêt of Aug. 26, 1562.

[5] B.M.R., MS Y 102 (1), entry of May 3, 1560.

[6] *Archivo documental español: negociaciones con Francia* (Madrid, 1950–59), Vol. 1, p. 327.

[7] De Thou, *Histoire universelle*, Vol. 3, p. 53; Lucien Romier, *Catholiques et Huguenots à la cour de Charles IX* (Paris, 1924), p. 250.

[8] *Hist. eccl.*, Vol. 1, p. 861; Vol. 2, p. 610.

[9] *Ibid.*, Vol. 1, p. 861.

of membership may be low. Evidence from another Norman city, St Lô, indicates that the Reformed movement was only marginally larger in the mid-1560s than it was late in 1561, and Rouen's first surviving Protestant baptismal register suggests a membership on the order of 16,500 people in 1565.[1] (It contains 662 baptisms.) If Rouen's Protestant congregation evolved along lines parallel to St Lô's, the church may already have had 15,000 members by the end of 1561. Whatever its exact size, it had clearly become dramatically large within just a few years of its formation. Fifteen to twenty per cent of the city's population was now Protestant.

It is arguable that a social movement can only become a mass movement when it appears to have a reasonable likelihood of success, or, at the very least, does not expose its members to excessive danger. Certainly the political situation looked increasingly promising for the Protestant cause after 1559, while the degree of risk involved in joining the movement declined. It is not necessary to trace in detail the twists and turns of court politics in the years immediately following Henry II's fatal injury in the jousts celebrating the Peace of Cateau-Cambrésis – a peace which, it should be recalled, was motivated largely by the French king's desire to end his international adventures so that he could devote himself fully to the task of stamping out heresy at home.[2] Suffice it to say that this obviously providential death inaugurated a period in which France was ruled by two adolescent monarchs, Francis II and Charles IX; that the accession of a young king always whetted the ambitions of the great families and set off political skirmishing around the problem of the composition of a regency; that Francis II's sudden illness and death in 1560 shortly before he was expected to punish the Prince of Condé for that Protestant champion's plots against the crown appeared to many Calvinists to be yet another 'evident miracle' which proved that God was working to thwart their enemies;[3] and that during the period following the accession of Charles IX, the calling of the Estates-General and of the Colloquy of Poissy, together with the proclamation of the first edicts of toleration, suggested that the monarchy was looking more favorably on Protestantism and might even be swayed to espouse it. In the midst of the rapid political turnabouts the crown's authority in the provinces was shaken. 'The kingdom was as if without a

[1] Figures for Rouen from A.D.S.M., E, Registres paroissiaux, Protestants de Rouen, 1565–6. On St Lô, *see* Appendix 1.

[2] The history of these years has been masterfully traced by Lucien Romier in his *Les origines politiques des guerres de religion* (Paris, 1913–14); *La conjuration d'Amboise* (Paris, 1923); and *Catholiques et Huguenots à la cour de Charles IX*.

[3] The phrase 'evident miracle' appears in J. L. Rigal, ed., *Mémoires d'un calviniste de Millau* (Rodez, 1911), p. 472. A similar idea is expressed in the 'Cantique solemnel de l'église d'Orléans sur la delivrance feit de son peuple le cinquiesme Decembre 1560', P. Tarbé, ed., *Recueil de poésies calvinistes (1550–1566)* (reprint ed., Geneva, 1968), pp. 27–9.

king. . . Justice lost all its force', wrote one Rouennais.[1] The lid of official surveillance which had previously checked the spread of Protestant literature was lifted, and works of propaganda flowed off the Genevan presses into France at a record pace.[2] The political developments of these years encouraged those with Protestant leanings who might previously have hesitated before joining an outlawed movement to embrace a cause whose time now appeared near, while the public preaching and psalm-singing combined with the flood of printed propaganda to provide many people with their first detailed exposure to Protestant doctrines. The resulting surge of new members in turn further heartened the Calvinists, for was their rapid growth not another proof of divine approval, yet another sign that the Reformation was approaching?

One misunderstands these years if one fails to appreciate the exuberance and exaltation which gripped many Protestants as they sensed the potential triumph of their cause. A Calvinist poem published in Lyon, 'The True Bulls-Eye of the Archers Who Aim at the Popeinjay', reveals their optimism clearly.[3] A procession of theologian–bowmen beginning with Wyclif take aim at the popinjay, the traditional target in the shooting competitions held annually in most French cities in this period (including Rouen). Following the shots of Calvin and Viret, the target totters precariously on its lofty perch, about to fall. A popular Huguenot song of these years is entitled, even more confidently, 'Regrets and Adieu to the Pope'.[4] And the widely hawked and influential woodcut of 'The Great *Marmite* Overturned' (see page 55) gives graphic expression to the same sentiments. Although the Pope and his minions try to keep people blindfolded and fenced off from the truth, they cannot prevent a shaft of light bearing the Holy Scriptures from descending from heaven and toppling the *marmite* (a pun meaning both stewpot and hypocrite). The fires of the Protestant martyrs help overturn the stewpot, which contains all the riches of the Roman Church. Meanwhile, assorted members of the first estate struggle vainly to hold it upright – when they are not otherwise engaged chucking their concubines under the chin or deflecting the wealth of the church into their own purses. This clever work compresses into a single image many of the basic themes of Protestant propaganda – that the

1 *Relation des troubles*, p. 12. *See also* J. H. M. Salmon, *Society in Crisis: France in the Sixteenth Century* (New York, 1975), pp. 134–5.

2 Geneva's presses recorded their peak output of the century in 1561. Robert M. Kingdon, *Geneva and the Coming of the Wars of Religion in France, 1555–1563* (Geneva, 1956), p. 99.

3 Jacques Pineaux, *La Poésie des Protestants de langue française, du premier synode national jusqu'à la proclamation de l'Edit de Nantes (1559–1598)* (Paris, 1971), pp. 80–81.

4 *Ibid.*, p. 81. Similarly confident sentiments appear in the 'pasquil' about the Pope reported in *Archivo documental español*, Vol. 3, p. 331; Tarbé, ed., *Recueil de poésies calvinistes*, pp. 47–8.

La Verité à du tout renuerſee
L'hypocriſie, & la marmite auſſy,
Elle ne peut plus eſtre redreſſee
Par ſeducteurs auec tout leur ſoucy,
Vn chaſcun d'eux y met la main ainſy
Que vous voyez, mais en vain il ſefforce,
Car Verité deſcend du Ciel icy
Qui va briſant de leur Canons la force,

'The Great *Marmite* Overturned'

Source: reproduced from the copy in the Cabinet d'Estampes, B.N.

laity has been duped by a corrupt and wealthy clergy, that Protestantism represents the pure and powerful light of the Scriptures, that the blood of the martyrs is the seed of the church – and it proved to be highly effective. Copies appear to have been widely circulated, and the Parisian theologian Thomas Beauxamis was stung badly enough by the engraving to respond soon thereafter with a *Resolution on Certain Portraits and Libels, Entitled with the Name of the Marmite* (Paris, 1562).[1] Despite his attempts to prove that the '*secte Calvinique*' was the true *marmite*, the phrases '*marmite*' or '*marmiton*' quickly became standard terms of derision used by the Huguenots to denote the Catholic Church and its clergy.[2]

A letter written to Calvin by an anonymous Norman minister describing his visit in August 1561 to the important trade fair of Guibray provides an exceptional glimpse of the atmosphere now reigning among Normandy's Huguenots.[3] Arriving in the company of several Rouennais merchants at the plain outside Falaise where the fair was held annually, the minister was surprised to find that placards against the Mass were being carried openly among the stalls. 'The abolition of the Mass! The ruin of the stinking Mass!...See how the merchants who peddle us their fine wares [i.e. the Catholic clerics who sell anniversary Masses and indulgences] are about to be done away with!' cried the hawkers. When several priests tried to silence the vendors, they were quickly surrounded by a menacing crowd shouting at them: 'Go out and glean, it's good weather...Learn how to work, you fine merchants, you've eaten too long without doing anything!' The language of Protestant pamphlets and of their peddlers was becoming the language of the crowd as well. After some initial hesitation caused by fears that his sermons might provoke trouble, Calvin's anonymous correspondent began to preach daily at the fair. His audience grew regularly, and he estimated the Sunday crowd at 5–6,000 people. That night, the *compagnons de boutique* began to sing psalms in front of their stalls. Some Parisian makers of rosary beads responded with their own, profane songs. Although told to keep quiet if they could not sing the praises of the Lord, they refused, whereupon some of the more zealous Huguenots started a 'tumult' and

1 The diary of Antoine Richart, *Mémoires sur la Ligue dans le Laonnois* (Laon, 1869), p. 493 reports that copies of this print were hawked in Laon in the wake of the Edict of January. A copy of the engraving is in the Bibliothèque Nationale and a drawn reproduction survives in the Fonds Leber of the B.M.R.

2 *See*, for example, such later Calvinist poems as 'The Despair of the Grey Friars at the Loss of the Overturned *Marmite*' (1562) and 'The Polymachy of the *Marmitons*, or the Pope's Gendarmerie' (1563), both from Lyon. (Montaiglon and Rothschild, eds., *Recueil de poésies françoises*, Vol. 7, pp. 51–65, 140–7.) In this latter poem Lucifer attempts to recruit the '*prestraille*' into an army which will attempt to vindicate the cause of his eldest son, the Pope, and set the *marmite* upright once more. All interested are urged to betake themselves to the lodgings of madame Idolatry, at the sign of the Abuse, on False Religion Street.

3 'Une mission à la Foire de Guibray: lettre d'un ministre normand à Calvin', *B.S.H.P.F.*, XXVIII (1879), pp. 455–64.

forced them to flee. Several hundred Protestants then began to move systematically through the fair, swords in hand, 'reforming' whatever singing or other 'dissolution' they encountered. At the fair's close, the minister could report with satisfaction that sales of rosaries and candles had been only a fraction of normal, while business had been ruined for the prostitutes who set up their tents near the fairground. (Then as now, it would appear, the travelling salesman and the lady of pleasure went together.)

The events at the fair of Guibray not only convey the exciting rapidity with which Protestant ideas seemed to be spreading in this period. They also demonstrate the speed with which many Protestants, once converted, passed from words to deeds, making public demonstrations of their faith and setting out to rid society of its abuses. Significantly, on the last day of the fair, the anonymous pastor chose to outline for his new converts what was entailed in living a Christian life. Until the true gospel was preached openly and legally throughout the realm, he told them, they should confine their energies to reading the Scriptures, reforming their own lives, teaching their families, and praying to God that he might show the light to the powers that be. These were the acceptable limits of political action as set forth by Calvin and the Reformed ministry. Calvin preached consistently that one must obey the duly constituted authorities and do nothing to reform the church without their permission. Even martyrdom was to be accepted without protest. The official organs of the Reformed Church in Normandy all shared Calvin's respect for the political order and his desire not to have their movement appear in any way seditious. At its meeting of 1560, the provincial synod affirmed its opposition to any acts of iconoclasm carried out without judicial authorization, while the consistory of the congregation of Rouen steadfastly condemned any acts of violence by members of the church, including attempts to rescue arrested Protestants being led off to execution.[1] But such pronouncements from the Reformed leadership could not keep some members of the faith from adopting more aggressive tactics in order to hasten the abolition of papistry and its abominations. While the consistory, which was dominated by men from the urban elite,[2] may have been moved by an understandable concern for public order, their concern was not shared by many humbler converts. Throughout France, and even

[1] *Hist. eccl.*, Vol. 1, p. 862; Library of the Remonstrant Church (Rotterdam), MS 404, synod of 1560, article 15. I consulted this latter document on microfilm at the Musée Historique de la Réformation, Geneva.

[2] Of the seventeen Calvinist elders of 1562 listed in *Relation des troubles*, p. 18, the occupations of eleven can be identified. One was a member of a sovereign court, three were lesser *officiers*, one a lawyer, five merchants, and one a tavernkeeper. Four others bore the noble title '*seigneur de*'. Since very few true noblemen resided in Rouen, these four individuals were probably merchants or officials who had purchased a noble estate.

in the neighboring areas of the Low Countries, the years 1560–62 saw a wave of illegal demonstrations and disturbances initiated by the mass of the Protestant faithful, especially the lesser nobility and the artisans.[1] The watchword of all might well have been that of the Protestant artisans of Agen, who, after systematically destroying the altars and statues in the Catholic churches of that city, declared 'if one tarried for the consistory, it would never be done'.[2] In Rouen alone there were at least nine incidents variously described in the documents as 'tumults', 'riots', and 'seditions' in the years 1560 and 1561, all of them arising out of actions taken publicly by Protestant converts who felt moved to rely on more than prayer to bring about the triumph of their cause. In fact, it is fair to say that, as a result of these actions, the confessional struggle began in earnest for the people of Rouen in 1560, not with the formal advent of civil war in 1562.

If the study of popular unrest has recently become one of the liveliest areas of historical research, it is primarily because historians have recognized that from the actions of a crowd it is possible to distill something of the consciousness of the otherwise voiceless men and women who comprise it. Outbursts of collective violence reveal better than any other events those issues which were agitating the common people systematically excluded from the normal channels of political decision-making in pre-industrial and early industrial Europe. What underlay the numerous incidents of popular violence which punctuated the years 1560–61 in Rouen and were to continue to trouble the city for a decade thereafter? Above all, the conflicts centered around attitudes toward a set of powerfully charged religious symbols which had long been considered sacred but which suddenly appeared to converts to Protestantism as profane, indeed profaning, in the sharp new light of Luther and Calvin's reinterpretation of Christianity. Religion does not appear to have been merely the mask of self-interest or class interest for these men. A close reading of all available accounts of the incidents of violence fails to reveal a single mention of epithets hurled or individuals singled out for attack that would suggest social or economic antagonisms at work.[3] Instead, the unrest grew out of and reflected two radically conflicting visions of the world and of the place of the sacred within it.

1 It would be tedious to list all such disturbances in France. Examples can be found in just about any local history. For evidence that this aggressive spirit spilled over the French border into the Low Countries, *see* Gerard Moreau, *Histoire du Protestantisme à Tournai jusqu'à la veille de la Révolution des Pays-Bas* (Paris, 1962), pp. 169ff.

2 Natalie Zemon Davis, 'The Rites of Violence: Religious Riot in Sixteenth-Century France', *Past and Present*, 59 (1973), p. 64.

3 As the next chapter will show, the available evidence also fails to suggest that the two faiths attracted their members from mutually antagonistic social groups.

The essence of Calvin's teachings as understood by his disciples in Rouen was neatly summarized in a letter which the Reformed congregation sent Anthony of Navarre in 1561 urging him to take up the defense of their cause. Our souls, so the letter states, have been 'repurchased and washed by the precious blood of the immaculate Lamb, preordained by God's decision before the foundation of the world to be offered in sacrifice by Himself one single time in order to sanctify the elect and thereby abolish on the cross the memory of our sins'.[1] Once one accepted this proposition and the corollary that all that was needed for salvation was to believe in the efficacy of this one great miracle, much of what was held by Catholicism to be sacred no longer seemed so. If perfect redemption was guaranteed once and for all by God's death on the cross, then any form of devotion which diverted attention away from this miracle was a dangerous product of human invention, perhaps concocted out of avarice, certainly a sign of man's stubborn desire to worship as he saw fit and not as God had ordained. To maintain that another saving miracle occurred every time a priest said 'hocus-pocus' over a wafer and that this wafer then became endowed with magical powers was simply absurd. To surround God's temple with graven images before which one prayed in order to be cured of disease was obvious idolatry of the kind condemned quite clearly in the Bible. The doctrine of transubstantiation, the veneration of images, the church calendar of feasts and fasts, and all the other accumulated beliefs and practices which had submerged the central importance of Christ's sacrifice were nothing but, in the words of this same letter, 'the merchandise of seducers'.[2] They were the wares of an enormous first estate which supported itself regally through the sale of indulgences, of anniversary Masses, of exemptions from Lenten restrictions, of dispensations of the ban on marrying within prohibited degrees of cousinage, and of all the other instruments of grace or pardon for which the medieval church made the believer pay hard cash. Outrage at this swindling was doubled by the fact that the swindlers seemed hypocrites to boot. The notoriously corrupt clergy could not even live according to its own rules.[3]

[1] *Mémoires de Condé* (London, 1743), Vol. 2, pp. 325–6.

[2] *Ibid.*, Vol. 2, p. 327.

[3] Was Rouen's clergy badly corrupt? While the detailed information necessary for a full assessment of its moral and educational level does not exist (in particular, no records of episcopal visitations have survived), references to individual instances of clerical immorality are sufficiently frequent to allow one to be sure that the city always contained members of the first estate who could be pointed out as examples of clerical corruption. The deliberations of the cathedral chapter (A.D.S.M., G 2165–80) record numerous instances of canons reprimanded for maintaining concubines, while among the shortcomings denounced as widespread by the Provincial Council of 1581 were simony and the ordination of the bastard sons of the clergy. Claude de Sainctes, *Le concile provincial des diocèses de Normandie tenu à Rouen l'an 1581* (Rouen, 1606), pp. 37–8. The thrust of a good deal of recent work in late medieval church history has been to suggest that the moral and educational level of the clergy was improving on the eve of the Reformation by contrast with the preceding centuries. This may

The forms of Protestant protest were so many expressions of these beliefs. For someone who had seen the light, the truth of the Reformed articles of faith seemed self-evident. One had only to show the light to others and surely they too would be converted. Much Calvinist agitation therefore took the form of attempting to present the confession of faith to the authorities, the assumption clearly being that, if the king or the parlement were to read these articles for themselves instead of listening to the calumnies of the clergy or the Guises, they would see that, far from posing a challenge to the established order, Reformed doctrine merely embodied the truth of the gospel. As Jacques Poujol has recently stressed, the Conspiracy of Amboise of 1560 was above all an *attroupement d'exaltés* from all over France who marched on Amboise in order to present the king with a copy of the confession of faith. The attempt to kidnap the monarch and remove him from the influence of the Guises was simply grafted onto this project by a band of zealous and adventurist lesser nobles.[1] When word reached the Protestant communities of France that the king was being attacked by these conspirators, it provoked considerable agitation among the mass of Huguenots, who protested publicly in several provinces, including Normandy, that they had not wished to offend His Majesty but simply to present him with a petition.[2] In Rouen, a copy of the confession of faith was also slipped anonymously under the door of the parlement on May 7, 1560, two months after the conspiracy. It was followed later in the year by a petition that the court live according to the reformation of the scriptures.[3] The frequent singing of psalms in public was another means by which the Calvinists attempted to carry their message to those who might not have heard it.[4]

While trying to obtain a public hearing for their views, the Protestants also sought to discredit the positions of the opposition. Public contradiction of a Catholic preacher was one method. On at least three different occasions, men with Protestant leanings became so incensed at what was being said from the pulpit that they stood up in church and attempted to refute the friar preaching.[5] Ridicule was also used. When the Cardinal of Bourbon

be true, but what was crucial insofar as people's perception of the clergy was concerned was not whether the percentage of clerics who failed to measure up to the church's standards had decreased slightly since their grandfather's day; it was whether or not enough corrupt clerics were still around so that the group as a whole was perceived as rotten by men already predisposed to think ill of it for reasons of doctrine. In the case of Rouen's clergy, we can be sure that this was so.

1 Jacques Poujol, 'De la Confession de Foi de 1559 à la Conjuration d'Amboise', *B.S.H.P.F.*, CXIX (1973), p. 171.

2 Abel Desjardins, ed., *Négociations diplomatiques de la France avec la Toscane* (Paris, 1865), Vol. 3, p. 413.

3 B.M.R., MS Y 214 (5), entries of May 7, 1560 and Dec. 18, 1560.

4 This point is made by Natalie Zemon Davis, 'The Protestant Printing Workers of Lyons in 1551', *Aspects de la propagande religieuse* (Geneva, 1957), p. 257.

5 This happened in August 1560, January 1561, and during Lent 1561. *Cal. S.P. For.* 1560/468 and 1561/886; *Hist. eccl.*, Vol. 2, p. 713; 'Discours abbregé', p. 190.

made one of his rare visits to the city late in 1561, he was not only the object of 'thousands of insults'; the Huguenots also decorated the archiepiscopal pulpit with a broadsheet showing a flock of geese, the prize traditionally awarded the king of liars in popular festivities of the period.[1]

Other Huguenot actions were taken in an attempt to desacralize objects the Catholics held to be sacred. Thus, the Host was consistently mocked in Calvinist verses of this period as a 'god of paste', a plain old wafer that the communicant chewed up, digested, and ultimately sent to the bottom of the latrine.[2] This point was made in symbolic fashion in 1560 when Rouen's Protestants ostentatiously refused to accord the Holy Sacrament the honor usually shown it during the Corpus Christi Day processions. They declined to drape their houses along the procession route with tapestries and then, according to one Catholic source, showered the clergy and parishioners of St Maclou with garbage as they marched solemnly down the rue Martainville.[3] Similar disrespect was shown saints' images and the crucifix. If the Spanish ambassador is to be believed, the Protestants hung several of both upside down from the public gallows in August 1560.[4] The iconoclastic incidents which had occurred at irregular intervals from the early 1540s into the 1560s, most often aimed at a statue of the Virgin located on the wall of the Archbishop's Palace,[5] were, of course, also symbolic statements denying the holiness of these objects. During Lent in 1562, the Protestants even dared mount an attack on one of the portals of the cathedral at the very moment when the prominent Franciscan friar Hugonis was pronouncing his lenten sermon inside. The crowd followed this attack by entering the cathedral, disrupting the preaching, and insulting the 'big fat [*gros et gras*] Hugonis', whose well-known weakness for the opposite sex made him a frequent target of Protestant mockery and earned him the ironic sobriquet, 'the pillar of our Holy Mother Church'.[6]

[1] *Archivo documental español*, Vol. 3, p. 257. Although the reports of the Spanish ambassador must always be handled with care since he was a highly partisan observer, this story is recounted in enough detail to have the ring of truth. It is partially corroborated by *Relation des troubles*, p. 10.

[2] Henri-Léonard Bordier, ed., *Le chansonnier huguenot du XVIe siècle* (Paris, 1870), pp. 153–4, 160. Calvinist derisions of the 'god of flour' is also mentioned briefly in A. N. Galpern, *The Religions of the People in Sixteenth-Century Champagne* (Cambridge, Mass., 1976), p. 156, whose analysis parallels mine here.

[3] *Hist. eccl.*, Vol. 1, p. 352; Dom J. T. Pommeraye, *Histoire des Archevesques de Rouen* (Rouen, 1667), p. 613, a work of considerable interest as it uses several memoirs of this period which have subsequently been lost.

[4] *Archivo documental español*, Vol. 1, p. 382.

[5] This statue was attacked in both 1545 and 1551. *Relation des troubles*, p. 8; B.M.R., MS Y 102 (1), entry of Oct. 30, 1551. The niche in which the statue stood can still be seen at the corner of the rue Saint-Romain and the rue de la République. It is empty.

[6] *Hist. eccl.*, Vol. 2, p. 713; Pommeraye, *Histoire des Archevesques* p. 614; Amable Floquet, *Histoire du Parlement de Normandie* (Rouen, 1840–41), Vol. 2, p. 376. On Hugonis *see* the accusations in the *Hist. eccl.*, Vol. 2, p. 713, and V. L. Saulnier, 'Autour du Colloque de Poissy: les avatars d'une chanson de Saint-Gelais à Ronsard et Théophile', *Bibliothèque d'Humanisme et Renaissance*, XX (1958), p. 64.

'Immodest' festive practices were yet another target of Protestant hostility. Just a few weeks prior to the disruption of Hugonis' preaching, Carnival week had seen the usual mummeries and parade of the city's festive organization, the *Conards*, broken up by the Protestant *menu peuple*.[1]

Finally, much of the extra-legal Protestant activity was directed simply at rescuing fellow Protestants from the clutches of the law. The ministers and consistory might insist that the authorities were not to be challenged and that martyrdom was a fate that had to be accepted if necessary; many within the congregation nonetheless rejected this position and acted on the belief that it was licit to defy the authorities attempting to punish those Protestants who participated in the frequent public demonstrations and disorders. In January 1560, a bookbinder being taken off to the stake was rescued by force as he passed the Carrefour de la Crosse in the center of town.[2] In August of the same year the lieutenant of the *bailliage*, de Brevedent, was attacked by a crowd of Huguenots in an attempt to force him to release a number of their imprisoned co-religionists.[3] In December a baker condemned to death for his role in a bloody conflict that had taken several lives in the parish of St Nicaise earlier in the year was rescued by force, leading the authorities to cease holding executions for religious reasons at the traditional site in the Vieux Marché and to move them instead to a balcony of the Bailliage, where the Protestants would have a harder time rescuing their co-religionists.[4] This practice either failed to achieve its purpose or else was discontinued soon thereafter, for a year later, in December 1561, a condemned iconoclast was again rescued from the stake.[5]

Inevitably, inexorably, the wave of Protestant demonstrations in the years 1560–61 provoked a Catholic reaction. The convert to Calvinism might see his old religious practices as superstitions, but to the unconverted the Holy Sacrament was still holy. The consecrated Host was more than a wafer; it was God's body. Simply to contemplate it was a meritorious act that enhanced one's chances for salvation; for the more credulous, it was also a guarantee that one would not die a sudden death that day. The notion that the Host contained great spiritual and even magical powers had been growing throughout the waning Middle Ages, and eucharistic devotions in which it was venerated with solemn marks of respect were

1 *Hist. eccl.*, Vol. 2, p. 713.

2 He was recaptured and executed the next day. *Cal. S.P. For.* 1560/708; 'Discours abbregé', pp. 186–7.

3 B.M.R., MS Y 102 (1), entry of Aug 15, 1560.

4 A.D.S.M., B, Parlement, Arrêts, Août–Octobre 1562, arrêt of Aug. 26, 1562; 'Journal d'un bourgeois', p. 6.

5 A.D.S.M., B, Parlement, Arrêts, Août–Octobre 1562, arrêt of Aug. 26, 1562; *Hist. eccl.*, Vol. 1, pp. 861–2.

central to sixteenth-century Catholicism. The Corpus Christi processions were the most spectacular examples of eucharistic devotion, but they were by no means the only.[1] When the Calvinists ridiculed the doctrine of the real presence, they therefore mocked more than a theological abstraction grasped only by Sorbonne doctors; they touched on one of the most sensitive points of doctrine for the average lay believer, much of whose hope for salvation might be structured around the belief that in adoring the Corpus Christi he or she was performing a meritorious act. The same point could be made with regard to Protestant iconoclasm, especially when directed against statues of the Virgin. At least nineteen separate confraternities were dedicated partially or totally to the Virgin Mary, and her birthday was the occasion for the poetic competition in her honor held by the *Puy des Palinods*.[2] A century later the local historian François Farin would write that the strength of devotion to the Virgin Mary was a special mark of Rouen. 'There is no gate of the city, no street, no corner, virtually no noteworthy house which is not adorned with the figure of that divine intercessor, sculpted with all of the decoration that the cleverest masters could add.'[3] One assumes that these statues had not all been erected in the intervening one hundred years.

Calvinist attacks on revered objects such as the consecrated Host or the statues of the Virgin not only shocked and offended those still Catholic; they made the Protestants seem a dangerous, polluting force within the body social. A sixteenth-century Catholic lived in a world filled with sacred objects and places – churches, shrines, cemeteries, the Host, etc. – all of them susceptible to pollution. When a Protestant mocked or attacked a ritual object with the intent to desacralize it, a Catholic saw this behavior as desecration, and desecration placed the community in danger. It was certain to be followed by some expression of divine wrath unless matters could be set right quickly. The initial reaction of the Catholic authorities to the development of Protestantism is exemplary in this regard. From 1528 on, in the wake of every incident of iconoclasm in the city, the cathedral chapter arranged a solemn procession which would wind its way through the streets to one or another of the city's religious houses, where a sermon

1 The development and importance of eucharistic devotions in the later Middle Ages is traced well by Peter Browe, *Die Verehrung der Eucharistie im Mittelalter* (Rome, 1967). Edouard Dumoutet's *Le désir de voir l'hostie et les origines de la dévotion au Saint-Sacrement* (Paris, 1926) is less rich but based more fully on French materials. Five confraternities in Rouen were dedicated in part or wholly to the adoration of the Eucharist. L. Martin, *Répertoire des anciennes confréries et charités du diocèse de Rouen approuvées de 1434 à 1610* (Fécamp, 1936), passim.

2 Martin, *Répertoire*, passim. A sense of the competition of the Palinods and of the poems written honoring the Virgin may be gained from A. Tougard, ed., *Les trois siècles palinodiques, ou histoire générale des Palinods de Rouen, Dieppe, etc.* Publications of the Société de l'Histoire de Normandie 31 (Rouen–Paris, 1898), passim.

3 François Farin, *Histoire de la ville de Rouen* (Rouen, 1668), Vol. 2, p. 60.

was usually delivered on the dangers of heresy.[1] The processions served a double function. The *chasse* of the Virgin or the Consecrated Host was usually carried in them, and thus they presented a dramatic, ornate public spectacle of reverence for a person or doctrine attacked by the Protestants, reaffirming their sacredness. At the same time, purificatory symbols such as the burning of candles and the ringing of the church bells were commonly included. The ceremony thus served as a rite of purification for a city soiled by heresy, thereby conveying very clearly to the onlooking crowds the message that the Protestants formed a force within society whose polluting actions required community atonement. That the message got through to the populace is shown by an incident which occurred in 1568, when the corpse of a Protestant mistakenly was included among the bodies being carted off from the Hôtel-Dieu for burial in the hospital's cemetery. To bury such a man in holy ground was to defile the ground, and when word of this error spread a mob rushed to the graveyard, interrupted the funeral, and dragged the cadaver off to a more fitting resting place, the town dump.[2] Few events demonstrate more strikingly that the Catholics came to view the Huguenots as agents of pollution.[3]

[1] *See here* my article 'The Catholic Response to Protestantism: Church Activity and Popular Piety in Rouen, 1560–1600', James Obelkevich, ed., *Religion and the People, 800–1700* (Chapel Hill, 1979), p. 171. Important processions sparked by the threat of heresy were held in 1528, 1531, 1534, 1535, 1539, 1542, 1551, 1559, and 1560. Important processions are described in detail in Farin, *Histoire de la ville de Rouen*, Vol. 2, pp. 29–32; Oursel, 'Notes pour l'histoire de la Réforme', pp. 161–2, 201–5.

[2] B.M.R., MS Y 214 (6), pp. 61–9; Archives Hospitalières de Rouen 1 E 2, entries of April 10 and Oct. 29, 1570; B.N., MS Français 15551, fo. 176, Bauquemare to Morvillier, April 9, 1570; René Rouault de la Vigne, 'Les Protestants de Rouen et de Quévilly sous l'Ancien Régime: Leurs registres de l'état civil, leurs cimetières', *Bull. Soc. Emul. S-I.*, ex. 1938, pp. 305–6. The possibility of Protestants being buried in Catholic cemeteries continued to arouse intense passions in France for the rest of the century, as is clear from Henry de Sponde's bitter attack on any such practices in *Les cimitieres sacrez* (Bordeaux, 1597). Significantly, the opposite of this practice in England, i.e. Catholic recusants being buried in the hallowed ground of an Anglican churchyard, seems to have provoked little popular opposition. The clergy often protested, but the bulk of the community seems to have been generally indifferent to the issue. Fear of pollution was apparently less strong. John Bossy, *The English Catholic Community, 1570–1850* (Oxford, 1976), pp. 140–41.

[3] Further evidence of this is provided in Natalie Zemon Davis, 'The Rites of Violence', pp. 57–9, an article which helped clarify my thinking on this issue considerably. The quickness of the Catholics to see the Huguenots as people whose very presence in the community endangered it was, of course, a corollary of the larger tendency for men in this period to intepret natural disasters as punishment for human failings. Earthquakes, plagues, floods, and celestial apparations were all warnings sent by an angry God to keep sinful men toeing the mark. Protestant iconoclasm became another form of sin to be placed alongside fornication, gambling, and immodest or unseemly dress as causes of such catastrophes. For the broader tendency to attribute natural disasters to human sinfulness, *see* J.-P. Seguin's study of the cheap broadsides which were the closest thing to a popular printed literature in the sixteenth century, *L'information en France avant la périodique* (Paris, 1964), passim, esp. pp. 53ff; and, more broadly, Keith Thomas, *Religion and the Decline of Magic* (New York, 1971), ch. 4. For cases of natural disasters or hardships blamed on Protestant iconoclasm, *see Relation des troubles*, p. 15 (quoted below, p. 104); 'Chroniques de la Confrérie du St Sacrement de Limoges 1560–1631', A. Leroux, ed., *Nouveaux documents historiques sur la Marche et le Limousin* (Limoges,

Anti-Huguenot feelings were further inflamed by a number of calumnies which Catholic preachers spread about the Protestants from the pulpit. First, just as the secret reunions of the early Christians under the Roman Empire had bred rumors that they engaged in wild debauchery and ritual cannibalism, so the early, often nocturnal Calvinist assemblies were said by Catholic preachers to be the scene of orgiastic lovemaking.[1] Charges that the Protestants were given to lechery proved surprisingly long-lasting; they continued to be levelled even after the Huguenots began to hold their services in public, when the Catholic populace could have seen for itself that the goings-on at a Reformed *prêche* were anything but lurid. The charge appears, for example, in a piece of doggerel which was circulating around Rouen in the mid-1560s and was written down by the curé of St Godard in the back of his parish register.

Ceux qui voudront lire [ces motz?] (page torn here)
Il cognoistront pour verité
Que le diable et les huguenotz
Sont d'une mesme voulonté.

Le diable a en grand horreur la messe;
Les huguenotz veullent que la dire l'on cesse.

Le diable veult que l'on destruisse l'eglise;
Les huguenotz c'est leur principalle entreprise.

Le diable hait la Vierge Marie;
Les huguenotz ne veulent que l'on la prie.

Le diable hait les saints qui sont en gloire;
Les huguenotz ne veulent faire memoire.

Le diable hait virginité et chastetté;
Les huguenotz paillardent...

Le diable hait jeusnes et abstinences;
Les huguenotz veulent toujours plaine pance.

...[illegible verse]

Le diable hait tutte religion;
Les huguenotz en veullent faire destruction.

Le diable hait de saintz les ymages;
Les huguenotz les brissent par les villaiges.

Le diable hait les croix de boys et de pierre;
Les huguenotz les jettent et mettent par terre.

1887), p. 331; Denis Pallier, *Recherches sur l'imprimerie à Paris pendant la Ligue (1585–1594)* (Geneva, 1975), pp. 172–3; Frederic J. Baumgartner, *Radical Reactionaries: the political thought of the French Catholic League* (Geneva, 1975), p. 32.

[1] This assertion was made in Rouen by a number of Catholic preachers. *Hist. eccl.*, Vol. 1, p. 229.

Le diable hait les gens de bien et preslatz;
Les huguenotz n'aiment que les appostatz.

Le diable hait que l'on faict du peché confession;
Les huguenotz dissent que ce n'est qu'alusion.

Le diable hait que l'on prie pour les trespassés;
Les huguenotz ne disent mot puys qu'ilz sont passés.

C'est chose donc bien veritable
Que huguenotz sont au diable semblable.[1]

In building up its picture of the Huguenots as literal demons, the poem focusses most of its attention on Protestant opposition to the fundamentals of 'all religion' – belief in the Virgin, in saints, in confession, in prayers for the dead, etc. But it also adduces charges of immorality against the Protestants: fornication and gluttony. To survive, hostile stereotypes usually contain at least a kernel of plausibility, even if blown out of all proportion by incomprehension and hatred. Just as the Roman accusations that the early Christians engaged in ritual cannibalism seem to have been based on distorted reports about the consumption of Christ's 'blood' and 'body' during the celebration of the Eucharist,[2] so the charges of lechery and gluttony were essentially exaggerations of what appeared to sixteenth-century Catholic authors as one of the most scandalous aspects of Protestantism, its denial of the need for clerical celibacy, periodic fast days, and abstinence during Lent. If the Protestants wished to do away with these, it was obviously because they were slaves to their carnal desires. They simply could not abide such restrictions. 'Who fails to see that this new faction gives free rein to all lasciviousness, given that it is an assembly of lustful apostates?', queried the Franciscan Thomas Beauxamis in the tract he wrote to counter the 'execrable portraits' of the '*Marmite* Overturned'.[3]

Not only were the Protestants lechers and gluttons, Catholic preachers charged; they were also seditious. This accusation was levelled from Catholic pulpits in Rouen as early as 1558, well before the Protestants actually undertook any concrete acts which threatened the king or the state, but again it did not take solid evidence to convince the more rabid Catholics of the truth of the charge, merely a degree of plausibility. Religion, all

1 A.C.R., R.P. 171. The page on which the poem is written is torn and the ink is badly faded, which is why certain verses are illegible. The poem is undated, but the register in which it is written covers the years 1565–7. A second piece of verse in the same hand, so faded that it is impossible to decipher more than a few phrases, follows, beginning 'La paix est faicte'. This is probably a reference to the peace of Longjumeau, the edict of pacification closest in date to the years covered by the parish register, thus suggesting that the poem might date from 1568.

2 Claude Lepelley, *L'empire romain et le christianisme* (Paris, 1969), p. 38.

3 Thomas Beauxamis, *Resolution sur certains pourtraictz et libelles intitulez du nom de Marmitte* (Paris, 1562), p. 12. *See also*, 'Chroniques de la confrérie du St Sacrement', p. 321.

learned men knew, was the surest foundation of the state, and many of the ceremonies in which the Protestants refused to participate were expressly understood by people at the time as rituals of amity and concord. Protestant non-participation ruptured that concord, thus clearly making them a threat to civic unity.[1] Of course, when levelled by a particularly intemperate preacher, the charge that the Huguenots were seditious could itself stir up sedition; in sermons denouncing the Protestants as threats to the city's peace, the curé of St Maclou and grand vicar of the cathedral, Adam Sécard, called on his auditors to stamp out this threat themselves if the authorities would not or could not do so.[2] The effect was ultimately to insure that the accusation became a self-fulfilling prophecy, for the eventual Huguenot recourse to arms was motivated in large measure by the desire of the Protestants to protect themselves against the sorts of attacks fostered by these accusations.

Just as Protestant beliefs led quickly to action, so too did Catholic. The Catholic reaction which developed in 1560–61 took a number of forms. The simplest was violence in response to specific Protestant outrages. The refusal of the Calvinists to drape their houses on Corpus Christi Day, 1560, provoked a riot during which the non-decorated houses were attacked and looted.[3] When the Huguenots interrupted the preacher in the church of St Vivien in August of that year, another riot ensued, claiming several casualties.[4] The Catholics may also have plotted a large scheme in 1561 to exterminate all of the city's leading Huguenots. The *Histoire ecclésiastique* recounts the scheme in ample detail,[5] and while the account provided by this Protestant work probably contains a degree of exaggeration, it is certain that in September 1561 one Pierre Quictart of Bourges – probably the same man as the 'Jean Guitard' identified by the *Histoire ecclésiastique* as a Guisard agent active in this plot – was executed after having been found with papers in his possession listing the names and indicating the wealth of the Reformed Church's leading members.[6] Protestant fears were not totally groundless.

Certain Catholics also attempted to employ economic sanctions against the Protestants. In 1560 a group of Catholic *drapiers drapants* decided to deny employment to all journeymen known to have attended Reformed

[1] John Bossy, 'Holiness and Society', *Past and Present*, 75 (1977), pp. 122, 131–3.

[2] *Hist. eccl.*, Vol. 1, p. 229. Sécard was consistently one of the most violent Catholic preachers and was reprimanded by the parlement as early as 1552 for having stimulated trouble with his 'parolles scandaleuses'. A.D.S.M., B, Parlement, Registres Secrets, Chambre des Vacations 1549–1556, entry of Nov. 7, 1552.

[3] *Hist. eccl.*, Vol. 1, p. 352; Pommeraye, *Histoire des Archevesques*, p. 613.

[4] *Cal. S.P. For.* 1560/468.

[5] *Hist. eccl.*, Vol. 1, pp. 857–61.

[6] 'Discours abbregé', p. 192.

services. The journeymen resorted to violence to preserve their livelihood. Six or seven fatalities resulted.[1]

Finally, some of the Catholic initiatives of these years were devotional in nature. As Huguenot attacks mounted against the Roman faith, the Catholics began to stage assemblies reaffirming their belief in certain contested doctrines. Thus, in response to Reformed denunciation of Catholic 'idolatry', a number of Catholics began to hold public, militant gatherings before the street-corner statues located through town. Such assemblies are known to have begun in Paris in 1559, where, according to De Thou, crowds of watercarriers, servants, and other elements of the *lie du peuple* gathered regularly before the statues of the Virgin and saints to light candles and sing canticles. Boxes were placed nearby and donations solicited from passers-by, who faced the prospect of being labelled Huguenots and beaten as such if they proved too niggardly.[2] By 1560 such wildcat devotions had clearly spread to Rouen as well, for in that year three chaplains were pursued by the authorities after they snatched a tennis racket from a youth and used it to break his collarbone when he would not genuflect before a statue, in front of which bands of children were said to assemble regularly in the evening to sing 'Ave Maris Stella'.[3]

In the following year, 1561, a number of Catholics sprang to the defense of the doctrine of the real presence by establishing the general Confraternity of the Holy Sacrament. This *Confrérie du Saint-Sacrement*, not to be confused with the secret seventeenth-century *Compagnie du Saint Sacrement*, was founded by twelve laymen. The association welcomed members from all of the city's parishes who were to assemble each week in a different church to hear a special Mass paid for by members on a rotating basis. This Mass was followed by a sermon, and then, in the afternoon, an *ave verum*, a *salve*, and a small procession around the church and its cemetery bearing the Holy Sacrament aloft. In addition to these small weekly processions, the confraternity also staged large bi-annual parades through the entire city 'to incite the populace to devotion'. Members of the four mendicant orders, the city militia, the students of the four paupers' schools, and a large number of children dressed in white carrying burning candles all participated in these larger processions, which, like the smaller weekly ones, were symbolic reaffirmations of the doctrine of transubstantiation.[4]

Did the actions of the confraternity represent a conscious response to Protestant attacks on this doctrine? Confraternities in honor of the Eucharist had been a common feature of Catholic religious life from the

[1] *Hist. eccl.*, Vol. 1, p. 353; 'Journal d'un bourgeois', p. 8; Floquet, *Histoire du Parlement de Normandie*, Vol. 2, p. 319.

[2] De Thou, *Histoire universelle*, Vol. 2, pp. 705–6.

[3] *Hist. eccl.*, Vol. 1, p. 353.

[4] A.D.S.M., G 9870.

later fourteenth century onward, and an earlier Confraternity of the Holy Sacrament had already been founded in Rouen in 1435.[1] One might therefore suspect that the foundation of this second confraternity at a time of growing Protestant strength was simple coincidence. It would appear not, however. Louis Marc, one of the twelve founders and the first head of the confraternity, was also one of the most zealously anti-Protestant figures in Rouen.[2] Furthermore a myth of anti-Protestant origins seems to have been passed down orally within the organization, for in a brief account of its foundation written in 1590 the confraternity is said to have been founded at a time when the Protestants were masters of Rouen and trampling the Holy Sacrament underfoot.[3] The statement is a significant revelation of the confraternity's image of itself as an organization devoted to rescuing the Host from those Protestants who would vilify it. Such a purpose struck a responsive chord among Rouen's Catholic population. In the confraternity's first year of existence, over 1,300 members enrolled.[4]

By late 1561, Rouen was becoming increasingly sharply polarized between two rival religious camps, each of which was becoming increasingly militant and well organized. The same was true throughout France, for the Catholic reaction, like the rapid growth of Protestantism, was a nationwide phenomenon. Proto-Leagues dedicated to the extermination of Protestantism sprang up in several provincial cities, while at court the leading Catholic noblemen grouped themselves into an informal association known as the Triumvirate which pushed for an end to the policy of religious conciliation being pursued by Catherine de Medici and her chancellor Michel de l'Hôpital.[5] The country was sliding rapidly toward civil war, and unlike many upheavals in early modern Europe, this would be a civil war that did not simply reach the local community as the distant echo of rivalries at court. The warring factions at the center had their analogues in the rival

[1] A list of the members of this earlier confraternity may be found in the British Museum, Add. MS 19743.

[2] He is one of the men accused in the *Histoire ecclésiastique* of participating in the plot to exterminate the city's Calvinists. I should mention here that there is nothing in the account books of the Confraternity of the Holy Sacrament which would indicate that it might have been an instrument of this or any other such plots. More generally, there is no evidence of any militant Catholic confraternities dedicated to the extermination of heresy such as one finds elsewhere in France.

[3] A.D.S.M., G 9870, fo. 1.

[4] A.D.S.M., G 9869. One cannot be absolutely precise about the number of people enrolled since this list of members is poorly bound and is missing 11 pages. It contains today 1,241 names. The missing pages would have included about 80 more members.

[5] On the Catholic reaction in the provinces, *see* Robert Boutruche et al., *Bordeaux de 1453 à 1715* (Bordeaux, 1966), p. 244; Guillaume and Jean Daval, *Histoire de la Réformation à Dieppe* (Rouen, 1878), p. 19. Events at court are traced best in Lucien Romier, *Catholiques et Huguenots à la cour de Charles IX* (Paris, 1924), pp. 99–110, and James Westfall Thompson, *The Wars of Religion in France, 1559–1576: The Huguenots, Catherine de Medici and Philip II* (Chicago, 1909), pp. 97–9.

religious parties throughout cities such as Rouen. But who composed the groups divided so sharply over religion in a provincial town such as Rouen? Did the rival confessions recruit their members from different social groups, or were they composed of individuals very much like one another except for the faith they held? These questions must be answered before delving into the actual events of the civil wars.

3

The sociology of the rival confessions

Ever since Marx argued so powerfully that 'sentiments, illusions, modes of thought and views of life' are a superstructure shaped by social conditions of existence, historians of any major ideological movement have been unable to avoid the question of that movement's relationship to the social and economic milieu in which it developed. In the case of the French Reformation, some scholars, notably Henri Hauser, have suggested a fairly rigid link between the rise of Protestantism and the struggles of the working classes. 'In Rouen in 1560', wrote Hauser in 1899, 'the workingman's cause and the cause of the Reform were one and the same'.[1] Other historians such as the pastor Mours, perhaps influenced by a desire to show that God does not discriminate on the basis of social class among those whom he calls to salvation, have denied any connection between the growth of the faith and the interests of any one social group.[2] Both groups have found support for their case without difficulty. Because the Reformation achieved its greatest early successes in the towns, the lists of early adherents to the cause are, not surprisingly, composed overwhelmingly of artisans. By overlooking the fact that the converts remained only a fraction of the total population of most cities, it is a relatively easy step from there to an equation between Protestantism and the working class. On the other hand, Protestantism did reach beyond the artisanal classes, attracting monks and poets, noblemen and merchants, even peasants. It is therefore possible to cite examples of believers drawn from every social stratum and geographic region of France and to deny on the basis of such examples any link between Reformation and society.

In recent years historians have begun to approach the sociology of religious choice with increasing sophistication. It is now clear that to investigate properly the social composition of a movement such as French Calvinism, the essentially impressionistic (and tendentious) methods of the

[1] Henri Hauser, 'La Réforme et les classes populaires', *Revue d'Histoire Moderne et Contemporaine*, I (1899–1900), p. 31.

[2] Samuel Mours, *Le Protestantisme en Vivarais et en Velay des origines à nos jours* (Valence, 1949), p. 16. The same theme is also sounded by E. G. Léonard, 'Les origines de la Réforme en France', *Calvin et la Réforme en France* (2nd ed., Aix-en-Provence, 1959), pp. 23–41; and Jean Delumeau, *Naissance et affirmation de la Réforme* (3rd ed., Paris, 1973), pp. 265–8.

past must be abandoned in favor of a statistical approach which seeks not only to establish a social profile of the movement's adherents, but to compare that with the contours of the larger society from which the converts were drawn. One must learn not just how many butchers, bakers, or candlestick-makers became Protestants, but also whether the percentage of such men within the movement was greater or smaller than their place within society as a whole.[1]

Rouen is not the ideal site for this sort of statistical study of Protestantism. Not only has no census survived which would allow one to reconstruct with statistical precision the social structure of the city as a whole; there also are no comprehensive lists of the members of the Reformed congregation. Rouen is not Montpellier, where a census was taken of the Protestant community in 1560,[2] nor Amiens, where a unique collection of inventories after death enables one to compare with exceptional precision the wealth, occupations, rate of book ownership and even clothing preferences of the city's Protestants and Catholics.[3] While the baptismal registers of Rouen's Reformed congregation have survived, they indicate the father's profession only rarely and cannot be trusted as a guide to the movement's social composition.[4] The notarial records would seem to hold out the promise of identifying the occupations of those whose names appear in the baptismal registers, but this source is immensely time-consuming to consult and would in any case underrepresent the poorer members of the congregation, who would rarely have used the services of a notary.

But given the importance of the issue of Protestantism's relationship to society, it is imperative that we confront it somehow. Fortunately documents do not lack entirely. While a total reconstruction of the Reformed congregation is impossible, four partial lists of Huguenots have survived from the period 1550–72. Each has a bias, but if the lists are subjected to critical scrutiny and their biases taken into account, they can provide a rough picture of the occupational structure of the Protestant community. Furthermore, Rouen is favored in one regard insofar as the sources are concerned. The membership rolls of the General Confraternity of the Holy Sacrament have survived, and they note systematically the occupation and parish of residence of the confraternity's members. It becomes possible therefore to analyze the sociology of a large Catholic association dedicated

[1] Two studies in particular have served as models of method: Natalie Zemon Davis, 'Strikes and Salvation at Lyon', *Archiv für Reformationsgeschichte*, LVI (1965), pp. 48–64; and J. van Roey, 'De correlatie tussen het sociale-beroepsmilieu en de godsdienstkeuze te Antwerpen op het einde der XVIe eeuw', *Sources de l'histoire religieuse de la Belgique, Moyen Age et Temps modernes* (Louvain, 1968), pp. 239–57.

[2] Emmanuel Le Roy Ladurie, *Paysans de Languedoc* (Paris, 1966), pp. 341–3.

[3] David Rosenberg of the University of Mississippi is now revising a study of Protestantism in Amiens that promises to be a major contribution to the understanding of the movement.

[4] The source is biased very strongly toward the upper levels of the socio-economic scale.

Table 2. *Emigrés from Rouen to Geneva, 1549–1560*

Professionals		*Artisans (cont.)*	
apothecaries	2	dyers	2
Merchants		weavers	1
merchants	4	damask-makers	1
mercers	3	serge-makers	1
Artisans		ribboners	1
a. artisanal elite		hatters	1
goldsmiths–coiners	7	c. food and drink trades	
printers	3	butchers	2
painters	2	pastry cooks	1
scribes	1	d. miscellaneous trades	
booksellers	1	joiners	7
b. cloth trades		shoemakers	4
hosiers	10	carpenters	2
tailors	3	miscellaneous, one each	11
wool-shearers	3	*Other*	
lace-makers	3	market gardeners	1
silk-workers	2	*No occupation given*	60

to upholding traditional beliefs and to compare it with the information available about the Protestants. A number of differences in social recruitment emerge from the comparison, differences which help to clarify the social context of religious choice in Rouen.

The first of the four surviving lists of Rouen's Protestants is composed of the 139 natives whose names appear in the Genevan *livre des habitants* between 1550 and 1560.[1] Like the overwhelming majority of the refugees who entered Geneva between these years,[2] the 79 Rouennais whose calling is noted in the document were virtually all artisans. (See Table 2.) The high percentage of artisans in Table 2 – fully 87 per cent of those refugees whose occupations are known – must consequently be attributed in part to the biases inherent in the source. Since artisans could pull up stakes and leave for Geneva more easily than could people tied to a parcel of land or an office, they were naturally particularly likely to emigrate to Geneva. Table 2, therefore, cannot be considered a reliable guide to the precise relative importance of the major social categories (merchants, professionals, artisans, etc.) within the Protestant congregation. It can, however, be used to make discriminations among different categories of artisans.

The same holds true for Table 3, a list of the victims of the St Bartholomew's Massacre in Rouen compiled by the Protestant martyrologist

[1] Paul-F. Geisendorf, ed., *Livre des habitants de Genève*, Vol. 1, *1549–1560* (Geneva, 1957–63), passim.

[2] Geisendorf analyzes the social composition of the entire group of French refugees in 'Métiers et conditions sociales du premier Réfuge à Genève (1549–1587)', *Mélanges Antony Babel* (Geneva, 1963), Vol. 1, pp. 239–49.

Table 3. *The victims of the St Bartholomew's Day Massacre*

Titled		*Artisans (cont.)*	
seigneur de	2	wool-shearers	5
bourgeois de Rouen	1	linen-finishers	5
Office-holders		lace-makers	4
huissiers	2	tailors	4
peseurs de laine	2	weavers	3
mesureurs	2	dyers	2
clerc au Greffe du Palais	1	spinners	1
courtier de vins	1	c. food and drink	
Professionals		inn- and tavern-keepers	6
procureurs	4	bakers	5
praticiens	1	butchers	2
ministers	1	oil-vendors	2
schoolmasters	1	d. miscellaneous trades	
Merchants		shoemakers	5
merchants	7	comb-makers	4
mercers	3	dealers in used clothes	4
couriers of the English	2	basket-makers	3
factor for the Flemish	1	locksmiths	3
Artisans		playing-card-makers	3
a. artisanal elite		plasterers	3
booksellers	5	balance-makers	2
goldsmiths	4	masons	2
painters	1	miscellaneous, one each	17
musicians	1	*Others*	
b. cloth trades		market gardeners	1
hosiers	18	lessor of horses	1
hatters	8	messenger	1
		No occupation given	43

Simon Goulard.[1] This table, like the preceding, is composed overwhelmingly of artisans, a fact which once again must be attributed at least partially to the biases inherent in the source. As we shall see, the wealthy were by and large spared in Rouen's St Bartholomew's Massacre.[2] But how reliable is this list? The work of a partisan chronicler might well appear suspect, especially since Goulard's estimate of the total number of victims claimed by the violence in 1572 is significantly higher than the other estimates which have come down to us. Furthermore, Pierre de l'Estoile wrote that Goulard 'often reports as dead those who are living and in good health...'[3] Still, reasons exist to believe that Goulard's identifications are generally trustworthy. Testing l'Estoile's accusation by examining the subsequent Protestant baptismal registers reveals that only 3 of the 184

[1] *Mémoires de l'estat de France sous Charles IX* (Middelburg, 1578), Vol. 1, pp. 295ff.

[2] *See below*, p. 128.

[3] Pierre de l'Estoile, *Mémoires-Journaux*, ed. Brunet, Champollion et al. (Paris, 1875), Vol. 1, p. 31.

Table 4. *Refugees from Rouen in Rye, November 1572*

Titled		*Artisans*	
gentlemen	3	a. artisanal elite	
Professionals		b. cloth trades	
preachers	1	tailors	1
apothecaries	1	drapers	1
		c. food and drink	
Merchants		cooks	1
merchants	25	bakers	1
mercers	3	d. miscellaneous trades	
		basket-makers	1
Others		coopers	1
mariners	13	carpenters	1
shipwright	1	playing-card-makers	1

names of male victims Goulard listed reappear in the post-1572 registers, a small rate of error even assuming that these 3 were actually the purported victims and not relatives with the same name. By contrast, most of Goulard's names appear in the first Protestant register, that of 1565–6, suggesting that he did not make them up out of whole cloth. Furthermore, it is understandable that a Huguenot polemicist might exaggerate the number of massacre victims, but it is harder to comprehend why he would falsify their names or occupations. Goulard lists by name only 214 of the 600 individuals he claims were massacred in Rouen, so clearly he resisted any temptation he might have felt to invent identities for the 386 others. This lack of completeness seems to have been common to many martyrologies. Recent critical studies comparing the facts given in the martyrologies concerning the identity, occupations, and circumstances of death of Protestant martyrs with the information available from court records find that many individuals are left out, but that the information about those who are listed by the martyrologists is quite accurate.[1] It would seem, then, that Goulard's list is probably worthy of credence.[2]

Table 4 has a quite different bias from the first two. Like Table 3, it grew out of the St Bartholomew's Day Massacre, for it is based on a

[1] *See, inter alia*, Léon-E. Halkin, 'Les martyrologes et la critique: contribution à l'étude du martyrologe protestant des Pays-Bas', *Mélanges Jean Meyhoffer* (Lausanne, 1952), pp. 52–70; E. Mahieu, 'Les martyrs montois dans les martyrologes', *Sources de l'histoire religieuse de la Belgique, Moyen Age et Temps modernes* (Louvain, 1968), pp. 389–402.

[2] It also provides a very important counterpoise to the preceding list. The roll of refugees to Geneva is almost surely biased in favor of those artisanal occupations producing goods or involving skills which could be marketed just as easily in one area as in another. Men engaged in those occupations which tied their practitioners to Rouen because they depended on raw materials or a marketing structure that was only available locally could not leave as easily for exile. Obviously, it is also these men who are particularly likely not to have fled Rouen in the four weeks between the St Bartholomew's Day Massacre in Paris and its local reenactment in Rouen and who thus are likely to be over-represented on this second list.

Table 5. *Office-holders tried by parlement as Huguenots, 1568–1569*

The following symbols represent the verdicts delivered: DO – deprived of office; ARO – the office-holder has already resigned his office as required by the edict of September 25, 1568; FIO – further investigation ordered; NV – no verdict reached before the volume closes.

All titles are given in French as English equivalents are often lacking.

Members of Major Jurisdictions	
Conseiller au Parlement	4 DO; 1 ARO
Notaire et Secrétaire du Roi	3 DO
Avocat du Roi en la Cour des Aides	1 DO
Général en la Cour des Aides	2 DO; 1 FIO
Conseiller au Siège Présidial	1 DO
Controlleur en la Chancellerie	1 DO
Conseiller Référendaire en la Chancellerie	1 DO
Lieutenant Criminel au Bailliage	1 DO
Trésorier de la Marine	1 ARO; 1 NV
Conseiller à l'Amiraulté	1 NV
Vicomte de Rouen	2 DO
Subaltern Officials of Major Jurisdictions	
Procureur Commis au Parlement	4 DO
Receveur et Payeur des Gages en la Cour des Aides	1 DO
Receveur et Payeur des Gages du Siège Présidial	1 FIO
Huissier au Siège Présidial	1 DO
Commis au Greffe de la Cour des Aides	1 NV
Référendaire en la Chancellerie	1 DO
Chauffecire en la Chancellerie	1 DO
Huissier en la Chancellerie	1 DO
Greffier au Bailliage	1 ARO
Clerc Sieger en la Vicomté de l'Eau	1 FIO
Sergent en la Vicomté de l'Eau	1 DO
Greffier aux Eaux et Forêts	1 DO
Officials Supervising Trade	
Controlleur en la Romaine*	1 DO
Priseur en la Romaine	1 NV
Visiteur en la Romaine	1 NV
Greffier Commis en la Romaine	1 NV
Collecteur de Deniers de la Vieille Tour†	1 DO
Clerc Sieger au Gros de Vin	1 DO
Clerc Sieger aux Brettes de Vin	2 DO
Commissionaire pour les Brettes de Vin	1 DO
Fermier du Quatrième de Vin	1 NV
Courtier de Vin	3 DO; 1 NV
Priseur de Vin	1 DO
Mesureur de Blé	1 DO
Mesureur de Sel	1 DO; 1 ARO
Mesureur de Voide	1 DO
Mesureur de Charbon	1 NV
Courtier de Draps	3 DO; 3 NV
Réal au Poix de la Laine	1 DO
Clerc Sieger au Poix de la Laine	1 DO
Controlleur et Receveur des Espiceries	1 DO
Commis des Fermiers de l'Imposition Foraine	1 DO
Fermier des Aides	1 NV

Table 5 *cont.*

Vendeur de Poisson	1 DO; 1 NV
Vendeur de Marc	1 NV
Lotisseur de Cuirs	1 DO
Lotisseur de Cuirs et d'Oranges	1 NV
Enquesteur	2 DO
Officier de Courbage et Passage des Chevaux Servant à Tirer les Bateaux Montant la Seine	2 DO
The Forces of Order	
Sergent	6 DO; 2 ARO; 3 NV
Sergent Royal	1 DO; 2 NV
Ecossais de la Garde du Roy	1 NV
Miscellaneous	
Receveur Général	1 NV
Tabellion Royal	1 NV
Trompette	1 NV
Maître des Portes	1 DO
Maître Fontainier du Roy	1 NV
Poste pour le Roy à Grande Couronne	1 NV

* The agency overseeing the port
† The Halle aux Toiles

census of refugees fleeing France after the massacre taken by the authorities of the small English port of Rye.[1] This list, however, overrepresents the role of two groups underrepresented in the previous lists, merchants and sailors. This is because the census was made on November 4, 1572, over six weeks after the massacre. By this time, most of those who had fled to England and disembarked at Rye had surely passed on to London or elsewhere. The only people likely still to be in a small Sussex port, apart from recent arrivals, would be those who could do business there – that is, merchants and sailors.

These first three lists are all samples of the total universe of Rouen's Protestants, and while each has a bias based on its origin, each nonetheless provides information about the relative importance of different social groups within the movement. Table 5 by contrast allows one to estimate the absolute size of one social group, the office-holders.[2] This list is derived from a special volume of the *Arrêts* of the Parlement devoted solely to cases arising out of the edict of September 25, 1568, which deprived all Huguenots holding royal offices of their positions.[3] In all, the court

[1] Published in W. J. Hardy, 'Foreign Refugees at Rye', *Proceedings of the Huguenot Society of London*, II (1887–8), pp. 573–4.
[2] I use the word 'office-holder' here to refer to any person who held a governmental position, no matter how minor. The more common '*officier*' generally designates only those government officials holding important posts.
[3] A.D.S.M., B, Parlement, Arrêts, Décembre 1568–Juin 1569.

instituted proceedings against 97 suspected Calvinists from Rouen, virtually all of whom seem indeed to have been Huguenots. Nobody investigated by the parlement was acquitted, and in the two cases where the accused could not clearly be proven a Protestant, further investigation was ordered. It is also unlikely that many Calvinist office-holders escaped the attention of the court, which, in the course of its investigation, called upon all of the city's curés to name those office-holders residing in their parish who did not take Easter communion.

From these lists it is apparent that Calvinism drew its adherents from virtually all strata of society and from a bewildering variety of occupations. Even the last group in the city one might expect to be touched by heresy, the important colony of merchants of Spanish descent, was affected; two Quintanadoines and two de Civilles are to be found in the Protestant baptismal registers.[1] Only the very lowest strata of society – street-sweepers, day-laborers, *laboureurs*, etc. – do not appear with any regularity on the lists of Protestants.

It would be banal, however, simply to conclude that the movement cut across all social boundaries and to press the analysis no farther. Close scrutiny of these four tables reveals that certain occupations or occupational groups are represented in numbers disproportionate to their importance within the total city population.

First, while the number of Protestant office-holders is far from negligible, these men nevertheless seem underrepresented proportionally, especially the members of the elite sovereign courts. The total number of several categories of minor officials in charge of trade is known; there were 40 *courtiers de draps*, 24 *courtiers de vin*, and 24 *mesureurs de blé*. It is also known that there were 47 sergeants of the various jurisdictions.[2] Totalling these categories, it is simple to calculate that 16 per cent of these minor officials were Protestant in 1568. Overall the Huguenots formed about 21 per cent of the city's population around this time.[3] These officers were thus underrepresented within the movement. The percentage of Protestants among the 65 members of the parlement fell even farther below the movement's strength among the population as a whole. Only 5 members of the court were Huguenot in 1567. The apparent reluctance of Rouen's *officiers* to join the Protestant movement conforms to the pattern of prudence found among the office-holding and governing classes of the German and Dutch cities and which was long thought to have governed

1 A.D.S.M., E, Protestants de Rouen, 1564–6, entries of March 29 and Aug. 9, 1565, Feb. 3, 1566. These men were not, as one might possibly suspect, of *marrano* origin.

2 A.C.R., A 16, fo. 110.

3 Philip Benedict, 'Catholics and Huguenots in Sixteenth-Century Rouen: The Demographic Effects of the Religious Wars', *French Historical Studies*, IX (1975), p. 224.

the behavior of most of the French robe as well.[1] Their prudence is hardly surprising, for the purchase of an office represented a sizeable investment in an immobile form of wealth that one would think twice about jeopardizing by becoming involved in an opposition religion. Several very recent studies have shown, however, that the *parlementaires* of both Paris and Toulouse were strongly compromised in the Protestant movement.[2] Whether the behavior of Rouen's *officiers* represented the norm or the exception among this class in France is now an open question.

In both Lyon and Antwerp, two cities comparable in size to Rouen, merchants appear to have been more heavily represented within the Protestant community than lawyers or governing officials.[3] This may well have been the case in Rouen too, but our lists are too fragmentary to allow any firm conclusions to be drawn here. It can be ascertained, however, that it was not the very wealthiest merchants who tended to become Calvinists in Rouen. Only 1 of the 46 merchants assessed 100 *livres* or more in 1565 to finance the construction of the *juridiction consulaire* was a Protestant.[4] Huguenot merchants seem instead to have come disproportionately from the ranks of those on the fringes of the elite of international traders. Figure 1 is a comparison of the wealth distribution of a sample of 77 merchants identified as Protestants on the basis of the Reformed baptismal register of 1565 with the wealth distribution of the entire population of individuals listed in the 1565 tax roll of merchants. It shows clearly that the 20–49 *livre* category is the only one where the sample of Protestants is represented in numbers significantly greater than their proportion within the total population would lead one to expect. In Antwerp, too, it is interesting to note, the very wealthiest merchants tended to remain Catholic while traders of middling stature were more likely to become Protestant.[5]

Among Rouen's artisans, several groups appear to have been involved

[1] On Germany, *see especially* Bernd Moeller, *Imperial Cities and the Reformation* (Philadelphia, 1972), pp. 62–3. On the Low Countries: Van Roey, 'Correlatie', p. 252; A. C. F. Koch, 'The Reformation at Deventer in 1579–1580: Size and Structure of the Catholic Section of the Population during the Religious Peace', *Acta Historiae Neerlandicae*, VI (1973), p. 50. On the French robe: Emile G. Léonard, *Le Protestant français* (Paris, 1953), p. 45.

[2] Twenty-two per cent of the Parisian *parlementaires* left the Catholic-controlled capital in 1562 'pour fait de religion'. Denis Richet, 'Aspects socio-culturels des conflits religieux à Paris dans la seconde moitié du XVIe siècle', *Annales: E.S.C.*, XXXII (1977), p. 768. In Toulouse, 30 of 80 members of the court were barred from office during the First Civil War, *Histoire des Protestants en France* (Toulouse, 1977), p. 61. Janine Estèbe, the author of the relevant chapter in this latter volume, also indicates, although without providing statistics, that the parlements of Grenoble and Bordeaux contained a significant Protestant minority.

[3] Natalie Davis, 'The Rites of Violence', *Society and Culture in Early Modern France: Eight Essays* (Stanford, 1975), p. 80n; Van Roey, 'Correlatie', p. 252. Richet suggests that the leading merchants also formed a significant element in Parisian Protestantism, 'Aspects socio-culturels', p. 767.

[4] Noel Boyvin, seigneur de Trouville, known to be Protestant because his son was baptized at the temple March 31, 1566.

[5] Van Roey, 'Correlatie', p. 254.

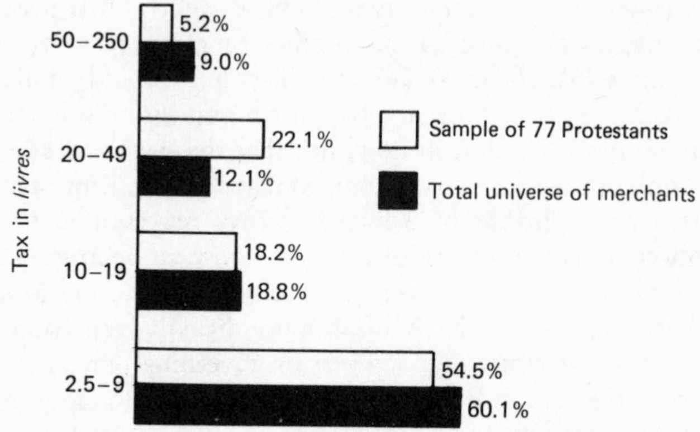

Figure 1. Distribution of wealth among Protestant and Catholic merchants

in the Protestant movement in numbers disproportionate to their importance within the city as a whole. The hosiers and the weavers were, as we know, Rouen's two largest occupations. Hosiers are well represented in the lists of Protestants, but more thoroughly proletarianized weavers appear far less often. The number of printers, goldsmiths, painters (a very small trade in Rouen), and other well-educated, high-status artisans also stands out, confirming the observation of the Catholic author Florimond de Raemond that 'those whose trades contain a certain nobility of the spirit were the easiest to ensnare'.[1] By contrast, there is a clear underrepresentation of members of those trades which involved processing or serving food and drink: bakers, butchers, fishmongers – where would a fishmonger be without Lent? – and tavern-keepers. These food and drink trades formed 13 per cent of the contingent of artisans marching in the *joyeuse entrée* of 1550, but account for only 8 per cent of the artisans in the tables here.[2]

[1] Quoted in Léonard, *Le Protestant français*, p. 45.

[2] For the importance of the food and drink trades in the *joyeuse entrée*, *see above*, p. 7. In Amiens, too, the food and drink trades remained Catholic almost to a man. Goldsmiths, on the other hand, tended disproportionately to become Protestant. David L. Rosenberg, 'Social Experience and Religious Choice: A Case Study, the Protestant Weavers and Woolcombers of Amiens in the Sixteenth Century' (unpub. Ph.D. dissertation, Yale University, 1978), Appendix II. The pattern of conversion revealed by this study differs strikingly from that in Rouen in one respect: the woolen trades were dramatically overrepresented within the Protestant movement in Picardy's capital where they were underrepresented within it in Rouen. This contrast can be accounted for by sharp differences in the organization and regulation of the woolen trades in the two towns. Amiens' cloth workers were not so thoroughly proletarianized as Rouen's seem to have been, while they were subjected to an exploitative system of regulation by the municipal authorities unique among the city's trades. This, Rosenberg convincingly argues, made Amiens' weavers particularly likely to respond to Protestant arguments that those in positions of authority within the church had corrupted the message of the Gospels for personal gain. Their experience with the secular authorities had taught them that this was just the sort of thing those in positions of power tended to do.

Finally, day-laborers and semi-rural groups such as *jardiniers* and *laboureurs* are particularly notable by their absence, a situation which corroborates the already well-known non-participation of these groups in the French Protestant movement.[1]

Just as it did socially, Protestantism touched virtually every sector of the city geographically but again tended to cluster in certain areas more than others. The best evidence about the residential distribution of the Huguenot population within the city around this time comes from the Catholic parish registers of 1572, where numerous Protestant families appear having their children baptized as Catholics following the St Bartholomew's Day Massacre.[2] These registers exist for only a minority of parishes, so they must be supplemented with the first Protestant 'parish' register to note place of residence, the seventeenth-century register of burials dating from the years 1626–9.[3] As one would expect, there are certain differences between the residential patterns revealed by these sources, fifty years apart from each other in date. Both, nonetheless, point toward the same area of the city as the main center of Protestant strength. As Map 6 shows, the Huguenots were clustered most densely in the southwestern quadrant of the city in the adjoining parishes of St Eloi, St Vincent, and St André-de-la-Ville. St Eloi was, and has remained ever since, the historic core of the Protestant community. Following the 1572 massacre more Huguenot children were rebaptized in the parish than in any other for which records have survived. A century later, in 1658, the parish was still said to be the center of the faith,[4] and today the old parish church is the Reformed Temple. While the parish registers of the adjoining parishes of St Vincent and St André have not survived from 1572, the percentage of Huguenots per one hundred inhabitants as revealed by the Protestant register of burials of 1626–9 was substantially higher in these two parishes than in any other. Moving away from these three southwestern parishes, the percentage of Huguenots gradually declines. Relatively few lived in the northern and eastern sections of the city, and fewest of all in the *faubourgs*, whose residents seem in general to have participated only marginally in the associational life of the city.

[1] Le Roy Ladurie, *Paysans de Languedoc*, pp. 341–4; Edmond Belle, 'La Réforme à Dijon des origines à la fin de la lieutenance générale de Gaspard de Saulx-Tavanes (1530–1570)', *Revue Bourguignonne*, XXI (1911), p. 44.

[2] This wave of Protestant rebaptisms is discussed below, p. 129. A table of the number of rebaptisms per parish may be found in my Princeton Univ. Ph.D. dissertation, 'Rouen during the Wars of Religion', p. 194.

[3] A.D.S.M., E, Protestants de Quévilly, sépultures, 1600–1629.

[4] Philippe Legendre, *Histoire de la persecution faicte à l'église de Rouen sur la fin du dernier siècle* (Rotterdam, 1704), p. 6. Legendre was one of the ministers of Rouen's Reformed Church and thus in a position to know where its members lived.

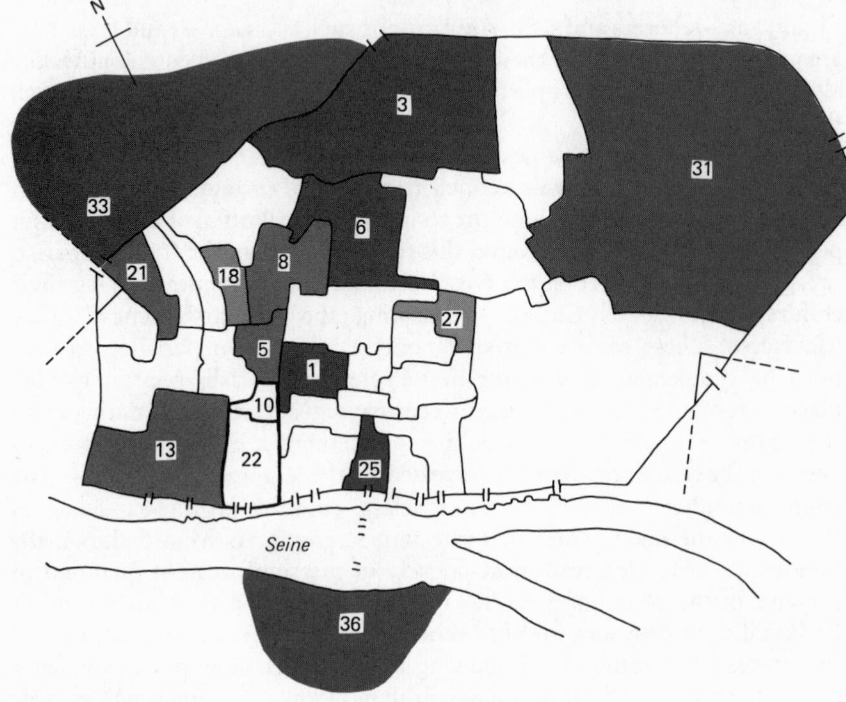

Map 6. Residential distribution of the Huguenot population

Quartier Beauvoisine
1. Notre-Dame-de-la-Ronde
2. Ste Croix–St Ouen
3. St Godard
4. St Herbland
5. St Jehan
6. St Laurent
7. St Lô
8. St Martin-sur-Renelle
9. St Patrice

Quartier Cauchoise
10. St André
11. St Cande-le-Jeune
12. Ste Croix-des-Pelletiers
13. St Eloi
14. St Etienne-des-Tonneliers
15. Ste Marie-la-Petite
16. St Michel
17. St Pierre-du-Chastel
18. St Pierre-l'Honoré
19. St Pierre-le-Portier
20. St Sauveur
21. St Vigor
22. St Vincent

Quartier Martainville
23. St Cande-le-Vieil
24. St Denis
25. St Martin-du-Pont
26. St Maclou

Quartier St Hilaire
27. St Amand
28. St Etienne-la-Grande-Eglise
29. St Nicaise
30. St Nicolas
31. St Vivien

Faubourgs
32. St André-hors-Ville
33. St Gervais
34. St Hilaire
35. St Paul
36. St Sever

The darker the shading, the greater the number of Protestants appearing in the Catholic parish registers of 1572 in comparison with the parish's total population. Parish registers exist for 1572 only for those parishes shaded. The two parishes whose boundaries are outlined are those which the number of Protestant burials in 1626–7 suggests to have been the centers of Huguenot strength in that era.

To be a Protestant in Rouen after 1557 involved a strong formal commitment to a set of religious principles clearly enunciated in a confession of faith. The same was hardly true of Catholicism. Everybody who was not an avowed Protestant was Catholic – at least in name. Great differences existed between individuals within the Roman Church, both in strength of attachment to Catholic tenets and in the way in which the elements of the faith were interpreted. Some believers held to tolerant, irenic forms of Catholicism. More were simply tepid in their commitment to the faith. As one Catholic chronicler recorded, the city contained many who were 'Catholic in name and *Politique* in faith, who hardly troubled themselves at all about the interests of the church'.[1]

It is the range of opinions and the unknowable but probably significant degree of apathy which existed within the Catholic community that make the membership rolls of the General Confraternity of the Holy Sacrament so valuable a source. Here was an organization devoted to reaffirming the doctrine of transubstantiation and the importance of eucharistic devotion. It drew its adherents from all parishes of the city and made no great financial demands on its members. (The requirement that they pay for a Mass on a rotating basis was waived for those who could not afford it.) An analysis of its membership can thus provide a rare opportunity to ascertain which strata of society and which sections of the city were not just Catholic in name but were particularly attached to traditional Roman doctrines and practices.

Table 6 lists the occupations of 1,241 *confrères* and *consoeurs* who joined the association in the course of the twelve months following its foundation in June 1561.[2] In many ways the list compares with the evidence available about the Reformed Church as a photographic negative compares with the final print. Where hosiers were more numerous than weavers among the Huguenots, the more proletarianized cloth-workers easily outnumber the more independent stocking-makers here. Where people in the food and drink trades represented 8 per cent of all artisans in the lists of Protestants and 'elite' artisans represented 13 per cent, the figures are reversed here,

[1] Dom J. T. Pommeraye, *Histoire des Archevesques de Rouen* (Rouen, 1667), p. 614.

[2] A.D.S.M., G 9869. I have chosen for the purposes of analysis the group of original members rather than all those who joined the confraternity between 1561 and 1600 because the notation of occupation becomes far less complete in the membership rolls after 1570. This precaution probably does not alter the results in any way, since comparison of the information available about the entire membership between 1561 and 1600 with this group of original members shows that, with the exception of the higher percentage of 'No Occupation Givens' among the former, there were no major differences between the two groups. In the case of the confraternity's numerous female members, I have recorded either their own occupation or their husband's, depending upon which is provided by the source. Often no occupation is noted at all for women. This accounts for nearly all of the 'No Occupation Givens' in the original group.

Table 6. *The original members of the Confraternity of the Holy Sacrament*

Clergy	
nuns	32
priests	15
chaplains	10
monks	8
curés	5
vicars	3
canons	1
Titled	
bourgeois de Rouen	3
seigneur de . . .	1
Office-holders	
huissiers	3
clercs	3
conseillers aux eaux et forêts	2
officiers de la vicomté	2
receveurs de la vicomté	2
sergeants	2
conseiller au parlement	1
courtier de vins	1
lieutenant au bailliage	1
mesureur de sel	1
tabellion	1
officier de la carue	1
conseiller au présidial	1
quêteur de vins	1
secrétaire de l'archéveché	1
visiteur de poissons	1
auneur de draps	1
Professionals	
procureurs	29
avocats	12
praticiens	9
apothecaries	2
clerks	2
apprentice apothecaries	1
surgeons	1
Merchants	
merchants	42
mercers	19
factors	2
Artisans	
a. artisanal elite	
painters	4
gold-beaters	3
goldsmiths	2
musicians	2
scribes	1
b. cloth trades	
weavers	75
hosiers	40
Artisans (*cont.*)	
dyers	21
tailors	18
linen embroiderers	13
ribbon-makers	9
linen-finishers	8
spinners	8
wool-shearers	6
wool-tailors	4
apprentice weavers	3
apprentice hosiers	1
c. food and drink	
bakers	19
butchers	16
fishmongers	13
tavern-keepers	12
inn-keepers	9
brewers	7
fruit-sellers	5
pastry chefs	5
grocers	4
salters	2
butter vendors	1
oil vendors	1
poultry sellers	1
tripe vendors	1
d. miscellaneous trades	
shoemakers	37
used-clothes dealers	24
coopers	18
needle- and pin-makers	13
pavers	12
playing-card-makers	12
tanners	11
plasterers	11
joiners	11
belt-makers	11
makers of leather thongs (*corroyeurs*)	9
comb-makers	9
candle-makers	8
hatters	8
saddlers	7
chautiers	7
sheath- and wallet-makers	6
tinsmiths	5
locksmiths	5
trunk-makers	4
pewterers	4
makers of tennis rackets	4
hook-makers	3
paper-makers	3
masons	3

Table 6 *cont.*

Artisans (cont.)		*Others*	
skinners	3	servants	28
dinants	3	market gardeners	13
carpenters	3	barrow-men	8
soap-makers	3	day-laborers	5
blacksmiths	2	dockworkers	5
nail-makers	2	washerwomen	3
pennetiers	2	*laboureurs*	2
gibletiers	2	carters	1
makers of church ornaments	2	*Children*	
miscellaneous trades, one each	15	daughter of...	19
		son of...	11
		No occupation given	328

with purveyors of food and drink accounting for 16 per cent of all artisans and those in the 'nobler' crafts less than 2 per cent. Other groups whose proportional representation was greater within this Catholic organization than within the Reformed congregation were, at one end of the social spectrum, the sub-artisanal occupations such as domestic service, street-sweeping, and market gardening and, at the other, the non-office-holding lawyers. From this last group were recruited the members of the city's festive organization, the *Conards*, which staged the popular mummeries so strongly attacked by the Calvinists. With their vital subculture, the lawyers were well integrated into the city's ritual and festive life, so it is hardly surprising that they reacted strongly to Huguenot attacks and remained committed to Catholicism. This was not only the case in Rouen; in Paris, the legal world of the *Basoche* was to form the hotbed of ultra-Catholic militancy at the time of the League.[1]

Rouen's *officiers* apparently tended to shun this Catholic confraternity just as strongly as they did Protestantism. Only one member of a sovereign court joined the association, and higher echelon officials in general played a modest role in it. The leading *officiers*' refusal to join undoubtedly reflects in part their general reluctance to mingle with the *vulgum plebus*; the members of the sovereign courts were highly conscious of their dignity and the dignity of their corporation, and they tried to keep a distance between themselves and the everyday activities of city life.[2] It is tempting as well to see the *officiers*' lack of involvement in both the Protestant movement and the Confraternity of the Holy Sacrament as an indication of their broader attitudes toward religion. Erasmian opinions appear to have been

[1] On the social composition of the Paris League, *see* J. H. M. Salmon, 'The Paris Sixteen, 1584–1594: The Social Analysis of a Revolutionary Movement', *The Journal of Modern History*, XLIV (1972), pp. 540–76, plus the important modifications suggested by Richet in 'Aspects socio-culturels', p. 779.

[2] Jonathan S. Dewald, *The Formation of a Provincial Nobility: The Magistrates of the Parlement of Rouen, 1499–1610* (Princeton, 1980), pp. 54–7.

prominent within this elite, highly educated milieu and would have led many *parlementaires* to scorn the external, ritualistic aspects of Catholicism even while caution and a concern for social order led them to shy away from outright heresy.[1] One must beware of painting too monolithic a portrait of religious opinions among this group, for it will become clear when we examine the First Civil War and, later, the Catholic League that certain *parlementaires* proved the most zealous of Catholic militants. Nevertheless, if there was any one stratum of Rouennais society within which Erasmian hopes for a *via media* took hold, it would seem to have been among the members of the sovereign courts and a few kindred spirits in the cathedral chapter.[2]

One of the most striking features of the Confraternity of the Holy Sacrament was the number of women who joined. *Consoeurs* represented fully 60 per cent of the association.[3] Can we conclude that women were more strongly and more traditionally Catholic than men? The hypothesis seems plausible. Husbands and wives frequently acted independently of one another in making religious choices. A list of Protestant abjurations from the period 1568–72 shows men abjuring independently of their wives, women abjuring independently of their husbands, and even husbands and wives abjuring at points several years apart.[4] A provincial synod of Normandy had to consider the question of whether elders of the Reformed Church ought to be suspended from their duties if their wives were '*tellement rebelle*' that they had their children baptized as Catholics.[5] A significant religious imbalance between the sexes thus could very well come about. And it appears that such an imbalance did come about. Although most sixteenth-century documents render married women invisible by noting only heads of households, the occasional documents which list both male and female Protestants in an apparently complete fashion suggest that far fewer women than men joined the Reformed Church. Thus, a list of Protestants returning to Catholicism in 1572 in the parish of St Laurent includes 36 men and 31 women, while among the refugees in Rye in the same year 75 men and 37 women appear.[6] Evidence about other

[1] On the Erasmian quality of *parlementaire* religious life, *see* Jonathan S. Dewald, 'The "Perfect Magistrate": Parlementaires and Crime in Sixteenth-Century Rouen', *Archiv für Reformationsgeschichte*, LXVII (1976), p. 285; George Huppert, *Les Bourgeois Gentilshommes: An Essay on the Definition of Elites in Renaissance France* (Chicago, 1977), p. 157.

[2] The presence of an Erasmian group within this latter corporation is shown in Philip Benedict, 'The Catholic Response to Protestantism: Church Activity and Popular Piety in Rouen, 1560–1600', James Obelkevich, ed., *Religion and the People, 800–1700* (Chapel Hill, 1979), p. 177.

[3] Seven hundred and forty-one of the 1,246 original members were women.

[4] A.C.R., R.P. 138.

[5] Library of the Remonstrant Church (Rotterdam), MS 404, synod of 1560, article 4. *See also here* Natalie Davis, 'City Women and Religious Change', *Society and Culture in Early Modern France: Eight Essays* (Stanford, 1975), p. 81.

[6] A.D.S.M., G 6802, fos. 37v–38; F. de Schickler, *Les églises du Réfuge en Angleterre*, Vol. 1 (Paris, 1892), p. 295.

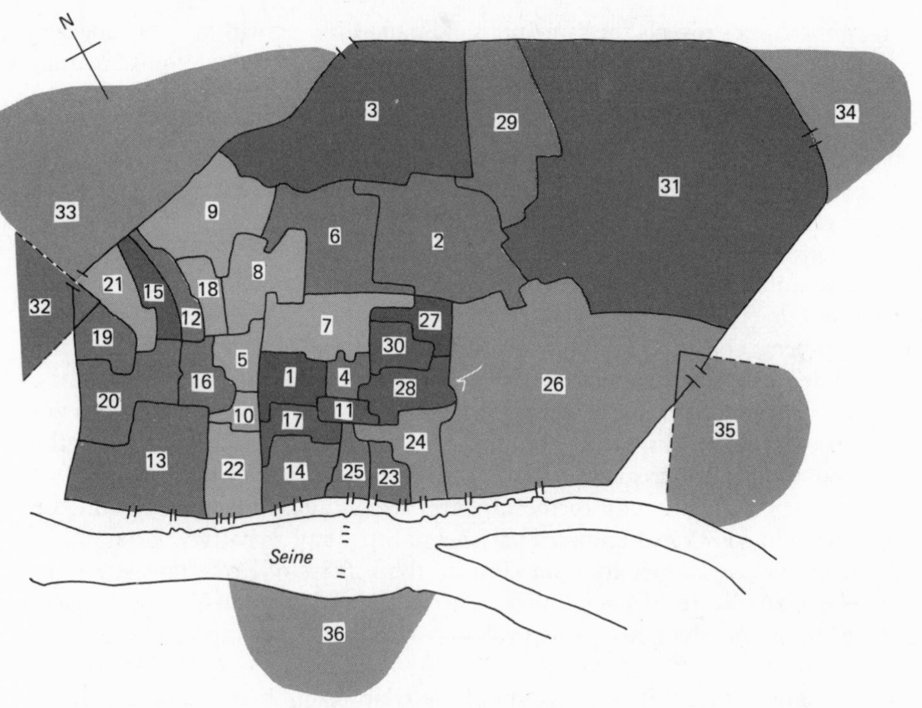

Map 7. Residential distribution of the *Confrères* of the Holy Sacrament

Quartier Beauvoisine
1. Notre-Dame-de-la-Ronde
2. Ste Croix–St Ouen
3. St Godard
4. St Herbland
5. St Jehan
6. St Laurent
7. St Lô
8. St Martin-sur-Renelle
9. St Patrice

Quartier Cauchoise
10. St André
11. St Cande-le-Jeune
12. Ste Croix-des-Pelletiers
13. St Eloi
14. St Etienne-des-Tonneliers
15. Ste Marie-la-Petite
16. St Michel
17. St Pierre-du-Chastel
18. St Pierre-l'Honoré
19. St Pierre-le-Portier
20. St Sauveur
21. St Vigor
22. St Vincent

Quartier Martainville
23. St Cande-le-Vieil
24. St Denis
25. St Martin-du-Pont
26. St Maclou

Quartier St Hilaire
27. St Amand
28. St Etienne-la-Grande-Eglise
29. St Nicaise
30. St Nicolas
31. St Vivien

Faubourgs
32. St André-hors-Ville
33. St Gervais
34. St Hilaire
35. St Paul
36. St Sever

(The darker the shading, the greater the number of members per 100 inhabitants.)
Source: A.D.S.M., G 9869.

communities reveals the same preponderance of men within the Protestant movement.[1] The prominence which women occasionally attained within the Reformed cause should not obscure the fact that women as a group seem to have been more likely than men to remain Catholic.

Map 7 sets forth the residential distribution of the *confrères* and *consoeurs* of the Holy Sacrament, plotting the number of members of this confraternity in relation to each parish's approximate total population.[2] The centers of the group's strength can be seen to have lain in the western parishes of the city, quite near to, and partially overlapping, the centers of Protestant strength. The popular quarters of the eastern half of town lodged fewer members, and the *faubourgs* fewest of all, suggesting once again that the residents of the extramural parishes participated but little in the life of the city. No common social characteristics unite the parishes most heavily represented within the confraternity. They stretch in a band from the predominantly mercantile parish of St Vincent through the artisanal areas in the heart of the city to the tanners' region along the Renelle and the *officier*- and lawyer-dominated parishes of St Lô and St Patrice. What unites them instead is their location close to the centers of Protestant strength. The Catholic residents of these parishes were presumably particularly aware of and alarmed by the growing strength of Calvinism.

In summarizing this examination of the relationship between occupational status and confessional choice, it is difficult to know whether to stress the similarities or the differences between Protestant and Catholic in sixteenth-century Rouen. Both religions attracted believers from a remarkably wide range of occupations and social strata, with the spread being perhaps slightly greater within Catholicism. Even the most basic unit of society, the family, could be riven by the confessional divisions. There were no perfect correlations between status and religion.

There is also no evidence that social or occupational rivalries were mirrored in the difference between Catholic and Protestant. The most important structural change occurring in Rouen's economy at this time was

[1] *Hist. eccl.*, Vol. 1, p. 68 (41 men and 19 women arrested in a raid on a Protestant assembly in Meaux, 1547); Louise Guiraud, *Etudes sur la Réforme à Montpellier* (Montpellier, 1918), Vol. 2, pp. 346–78 (757 men and 343 women on a 1560 'rôle...des assistants aux assemblées calvinistes'); F. de Schickler, *Les églises du Réfuge en Angleterre*, Vol. 1, p. 295 (242 male and 167 female refugees from Dieppe in Rye); 'Etat nominatif des Protestants de la Vicomté de Coutances en 1588', *B.S.H.P.F.*, XXXVI (1887), pp. 246–58 (444 men and 122 women).

[2] In preparing this map, I relied on the number of baptisms in each parish's parish registers as a guide to its total size. Since parish registers were not maintained for all parishes until the early seventeenth century, I have therefore used the average number of yearly baptisms for the period 1574–6 where possible and, where these do not exist, substituted those for 1599–1601 or, in a very few cases, 1609–11. This procedure should not introduce major distortions into the map since the population of the city changed but little between these three periods, as, presumably, did the relative size of the different intramural parishes.

the steady migration of industrial production away from the city to the surrounding countryside. It was a development which produced considerable conflict between the mercers, who organized the putting-out system which enabled industry to move to the countryside, and those city artisans who suffered from the rural competition. Frequent lawsuits were initiated by the aggrieved guilds – the hosiers, hat-makers, belt-makers, linen dyers, pewterers, and small metalware producers[1] – yet despite the social antagonisms, the differences visible between the mercers' religious leanings and those of their economic rivals are insignificant.[2] Another socio-economic rivalry that may have been growing stronger at the time is that between masters and journeymen within many crafts. The classic argument of Henri Hauser, that barriers to mastership were rising even higher and the artisan class was becoming increasingly polarized between a hereditary elite of master capitalists and a large number of permanent journeymen, receives at least modest corroboration from local evidence.[3] While the available lists do not permit discrimination between masters and journeymen among Rouen's Protestants, Natalie Davis' work on Lyon reveals no significant differences in the pattern of confessional choice between these two groups.[4]

If the social differences between Catholic and Protestant should not be exaggerated and cannot be made out to be the reflection of competing economic interest, neither should they be unduly minimized. The comparison of the members of the Reformed Church and the Confraternity of the Holy Sacrament has revealed clear and extremely suggestive divergences between the social composition of the two groups. If one cannot speak of perfect correlations, one can speak of statistical tendencies linking certain

[1] A.D.S.M., 5 E 464, 5 E 617, and 5 E 589 all contain documents pertaining to this ongoing rivalry. The last reveals particularly well the bitterness with which the mercers came to be regarded. According to a 1581 suit brought jointly by the hatters, hat-band-makers, hat-embroiderers, hosiers, belt-makers, brooch- and clasp-makers, spurriers, tinkers, sword-gilders, linen dyers, cloth retailers, and apothecaries the mercers had been born '*in perniciem*', selling such wares of sin as dice, masks, and cards. Following this tainted birth, they had gone on to attempt to engross all other trades in an avaricious quest to become 'merchants of everything'.

[2] A comparison based on Tables 2, 3, and 6 of the mercers' religious affinities and those of members of the trades which brought suit against them in 1581 reveals the following:

	Protestants	*Confrères* of the Holy Sacrament
Mercers	9	19
Members of rival guilds	49	103

[3] The number of new master weavers who were themselves sons of masters rose from 70 per cent in the 1550s to 97 per cent around the end of the century. A.D.S.M., G 7228–57, 7754–94. Among the goldsmiths the figure rose from 25 per cent in the 1550s to approximately 45 per cent throughout the last decades of the sixteenth and first decades of the seventeenth centuries. A.D.S.M., 5 E 609. These are the only two crafts for which such information is available. The fundamental work on this question remains Henri Hauser, *Ouvriers du temps passé* (Paris, 1899), pp. 119–27.

[4] Davis, 'Strikes and Salvation', p. 49.

trades with one faith or the other, or, perhaps better yet, of 'elective affinities' between the kinds of people who tended to cluster in certain occupations and the church whose doctrines they preferred. Both the Reformed Church and the Confraternity of the Holy Sacrament appealed most strongly not to the official elite, but to those from lower down the social scale. If stark class differences did not divide the two groups, it does appear that traditional Catholics tended to come disproportionately from the food and drink trades and from the levels of society teetering precariously near mendicity – domestic servants, street-sweepers, and the like. Clothworkers also seem overwhelmingly to have remained Catholic, and the same may have been true of lawyers. Protestants by contrast were more likely to be recruited from the ranks of the artisanal elite. More were hosiers than weavers. And among the merchants, the Calvinists tended to come not from the very wealthiest families, but from the strata just below.

In the absence of any diaries or journals in which individuals reveal their reasons for choosing one faith or the other, one can only attempt to infer why members of certain social groups were especially attracted to a given religion from the social characteristics associated with the group. The reluctance of both the wealthiest international merchants and the members of the sovereign courts to become involved in Protestantism is probably attributable to the prudence of high position. Yet the religious conflicts reflect no simple struggle of 'outs' versus 'ins', for among the converts to Protestantism in 1559–62 were three of the city's six ruling *conseillers-échevins*. The contrasting statistical tendencies visible among the different groups of artisans tend to confirm the insights both of such contemporary observers as Ronsard and Florimond de Raemond, as well as of such recent scholars as Emmanuel Le Roy Ladurie and Natalie Davis.[1] The more strongly Protestant trades were those in which the literacy rate was higher, suggesting once again the importance of this factor for the success of a faith which stressed private Bible reading so strongly.[2] Two hypotheses might

[1] Ronsard's opinions are reflected in the quotation at the beginning of this section, especially the comment that 'Ceux qui sçavent un peu' were those attracted to Protestantism.

[2] The link between literacy and Protestantism has been stressed especially by Le Roy Ladurie, *Paysans de Languedoc*, pp. 344–51. Using Natalie Davis' classification of trades into those in which literacy was high, medium, and low, one arrives at the following cross-tabulation:

Trades in which literacy …	Protestants	*Confrères* of the Holy Sacrament
High or very high	40 (23%)	75 (15%)
Medium	96 (56%)	287 (56%)
Low	35 (21%)	152 (29%)

Trade classification from Natalie Davis, 'Printing and the People', *Society and Culture in Early Modern France: Eight Essays* (Stanford, 1975), p. 210. It is probable that this table significantly understates the difference in literacy between the two groups, since the classification of literacy levels is based on evidence from Lyon, where the occupational structure was somewhat different from Rouen. All of the 'textile and clothing trades' are classified as ones of medium literacy, but Rouen's

explain the divergent behavior of the hosiers and the weavers. Davis has argued that Calvinism tended to attract more adherents from newer trades than old; recent immigrants to the city, perhaps a bit bewildered by urban life and in need of a community to which to belong, were more likely to be found in expanding new industries, while these trades were less well integrated into the confraternal and associational life of the city than were the older crafts whose traditions were long established. For both these reasons, members of these trades were attracted to Protestantism.[1] Although already declining by 1560, the hosiery trade was a relatively new industry in Rouen, considerably newer than the weaving industry, and it seems to have recruited certain of its workers from outside the city.[2] This might explain the number of Protestants within its ranks. Alternatively, the stress in Protestantism on a direct, unmediated relationship between the individual and God may have meant that the Reformed congregation tended to draw its adherents from the more independent artisans, while people in situations of personal dependence may have been more likely to find the Catholic panoply of saints, guardian angels, and other mediators between man and God reassuringly analogous to their own place in the social hierarchy.[3] This could also explain the hosier–weaver split. Finally, Davis has argued that a link existed between Calvinism and those individuals with a strong sense of self-confidence born out of pride in their calling.[4] This could well account for the connection between Protestantism and those crafts claiming to be the nobler arts.

Given the available evidence, all of these suggested links must remain tentative, but when combined they do present a convincing image of the sort of city dwellers especially likely to convert to Protestantism: people from somewhat below the very highest status occupations, but with the degree of literacy, self-confidence, and personal independence needed to reject the tutelage of the clergy and embrace the idea of a priesthood of all believers.[5] This is also the image of the Protestant which emerges from

textile trades were far more heterogeneous in organization and social composition than Lyon's, where there was no large group of proletarianized *ouvriers de draperie*. These individuals almost surely fell into the low literacy category. Similarly, one suspects that Rouen's numerous producers of small metalwares – pots, pans, pins, etc. – do not really belong in the high literacy category alongside the goldsmiths and pewterers. If these groups were shifted, the discrepancy between Catholic and Protestant in both the upper and lower literacy categories would widen significantly.

1 Davis, 'Strikes and Salvation', p. 50, and especially, 'Rites of Violence', pp. 80–81.

2 *See above*, pp. 13–15.

3 The recent anthropological study of William A. Christian Jr., *Person and God in a Spanish Valley* (New York, 1972), pp. 173–4, suggests how the mechanics of social intercourse in a hierarchical society seem replicated in prayers to saints or other intercessory figures.

4 Davis, 'Strikes and Salvation', pp. 52–4.

5 *See here* the remark of Gentian Hervet, *Discours de ce que les pilleurs, voleurs, & brusleurs d'eglises disent qu'ilz n'en veulent qu'aux moynes & aux prestres* (Reims, 1563), unpaginated, that it was those 'se fians par trop a leurs espritz, sans demander l'advis des gens doctes' who were led into Protestantism.

the studies of such communities as Lyon, Montpellier, Antwerp, and Deventer.[1] Such a picture of the attributes associated with conversion to Protestantism would also explain why women were less likely to convert than men. Literacy was significantly lower among women, and while we have seen that certain women enjoyed a degree of economic independence at this time, this was more the exception than the rule.[2]

The social analysis of ideological movements has long been plagued by reductionism. Too often, a movement is either presented simply as a crude vehicle for the social and political aspirations of a specific group or class which can be shown to have been strong within it, or else all links whatsoever are denied between it and the larger society in which it developed.[3] The relationship between confessional conflict and its social context suggested here is more complex. Any of a number of social variables (literacy, wealth, occupational status, length of residence in the community) – only some of which could be adequately investigated in Rouen – may predispose individuals in different occupations or social strata toward different religious choices, the key to each individual's choice being a certain 'fit' between the nature of those beliefs and that individual's personality and social experience. Once the choice is made, it involves accepting an all-encompassing intellectual system composed of a complex, interrelated set of metaphysical postulates and moral rules which is far more than a simple expression of the interest which may have led the individual to embrace the faith in the first place. This belief system will then shape the convert's subsequent behavior, very often along lines that have nothing to do with his self-interest. In short, a two-stage process is involved. Social factors predispose men to choose one set of religious beliefs or another; these beliefs in turn motivate much of their subsequent action.

1 David Rosenberg's research on Amiens, however, reveals a different pattern. *Protestantism there was a phenomenon primarily of the city's textile workers*, who were not especially highly literate, whose trade was considered 'base', and who were in many ways less independent than other workers in the city since the authorities felt the textile workers 'too irresponsible' to set their own work regulations as other guilds did. Rosenberg, 'Social Experience and Religious Choice', passim. There may have been a Protestantism of resentment and of the exploited as well as a Protestantism of the literate and self-assertive. The textile towns of Hainault and Flanders, often major centers of Calvinism, may also conform to the Amiens pattern.

2 *See above*, Chapter 1, p. 24. Significantly Natalie Davis finds that those women who became Protestants in Lyon 'include more than a random number of widows, of women with employ of their own...and of women with the curious nicknames associated with public and eccentric personalities', 'City Women and Religious Change', p. 81.

3 A typical example of such reductionism is Mours' comment in his generally excellent monograph, *Le Protestantisme en Vivarais et en Velay*, p. 16. 'Le fait', Mours writes, 'que la Réforme obtint des adhésions dans toutes les classes de la société...prouve que toutes les explications qu'on a voulu donner à sa rapide expansion – causes économiques, sociales, voire raciales – se révèlent sinon fausses, du moins grandement insuffisantes. Pour nous, il ne fait pas de doute, la Réforme fut avant tout un puissant mouvement de réveil de la foi chrétienne.' Cannot a movement be a revival of Christian faith even if it does not draw its members from all social classes? Even if such a movement does draw its members from all social classes cannot its expansion have social causes?

In concluding, however, it should be recalled that the sorts of affinities suggested in this chapter between Calvinism and the social experience of printers, goldsmiths, or hosiers cannot alone explain the rise of Protestantism in France. For a new religion to spread as Calvinism did in Rouen, it is necessary not only that there exist within society groups of people to whom the faith will appeal; there must also be the necessary social 'space' for the new religion to develop freely. Here historical contingency played a crucial role in the rise of Protestantism. The social groups which were to form the backbone of the Protestant movement existed well before the late 1550s, but Calvinism only became a major force in French society when the fluid political situation which prevailed between 1559 and 1562 blurred the lines of authority sufficiently to create a situation in which the Reformed cause could develop without undue harrassment. This may well be a point with more general implications for understanding the timing and extent of success enjoyed by Protestantism throughout Europe. While recent work on the Reformation's growth as a popular movement has tended to focus on either the social origins of the early converts or the ideological content of Protestant propaganda, the political context in which the movement developed – or failed to develop – also bears on the new religion's fate in different parts of Europe. When the German Reformation is seen from the vantage point of France, it is immediately apparent that an essential reason for Lutheranism's growth into a huge mass movement within only a few years of the posting of the 95 theses lies in the exceptional latitude given Protestant preachers and pamphleteers by the German princes and the burgermeisters of the Free Imperial Cities, who simply ignored the imperial edicts outlawing the dissemination of Luther's writings. An exception which proves the rule is Cologne, where the city fathers strictly enforced the edicts lest the emperor be given an excuse to intervene against them in their continuing struggle with the bishop or cut off their crucial trading connection with Habsburg Antwerp. Protestant ideas filtered into the city despite the careful surveillance, but Lutheranism never developed into a mass movement capable of forcing the Reformation on a recalcitrant oligarchy as it did in most other imperial cities. Cologne remained the 'German Rome'.[1] In the Low Countries, the great period of Calvinist expansion, the *Wonderjaar* of 1566, took place, as in France, at a time when the political situation was confused and central authority momentarily weakened.[2] And if Protestantism never enjoyed much success in Spain and soon saw its early gains rolled back in Italy, a great deal of the credit must surely go there to the Inquisitions in these lands, not to

[1] R. W. Scribner, 'Why was there no Reformation in Cologne?', *Bulletin of the Institute of Historical Research*, XLIX (1976), pp. 217–41. The author uses the same metaphor of necessary social 'space' that I have adopted here.

[2] Phyllis Mack Crew, *Calvinist Preaching and Iconoclasm in the Netherlands, 1544–1569* (Cambridge, 1978), pp. 151–5.

the absence of a potential audience for Protestantism. The degree of latitude afforded Protestantism in different countries and at different periods must be kept in mind in any analysis of the movement's appeal.

The subsequent history of Protestantism in Rouen will prove this point only too well. As we shall see, the series of civil wars which was to begin in 1562 soon embittered relations between the two confessions so greatly that Protestantism's social 'space' was drastically reduced. The Reformed movement lost its original momentum. Within a decade, the pressure of events would markedly transform it.

4

'The most difficult inhabitants of the kingdom'

Confessional antagonisms began to shake Rouen as early as 1560, but the effervescence of these first years was only a prelude to more bitter struggles to come. The outbreak of the First Civil War in April 1562 initiated a series of developments whose cumulative effect was to raise the religious rivalries to a new pitch of hatred. The Huguenot minority seized control of the city at the commencement of the civil war and maintained a domination which was to chafe ever more harshly on the city's Catholics as the twin pressures of war and popular militancy pushed the authorities to adopt increasingly punitive measures. The Huguenot domination ended with the capture of the city by royal forces in October, but the price of deliverance for the Catholics was a violent sacking of the city. The event restored the Catholics to an ascendancy that they never subsequently relinquished, but their domination was not unqualified. Following the edict of pacification which ended the First Civil War early in 1563, the Protestant congregation was re-established and those of its members who had fled the city in the wake of its fall returned. The faith's growth was checked by the events of the civil war; its militance was not. The fluid religious situation of the period prior to 1562 gave way to a more rigidly polarized one in which two clearly defined groups faced each other across a gulf of misunderstanding and hatred, their ideological antagonisms now intensified by increasingly sharp differences in personal behavior, not to mention the accumulation of grievances and thirst for revenge that inevitably accompany and serve to prolong civil war. Major outbreaks of violence, far more deadly in general than the incidents which had occurred prior to 1562, became an almost annual affair, and Rouen became the despair of a crown trying to pursue a policy of moderation and pacification.

The spark which touched off this process came from beyond Normandy's borders. On March 1, 1562, the duke of Guise was passing through the small town of Vassy in Champagne when he happened upon a Protestant assembly being held inside the city in violation of the terms of the edict of January. The duke's impetuosity mastered him. He and his retainers fell upon the worshippers. Called to court to account for the massacre, Guise chose to go instead to Paris, where he was acclaimed a hero by the Catholic populace. At Paris he managed to rally the vacillating Anthony of Navarre to the side of the arch-Catholic noblemen known collectively as the Triumvirate. He then sent a large force to the court at Fontainebleau to overawe Catherine de Medici and, in effect, kidnap young Charles IX. Meanwhile, the Protestant chieftain, Condé, refused Catherine's desperate plea that he come to court and assume the role of protector of the king. Acting perhaps out of cowardice, perhaps out of a desire for war, he chose instead to march to Orleans, assemble the Calvinist nobility, and issue a manifesto announcing that the violent designs of the Guises had compelled him to take up arms to defend the king. It was effectively a declaration of civil war.[1]

In Rouen, news of the massacre of Vassy and of the ensuing actions of the duke of Guise provoked an alarmed reaction from the city's Protestants. Both their fears and their militance (two sides of the same coin?) were aroused by letters circulating in Huguenot circles warning of future Vassys and instructing all churches to be ready to succor their neighboring congregations, with arms if necessary. Rouen's Huguenots immediately began to mount an armed guard around their assemblies. When two army captains entered the city early in April bearing a commission from the now-captive king directing them to levy troops, the Calvinists, fearful that the troops were intended for use against them, attacked these recruiters and drove them from town.[2] Six days later the pro-Guise *bailli*, Villebon d'Estouteville, returned to Rouen. The Calvinists later explained that they came to suspect Villebon of plotting to seize the arms in the Hôtel de Ville and that they took up arms against him to forestall the plot,[3] but Condé had recently issued his first manifesto of civil war and uprisings similar to that which ensued in Rouen were beginning in cities throughout France, suggesting that the claim of self-defense needs to be treated with caution. In any case, on the night of April 15 the Huguenots occupied the convent of the Celestines and the Hôtel de Ville, then besieged Villebon in the Château. He was soon forced to surrender and leave town. The uprising

1 Lucien Romier, *Catholiques et Huguenots à la cour de Charles IX* (Paris, 1924), pp. 318–51.

2 For local events, *see Cal. S.P. For.* 1562/997; 'Discours abbregé et memoires d'aulcunes choses advenues tant en Normandye que en France depuis le commencement de l'an 1559, et principalement en la ville de Rouen', ed. A. Héron, *Deux chroniques de Rouen* (Rouen, 1900), p. 193; *Journal d'un bourgeois de Rouen, mentionnant quelques événemens arrivés dans cette ville depuis l'an 1545 jusqu'à l'an 1564*, publication of *La Revue de Rouen et de la Normandie* (Rouen, 1837), pp. 8–9; *Hist. eccl.*, Vol. 2, pp. 713–15. The letters circulating among the Protestant communities are discussed in Romier, *Catholiques et Huguenots*, pp. 324–5.

3 *Remonstrance des habitans de la ville de Rouen, addressée aux Presidents et Conseillers du Parlement, ayans abandonné le service de Dieu et du Roy pour tenir un conventicule à Louviers* (n.p. [surely Rouen], 1562), unpaginated.

caught the Catholics within the city totally unprepared. As the Catholics were to do on St Bartholomew's Day a decade later, the Protestants had so quickly and so decisively taken control of the situation that their adversaries were too stunned to resist. The gates were secured and the personnel of the night watch changed to ensure Protestant military control of the city. The Huguenots were the effective masters of Rouen.[1]

The expulsion of the crown's agent Villebon represented a direct challenge to royal authority, but it did not necessarily condemn the city to an armed confrontation with the king. The Huguenot coup was originally more a defensive reaction than an attempt to initiate major changes either in religion or in city government. Although the municipal register of deliberations from 1559 through 1562 was either lost or destroyed when the city fell to the royal forces in October, enough evidence survives to indicate that the initial actions of the new authorities were anything but revolutionary. The rebel spokesmen stressed in their public pronouncements their continued obedience to the king, declaring that they had only taken up arms to prevent a repetition of Vassy. The Catholic members of the Council of Twenty-Four were permitted to continue participating in the body's deliberations. The parlement continued to sit. The often incendiary members of the mendicant orders were warned that they would be expelled if they stirred up any trouble, and some fled the city, but the clergy was nonetheless allowed to continue celebrating Mass. Finally, as a warning to those who might contemplate violence against the remaining clerics, a soldier who had injured the prior of the Celestines during the takeover was executed.[2]

The subsequent months of Protestant domination witnessed a classic example of militant elements on both sides forcing a confrontation that more moderate individuals hoped to avoid. The first step came from the Protestant side. Appeals for calm by the Protestant ministers and elders proved no more effective now than in the preceding years in deterring the zealots within the church from taking direct action. On May 3 and 4 a wave of iconoclasm broke over the city. Armed Huguenots went systematically from church to church, confiscating objects of precious metal, smashing or defacing sculptures, altars, and baptismal fonts, and dragging all tapestries, pews, coffers, and music books into the streets, where they were consumed in great bonfires.[3] The city's scarred churches still bear witness today to the thoroughness with which the entire operation was carried out.

[1] The best account of the Huguenot takeover is 'Discours abbregé', pp. 194–5.

[2] *Hist. eccl.*, Vol. 2, pp. 716–18; 'Discours abbregé', pp. 195, 197; E. Le Parquier, *Le siège de Rouen en 1562* (Sotteville-lès-Rouen, 1907), p. 14, an excellent and very thorough narrative of the events of 1562.

[3] The *chartrier* of the parish church of St Vincent provides a particularly vivid glimpse of the extent of the destruction. Paul Baudry, *L'église paroissiale de Saint-Vincent de Rouen* (Rouen, 1875), pp. 33–5. *See also* 'Discours abbregé', pp. 199–200.

A hastily-penned 'Apology of the Ministers and Elders of the Reformed Church in the City of Rouen' provides the only surviving indication of the identity of the iconoclasts – a statement that children initiated and played a major role in the destruction.[1] The pamphlet is, however, coyly disingenuous; it seeks to convey the impression that the iconoclasm was a spontaneous outburst of zeal carried out in complete disregard of the Reformed leadership, while at the same time indicating a degree of tacit approval in the claim that the iconoclasm was a providential act which demonstrated divine displeasure at Catholic 'idolatry'. The degree of organization apparent among the iconoclasts, said to have 'assembled into several bands',[2] leads one to suspect that more than children were involved. The destruction probably was the premeditated effort of a group within the church wishing to push through more drastic measures than the magistrates dared undertake.

The result of the iconoclasm certainly was to overturn the old order thoroughly. Not only were the 'idols' torn down; the bands of iconoclasts also invaded the houses of the city's Catholics, seizing their arms. An exodus of alarmed Catholic merchants, officials, and priests soon developed in the direction of Louviers and Beaumont-le-Roger. It was intensified when, on May 10, the parlement decided that it could no longer continue to sit safely within Rouen. By the end of the month only a handful of Catholic clerics and *officiers* remained in the city, most of them men with relatives among the Protestant leadership. Priests no longer dared appear in public in their clerical habits. Catholic services ceased.[3]

The flight of the parlement and of many Catholic members of the city government naturally left the Protestants in more complete political control of the city than before. The three Catholic *conseillers-échevins* ceased to participate in the meetings of the Council of Twenty-Four, leaving the three Protestants to dominate municipal government until July 4, the normal date for elections, when a new, all-Protestant Council was voted into office. An extraordinary 'Council Established by the People', dominated by the Reformed elders, also began to function.[4] Its exact competence *vis-à-vis* the Council of Twenty-Four cannot be determined, the loss of the

1 *Apologie des ministres en anciens de l'Eglise reformee en la ville de Rouen sur le brisement des images* (n.p. [surely Rouen], 1562), unpaginated.

2 'Discours abbregé', p. 198.

3 'Discours abbregé', p. 200; *Journal d'un bourgeois*, p. 10; Le Parquier, *Siège de Rouen*, pp. 9–14. On the flight of the city's merchants and their destinations: A.D.S.M., B, Parlement, Arrêts, Août–Octobre 1562, arrêts of Oct. 3, 12, 17, and 21; Novembre 1562–Mars 1563, arrêts of Jan. 11, Feb. 27, March 9, 17, 21, and 24, all arrêts referring to merchants who left the city during the period of Huguenot domination.

4 A.D.S.M., G 2165, entry of June 3, 1562; *Relation des troubles excités par les calvinistes dans la ville de Rouen depuis l'an 1537 jusqu'en l'an 1582*, publication of *La Revue de Rouen et de la Normandie* (Rouen, 1837), p. 18; Le Parquier, *Siège de Rouen*, pp. 14–15.

municipal registers of deliberations making all of the actions of the new Protestant authorities very difficult to follow. The *Histoire ecclésiastique* does boast, however, of efforts to improve the system of poor relief within the city, measures which were probably necessitated by the economic disruption caused by the flight of many of the leading merchants and the campaigning which soon began in the region.[1] It also seems that the officials continued to try to follow a moderate line, resisting pressure from certain inhabitants that all Catholics be expelled in retaliation for the banishment of the Huguenots from Paris early in June.[2]

For her part, Catherine de Medici was also discovering the difficulties of moderation. She opened negotiations with the Rouennais soon after the initial uprising in April and continued them even after the iconoclasm of May, hoping to arrange a settlement whereby the city would admit the crown's officials in return for a promise of leniency for its rebellion. Her efforts ran afoul of the hard-liners on the Catholic side. Ever distrustful of the house of Lorraine, the Rouennais insisted on the revocation of the special commission recently given the duke of Aumale, Guise's brother, as lieutenant-general of Normandy with powers to raise troops throughout the region. Catherine could not persuade the Triumvirs to consent to a measure depriving a leading member of their faction of his position, and she was in too vulnerable a position to act without them. On May 28 Aumale appeared before Rouen and demanded that the city open the gates to him. When the inhabitants refused, he began a diffident siege. Negotiation had given way to open conflict.[3]

The forces at Aumale's command were too weak to pose an immediate threat to Rouen's defenses, but they maintained intermittent pressure on the town for over a month. Under their harrassment, and with the city steadily filling up with Protestant soldiers who had come to aid in its defense, the atmosphere grew steadily grimmer. The soldiers who entered the city proved prone to rob the natives when not otherwise engaged in the raids that were a mixture of iconoclasm and simple pillage launched against such nearby towns as Darnétal, Elbeuf, and Caudebec.[4] Religious antipathies were heightened further when the parlement's more zealously Catholic members assembled at Louviers in early August and formed a skeleton court which embarked on a campaign of terror against the

[1] *Hist. eccl.*, Vol. 2, p. 728.

[2] Le Parquier, *Siège de Rouen*, pp. 33–4. The Protestant masters of Orleans were not so moderate. They expelled all Catholics at this point. Bernard de Lacombe, *Les débuts des guerres de religion (Orléans, 1559–1564): Cathérine de Médicis entre Guise et Condé* (Paris, 1899), pp. 198–9.

[3] B.N., MS Français 15876, fo. 41; *L.C.M.*, Vol. 1, pp. 322–3; Le Parquier, *Siège de Rouen*, p. 33.

[4] A.D.S.M., G 2165, entry of June 3, 1562; *Hist. eccl.*, Vol. 2, p. 731; Le Parquier, *Siège de Rouen*, pp. 16, 31–2, 37; H. Voiment, *Notes chronologiques sur l'ancien bourg de Darnétal (près Rouen), XIVe siècle – 1805* (Evreux, 1900), p. 11; H. Saint-Denis, *Histoire d'Elbeuf* (Elbeuf, 1894), Vol. 2, pp. 237–9.

Huguenots. A harsh *arrêt* banned Protestant worship in all royal-controlled portions of the province, forbade Calvinists to hold royal offices, and declared those responsible for the destruction of church property guilty of *lèse-majesté* and forfeit of all their goods and inheritances. Those Huguenots unlucky enough to fall into the court's hands were hanged in a series of mass executions. The authorities in Rouen were moved to retaliation. They imprisoned a number of Catholics, forced all others to make a public profession of the Reformed articles of faith, and seized the property of those who had 'deserted' the city.[1]

The mounting violence on both sides destroyed any remaining chances for negotiation. As the royal armies started to add victory to victory in central France, the military situation began to appear ominous for the Rouennais. Their reaction was to look beyond France's borders for reinforcement. On August 15 a deputy of the city embarked for England with the Vidame of Chartres to open negotiations with Queen Elizabeth. Three weeks later, with the main body of royal forces now heading north after taking Bourges, the city authorities addressed an urgent appeal to the Virgin Queen that she intervene to save a city 'that is and wishes to render itself yours'. These overtures finally resulted in the treaty of Hampton Court, signed on September 20, by which the Protestants handed Le Havre over to Elizabeth in return for a pledge of a 6,000-man relief force to aid Rouen and Dieppe.[2]

Inviting the assistance of France's traditional enemy was not a universally popular policy within the Huguenot camp. Plots to block the landing of the English troops were soon uncovered, and news of the signature of the treaty led several Calvinist noblemen to leave Rouen in disapproval.[3] In the end, the objections of these men proved justified, for the treaty turned out to be of little avail to the Rouennais. Only after the English had securely garrisoned their prize of Le Havre did they send any troops to Rouen. By the time the first company of 200 Scots arrived on October 4, the city was already besieged by some 30,000 royal soldiers under the command of the king of Navarre, for the signing of the pact had only spurred the royal forces to move north rapidly. Before the second and final contingent of 300 English soldiers arrived, the attacking forces had captured the Fort Ste Catherine.[4]

1 B.M.R., MS Y 214 (5), fos. 386ff.; A.D.S.M., B, Parlement, Arrêts; Août–Octobre 1562, arrêt of Aug. 26, 1562; *Memoires de Condé* (London, 1743), Vol. 4, p. 40; Le Parquier, *Siège de Rouen*, p. 36. A.D.S.M., B, Parlement, Arrêts, Novembre 1562–Mars 1563 and Avril–Septembre 1563 contain numerous cases brought by leading Catholic 'deserters' for reimbursement of the sums confiscated from them.

2 Le Parquier, *Siège de Rouen*, p. 38; James Westfall Thompson, *The Wars of Religion in France 1559–1576: The Huguenots, Catherine de Medici and Philip II* (Chicago, 1909), pp. 163–5.

3 Jacques-Auguste De Thou, *Histoire universelle* (The Hague, 1740), Vol. 3, p. 184; Le Parquier, *Siège de Rouen*, p. 39.

4 Le Parquier, *Siège de Rouen*, p. 40.

The royal forces had an overwhelming superiority in both arms and men, so their capture of the Fort Ste Catherine, the citadel which commanded the town from the southeast, was expected to lead quickly to Rouen's surrender. Once again Catherine de Medici pressed for a negotiated settlement, not wishing to subject one of the kingdom's richest cities to a damaging attack and the possibility of a sacking once it was captured. Once again, negotiation failed. Within the city the merchants and bourgeois seem to have been willing to compromise, but the more zealous inhabitants, primarily the artisans and the refugees from Lower Normandy and Maine who had taken shelter in the city, backed the military commander Montgommery in deciding to resist.[1] The Spanish ambassador Chantonnay described the course of the siege with exasperation: 'They fight, they negotiate, they get angry, they calm down; and in the end they lose a great deal of time.'[2] Finally discussions between the two sides broke down for good over the Rouennais' insistence that all Protestant ministers be allowed to remain in the city if it surrendered.[3] On October 21 the attackers launched a full-scale offensive. The walls were breached in five days. Those Protestant leaders who could fled in ships that had been kept anchored along the Seine in case of such an eventuality. Others slipped out of town by night in the midst of the confusion of the next few days, scattering throughout the portions of Normandy still under Protestant or English control: Caen, Dieppe, Le Havre, and the Pays de Caux.[4] Several were captured, among them the *conseillers-échevins* Vincent de Gruchet and Noël Cotton and the city's noted pastor, Augustin Marlorat.

The leaders of the royal army attempted to save the Norman capital from the customary fate of a captured city, a sacking, by announcing a bonus in pay when the walls were breached.[5] The soldiers were not about to be bought off so cheaply. The reports of the violence which ensued contain great discrepancies. The Spanish ambassador, whom long experience had rendered somewhat blasé about these matters, thought that all went

[1] J. Le Laboureur, *Les mémoires de Messire Michel de Castelnau...illustrez et augmentez de plusieurs Commentaires et Manuscrits* (Paris, 1659), Vol. 1, pp. 107–8; Le Parquier, *Siège de Rouen*, p. 58. In Orleans in 1563 and in La Rochelle in 1572 this same division between hard-line artisans and conciliatory bourgeois surfaced inside a Huguenot-controlled city under siege. Lacombe, *Les débuts des guerres de religion*, pp. 322–3; Etienne Trocmé, 'La Rochelle de 1560 à 1628: Tableau d'une société réformée au temps des Guerres de Religion', unpublished thèse de théologie protestante (Paris, 1950), pp. 196–7.

[2] *Mémoires de Condé*, Vol. 2, p. 99.

[3] Le Parquier, *Siège de Rouen*, p. 59.

[4] On the flight of the Protestants, *see Archivo documental español: Negociaciones con Francia* (Madrid, 1950–59), Vol. 4, pp. 350–51. Their destinations are revealed by A. D. Calvados, C 1565–66; A.D.S.M., B, Parlement, Arrêts, Novembre 1562–Mars 1563, arrêt of Dec. 9, 1562; Guillaume and Jean Daval, *Histoire de la Réformation à Dieppe* (Rouen, 1878), p. 42; Mario Battistini, ed., *Lettere di Giovani Battista Guicciardini a Cosimo e Francesco de' Medici scritte dal Belgio dal 1559 al 1577* (Brussels–Rome, 1949), p. 193.

[5] Le Laboureur, *Mémoires de Castelnau*, p. 108; Le Parquier, *Siège de Rouen*, p. 65.

'*dulcemente*'. The houses of the Huguenots were thoroughly looted, but those Catholics who could get to their houses in time were able to buy off the soldiers at a going rate of 200 *écus* (in fact, a sum well beyond the means of most). Such objects as were taken were, as usual, sold for a tiny fraction of their worth to merchants, who were in turn ordered to sell the wares back to their original owners for what they had paid.[1] Local chroniclers recount the sack with a good deal less *sang-froid*:

Horrible thing to see! The entry of the soldiers unleashed the cruelty and furor of war on all people whom the soldiers happened to encounter in the streets, men and women, Huguenots and Catholics, with such fury that it took two days to recover the bodies from among the garbage on the pavement, and no matter what orders were issued by the king, order could not be restored.[2]

The violence lasted three days,[3] and not even the Catholic churches were spared by their liberators, a fact which is evident from the treasury accounts of two parish churches noting expenditures for the purpose of reacquiring pillaged objects from merchants of Pontoise and Lyons-la-Forêt.[4] These entries also corroborate the reports of chroniclers that merchants descended on the city from throughout the region and as far away as Paris to purchase at bargain rates the booty amassed by the soldiers.[5] As for deaths among the defenders and inhabitants of the city, Chantonnay reports that the common estimate was a thousand victims.[6]

The sacking of the city by the royal forces was a bloody end to the only period of political control which Rouen's Protestants would ever attain. It was not, as is often asserted, the start of a period of numerical decline for the congregation. Catholicism was quickly restored to a dominant position within the city; the *parlementaires* who had gathered at Louviers entered the city on the heels of the royal troops, voided the municipal elections

1 *Archivo documental español*, Vol. 4, pp. 353, 367. *See also* Abel Desjardins, ed., *Négociations diplomatiques avec la Toscane* (Paris, 1859–76), Vol. 3, p. 497 for a similar account which corroborates certain details of Chantonnay's report.

2 'Discours abbregé', p. 267. This more somber view of the sack is also reflected in *Le vary pourtraict de la ville de Rouen assiegée et prise par le roy Charles 9* (Paris, n.d.), single page map with text.

3 Three days is the duration claimed by the best eyewitness account: 'Discours abbregé', p. 267. Other accounts differ widely on this score. *Hist. eccl.*, Vol. 2, p. 784, declares that the sack lasted 24 weeks. The Catholic *Relation des troubles*, p. 24, states that the city was pillaged for no more than 24 hours, the figure also supplied by *Le vary pourtraict*.

4 A.D.S.M., F, Dépot Association Diocesaine, Eglise St Vincent, Inventaire des Titres du Trésor, Vol. 1, pp. 560–61; A.D.S.M., G 7755.

5 *Relation des troubles*, p. 41. According to the author, this is just one example of the way 'ce peuple inepte de Paris, presque sot de nature' had always preyed on the hard-working Normans, bleeding them dry of food and precious metals.

6 *Archivo documental español*, Vol. 4, p. 353.

which had been held in July on the grounds that the Catholics had not been allowed to vote freely, and ordered a new round of balloting which yielded a Council of Twenty-Four without a single Reformed member.[1] Yet if the Protestants would never again elect so much as a single one of their number to the Council, their movement was by no means broken. Many Huguenots chose to stay in Rouen after the city's fall, and when the edict of Amboise brought an end to the First Civil War and granted those who had fled the city the right to return and to resume worshipping freely, the congregation quickly regrouped. With their impressive totals of 662 baptisms per year, 21 per cent of the total number of baptisms in the city, the Reformed baptismal registers of 1565–6 suggest a community that was probably larger in size than it had been prior to the First Civil War. In other Norman Protestant congregations, the figures indicate clearly that the movement grew in strength between 1561 and 1564.[2] Furthermore, Rouen's congregation was a group which had not lost hope of attracting new converts and perhaps even returning to power; its assertiveness was scarcely diminished. No sooner was the peace of Amboise announced than some bold members of the faith began singing psalms in public.[3] The following year witnessed two incidents of iconoclasm and another in which a Catholic preacher was publicly contradicted by a Protestant in the audience.[4] Proselytization was resumed, and from a secret press somewhere within the city the Geneva-trained printer Abel Clémence began turning out large numbers of psalters and theological works, both for local consumption and for export to Flanders, Holland, and England.[5] In 1566 the Huguenots mounted a major effort to elect several of their own to the Council of Twenty-Four, while the outbreak of the Second Civil War in 1567 was, as we shall see, the occasion for an abortive plot to seize the city militarily once again.[6]

Instead of marking the end of the Protestant movement as a major political challenge in Rouen, the chief result of the events of 1562 was to exacerbate Catholic hostility. Many cities were seized by the Protestants at the outbreak of the First Civil War, but the course of events during the six months of Huguenot domination in Rouen was such as to stimulate

[1] A.C.R., A 18, entries of Oct. 31 and Nov. 7, 1562.

[2] Philip Benedict, 'Catholics and Huguenots in Sixteenth-Century Rouen: The Demographic Effects of the Religious Wars', *French Historical Studies*, IX (1975), pp. 223–5. *See also* Appendix 1, p. 254.

[3] A.C.R., A 18, entry of April 6, 1563.

[4] B.M.R., MS Y 102 (2), p. 22; J. T. Pommeraye, *Histoire de l'Eglise Cathédrale de Rouen* (Rouen, 1686), p. 141.

[5] George Clutton, '"Abel Clemence" of "Rouen": A Sixteenth-Century Secret Press', *The Library*, 4th series, XX (1939), pp. 136–53; H. de la Fontaine-Verwey, 'Une presse secrète du XVIe siècle: Abel Clémence, imprimeur à Rouen', *Mélanges Frantz Callot* (Paris, 1960), pp. 81–9; Gérard Moreau, *Histoire du Protestantisme à Tournai jusqu'à la veille de la Révolution des Pays-Bas* (Paris, 1962), p. 167.

[6] *See below*, p. 118.

particularly violent resentments. Moderation had gradually crumbled before militance on both sides, and the ultimate consequence of the Huguenot takeover had been a devastating sacking – ample confirmation of the Catholic view that the Huguenots were a seditious element whose presence in a community only brought disaster. In most other cities the period of Protestant domination did not end amid bloodshed and pillage; instead the Huguenots voluntarily relinquished power after a negotiated settlement, a denouement far less likely to increase hatred of them. Memories, first of the iconoclasm and then of the sacking, would haunt Rouen's Catholics for decades. The plague, earthquake, and floods of 1580–82 were proof to one that 'the elements...are still irritated' by the 1562 image-smashing.[1] Numerous *doléances* trace all subsequent economic ills back to the sack.[2] While religious passions had already been running high, the resentments accumulated during the period in which the Catholics watched impotently as their shrines were defiled, their consciences forced, their goods confiscated, and then their houses pillaged or held up for ransom in what was supposed to be their deliverance were to lend a new bitterness to future events born of old scores to settle. In the ensuing decade, the Catholics replaced the Protestants as the party taking the offensive within the city.

The course of events in Rouen during 1562 was not the only development adding fuel to the fire of anti-Protestant sentiment. Another development, this one common to many communities, also intensified Catholic resentment: the growing chasm between the two religions in terms of their behavior and self-image. The events of 1562 may not have broken Protestantism; they did brake its growth. New conversions became rare, and as a result the Huguenot community increasingly became a well-defined group. It also became increasingly a group apart, for conversion to Protestantism had entailed adopting a new set of moral priorities, brought the convert into a new cultural universe, and often produced in him a new self-image. With conversions now less common and the Protestants increasingly set in their ways, the degree of Protestant 'otherness' became marked.

Lacking better evidence, one of the best guides to the Huguenots' self-image is provided by the names they chose to bestow on their children. Over a generation ago Lucien Febvre first pointed out that people often select for their children the names of beloved saints, biblical figures, or other people worthy of emulation, and that the study of names can therefore reveal a good deal about a group's culture and values.[3] A comparison of the names chosen by Catholic and Protestant families in Rouen bears out Febvre's

[1] *Relation des troubles*, p. 15.
[2] For example, A.C.R., A 19, entry of May 16, 1571.
[3] Lucien Febvre, 'A Amiens: de la Renaissance à la Contre-Réforme', *Au coeur religieux du XVIe siècle* (Paris, 1957), pp. 278–81 (article originally published 1941).

Table 7. *The most popular names*

Boys		Girls	
		Catholics*	
Jean	70	Marie	63
Guillaume	30	Catherine	41
Pierre	27	Marguerite	33
Nicolas	26	Jeanne	28
Jacques	22	Anne	26
		Protestants†	
Jean	46	Marie	113
Abraham	42	Judith	38
Isaac	41	Sara	31
Pierre	36	Susanne	27
Daniel	33	Anne	17

* Based on a sample of 650 names drawn from the parish register of St Maclou 1578–79.
† Based on the entries in the Huguenot baptismal register of 1565

insight. As part of his attack on the cult of saints, Calvin forbade his followers to bestow saints' names on their children. This prohibition was not universally obeyed among Calvinists,[1] but in Rouen it was followed strictly. Table 7 shows the pattern of names that came to characterize the rival faiths. Among the Catholic sample, the five most popular men's names were precisely the same five Febvre found in Amiens, with the only difference being that Guillaume rated higher in popularity in Rouen (still memories of the Conqueror?). The rank order among the Protestants was completely different; the highly popular Jean still came first, but it was challenged closely by two utterly non-traditional names of Old Testament origin, Abraham and Isaac. Another Old Testament name, Daniel, stood fifth in popularity, while the two traditionally popular choices which were saints' names, Guillaume and Nicolas, were not bestowed on a single Protestant child in 1565. The pattern of popularity among the girls' names chosen by Catholic parents was slightly different in Rouen than in Amiens, but the contrast between Catholics and Protestants remains equally sharp here, as it does in the complete figures provided in Appendix 2. Saints' names were overwhelmingly Catholic, Old Testament names predominantly Protestant, and the names of the apostles and other New Testament figures cut across confessional lines. The percentage of Protestant names drawn from the Old Testament is particularly noteworthy. Fully 50 per cent of

[1] *See* Willy Richard, *Untersuchungen zur Genesis der reformierten Kirchenterminologie der Westschweiz und Frankreichs mit besonderer Berücksichtigung der Namengebung* (Bern, 1959), Romanica Helvetica LVII, pp. 191–217. I would like to thank William Monter for calling this work to my attention.

the names in this first Huguenot baptismal register were of Hebrew origin, among them such attention-grabbing monickers as Melchizadeh and Roboam. (The mortification of the unfortunate children given these names is easy to imagine.) The clear sense of identification with the ancient Hebrews revealed by these names was of course a product of the constant Bible reading of the Protestants. It could well have also been the product of the parallels which the Calvinists saw between themselves and the Hebrews. They too were God's chosen people, the elect, living in the midst of a hostile and unregenerate mass of humanity around them. The image of the Huguenot sketched by Ronsard in his 'Remonstrance au Peuple de France' looks very much like the stock figure of the English Puritan in anti-Puritan satire: stern of visage, sober of language, discoursing constantly of Jacob and the predestined. The accuracy of the picture cannot be fully verified, but it is clear that the Protestants often named their children Jacob and felt a strong bond with the ancient Hebrews. Significantly, the percentage of Old Testament names among the Protestant children in Rouen is over 20 per cent higher than the percentage of such names bestowed on infants in Geneva in this period, a disparity which reflects the difference between a minority Reformed congregation whose members had all joined out of conviction and a community where the faith was imposed on all by law.[1] It also seems revealing that of all the prominent figures in the Old Testament, the ones after whom the Calvinists most frequently named their children – Abraham, Isaac, and Daniel – were individuals whose lives represented dramas of obedience to God's will and of suffering for that obedience. However militant the actions of the Huguenots, it was not the warrior-kings or the lawgivers to whom they felt the closest bond. In their own eyes they were servants of God's will whose faith was being constantly tested.

If the Huguenots thought of themselves as chosen people, their sense of themselves as such could have been reinforced by a sense of their moral superiority. Reformed Church discipline enforced a strict code of behavior. All members of the faith were to abstain from blasphemy, to dress modestly, and to avoid all games of chance and those 'involving avarice, lewdness, scandal, or notorious wasting of time'. Believers were also to abstain from dancing, to shun popular festivities, and to avoid 'those who perform sleight of hand tricks, acrobatics, or stage marionette shows'.[2] Such restrictions cut the Calvinists off from common festivities and amusements and from

[1] *Ibid.*, p. 202. Richard's meticulous study demonstrates that the study of names can be an excellent index of the strength of popular commitment to Calvinism in a given area. Just as fewer Old Testament names were chosen in Geneva than in Rouen, so the number declines even more sharply in passing from Geneva to the small towns and villages of the Pays de Vaud, where saints' names also lingered on in large numbers. While formally Calvinist, these communities were clearly only lightly touched by a Reformed spirit as late as the 1570s.

[2] Issac d'Huisseau, *La discipline des Eglises Réformées de France* (n.p., 1656), pp. 101–3.

that center of popular sociability, the tavern. Of course, it was not to be expected that every convert would heed these restrictions. Precisely for that reason, they were backed by a rigorous system of formal and informal sanctions. It was every believer's Christian duty to admonish privately their brothers whom they observed misbehaving. Those who disregarded such fraternal admonitions or misbehaved in especially heinous or notorious fashion were to be denounced to the church consistory, an assembly of pastors and elders which would rebuke sinners for their bad behavior and seek to obtain a promise from them that they would not repeat their offense. The consistory had the right to hand out punishments which might vary from requiring a public confession of guilt before the entire congregation to expulsion from the Lord's Supper.[1]

The consistory records of Rouen's Reformed Church have not survived, but a sense of the kind of surveillance exercised by this assembly can be obtained from the records of the refugee French Church of Threadneedle Street, London, which from earliest days always contained a significant number of Rouennais exiles among its members.[2] Believers were reprimanded for a wide range of offenses varying in gravity from attempted rape (seduction, the man claimed) through mistreatment of apprentices, gambling at tennis, and stealing from the *plattelet des povres*.[3] As Table

[1] *Institutes of the Christian Religion*, IV, xii, 2. R. N. Caswell, 'Calvin's View of Ecclesiastical Discipline', *John Calvin*, Courtenay Studies in Reformation Theology I (Appleford, Berks., 1966), pp. 210–26, is a clear explication of the theory of Reformed discipline, while a sense of the consistory in action can be obtained from the introduction to Elsie Johnston, ed. *Actes du consistoire de l'église française de Threadneedle Street, Londres*, Vol. 1, *1560–1565* (Frome, 1937), Huguenot Society of London Publication XXXVIII, p. xxv. Naturally it is very difficult to know how zealously the average Calvinist discharged his duty to admonish a misbehaving neighbor. One has difficulty imagining a simple weaver rebuking a nobleman for an indiscretion. Still, an occasional case shows that certain converts took their duty so seriously that they allowed it to overcome even simple prudence. The arrest of Thomas de Sainct-Pol, a resident of Soissons martyred for the faith, came when 'he could not suffer the blasphemies' of a man with whom he was doing business and so admonished him for them. 'The other, being irritated, immediately suspected him as a Lutheran (as they called them) because of this remonstrance unaccustomed among Papists.' Jean Crespin, *Histoire des martyrs persecutez et mis a mort pour la verité de l'evangile, depuis le temps des apostres jusques a present* (*1619*) (Toulouse, 1889), Vol. 1, p. 559.

[2] Two volumes of the London consistory records from 1560–65 and 1571–7 have been edited by Elsie Johnston and Anne M. Oakley respectively and published by the Huguenot Society of London (Publications XXXVIII and XLVIII). At least 26 of the individuals who appear in these volumes are from Rouen. The significant percentage of Rouennais within the congregation can also be seen from the church's 1560 list of members, *Actes du consistoire*, Vol. 1, pp. 1–4 (5 of 20 individuals whose place of origin noted from Rouen) and from *Returns of Aliens Dwelling in the City and Suburbs of London from the Reign of Henry VIII to that of James I*, Publications of the Huguenot Society of London X (Aberdeen, 1900–8), Vol. 1, pp. 287–92 (7 of 101 'strangers in London of ye French Chirch' from Rouen, more than from any other city).

[3] *Actes du consistoire*, passim, esp. Vol. 1, pp. 10, 15 and Vol. 2, pp. 12, 100. Significantly, two offences for which nobody was reprimanded were usury and false business practices. E. W. Monter, *Calvin's Geneva* (New York, 1967), p. 219, points out that while Calvin may have loosened theoretical strictures on lending at interest, in practice Geneva was one of the few cities where usurers were ever caught and punished. Genevan enforcement of strictures against lending at excessive rates of

Table 8. *Offenses handled by the consistory of the French Church of London, 1560–1565, 1571–1577*

Cases ending in excommunication	
Domestic quarrels	4 (6%)
Quarrels with others	16 (24%)
'Scandalous living'	5 (7%)
Fornication, bigamy, or other sexual offense	15 (22%)
Drunkenness	15 (22%)
Assault	1 (1%)
Gambling	2 (3%)
Clandestine marriage or marriage outside church	2 (3%)
Consulting magician	1 (1%)
Denying doctrine of church or authority of consistory	7 (10%)
All offenses before consistory	
Domestic quarrels*	38 (9%)
Quarrels with others	92 (22%)
Fornication, bigamy, or other sexual offense	51 (12%)
Papistical 'pollution'	105† (25%)
Marital jurisprudence	22 (5%)
Clandestine marriage or marriage outside church	9 (2%)
Drunkenness	53 (12%)
Assault	10 (2%)
General scandal	9 (2%)
Murder	2 (0.4%)
Gambling	5 (1%)
Theft	3 (0.7%)
Magical practices	3 (0.7%)
Blasphemy and swearing	2 (0.5%)
Denying doctrine of church or authority of consistory	12 (3%)
Miscellaneous offenses, one each‡	10 (2%)

* Includes quarrels with kin, servants, or apprentices.

† Ninety-five of these cases grew out of the St Bartholomew's Day Massacre, in the wake of which many Rouennais Protestants briefly attended Catholic services before fleeing to England. This is discussed below, pp. 128–9.

‡ Includes working on Sunday, false accusation, 'rebellion' to elders, attempted suicide, mistreatment of worker, dancing.

N.B.: Percentage figures given do not add up to 100 per cent because percentages have been rounded off. This table does not include matters of church governance and administration dealt with by the consistory. These occupied roughly a quarter of the body's deliberations.

8 shows, drunkenness and sexual misconduct seem to have been particular problems for this refugee church, perhaps as a result of the loneliness and disruption of normal family life caused by exile.[1] Of course, much of the

interest may well have been the exception among Reformed churches. As in London, nobody appears to have been punished for this offense in the Languedoc congregations studied by Janine Estèbe. J. Estèbe and B. Vogler, 'La genèse d'une société protestante: étude comparée de quelques registres consistoriaux languedociens et palatins vers 1600', *Annales: E.S.C.*, XXXI (1976), pp. 362–88.

[1] The high incidence of these offenses emerges clearly when compared with the statistics compiled from the consistory records of Geneva and Montauban. (E. W. Monter, 'The Consistory of Geneva,

behavior which Reformed discipline sought to repress was also condemned by Catholic moralists, but thanks to both the self-discipline which a good Calvinist sought to exercise over himself and the external discipline exercised by the consistory over the less good Calvinists, the Huguenots clearly stood apart within the community because of their moral rigor.

Moral rigor shades over easily into self-righteousness, and the elect are rarely loved when they let the remainder of the community know that it is damned. Protestant patterns of behavior intensified Catholic bitterness toward the Huguenots. Janine Estèbe has noted that Catholic authors frequently taxed the Calvinists as arrogant,[1] and it is easy to see how the accusation might have been levelled when one reads the remonstrance which the Reformed congregation addressed to Charles IX in 1566 complaining of unfair practices in the municipal elections of that year. Although, so the Huguenots claimed, they outnumbered the Catholics in votes by as much as ten to one in certain *quartiers*, the Catholics had nonetheless managed to win all of the places on the Council by barring Protestant voters from the polling places or neglecting to count their votes. Furthermore, a number of those elected were patently ineligible or unfit for their new positions; one was even known to be entirely 'lacking in sense or reason'. Why did the Catholics choose such incompetents? The reason is plain, the remonstrance concludes. They lacked better candidates, because 'all of the other honorable, ancient and peaceful houses and families are of the Reformed Religion'.[2] Such an inflated sense of their numbers and worth could hardly fail to transmit itself to the Catholics and to provoke in them the urge to teach the Huguenots a lesson or two. Indeed, in a letter to the king reporting several incidents of violence which broke out in 1568, the governor Carrouges placed part of the blame on the 'insolent words' of the Huguenots, who 'cannot refrain from acting in a haughty manner'.[3]

One last stimulus also increased Catholic hostility toward Protestantism in the years after 1562: economic hardship. Although the decade following the outbreak of the First Civil War was not entirely without bright spots, the overall performance of Rouen's economy was mediocre at best and there were to be years of real hardship. The First Civil War naturally interrupted

1559–1569', *Bibliothèque d'Humanisme et Renaissance*, XXXVIII (1976), pp. 467–84, esp. 479; Estèbe and Vogler, 'Genèse d'une société protestante', passim.) Drunkenness and frequenting taverns accounted for just 5.3 per cent of the excommunications in Geneva and 1.4 per cent of the cases in Montauban. Sexual misconduct accounted for 8.4 per cent of the Genevan excommunications and 7.5 per cent of the cases in Montauban. The link between the high percentage of the latter offense in London and the fact that this was a church of refugees is very clear, since many of the cases involve individuals separated from their spouse by exile.

[1] Estèbe, *Tocsin pour un massacre: la saison des Saint-Barthélemy* (Paris, 1968), p. 67. Estèbe's excellent evocation of Huguenot behavior has strongly influenced this entire section.

[2] Bibliothèque Publique et Universitaire de Genève, Archives Tronchin, Vol. 8, fos. 76–9.

[3] B.N., MS Français 15546, fo. 79, Carrouges to Charles IX, May 21, 1568.

trade, and commerce continued to be sorely hampered even after the conflict ended, since the English maintained control of Le Havre, their prize for signing the treaty of Hampton Court, and turned that city into a pirates' nest. Only when a military campaign early in 1564 ousted the English from Le Havre could ships move safely up and down the lower Seine, and only then did many of the merchants who had fled Rouen in 1562 return.[1] Another calamity struck early in 1565 when the ice and high water of a sudden February thaw battered the ships anchored before the city, sinking many and irretrievably damaging the cargoes of others. The losses suffered by the city's merchants were estimated as being only slightly less great than those incurred during the sacking of 1562.[2] This disaster aside, the city's commerce enjoyed a period of recovery and even expansion between 1564 and 1568, the result both of the steady growth of the *carrera de Indias*, with its positive consequences for the Norman linen industry, and of the diversion of English trade away from Antwerp following the Anglo-Spanish quarrel over the privileges of the English Merchant Adventurers. Some of the British cloth which had previously been funneled through the great entrepôt on the Scheldt now came to be sent toward the Mediterranean via Rouen, and this stimulated business among the city's cloth finishers and retailers, since the cloth was imported in its raw state and then bleached and dyed in France. But these benefits were counterbalanced by difficulties in other sectors of the economy, notably the continuing decay of the hosiery and woolen industries, whose difficulties continued unabated through the 1560s.[3] Furthermore, the outbreak of the Third Civil War in 1568 then provoked disruption anew in the city's trade. Huguenot and English corsairs began to plague Channel shipping, and the French crown halted all commerce with England for nearly eleven months as retaliation for the assistance which the English lent the Huguenots in this conflict. Two indicators provide telling evidence of the effect of these developments on the city's general welfare. The number of baptisms celebrated in the city declined by 10 to 15 per cent between 1564 and 1575, while house rents, a good guide to the economic well-being of a city, rose but feebly, lagging well behind the general movement of prices.[4]

Beneath general economic indicators such as these lie hundreds of individual dramas of families thrown out of work or forced into debt because the supply of raw materials needed for their livelihood was

[1] The commercial *conjoncture* of these years is treated in detail in my 'Rouen's Foreign Trade During the Era of Religious Wars (1560–1600)', forthcoming.

[2] A.C.R., A 19, entries of March 7, 1565 and May 16, 1571 (a long remonstrance recounting the economic difficulties of the preceding nine years); 'Discours abbregé', p. 316.

[3] *See above*, ch. 1, pp. 13–15. Between the 1550s and the 1560s, the number of *lettres de draperie* issued to new master weavers fell from 396 to 329.

[4] *See* Appendixes 3 and 4; Benedict, 'Catholics and Huguenots', passim, esp. p. 232.

disrupted by trade blockades or the prosperity of their guild undermined by rural competition. Their hard times cannot be considered the chief cause of religious hatred, but given the Catholic propensity to trace whatever difficulties befell the city back to the events of 1562 and to interpret hardship as divine punishment for a community which permitted heretics to live in its midst, economic ills undoubtedly added more fuel to an already volatile situation. In the one instance from this period when those involved in an incident of religious violence were identified, many of the rioters were said to be artisans who had left their trades to fight in the civil wars and had subsequently been unable to resume their old occupations for lack of work.[1] When a bad harvest cut into the city's grain supply and a riot threatened to break out at the Halle au Blé in 1573, some in the crowd insisted that the Huguenots were to blame.[2] Economic difficulties did not call into being the religious rivalries, but they could exacerbate them.

The net result of all of these developments was to breed in the Catholics a bitter *esprit de revanche* that was quick to find expression in violence against the Huguenots, those 'enemies of God, of our faith and of all virtue, enemies of the king, of the law, of tranquility and of every republic', as one Catholic tersely described them.[3] Occasionally a document happens to illuminate a scene from everyday life; when it does, the depth and pervasiveness of the religious hatreds stand starkly revealed.

The savagery to which the Catholics could be aroused is shown by an incident of February 1563, when the crowd that had assembled to witness the execution of two convicted criminals, one Catholic and one Protestant, staged a savage morality play illustrating the right and wrong way to die. After the execution of the Catholic criminal, whose last words and deeds showed him to have died reconciled to the Roman Church, his body was carried reverently by the onlookers to the consecrated ground of a nearby cemetery, where he received a proper burial. The Protestant refused to recant his faith and consequently suffered a crueler end. Although he was condemned to be hanged until dead and then burned at the stake, the mob would not allow him the relative luxury of a death by hanging. It forced the executioner to cut the rope and light the bonfire at the man's heels. Before he had breathed his last, the mob then seized him, began to hack his body brutally, and finally dragged what remained of his corpse to the Seine, where it was thrown in and left to float downstream.[4]

Catholic mobs could be no less quick to act than they were brutal in heaping indignities on the Huguenots once provoked. In 1565 a royal sergeant happened to spot a priest carrying an illegal weapon. '*Mort Dieu*,

[1] B.N., MS Français 15546, fo. 79, Carrouges to Charles IX, May 21, 1568.

[2] A.D.S.M., B, Parlement, Registres Secrets, entry of May 27, 1573.

[3] *Relation des troubles*, p. 3.

[4] *Archivo documental español*, Vol. 5, p. 65.

these Papists, they ought all to be killed', the sergeant is reported to have muttered as he went to arrest the man. Instead it was he who was killed. When the inevitable crowd gathered to watch the priest's arrest and realized that the sergeant was Protestant, it began to stone him, apparently at the priest's urging. The sergeant died from the barrage.[1]

Even the most quotidian of encounters could be poisoned by the pervasive religious suspicion. In April 1566 the cathedral chapter received a complaint from the tenant of one of its houses, in front of which repairs were being made. The tenant maintained that the repairs were not needed. Obviously, he claimed, these must be Huguenot workmen trying to harrass the good Catholics of the city by making them pay for unnecessary repairs.[2]

In such a climate, continued religious violence was almost inevitable. Certain of the factors contributing to the tensions were ones common to most communities, but the specific sequence of events which occurred in Rouen in 1562, plus the particularly volatile situation caused by the presence of a still large and aggressive Protestant minority amid an aroused Catholic majority, guaranteed that Normandy's capital would be particularly troubled. Its inhabitants became, according to an exasperated Catherine de Medici, the most difficult of the kingdom.[3]

While sharp differences of ideology and comportment, the thirst for revenge aroused by the events of 1562, and a general climate of economic malaise all combined to sow the seeds of violence, royal policy sought to keep the violence under control and to reconcile the two religions. Catherine de Medici's actions may have been motivated, as it was once fashionable to assert, by a mother's desire to keep her sons' inheritance intact. They may have been the fruit of a hothouse court culture which kept Renaissance ideals of toleration alive long after they had given way to sterner passions in most of the kingdom. Most probably, simple political calculation sufficed to dictate them. In any case, the overriding concern of royal policy throughout the years following 1562 was, as a letter to the city explained in 1564, to maintain a 'just balance' between the two faiths.[4] The crown pursued this line as vigorously as it could, but as often as not royal efforts, and the efforts of the crown's representatives in Rouen, proved inadequate. Such a balance could not be struck while the local situation remained so volatile.

The tensions between the royal policy of mediation and the Catholic desire for revenge manifested themselves as soon as Rouen fell to the royal

1 A.D.S.M., G 2167, entry of May 31, 1565.
2 B.M.R., MS Y 102 (2), p. 34.
3 Catherine's comment is reported in A.C.R., A 18, entry of Aug. 30, 1564.
4 B.N., MS Français 17832, fo. 82, Charles IX to *échevins* of Rouen, June 28, 1564.

forces in October 1562. The *parlementaires* who returned from Louviers urged that harsh punishment be meted out so that the rebellious Protestants would be taught a lesson they would not soon forget. Catherine opted instead for the execution of just four leading actors in the revolt (among them the pastor Marlorat). She preferred to use the occasion to extract tribute from the conquered city. A general pardon was granted all others implicated in the Protestant takeover in return for an enormous forced loan of 140,000 *écus*.[1]

As soon as the court and the great nobles began to leave Rouen to continue the military campaign against other Huguenot-controlled cities, a reaction set in against those Protestants who had not fled the Norman capital in the wake of its capture. On November 6, Guise and Montmorency marched off with the bulk of the royal army to begin the campaign against Condé which was to culminate in the battle of Dreux. Six days later Catherine and Charles followed them, and on November 15 the mortally wounded Anthony of Navarre, who had received a ball in the shoulder during the siege, was borne toward Les Andélys by a specially constructed houseboat to spare him the agony of a journey over Normandy's rutted roads.[2] No sooner had they left than the municipal authorities instituted a series of measures against Rouen's Protestants. The Huguenots were disarmed and subjected to a special tax to be used to repair the breaches in the town's walls, Protestant incumbents were ousted from a variety of minor municipal positions such as *concierge* of the Hôtel de Ville, the royal garrison left behind in the city was quartered in Calvinist homes, and an all-Catholic militia was formed.[3]

The aroused Catholics would brook no compromise with heresy. Shortly after returning to Rouen from his chateau in Burgundy where he had spent the period of Huguenot domination, the moderate first president of the parlement, Saint-Anthot, urged that the Protestant members of the court be allowed to rejoin it. For this he found himself threatened by a large mob as he left the Palais de Justice on his mule in the evening of January 18. After showering him with insults, the crowd allowed him to pass unharmed, but it turned on several suspected Huguenots unlucky enough to be in the vicinity and killed three of them, including the *avocat du roi au bailliage*, Mustel de Boscroger, whose corpse was left on the pavement to rot.[4]

1 B.N., MS Français 3216, fo. 82, Moreau to Gonnart, Nov. 5, 1562; *Memoires de Condé*, Vol. 2, p. 104; 'Discours abbregé', p. 267; De Thou, *Histoire universelle*, Vol. 3, p. 335.

2 'Discours abbregé', pp. 272–4.

3 A.C.R., A 18, entries of Nov. 7, 15 and 16, 1562; 'Discours abbregé', pp. 272–8; *Hist. eccl.*, Vol. 2, pp. 784–5.

4 A.C.R., A 18, entries of Jan. 20 and 21, 1563; 'Discours abbregé', p. 280; *Archivo documental español*, Vol. 5, p. 56; Charles Marchand, *Le Maréchal François de Scépeaux de Vielleville et ses Mémoires* (Paris, 1893), pp. 225–6.

Until the crown was able to find reliable men to fill the leading royal offices, the difficulties of maintaining order were compounded by the partisanship and personal rivalries of the monarchy's chief representatives. The ultra-Catholic Villebon stood by idly during the attack on Mustel de Boscroger. His inactivity in turn infuriated a new royal lieutenant-general, the maréchal de Vielleville, who had recently been sent to Rouen to defend it against possible advance by the English still at Le Havre. Vielleville, who had married his daughter to a Protestant and may well have had Calvinist sympathies, rebuked Villebon for his inaction during a dinner at the maréchal's lodgings at St Ouen. The quarrel quickly escalated into a sword fight in the course of which Villebon was wounded in the hand. Word of his injury rapidly circulated through the city, prompting an angry Catholic crowd to gather before St Ouen and besiege Vielleville and his men in the Abbey. A company of royal soldiers had to be hastily summoned to disperse the crowd. A new lieutenant-general was also quickly dispatched, the count of Brissac, who relieved both Vielleville and Villebon of their duties.[1]

When the signing of the edict of Amboise ended the First Civil War in March 1563, it was thus Brissac's unenviable responsibility to see to it that the edict's provisions were put into effect. The treaty provided for the return and reinstatement of all individuals who had been forced to flee their homes or abandon their offices during the civil war. It also permitted Reformed services to be re-established on the estates of all noblemen possessing *plein fief de haubert*.[2] Since several such noblemen with Protestant leanings lived in the vicinity of Rouen, the Rouennais recognized at once that the edict would allow the re-establishment of Protestantism in the city. Their resistance was fierce. The parlement originally refused to register the edict, while the Council of Twenty-Four petitioned the Queen Mother to exempt Rouen from its provisions and then, when this petition was denied, passed a law eviscerating the edict by barring any Huguenot who had aided in the seizure of the city from returning and disarming all those who were allowed to re-enter the city, thus placing them at the mercy of the still-armed Catholic populace.[3] Late in April, over a month after the edict of pacification had been promulgated, many of Rouen's Protestants had not even been permitted back into the city, much less restored to office. They were gathered in nearby villages, knocking on the gates demanding to be

[1] A.C.R., A 18, entry of Jan. 24, 1563; 'Discours abbregé', pp. 282–3; *Archivo documental español*, Vol. 5, p. 65; Marchand, *Vielleville*, pp. 220–30. The account of this incident in Vielleville's *Mémoires*, Michaud and Poujoulat, 1st ser., Vol. 9, pp. 332–40 contains a large element of embellishment.

[2] The full text of the edict may be found in Isambert, Decrusy, and Taillandier, *Recueil général des anciennes lois françaises depuis l'an 420 jusqu'à la Révolution de 1789* (Paris, 1821), Vol. 14, pp. 135–40.

[3] A.C.R., A 18, entries of April 6 and 18, 1563; *Négociations diplomatiques avec la Toscane*, Vol. 3, p. 504; 'Discours abbregé', pp. 290, 294.

let in. The gates were not finally opened until a series of incidents had raised the specter of renewed warfare. On April 24 two delegates were sent by the Protestants still outside the walls to urge Brissac to allow them to return. Before they could even reach the city, they were set upon and killed by a group of boatmen and soldiers along the Seine. In retaliation, the Calvinists demolished the suburban church of Grand Quévilly and attacked several houses in nearby Croisset. News of these incidents led the crown to send stinging letters to the parlement and the Council of Twenty-Four, and the edict of pacification was finally registered and put into effect.[1]

The resistance against registration of the edict of pacification augured poorly for the crown's balancing act. For the next year after the Protestants were finally able to re-enter the city, relations between the two faiths remained a continuing problem for the authorities. A contingent of royal troops sent to protect the returning Huguenots remained in the city for most of the year and was able to contain most potential violence. Nonetheless, an uninterrupted stream of mutual recrimination fills the registers of deliberation of the city council and the letters sent by the town to court. The Protestants claimed that the authorities impeded their attempts to regain their seized goods and reassume their former offices. The Catholics were alarmed by recurrent rumors that the Huguenots were stockpiling arms or planning an uprising.[2] The profound split in the community was even manifested when Charles IX entered the city in August 1563 to a reception that was deliberately kept modest to avoid burdening the city with the expense of an elaborate royal entry so soon after the hardships of the civil war. All Huguenots were systematically excluded from the small honor guard of leading inhabitants that marched out to greet the young king. A few days later, when the prince of Condé and the cardinal Châtillon arrived in the city, the Protestants formed their own guard of honor and rode out to greet them.[3] In the place of the one spectacular entry of 1550, the city now staged two.

In March 1564 the tensions between the two parties provoked renewed violence. On March 5 several hundred armed Protestants returning from their services at the fief of the baroness d'Esneval in Pavilly exchanged insults with worshippers leaving a Lenten sermon at the suburban chapel of St Maur. One source suggests that the Protestants threw stones at the chapel; another that they sang psalms loudly, interrupting Mass.[4] Whatever the spark, the subsequent fighting claimed at least two lives and threw the

[1] A.C.R., A 18, entry of April 30, 1563; 'Discours abbregé', pp. 291–2.

[2] A.C.R., entries of June 11 and 28, 1563; B.N., MS Français 15878, fo. 32, *Conseillers, manans, et habitans de Rouen* to Catherine de Medici, June 12, 1563; 'Discours abbregé', pp. 296–8.

[3] A.C.R., A 18, entries of Aug. 4, 6, and 14, 1563; *Archivo documental español*, Vol. 5, pp. 353–4, 377. The Huguenots' greeting to Condé and Chatillon 'parescia otra entrada' to the Spanish ambassador.

[4] A.C.R., B 2, entry of March 5, 1564; *Archivo documental español*, Vol. 6, pp. 150–51.

Catholics into an uproar. Three days later, following a meeting called by a priest of the poor weaver's parish of St Nicaise, a crowd assembled in the courtyard of the Palais de Justice and, through its spokesman, the *procureur* Jean Le Pelletier, demanded that the parlement take action against the illegal Huguenot assemblies which they alleged were being held within the city. On the same day, a group of Protestants in the heavily Calvinist parish of St Eloi attacked and smashed several statues in the parish church. Another Catholic crowd gathered the next day and confronted the lieutenant-general, jostling and insulting him. Order was not fully restored until March 10.[1]

In June the arrival of the governor of Normandy, the duke of Bouillon, threw the Catholics into a new uproar. The duke was one of the leading Protestant noblemen of the realm, and although he had been governor of the province since 1556, this was his first extended visit to Normandy since his conversion to Calvinism. His arrival awakened Catholic fears of a new period of Huguenot domination, fears which were only intensified by Bouillon's actions in the week following his arrival. It became his custom to travel about town accompanied by a large armed guard, which he augmented by moving a garrison of troops from Bayeux to Rouen. He also revived the case of Mustel de Boscroger, the *avocat du roi* killed by the mob in 1563, imprisoning several of those implicated, including the *ancien conseiller*, Richard Papillon. Finally, he ordered the reinstatement of all Protestant municipal officials of 1562.[2] A number of Huguenots who had not dared return home since the city's capture by the royal forces now did so. Rumors flew that even the feared and hated Protestant military commander of 1562, Gabriel de Montgommery, was back in town.[3] The Catholic population reacted with alarm. Some may even have left the city out of fear for their safety. The Council of Twenty-Four addressed a series of petitions first to Bouillon and then to court, each one protesting Bouillon's measures in terms stronger than the last.[4] Catherine responded to these petitions with anger, and it was at this point that she told Rouen's delegates that theirs was the most difficult city of the realm. Apparently it paid to be difficult. The constant complaints finally convinced the court of the dangerous situation provoked by Bouillon's actions. A number of his measures were ordered overturned. Bouillon reacted petulantly to the

[1] A.C.R., A 18, entries of March 7, 8, and 13, 1564; A.C.R., B 2, entry of March 5, 1564; A.D.S.M., B, Parlement, Arrêts, Janvier–Mars 1564, arrêt of March 20, 1564; J. T. Pommeraye, *Histoire de l'Eglise Cathédrale de Rouen* (Rouen, 1686), p. 141; E. Le Parquier, 'Un épisode de l'histoire de Rouen en 1564', *B.S.H.P.F.*, LXII (1913), pp. 414–24.

[2] A.C.R., A. 18, entries of July 22 and 25, 1564; 'Discours abbregé', pp. 308–10, 314.

[3] A.C.R., A 18, entry of July 5, 1564. *Archivo documental español*, Vol. 6, p. 165, also reflects Catholic fears of an uprising led by Montgommery.

[4] A.C.R., A 18, entry of July 25, 1564 reports that people were leaving town but could not be corroborated. For the delegations of protest: A.C.R., A 18, entries of July 1, 6, 10, and 25, 1564.

rebuke, retiring in a pout to his duchy on France's eastern border where his authority was subjected to no such vexing counter-orders from above.[1]

With Bouillon's departure, royal authority within Rouen devolved upon the latest lieutenant-general, Taneguy Le Veneur, sieur de Carrouges. As one of Brissac's lieutenants, Carrouges had already exercised a degree of authority within the city for nearly a year and had earned the respect of the Council of Twenty-Four as a strong and able peace-keeper.[2] For the next twenty-five years he was to remain the crown's chief representative in Rouen, holding at one point or another the offices of lieutenant-general of Normandy, governor of Rouen and Upper Normandy, *bailli* of Rouen, and captain of the Château and Vieux Palais, not to mention those of *conseiller d'état* and Knight of the Order of St Michael. The standard image of the provincial governors during the Wars of Religion is of great noblemen who seized on the weakness of the crown to make themselves semi-sovereign in their provinces.[3] Carrouges represents a different breed of royal lieutenant. He was the scion of an originally modest noble family whose title dated back to the fourteenth century but which had only ascended into the upper ranks of the provincial nobility early in the sixteenth century as a result of a royal favor. (Taneguy's great-uncle Jehan Le Veneur, bishop of Lisieux, was 'well loved by Francis I' and had gained from him a cardinal's hat and the position of *grand aumonier de France*.)[4] Carrouges continued the family tradition of fidelity to the crown, and it was his loyal service which brought him his offices and titles. Although linked by marriage to the house of Lorraine, none of his actions in Rouen show the favoritism toward the party of the Guises of which certain of his enemies accused him.[5] On the contrary, his overriding concern seems always to have been to carry out royal orders scrupulously, and it is significant that on

[1] Amable Floquet, *Histoire du Parlement de Normandie* (Rouen, 1840–42), Vol. 3, p. 22.

[2] Carrouges appears in local documents for the first time in A.C.R., A 18, entry of July 24, 1563. In a letter to the king written July 10, 1564, the Council of Twenty-Four contrasted Carrouges' behavior with Bouillon's, claiming that when violence threatened Carrouges went out among the people without fear to quell it, whereas Bouillon dared not be seen in public without a heavy guard and aroused violence through his suspicious actions.

[3] A typical statement of this view is J. H. Shennan, *Government and Society in France 1461–1661* (London, 1969), p. 61: 'Before the Wars of Religion the governors, like the bailiffs, tended to act only in an honorary capacity whilst their functions were taken over by a lieutenant, assisted by a council and by a captain-general who fulfilled the governor's military role. With the outbreak of war, however, the governors became resident once more. Now they controlled the provinces, promulgating ordinances, nominating important officials, seizing royal revenues, raising armies, defying the crown whose unifying grip over the country was progressively loosened.'

[4] B.N., Pièces Originales 2958 (dossier 65,745).

[5] Le Laboureur, *Mémoires de Castelnau*, Vol. 1, p. 535; and Claude Groulart, *Mémoires*, Michaud and Poujoulat, 1st ser., Vol. 11, p. 554, both suggest that Carrouges was a Guise client. He may well have profited from the early support of the family to gain office in Normandy, but this does not seem to have affected his subsequent conduct, which can easily be followed through his numerous letters in the Fonds Français of the B.N.

the eve of the League Catherine de Medici was to express the utmost confidence in his loyalty.[1] Carrouges proved the answer to the crown's search for a man who could be counted on to act energetically to keep order in Rouen. For the next three years, the city was untroubled by any major outbreaks of popular violence. Even the bitterly contested municipal elections of 1566 were conducted without violent incident.

The fragile peace which Carrouges was able to maintain within Rouen was finally upset by events taking place outside the city. The movement along France's eastern border of the large Spanish army sent in 1567 to quell the first flickers of revolt in the Low Countries seemed to the Protestants confirmation of their fears that Catherine de Medici and the duke of Alva had secretly agreed at the interview of Bayonne to exterminate them. Alva's forces were the troops sent to do so. It was to forestall this presumed Spanish intervention that the Huguenots touched off the Second Civil War with an unsuccessful attempt to seize the king at Meaux and remove him from the baneful influence of his mother and Catholic counsellors. Plans were made in Rouen to co-ordinate a local uprising with this attempt to kidnap the king, but when the news of the failure of the 'enterprise of Meaux' reached Normandy, the men involved in the plot fled the city rather than attempting their coup.[2] The municipal authorities quickly disarmed the remaining Protestants and tightened up the town's defenses. Rouen was thus secured for the crown at the outbreak of this conflict.

The Second Civil War lasted from September 1567 through March 1568 and initiated a pattern of events that was to be repeated during the Third Civil War which quickly followed in September 1568 and then again during all subsequent civil wars except the Seventh (1579–80). With each outbreak of fighting, the measures of toleration granted Protestantism were revoked. All Calvinist office-holders were deprived of their positions, and strict measures of surveillance were instituted against the Huguenots.[3] Reformed services ceased. The particularly committed or militant members of the

1 *L.C.M.*, Vol. 8, p. 252, Catherine to Brulart, April 15, 1585: 'J'ay veu aussi ce que m'avez escript de Rouen, estant bien eize que le sieur de Carouges y soit; car, outre que c'est un très homme de bien, il a beaucoup d'auctorité audict Rouen et l'amitié des habitants.' When the League took power in 1589, Carrouges was ousted from the city, hardly the usual fate of clients of the Guise. Even Harding's thorough study of the governors, *Power Elite*, highlights primarily those governors who defied the crown. One wonders how large the group of officials like Carrouges who advanced through loyal service was.

2 A.D.S.M., G 2168, entry of Sept. 26, 1567; 'Discours abbregé', pp. 322–3; Thompson, *Wars of Religion in France*, pp. 305–21; Jean H. Mariéjol, *La Réforme et la Ligue*, Vol. 6, part 1 of Ernest Lavisse, *Histoire de France* (Paris, 1904), pp. 93–7.

3 For these measures, see A.D.S.M., B, Parlement, Arrêts, Novembre 1567–Février 1568, arrêt of Dec. 10, 1567; Isambert, Decrusy, and Taillandier, *Recueil général des anciennes lois françaises depuis l'an 420 jusqu'à la Révolution de 1789* (Paris, 1821), Vol. 14, p. 228; A.C.R., A 19, entries of Oct. 1, 4, 9, and 10, 1567, Sept. 4, 1568.

faith then usually left their homes, either to participate in the fighting or to seek refuge in an area where they could worship freely. Whatever goods they left behind were confiscated.[1] Those Protestants who were less dedicated, or perhaps simply more tied down by family and business, meanwhile remained behind and tried their best to accommodate themselves to a situation in which they were burdened with special taxes and became the natural target of Catholic suspicion and hostility. During the Second Civil War many Protestants reputed 'factious' were jailed.[2] During the Third Civil War troops were billetted in Reformed households; they used the opportunity to extort food and money from their hosts with even greater impunity than was customary in such situations.[3] Catholic vigilantes also mounted a campaign during this conflict to enforce religious uniformity, forcing a number of Huguenots to attend Mass against their will in 1568 and petitioning the parlement in 1570 to banish all those who abstained from taking Easter communion.[4] Each period of civil war also saw special measures taken to guard the city against attack. Residents were ordered to lay in provisions in case of fighting in the area, the guard was reinforced at such strategic points as the city's gates, bell-tower, and powder magazine, and Protestant inn-keepers were forbidden to lodge any strangers.[5]

These precautionary measures were not really tested in either the Second or the Third Civil War. The fighting in both conflicts skirted Normandy and was centered primarily in the South and West. But even though Rouen was spared the direct effects of these conflicts, each nonetheless served to reinforce the Catholic belief that Protestantism was by nature seditious. When each civil war ended with a new edict of pacification, those Protestants who had left the city therefore returned to face even greater hostility. Following the peace of Longjumeau ending the Second Civil War, anti-Huguenot violence was so widespread throughout France that the Protestant historian La Popelinière claimed

[1] That Reformed services ceased and did not simply begin to be held secretly is clear from the Reformed baptismal registers from throughout France, which typically cease noting baptisms in periods of civil war in cities where the Protestants were not in control. (*See* Appendix 1). Random references such as *Actes du consistoire*, Vol. 1, pp. 69, 80, and A.D.S.M., G 2554 (reference to Michel le Sueur who left the house he was renting from the cathedral chapter to go to war) show that certain of the city's inhabitants left to fight in the civil wars. The movement of many Protestants to England or other places of asylum is clear from F. de Schickler, *Les églises du Réfuge en Angleterre*, Vol. 1 (Paris, 1892), pp. 147–8. B.M.R., Fonds Leber 3983 contains printed copies of royal letters-patent of Dec. 10, 1567, Jan. 25, 1568, and May 5, 1569 ordering the seizure of all goods belonging to those Protestants who have left their houses. *See also* Antoine Fontanon, *Les Edicts et Ordonnances des Roys de France depuis S. Loys jusques à present* (Paris, 1580), Vol. 2, pp. 1811–12, 1819–20.

[2] A.C.R., A 19, entries of Nov. 28, 1567 and Jan. 1, 1568.

[3] A.C.R., A 19, entry of Nov. 16, 1569.

[4] *Cal. S.P. For.* 1568/2596; A.C.R., A 19, entry of April 5, 1570; B.M.R., MS Y 214 (6), pp. 54–61.

[5] A.C.R., A 19, entries of Oct. 1, 4, 9 and 10, 1567, Sept. 4, 1568.

more of his co-religionists were killed during the subsequent months of 'peace' than during the first two civil wars combined.[1] The Rouennais did their best to show that they were still the most difficult inhabitants of all. The announcement of the measures of toleration contained in the edict of Longjumeau touched off three days of rioting. Mobs coursed through the Palais de Justice, preventing the *parlementaires* from registering the edict and forcing them to flee for their lives. Huguenot shops and houses were looted. Booksellers were singled out for special attention, and their wares were thrown into the street and burned.[2] Once order was restored the parlement was able to register the edict of pacification safely, but as the Huguenots who had left the city began to return home, new incidents of violence broke out. On April 23 several returning Protestants were set upon and slain.[3] On May 20 a crowd tried to prevent a Calvinist from taking his child to be baptized. Several days later a mob rescued a man taken prisoner for his role in these disturbances, looted several houses belonging to Protestants, and clashed with Carrouges' guard.[4] The lieutenant-general's letters of these months are filled with increasingly desperate pleas that a garrison of royal soldiers be sent to the city and kept there. No other force could pacify the city and preserve the king's authority from giving way to popular license, he wrote, and he would rather resign than suffer the disgrace of not being able to keep the city loyal.[5] A contingent of troops was finally dispatched late in May, but its approach touched off new unrest. With rumors flying that many of the soldiers were Huguenots and others infected with the plague, a crowd gathered before Carrouges' *hôtel* and would not disperse until he agreed to close the town gates to the royal troops. Only after the *conseillers-échevins* agreed under pain of royal displeasure to allow the troops to enter the city secretly by night were the soldiers admitted and calm restored.[6]

The immediate reaction to the edict of St Germain ending the Third Civil War was less violent. The parlement registered the edict without

1 Lancelot Voysin, sieur de la Popelinière, *La vraye et entiere histoire des troubles...advenues...depuis l'an 1562* (La Rochelle, 1573), Book 4, fo. 113v.

2 A.C.R., A 19, entry of April 6, 1568; Bibliothèque de l'Institut, Collection Godefroy 257, fo. 108, *gens du roy du parlement de Rouen* to Charles IX, April 3, 1568; B.N., MS Français 15545, fo. 115, *échevins* of Rouen to Charles IX, April 3, 1568 and fo. 116, Charles IX to parlement of Rouen, April 5, 1568; 'Discours abbregé', pp. 345–6.

3 'Discours abbregé', p. 346; B.N., MSS Français 15545, fo. 170, Carrouges to Charles IX, April 23, 1568; 15546, fo. 211, parlement of Rouen to Charles IX, June 14, 1568.

4 A.D.S.M., G 2168, entry of May 25, 1568; B.N., MS Français 15546, fos. 79, 86, Carrouges to Charles IX, May 21 and 23, 1568.

5 Especially beseeching are B.N., MSS Français 15545, fo. 170, Carrouges to Charles IX, April 23, 1568; 15546, fo. 212, Carrouges to duke of Anjou, June 15, 1568; and 15546, fo. 225, Carrouges to duke of Bouillon, June 16, 1568, the one case I have found where Carrouges addressed a letter to his nominal superior, the governor.

6 A.C.R., A 19, entries of June 2 and 3, 1568; B.N., MSS Français 15546, fo. 126, Carrouges to duke of Anjou, May 29, 1568; and 15560, fo. 128, *échevins* of Rouen to Charles IX, May 30, 1568; 'Discours abbregé', p. 347.

incident. It nonetheless proved every bit as difficult to enforce as the preceding one. The Lenten–Easter season was always the prime period of the year for confessional violence (five of the seven major incidents of religious rioting between 1563 and 1571 took place in the months of March and April), and on March 18, 1571 the bloodiest affray yet broke out between the members of the two faiths. Some 500–600 armed Calvinists on their way to Sunday services at Bondeville happened to pass a vicar carrying the Host to a man on his deathbed in the *faubourgs*. Several Catholics in the vicinity knelt down in honor of the Corpus Christi and cried to the Huguenots to doff their bonnets. The Calvinists replied with words of disrespect and rocks were thrown. When the guards manning the Porte Cauchoise tried to intervene, they were driven back. This first skirmish was of brief duration, but more serious fighting broke out later in the day when the Huguenots returned from their services. Children in the *faubourgs* began to cry '*Au Huguenot*' as they passed, and a crowd of men aroused by the earlier scuffle quickly assembled and attacked the Protestants. The Reformed chronicler Simon Goulard, whose estimates of victims tend to be rather high, reports that over 40 Protestants were left dead following the pitched battle which ensued.[1]

As so often happened, attempts to apprehend those involved in the riot only provoked further violence from a populace which clearly felt that the behavior of the mob did not warrant punishment. On April 3, five men were arrested for their role in this 'Massacre of Bondeville'; they were rescued the same day by an angry crowd which almost killed several of the guards. Even the Council of Twenty-Four, usually unalterably opposed to the presence of troops in the city, realized that a royal garrison was necessary to restore calm and urged the king to send one.[2] This was quickly done, for the crown was actively pursuing a policy of reconciliation during this period. A commission headed by the duke of Montmorency and accompanied by a large force of soldiers was dispatched to hand out an exemplary punishment. The *commissaires* condemned 66 individuals to death for their role in the clash and fined other rioters a total of 4,000 *livres*. They also purged all unreliable individuals from the privileged militia companies and attempted once again to reorganize the large town militia in such a fashion as to make it an effective peace-keeping force.[3] But even

[1] The best account of this incident is A.C.R., B 3, entry of March 18, 1571. *See also* A.D.S.M., B, Parlement, Registres Secrets, entries of March 18 and 19, 1571; *Mémoires de l'estat*, Vol. 1, p. 42. De Thou, *Histoire universelle*, Vol. 4, p. 483 is less reliable.

[2] A.D.S.M., B, Parlement, Registres Secrets, entry of March 20, 1571: 'ceulx de la ville avoient respondu qu'ilz aimoient mieulx qu'il y eust une garnison que continuacion (?) de sedition et que s'ilz y mettoient la main que l'on leur couperoit la gorge'.

[3] A.C.R., B 3, entries of April 18, May 6, May 16, 1571; A.D.S.M., B, Parlement, Registres Secrets, entry of May 5, 1571 and Arrêts, Septembre 1572–Janvier 1573, arrêt of Oct. 11, 1572; Crespin, *Histoire des martyrs*, Vol. 3, p. 720.

harsh measures such as these were to prove no more successful in putting an end to confessional violence within the city than previous royal attempts at pacification, especially since their efficacy was undermined by popular harrassment and royal equivocation. The officials trying to arrest those sentenced to death found their efforts impeded by many town dwellers. Most of those convicted managed to flee to safety before they could be apprehended. A few subsequently seem to have been able to obtain royal pardons.[1] They were thus able to return home in time for the event which marked the culmination of this period of intense confessional violence and the major turning point in the early decades of the civil wars: the St Bartholomew's Day Massacre.

[1] A.C.R., B 3, entries of May 28 and Aug. 23, 1571; A.D.S.M., B, Parlement, Arrêts, Septembre 1572–Janvier 1573, arrêts of Oct. 6 and 11, 1572; Crespin, *Histoire des martyrs*, Vol. 3, p. 720; De Thou, *Histoire universelle*, Vol. 4, p. 606.

PART II

In the wake of St Bartholomew's Day, 1572–1584

La Rochelle is ready to resist to the last these cruel tyrants. The inhabitants of Montauban and of several other cities of the region seem decided to do the same. Those of Nimes, of the Cévennes and Vivarais are still all on our side, as are Sancerre and Berry. But in the rest of France the defection has been and continues to be incredible. Nevertheless this defection is far from satisfying the beasts of prey. It has been resolved to kill, along with their families, even the innumerable people who have apostasied. This was decided on October 27. The execution has only been held off to attempt to win back with false promises the cities which are still holding firm, to calm the anger of foreigners, and to get as many of the fugitives to return home as possible.

Theodore Beza to Thomas Tilius, Dec. 3, 1572 (*B.S.H.P.F.*, VII (1858), 16–17)

There is hope that now things will go well in France.

Letter of an anonymous Catholic of Lyon, Aug. 30, 1572 (Archives d'Etat de Genève, pièce historique 1929)

5

A massacre and its impact

Historians have long recognized the St Bartholomew's Day Massacre as an important turning point for both French Protestantism and the Wars of Religion. This has been so for two reasons. First, most of the faith's noble leaders were either killed or imprisoned in the course of the event, so the Protestant movement, of necessity, took on a more radical, democratically organized, and urban-based character in subsequent years. In those regions of the Midi and the Center-West where the Huguenots were politically and militarily dominant, they effectively renounced obedience to the crown and usurped many governing and tax-collecting functions, forming their own state-within-a-state. Second, because Charles IX was generally thought at the time to have given the order for the general massacre, more forthright theories of the right of resistance to a tyrant king were enunciated and came to be accepted within the movement. During the first civil wars the Protestants had always maintained that they were loyal to the monarch; they merely were trying to save him from his evil counsellors. Now they began to claim that a higher loyalty to the true religion could permit the lesser magistrates to disobey their sovereign when he transgressed against fundamental principles of law or religion. In Rouen – and in many other cities as well – the event was also a turning point for a third and quite different reason: it radically transformed the Huguenot community. The preceding decade had been hard for the Calvinists in those regions where they were physically outnumbered and politically vulnerable. The constant hostility of their neighbors and intermittent proscription by the crown had made their lives one of danger, uprooting, and sacrifice. The effect of the massacre was to crystallize their growing sense of disillusionment, precipitate a wave of defections, and alter the attitudes of those who remained faithful to the cause. By the wake of 1572, the large and still militant minority of the mid-1560s would give way to a far smaller and more docile group that would henceforward never again pose a serious political threat to local Catholic dominance.[1]

[1] For the traditional assessment of the massacre's impact, *see* such basic works of synthesis as Emile G. Léonard, *Histoire générale du Protestantisme* (Paris, 1961), Vol. 2, pp. 125–6; J. H. M. Salmon, *Society in Crisis: France in the Sixteenth Century* (New York, 1975), pp. 187–93. A few authors,

For such a critical event, the precise details of Rouen's local St Bartholomew's Day Massacre are dismayingly vague. Although the actions leading up to the violence can be amply reconstructed, only four accounts of the actual massacre survive, all quite brief.[1] Local administrative records are mute about what transpired on the four days from September 17 to 20, 1572, when the massacre took place.

Historians are now generally agreed that the series of massacres that took place throughout France in August and September were not the product of a premeditated royal scheme to exterminate the Huguenots. Even when Charles IX succumbed to his mother's browbeating on the night of August 23 and ordered the murder of the leading Protestant noblemen gathered at court for the marriage of Henry of Navarre to Marguerite of Valois, he neither expected nor desired the general massacre which subsequently ensued. The king's orders for a selective strike were distorted into a call for a general massacre by ultra-Catholic elements at court and in the Parisian municipal government. What developed in Paris and then spread to a dozen provincial cities were mass religious riots essentially similar in motivation to the numerous disorders which had already punctured the country's tranquility, albeit of far greater proportions.[2]

The extant correspondence between Charles IX and Rouen's municipal officials corroborates that Charles IX did not wish the violence to spread beyond a limited strike against a few Huguenot leaders. On August 24, shortly after the mass bloodbath began in Paris, Charles wrote to Carrouges alerting him that the situation had gotten out of hand in the capital and resulted in a 'great and lamentable sedition'. 'I pray you, as soon as you have received this present letter, to have announced in every area under your charge that everybody both in the cities and in the countryside is to

notably Estèbe have partially anticipated the following argument that the massacre was also a major watershed for both Protestant numbers and values in those communities where the Huguenots were in the minority, Janine Estèbe, *Tocsin pour un massacre: La saison des Saint-Barthélemy* (Paris, 1968), pp. 164–6, and *Histoire des Protestants en France* (Toulouse, 1977), pp. 67–8. Robert Kingdon has shown that the massacre was also a turning point for yet another reason: it marked the effective end to the challenge posed to the centralized, presbyterian structure of the Reformed Church by the congregationalist followers of Jean Morély, *Geneva and the Consolidation of the French Protestant Movement, 1564–1572* (Geneva, 1967), passim, esp. p. 202.

[1] The fullest accounts of the massacre in Rouen are those of Goulard, *Memoires de l'estat de France sous Charles IX* (Middleburg, 1578), Vol. 1, pp. 293ff; and Jacques-Auguste De Thou, *Histoire universelle* (The Hague, 1740), Vol. 4, pp. 606–7. The only accounts by known eyewitnesses are a brief phrase written on the title page of a book by an unknown hand (published by N. Weiss, 'Un témoin de la Saint-Barthélemy à Rouen, 17–20 Septembre 1572', *B.S.H.P.F.*, L (1901), pp. 445–8); and a letter written by a Spanish merchant in Rouen, now in the Ruiz archives in Valladolid. The full text of this last, previously unpublished document may be found in note 4, p. 128.

[2] The best recent discussions of responsibility for the massacre are Estèbe, *Tocsin pour un massacre*, pp. 179–88; Ilja Mieck, 'Die Bartolomäusnacht als Forschungsproblem: Kritische Bestandaufnahme und Neue Aspekte', *Historische Zeitschrift*, CCXVI (1973), pp. 73–110.

remain in peace and security in his house, not taking up arms or giving offense to one another on pain of death. My last edict of pacification is to be maintained and observed with greater care than ever before.'[1] The lieutenant-general immediately reported the contents of this letter both to the Council of Twenty-Four and to the authorities of the other cities under his command.[2] The guard that had already been posted around Rouen two days previously on receipt of the news of the first unsuccessful attempt on Coligny's life was quickly reinforced. In an unprecedented measure of vigilance, the *conseillers-échevins* then passed the next several nights at the Hôtel de Ville to keep as close a watch as possible over the town.[3] Several days later, in response to another letter from the king, they ordered the Protestants rounded up and imprisoned for their own protection. Many went willingly, thinking themselves more secure in detention than in their homes; others chose to leave immediately for the safety of England or trusted to the strength of their bolts and locks.[4] Through these precautionary measures, the city authorities managed to maintain order within Rouen for almost four weeks following the massacre in Paris, although several nearby châteaux belonging to Protestant noblemen were attacked and looted by Catholics from the city.[5]

What finally broke this calm and touched off the local massacre on September 17? Here is where the sources are mute. In many provincial cities the violence was sparked by the arrival of couriers bearing reports that the king wished the Protestants exterminated. While we know today that Charles IX did not plan or approve of a general massacre of all France's Calvinists, contemporaries hearing of the events in Paris could hardly be so sure of the king's intentions, and in towns where anti-Huguenot feelings ran particularly high because of the events of the preceding decade, the arrival of reports suggesting that the king looked with favor on a massacre was all the encouragement local Catholics needed.[6] Perhaps the arrival of such reports precipitated Rouen's massacre. Perhaps a group of hardened Catholics simply decided, after waiting in vain for four weeks for such a royal command, that they had better strike in any case on September 17. All that is known for sure is that on that day Catholic zealots gained control of the city, locked the gates to prevent the Calvinists from escaping, broke

[1] A.C.R., Chartrier, tiroir 400 (2), Charles IX to Carrouges, Aug. 24, 1572. This letter has been published by C. R. H. L. d'Estaintot, *La Saint Barthélemy à Rouen, 17–21 Septembre 1572* (Rouen, 1877), pp. 3–5.

[2] A.C.R., B 3, entry of Aug. 26, 1572; C. Osmont de Courtsigny, 'Jean LeHennuyer et les Huguenots de Lisieux en 1572', *B.S.H.P.F.*, XXVI (1877), pp. 151–3.

[3] A.C.R., B 3, entry of Aug. 27, 1572.

[4] *Memoires de l'estat*, Vol. 1, p. 294; d'Estaintot, *La Saint Barthélemy à Rouen*, pp. 12–13.

[5] *Memoires de l'estat*, Vol. 1, p. 294.

[6] Philip Benedict, 'The Saint Bartholomew's Massacres in the Provinces', *The Historical Journal*, XXI (1978), pp. 205–25.

into the jail where the Huguenots were being detained, and systematically butchered them. Led by Laurent de Maromme, an official in the ecclesiastical courts who had previously been banished from Rouen for his role in the Massacre of Bondeville and who can also be connected with the disorders in 1568 following the peace of Longjumeau, the mob then gave itself over to a disorganized campaign of looting and violence which lasted for four days.

Estimates of the number of those killed in these four days range from 'three to four hundred' to 'over four hundred' to 'around five hundred' to Simon Goulard's probably excessive 'over six hundred'.[1] The victims were drawn predominantly from the lower strata of society and were distinctly humbler in station than were the massacre victims in other cities; only 19 per cent of the male victims listed by Crespin in his martyrology came from the urban elite of merchants, lawyers, and officials, as opposed to 33 per cent in Troyes and 53 per cent in Orleans.[2] Rouen's richer Protestants were able to escape by early flight, by influence, or by paying off their would-be executioners. As one local chronicler put it, 'The rich escaped by a bridge of silver, and the poor were put to death.'[3]

If the precise events of the four days of the massacre are obscure, the striking developments of the subsequent days and weeks are clear. Ten days after the massacre, a Spanish merchant in the city, Pedro Ortiz de Valderrama, sent this report to Simon Ruiz in Medina del Campo:

> Thanks be to God, today we are in peace, and all those of them [the Huguenots] who show themselves in public are making honorable reparations in the parish in which they live and a profession to live and die in the Catholic faith and are returning to baptize their sons and daughters who were baptized according to their fashion and some of them who were married in their manner are even returning to be married in the Catholic Church. All these are things to praise God for.[4]

[1] Weiss, 'Un témoin de la Saint-Barthélemy', p. 446; Ruiz, caja 17, 227, Pedro Ortiz de Valderrama to Simon Ruiz, Sept. 30, 1572; De Thou, *Histoire universlle*, Vol. 4, p. 606; *Memoires de l'estat*, Vol. 1, p. 410.

[2] Natalie Zemon Davis, 'The Rites of Violence', *Society and Culture in Early Modern France: Eight Essays* (Stanford, 1975), p. 80.

[3] *Rélation des troubles excités par les calvinistes dans la ville de Rouen depuis l'an 1537 jusqu'en l'an 1582*, publication of *La Revue de Rouen et de la Normandie* (Rouen, 1837), p. 36. *See also* Weiss, 'Un témoin de la Saint-Barthélemy', p. 446.

[4] Ruiz, caja 17, 227. Here is the full text of the paragraph of this unpublished letter pertaining to the massacre in Rouen. 'Las cosas pasadas por aca ya las sabra V.M. que parece ha sido una cosa divina mas que umana, y en este pueblo abiamos estado quietos fasta los 16 y 17 deste que el populaço se lebanto y mataron mas de 400 personas y algunas mujeres entre ellas desta ley nueva, pero a dios gracias hoy estamos en paz, y todos los que dellos se muestran publicamente acen reparacion onorable en la parruechia donde residen y profesion de bibir y morir en la ley catolica y acen tornar a batiçar los hijos y hijas que an sido batacados a su modo y tambien algunas de los que an sido casados a su manera tambien se tornan a casar a l'ayglesia catolica. Todas estas son cosas para alabar a dios. Tiene el mayor tanta voluntada de lo reducir todo desta manera, que esperamos en dios le dara gracia de acabar tan buena y santa cosa plegue a el asi sea.'

Numerous other sources confirm Valderrama's report. The Catholic parish registers reveal a flood of acts in the days and weeks following the massacre in which young Abrahams, Isaacs and Saras, ranging in age from one to twelve, are 're-presented for baptism', 'confirmed by baptism' or simply 'rebaptized'.[1] Theologically speaking, these rebaptisms may well have been unnecessary and even improper; Catholic doctrine considered valid any baptism with water in which the Trinity was invoked, even one performed by a heretic. The provincial council of Normandy which assembled in 1581 was specifically to denounce the rebaptism of Calvinist children as an abuse tending toward Anabaptism.[2] But whatever the official theology, laymen and even many parish priests obviously considered baptism above all else a rite of initiation into a specific religious community and demanded these rebaptisms to mark the reintegration of the erstwhile heretics back into the Catholic fold.[3]

While many Huguenots headed to their parish churches to have their children rebaptized, others flocked to the cathedral where they submitted to a formal ceremony of abjuration. After confession of their sins, they were made to approach and revere the Host, while carrying that symbol of purification, a burning taper.[4] It was a ceremony almost expressly designed to humble the erstwhile heretics by making them show their acceptance of the most violently rejected Catholic doctrine, transubstantiation. The abjuration Rouen's Protestants were required to sign reveals the same desire to humble the Huguenots. Not only did they have to renounce their faith; they also had to admit they had deserved any legal punishment they might have received for their beliefs.

I, Jehan le Grand, linen-worker living in the parish of St Gervais-lès-Rouen and recognizing the true catholic and apostolic faith, anathemise, detest, and abjure all extant heresies and in particular the heresies and false doctrine of the so-called new religion to which I previously adhered for a certain time..., proclaiming with heart and mouth that I shall live and die in the faith and religion of the catholic, apostolic, Roman church..., receive and hold all that it holds and approves

1 A.C.R., R.P.'s 34, 87, 138, 172, 246, 266, 287, 429, 500, 566, and 616; A.D.S.M., E, St Amand St Sever, St Vivien, Notre-Dame-de-la-Ronde. It is an easy matter to deduce in most cases that these are Huguenot children being rebaptized. In some registers there are even marginal notations such as 'huot' which made the fact explicit.

2 Claude de Sainctes, *Le Concile provincial des diocèses de Normandie tenu à Rouen, l'an 1581* (Rouen, 1606), p. 19.

3 The social meaning of baptism as a ritual of initiation into a specific community is also made clear by the behavior of English Catholics. For judicial reasons and in order to be able to disprove any future charge of illegitimacy, it was useful to have one's baptism recorded in the parish register kept by the local Anglican clergyman. The Catholics nonetheless sought wherever possible to have a proper Roman baptism performed, even though an Anglican one would be equally valid. Often when they then went to the minister to have their Catholic baptism recorded he would insist on a second, Anglican baptism. John Bossy, *The English Catholic Community, 1570–1850* (Oxford, 1976), p. 134.

4 Dom J. T. Pommeraye, *Histoire de l'Eglise Cathédrale de Rouen* (Rouen, 1686), p. 149.

concerning the holy sacraments of the church and the doctrine of the faith, and reject all that it reproves. I further confess that those who believe or dogmatize to the contrary are deserving of the penalties inflicted by law against the heretics, to which laws I submit myself to be punished accordingly in the event that I should ever violate in any manner this present abjuration which I have signed with my own hand.[1]

So many Huguenots went to the cathedral in this period to make their abjuration that the harried grand vicars had to ask to be excused from participating in the regular church service in order to administer the ceremony to all who demanded it.[2]

Some Protestants caviled at the extreme obeisance to Catholicism's sacred symbols involved in these ceremonies but still made gestures of reconciliation to the Roman Church when they first dared appear in public. The account books of several of the city's parishes contain lists recording monetary donations made by numerous Huguenots 'reduced' to Catholicism.[3] From these lists and from the rebaptisms recorded in the parish registers, it can be calculated that at least 3,000 Protestants made some sort of formal act of reconciliation to the Roman Church in the wake of the massacre. The number may well have been considerably higher.[4] Furthermore, many others who did not have their children rebaptized or make donations to the church nonetheless began to attend Mass in these years.[5] The exact size of the wave of conversions cannot be calculated, but it was obviously quite a considerable phenomenon.

While many of Rouen's Protestants headed directly for their parish church when they first dared to appear in public, others slipped out of town. A major movement of emigration developed. England was the chief destination. The French ambassador reported the arrival in London of 'fairly large numbers' of refugees from Rouen, while the census of aliens taken on November 4 in Rye revealed 174 Rouennais still in that small Sussex port, not counting those who had already passed through on their way to other destinations in England.[6] The census also notes the arrival of an additional 11 families within the next five days, an indication that

[1] A.C.R., R.P. 138.

[2] A.D.S.M., G 2170, entry of Nov. 20, 1572.

[3] A.D.S.M., G 6802, 6889, 7329, 7373, 7527, and 7757.

[4] For the calculation of this estimate and the reasons why it probably underestimates the number of formal converts, *see* Philip Benedict, 'Catholics and Huguenots in Sixteenth-Century Rouen: The Demographic Effects of the Religious Wars', *French Historical Studies*, IX (1975), pp. 228–9.

[5] This can be deduced from the consistory records of the French church of London. Of a large number of refugees from Rouen who admitted that they had attended Mass in the wake of the massacre, only 3 confessed to having signed a formal abjuration, had their children rebaptized, or donated money to their parish church.

[6] W. J. Hardy, 'Foreign Refugees at Rye', *Proceedings of the Huguenot Society of London*, II (1887–8), pp. 573–4. The report of the French ambassador is quoted by F. deSchickler, *Les églises du Réfuge en Angleterre* (Paris, 1892), Vol. I, pp. 187–8.

the emigration was still continuing six weeks after the massacre in Rouen. A substantial colony of Rouennais also joined the 'Walloon' congregation at Southampton, which in fact became predominantly French after 1572.[1] Other refugees from Rouen may have headed to Zeeland,[2] while a handful also made their way across France to Geneva, although this was an extremely perilous voyage since Guise's men patrolled the roads of eastern France in the wake of the massacre to intercept Huguenots fleeing to Germany or Switzerland.[3] Unlike the first wave of emigration to Geneva in 1549–60, the one which followed the St Bartholomew's Day Massacre came predominantly from the nearby provinces of southeastern France.

It might be thought that the abjuration or flight of so many Huguenots was merely a temporary reaction of fright – perhaps even, in the case of the abjurations, something wrung from them at the point of the halberd – and that, once order was restored and the Huguenots were able to worship freely, those who had converted or fled would return to the fold. A glance forward at the subsequent evolution of the Protestant congregation reveals that this was not the case.

Initially it looked to France's Catholics as if Protestantism might never recover. The wave of Huguenot conversions that followed the massacre seemed to many to portend the end of the Calvinist movement and the beginning of an era of restored religious unity. After dealing some of the Protestants an exemplary punishment, it was as though God was now leading the others peacefully back into the fold. Ortiz de Valderrama called the massacre and its sequel 'more a divine thing than a human one' and concluded his account of the event to Ruiz with the pious hope that God would grant the remaining Huguenots grace enough that they might all be reduced to Catholicism.[4] 'There is great hope that now things will go well in France', was the reaction of a Catholic in Lyon to the event.[5] Even the king himself was encouraged by events to think that Protestantism was on the verge of being eliminated and that the Wars of Religion might be brought to an end. Attempting to make the best of the unexpected situation in which he found himself, he barred all Calvinists from royal offices

[1] H. M. Godfray, ed., *Registre de l'église wallonne de Southampton*, Publications of the Huguenot Society of London IV (Lymington, 1890), passim. Between 1568 and 1572, 84 per cent of the marriages celebrated in this church involved refugees from the Walloon provinces; between 1573 and 1598, 67 per cent involved refugees from France.

[2] In 1585 Francesco de Fontaneda and Juan Pasqual reported to Simon Ruiz that many of the Huguenots who left the city in that year headed for Zeeland. It seems probable that if this was one of their places of refuge in 1585, it had also been one in 1572. Ruiz, caja 104, 113.

[3] Fourteen refugees from Rouen appear in the Genevan *livre des habitants* of the period 1572–4. Paul-F. Geisendorf, ed. *Livre des habitants de Genève* (Geneva, 1963), Vol. 2, *1572–1574 et 1585–1587*, passim. On the dangers of the voyage across France, *see* B.N., MS Dupuy 333, fo. 72; A. Kluckhohn, ed., *Briefe Friedrichs des Frommen Kurfursten von der Pfalz* (Braunschweig, 1872), Vol. 2, p. 488.

[4] Ruiz, caja 17, 227.

[5] Archives d'Etat de Genève, pièce historique 1929.

in an effort to spur further conversions.[1] Reformed services ceased in Rouen.[2]

Subsequent events dashed Catholic hopes that the massacre was the end of Protestantism. In a letter of late December Ortiz de Valderrama continued to maintain that the massacre and subsequent conversions 'surely were a work of God', but he had to report to Simon Ruiz that the Huguenots had risen against the crown in a number of cities, most notably La Rochelle.[3] The Fourth Civil War which ensued saw Charles fail to conquer the rebellious cities. He was forced to grant a new edict allowing freedom of conscience in July 1573. The survival of a chain of Huguenot strongholds stretching across southern France and up the west coast into Poitou guaranteed that Protestantism would not be eliminated and that the civil wars would continue for decades. But if Protestantism was not eradicated, it nonetheless had been dealt a stunning blow. When Rouen's Reformed Church began to rise from the ashes of the massacre in the years following the edict of pacification of July 1573, the church that reassembled was merely a shadow of its former self.

Initially, the church's recovery was extremely slow. Only a handful of Huguenots dared return from exile to re-establish the congregation in October 1574. Most remained understandably distrustful of royal assurances of protection.[4] The spectacularly unsuccessful efforts of Charles's successor, Henry III, in the Fifth Civil War of 1575–6 led, however, to the generous terms of the so-called peace of Monsieur, and more were emboldened to return. These men soon found their services interrupted once more, when the pressure brought to bear by the first Catholic League led the king to outlaw Protestantism once again in February 1577. The liberal terms of the peace of Monsieur had provoked a number of leading Catholic noblemen to form the League, a nationwide association theoretically pledged to the elimination of heresy but in this instance motivated every bit as much by the desire of these men to hold onto certain provincial governorships which they were in danger of losing under the terms of the peace. Henry III chose to meet the threat posed by this organization by co-opting it; he joined the League himself, assumed its direction, and set out upon the Sixth Civil War at its head in February 1577. But he was

[1] A.D.S.M., B, Parlement, Registres Secrets, entry of Oct. 6, 1572.

[2] I have not been able to find a copy of the official measure banning Protestantism, but the Protestant baptismal registers indicate that the congregation ceased to gather.

[3] Ruiz, caja 17, 230, Pedro Ortiz de Valderrama to Simon Ruiz, Dec. 24, 1572: 'En las cosas pasadas de por aca cierto ha sido cosa de dios, y sino es La Rrochela y ostros 2 o 3 villas todo esta ha debocion del Rey y la tierra pacifica pero estas no an querido obedecirlo. Es permision de Dios para que todos sean castigados de tantos malos como an fecho...'

[4] The Reformed baptismal registers show the slow recovery of the church. Although they declare it was re-established in October 1574, no baptisms are recorded until 1576. *See also* the remarks in Guillaume and Jean Daval, *Histoire de la Réformation à Dieppe* (Rouen, 1878), p. 120.

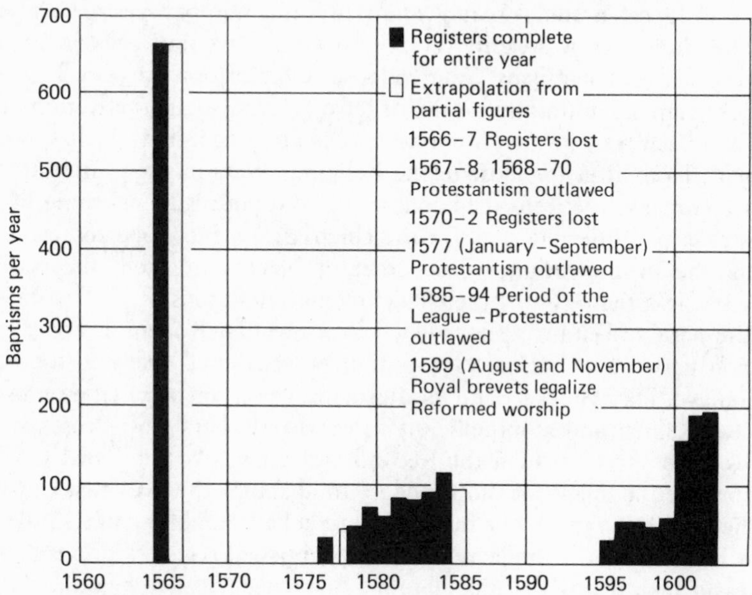

Figure 2. The numerical evolution of the Protestant community
Source: Huguenot baptismal registers, A.D.S.M., E, Protestants de Rouen et de Quévilly.

playing a double game. Even while he outlawed Protestantism throughout the realm, he sent letters to his local officials ordering them to protect the Huguenots in their jurisdiction and to reassure them that the reports being bruited about that he wished their extermination were false.[1] During this civil war Rouen's Protestants do not seem to have been molested, burdened with special taxes, or otherwise harassed as they had been during earlier periods of conflict, and following the edict of Poitiers ending this brief war in September 1577, services resumed immediately at the Protestant temple.[2] This time they were to prove of longer duration. The congregation was able to assemble freely for the next eight years, the longest uninterrupted period of toleration in the era of the Religious Wars.

Figure 2 presents the numerical evolution of the Protestant congregation as revealed by its register of baptisms. A glance reveals that the congregation which finally began to assemble regularly in 1578 contained just a tiny fraction of the membership of the mid-1560s. In 1579, the first full year for which services were held at the temple without interruption, only 70

[1] A.C.R., A 19, entry of Feb. 12, 1577; A.D.S.M., B, Parlement, Registres Secrets, entry of Feb. 8, 1577.

[2] Again, the reopening of the church is evident from the Reformed baptismal registers.

baptisms were celebrated – barely one-tenth the number performed in 1565. The church grew steadily for the next six years, but even in 1584 there were just 115 baptisms. The collapse in size from 1565 levels was dramatic. From a community on the order of 16,500 souls, the Reformed church had been transformed into one of 1,500 to 3,000. This decline was permanent. Even after the close of the Religious Wars in 1594, under the reign of Henry IV, the Reformed community did not regain anything like its old strength. While the ranks of the congregation increased somewhat following the promulgation of the edict of Nantes in 1598, they still remained at less than a third their level of the mid-1560s.

The dramatic and enduring decline which occurred in Rouen's Protestant population between 1565 and 1577 cannot be attributed solely to the St Bartholomew's Day Massacre and its aftermath. In certain other cities, most notably Caen, Gien, and Montpellier, it is clear that the harsh anti-Protestant measures which accompanied the Second and especially the Third Civil Wars prompted as many or more people to abandon the Calvinist cause as did the events of 1572.[1] The measures surely had something of a similar effect in Rouen, even if the lacunae in the baptismal registers prevent us from measuring it precisely. Still, all of the surviving evidence suggests that the St Bartholomew's Day Massacre must be accounted the primary cause of the numerical collapse of Rouen's Protestant community. Huguenots were barred from holding royal office in both 1568 and 1572, but only during the latter year did the number of expelled officials who appealed to the parlement for reinstatement on the grounds that they had abjured their faith take on important proportions. Twenty-six such requests for reinstatement appear among the court's *arrêts* for the years 1572–3, against just one in 1568–9.[2] Similarly, the Catholic parish registers contain none of the numerous rebaptisms after the first edicts of proscription that one finds in 1572, only an abjuration signed by 12 men.[3] There are no records of payments by Huguenots 'reduced' to the Roman Church in 1568 in the parish account books.

What explains this stunning wave of defections precipitated by the St Bartholomew's Day Massacre? One thing is clear. The decline was not

[1] *See* Appendix 1. There is also evidence of a similar movement back to the Catholic Church in these years in Lyon, Dijon, and Provins. *See* Richard Gascon, *Grand commerce et vie urbaine au XVIe siècle: Lyon et ses marchands (vers 1520–vers 1580)* (Paris–The Hague, 1971), Vol. 2, p. 523; Edmond Belle, 'La Réforme à Dijon des origines à la fin de la lieutenance-générale de Gaspard de Saulx-Tavanes (1530–1570)', *Revue Bourguignonne*, XXI (1911), p. 142; Claude Haton, *Mémoires de Claude Haton contenant le récit des événements accomplis de 1553 à 1582, principalement dans la Champagne et la Brie*, ed. Felix Bourquelot (Paris, 1857), Vol. 2, pp. 551–4.

[2] A.D.S.M., B, Parlement, Arrêts, Septembre–Décembre 1568, Janvier–Avril 1569, Septembre 1572–Janvier 1573, Février–Avril 1573, Mai–Juillet 1573.

[3] A.C.R., R.P. 138.

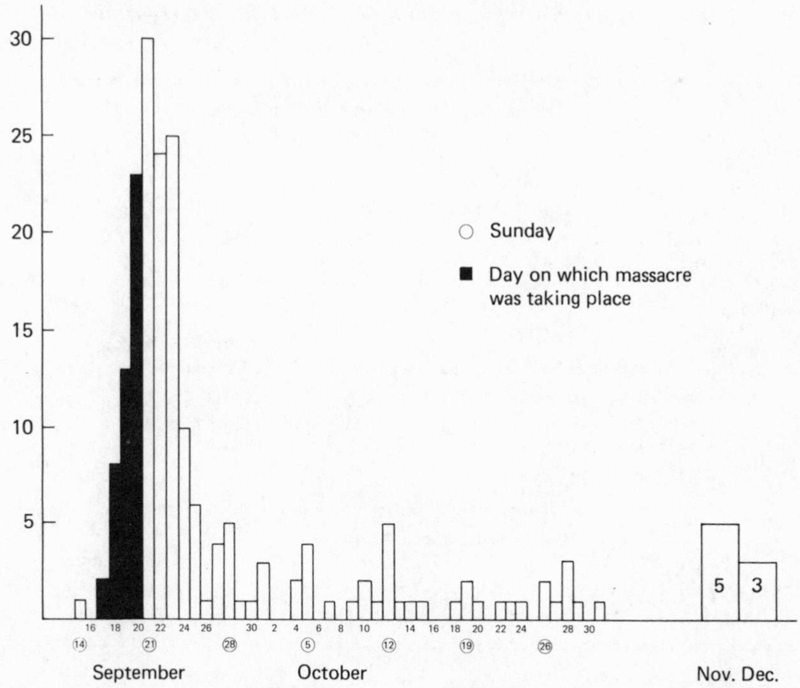

Figure 3. Number of Protestants rebaptized in 1572 by date of ceremony

simply the product of force. There is evidence that, in the days following the massacre, a few Protestants were compelled to participate in Roman services; one Jean Bossin, for example, told the consistory in London that he had been dragged to the Papist temple and made to worship the idols there.[1] But these cases were the exception. Most of those who confessed to the consistory in London that they had permitted themselves to be 'polluted by idolatry' in the aftermath of the massacre did not claim any such extenuating circumstances. The dates of the Huguenot rebaptisms recorded in the parish registers are also revealing. As Figure 3 shows, only a quarter took place during the four days on which the massacre actually raged, while half came in the week after order was restored and the remaining fourth spaced themselves out into December, with small peaks occurring each Sunday. It is not a pattern which suggests constraint. Nor do the actual entries in the parish registers suggest in any way that the children being baptized had been snatched from their families or dragged

[1] *Actes du consistoire de l'église française de Threadneedle Street, Londres*, Vol. 2 (*1571–7*), ed. Anne M. Oakley, publications of the Huguenot Society of London XLVIII (London, 1969), p. 101.

Table 9. *Comparative evolution of Protestant congregations, 1560–1600*

Average number of baptisms per year in towns for which baptismal registers well maintained

Caen		Gien		Montauban		Monoblet (Languedoc)	
1564–8	430	1563–5	111	1565–71	571	1563–71	29
1570–2	270	1570–2	65	1573–7	600	1573–7	27
1578–84	152	1578–85	60	1578–84	648	1578–84	32
1591–4	187	1591–1600	57	1585–94	606	1585–94	26
1595–1600	231			1595–1600	602	1595–1600	28

Montpellier		La Rochelle		Verteuil-Ruffec (Angoumois)	
1563–8	413	1564–9	539	1570–1	253
1570–2	211	1573–7	935	1578–84	193
1575–84	253	1578–84	674	1588–93	250
1585–94	320	1585–94	728		

Average number of baptisms per year in towns for which registers fragmentary

Loudun		La Baume-Cornillan (Dauphiné)		Saintes	
March 1566–Sept. 1567	150	June 1571–Aug. 1572	338	Oct. 1570–Aug. 1572	102
June 1576–Feb. 1577	120	March 1579–April 1580	214	1576, 1578–9, 1582–4	82

forcibly to the baptismal font. Parents and godparents presented the children exactly as in normal baptisms.[1] Finally, the most conclusive evidence of all that the reduction in Huguenot strength was not simply the result of force can be obtained by setting Rouen's experience in comparative perspective. An examination of Protestantism's numerical evolution in a number of communities throughout France reveals a similar decline in Huguenot numbers after 1572 in many cities which did not directly experience massacres.

Where they survive, the baptismal registers of the various Reformed congregations form the most reliable sources for the comparative study of Protestantism's numerical evolution. A well-maintained series of such registers stretching back to the years prior to 1572 is a rare find, but good sets of such registers do exist for seven congregations in addition to Rouen's. In three more cases fragments of registers have come down to us which are sufficiently complete to allow at least a rough comparison of the level of baptisms before and after 1572. Table 9 sets forth the movement of baptisms in these ten congregations.[2] The documents are naturally most

[1] Cf. here the entry from the parish register of St Ayoul, Provins, which makes it clear that in this case force was involved in a rebaptism. Haton, *Mémoires*, Vol. 2, p. 1,131.

[2] Complete year-by-year figures and a full discussion of the sources used in constructing this table may be found in Appendix 1.

numerous for congregations which suffered relatively little disruption over the course of the Religious Wars, and most of the registers thus come from the regions of greatest Protestant political strength, the Midi and Center-West. In none of the ten communities is any violence known to have occurred in 1572. Still, as can be seen, a significant decline occurred in the number of baptisms in two congregations. In Caen, where the number of such acts had already fallen by 37 per cent between 1568 and 1570, a further decline of 44 per cent occurred after 1572. In La Baume-Cornillan (Dauphiné), the massacre provoked a drop of 37 per cent. A decline on the order of 20 per cent can also be observed in the smaller congregations of the Center-West: Saintes, Loudun, and Verteuil-Ruffec (Angoumois).

The numerical evolution of Protestantism in certain other cities can be determined from different sources. For Bayeux a register of abjurations was kept by the *officialité*. It lists no fewer than 1,802 renunciations of Protestantism made by residents of the city and surrounding countryside in the months following the St Bartholomew's Massacre.[1] In Le Havre evidence of a decline in Huguenot numbers comes from the Catholic parish registers, which reveal that 309 Huguenot children were 'reconciled' to the Roman Church in the weeks following the massacre, a substantial number for what was still only an infant port.[2] In Amiens one Huguenot baptismal register survives from the sixteenth century, that of 1564–5. It records 147 baptisms between July 1564 and June 1565, a figure equivalent to a total Huguenot population of about 3,500 people.[3] A census made of the members of the Reformed Church in 1580 lists by contrast just 216 adult males, a figure equivalent to a total population of less than 1,500.[4] A letter written by the *échevins* of the city in 1576 explains the intervening decline: 'The majority of those who were of the *religion prétendue réformée*...left it four years ago.'[5] Finally, simple literary evidence such as this last letter attests to a large number of conversions in many other cities. Jesuit fathers boasted of the same press of Huguenots wishing to abjure their faith in Lyon and Toulouse as that which overwhelmed the vicars of the cathedral in Rouen in 1572.[6] The parlement of Dauphiné informed the king that 'the majority of *officiers* and an infinity of others' in that province returned to the Catholic Church immediately upon hearing the news of the massacre

[1] Eugène Anquetil, ed. *Abjurations de Protestants faites à Bayeux: Guerres de religion (1570–1573)* (Bayeux, n.d.), p. 4 and passim.

[2] A.D.S.M., E, St François-du-Havre, 1572; Notre-Dame-du-Havre, 1572.

[3] A. D. Somme, I 2.

[4] A. Dubois, ed. *La Ligue: Documents rélatifs à la Picardie d'après les registres de l'échevinage d'Amiens* (Amiens, 1859), p. 20; Robert Fossier et al., *Histoire de la Picardie* (Toulouse, 1974), p. 251.

[5] Fossier et al., *Picardie*, p. 252.

[6] Austin Lynn Martin, ed. 'Jesuits and the Massacre of St. Bartholomew's Day', *Archivum Historicum Societatis Iesu*, XLIII (1974), pp. 113, 116, 118.

in Paris.[1] Reports of similar developments come from Paris, Orleans, Troyes, Dijon, Meaux, Clairac and Ste Foy in Guyenne, and much of Bas-Poitou.[2] In Castres and Millau, on the other hand, contemporary memoirs suggest that few or no conversions took place.[3] Of all the cities, local massacres occurred only in Paris, Lyon, Toulouse, Orleans, and Meaux.

Rouen's Reformed community was thus anything but unique in suffering a dramatic decline in size as a consequence of the St Bartholomew's Day Massacre. Reliable quantitative evidence about four other Reformed congregations north of the Loire shows a marked drop in each one's membership (see Map 8), while literary evidence suggests that a similar decline affected the Huguenot communities throughout virtually all of northern and eastern France. South of the Loire Protestantism's evolution was a bit more complicated. Calvinist numbers remained stable or even increased in size due to an influx of refugees in certain areas – parts of Languedoc, Montauban, La Rochelle – but in other regions, notably much of Dauphiné, the movement's strength tumbled just as it did in the North. In all, Beza seems to have been quite well informed when he wrote to Thomas Tilius that the inhabitants of La Rochelle, Montauban, Nimes, the Cévennes, the Vivarais, Sancerre, and Berry were ready to resist, but that elsewhere 'the defection has been and continues to be incredible'.[4] Only Montpellier and the smaller congregations of the Center-West can be added with confidence to Beza's list of areas where Protestantism was holding firm, and even in the latter area a drop in Huguenot strength of approximately 20 per cent occurred following the massacre. It was apparently not so much the fact of experiencing a massacre itself that caused the decline in size of Rouen's Reformed community (although this may explain why its decline was greater than that of any of the other communities for which we have reliable quantitative evidence). Other considerations must obviously be invoked as well, chief among them the psychological impact which the event had on all Protestant communities in positions of relative insecurity.

[1] B.N., MS Français 15555, fo. 153, Oct. 22, 1572. *See also* Peter France, 'Les Protestants à Grenoble au XVIe siècle', *Cahiers d'Histoire*, VII (1962), p. 327.

[2] Charles Pradel, 'Un marchand de Paris au seizième siècle (1564–1588)', *Mémoires de l'Académie des Sciences, Inscriptions et Belles-Lettres de Toulouse*, 9th ser., II (1890), p. 422; Charles Read, ed. 'La Saint-Barthélemy à Orléans racontée par Joh.-Wilh. de Botzheim, étudiant allemand témoin oculaire', *B.S.H.P.F.*, XXI (1872), p. 385; B.N., MS Dupuy 698, fo. 392; Belle, 'La Réforme à Dijon', pp. XV, 147; 'La Saint-Barthélemy à Meaux', *Bulletin de la Société de l'Histoire de France* (1838), no. 4, p. 5; Estèbe, *Tocsin pour un massacre*, p. 165; B.N., MS Français 15555, fo. 88, de Saussay to Charles IX, Sept. 18, 1572.

[3] Jean Faurin, 'Journal sur les guerres de Castres', M. de la Pijardière, ed., *Pièces fugitives pour servir à l'histoire de France* (2nd ed., Montpellier, 1878), no. 15, pp. 63–4; *Mémoires d'un calviniste de Millau*, ed. J. L. Rigal (Rodez, 1911), pp. 241–4.

[4] 'Deux lettres de Théodore de Bèze sur la Saint-Barthélemy', *B.S.H.P.F.*, VII (1858), p. 17.

Map 8. The impact of the massacre

(Protestant congregations whose numerical evolution is known from reliable quantitative evidence are indicated in all capital letters. Those about which only literary evidence exists are in lower case. The congregations which experienced a significant decline in size after 1572 are denoted by boxes around them.)

The regions in which Calvinist numbers held firm were all areas in which the Protestants could feel reasonably confident about their ability to defy the central government or where the local authorities were able to ensure that there was little likelihood of the massacre being repeated locally. In most of these cities or regions – La Rochelle, Nimes, Montauban, Sancerre, the mountainous fringes of Languedoc – the Protestants were already politically dominant. Furthermore, La Rochelle, Montauban, and Sancerre were all strongly fortified cities, while the Cévennes and Vivarais are among the most rugged regions of France, natural territory for resistance movements from the days of the Albigensians down to the *maquis* of the twentieth century. This combination of an entrenched Protestant majority and a readily defensible location rendered these areas immune to the worst fears of annihilation which ran through the Protestant communities after the massacre. The relative stability of congregations such as Saintes and Gien is probably explained by the fact that their members could retire safely to the nearby sanctuaries of La Rochelle and Sancerre.[1] As for Montpellier, it was a somewhat different case. Despite a large Protestant population, the city was controlled by the Catholics, and a large wave of Huguenot defections had already taken place in 1568. No such phenomenon reproduced itself in 1572 because the *politique* governor of the area, Joyeuse, went out of his way to ensure that no violence broke out and to reassure the Protestants of their perfect safety.[2]

Even in these areas where Protestant numbers held firm, the Huguenots were extremely skittish in the wake of the massacre. A Protestant memoir from Annonay, in the Vivarais, reports that news of the killings in Paris 'threw so great a fright into the *religionnaires*...that they would flee at the least rumor or movement by the Catholics, although not a soul was pursuing them'.[3] The ministers of the Reformed Church of Nimes were sufficiently alarmed to contemplate organizing the emigration of the entire congregation – nearly 20,000 people – to Switzerland or the Low Countries.[4]

If near-panic prevailed in these predominantly Protestant regions, sheer terror reigned among the Huguenots in Catholic-controlled areas such as Rouen. In these areas the Calvinists had been exposed to the constant hostility of their neighbors for over a decade. They had no powerful protectors whom they could trust to defy the king's orders or stay the anger of the Catholic crowds. Against this backdrop of insecurity, the arrival of reports of the savage violence which had taken place in Paris precipitated the worst fears of annihilation. Even where no actual violence broke out, rumors ran rife for months following St Bartholomew's Day of impending massacres even more awful than the first. And most Protestants, despite the church's exaltation of martyrdom, were not eager for a martyr's fate. To save their lives they were willing to convert.[5] The massacre in Rouen

[1] The supposition that Gien's Protestants took refuge in Sancerre is confirmed by Géralde Nakam, ed., *Au lendemain de la Saint-Barthélemy, guerre civile et famine: Histoire mémorable du siège de Sancerre (1573) de Jean de Léry* (Paris, 1975), pp. 47–8. A sharp increase in the number of Huguenot baptisms in La Rochelle suggests a wave of refugees taking shelter in that city as well. *See* Appendix 1.

[2] Jean Philippi, *Mémoires*, Petitot, 1st ser., Vol. 34, p. 379.

[3] Achille Gamon, *Mémoires*, Petitot, 1st ser., Vol. 34, p. 314.

[4] Victor Carrière, 'Les lendemains de la Saint-Barthélemy en Languedoc', *Revue d'Histoire de l'Eglise de France*, XXVII (1941), p. 224.

[5] Thus, Jehan Rouille wrote Jacques and Pierre Fabvre from Paris: 'Or, pour abréger mon dire, je vous prie, tant qu'il m'est possible, si voulez sauver vostre âme, garentir vostre vie présente, sauver vos biens, vostre famille hors de pauvreté, de croire mon conseil, c'est que, le plus tost que faire pourrez, vous et toute vostre famille vous ayez à faire actuelle profession de la religion catholique,

played a particularly significant role in spreading this sense of panic throughout the communities of northern France, since, coming as it did four weeks after the initial wave of violence, it seemed to confirm the rumors of further massacres. Virtually all of the Protestant conversions in Le Havre occurred within the week following the massacre in Rouen, while a deputy of the governor of Amiens wrote that the news of the event had so agitated his previously peaceful city that he feared he could no longer guarantee the safety of its Protestants.[1] Panic, escalating as the weeks passed and as news of more and more local massacres filtered in to the Huguenot communities throughout France, must obviously be accounted the force which precipitated the bulk of the Protestant conversions.

But decisions made in fright are often repented in tranquility. Fear of further violence may have triggered the wave of Huguenot conversion and flight in 1572, but fear alone cannot explain the permanence of so many of the conversions of this year. Once the first months of panic had passed, once Protestantism had become legally tolerated once again, only a minority of those who had either converted or sought exile in 1572 resumed Protestant worship in France. Most chose to remain Catholic or stay in exile.[2] As Calvinist authors noted with incomprehension, there were even certain Protestants who originally fled to safety in 1572 but subsequently returned home, converted, and lived lives of zealous Catholic piety ever after.[3] Additional considerations must have reinforced and confirmed the

et que, en premier lieu, vous preniez acte de vostre évesque ou curé comme il vous aura ouy en confession, vous repentant de l'abus auquel par trop longtemps vous avez adhéré, et que doresnavant vous promestiez de vivre catholiquement; comme il vous aura vu assister à la messe et aux services de l'Eglise; prenez acte comme il vous aura administré le Sainct Sacrement de l'hostel; bref faictes tous actes d'homme de bien et catholique...Plus de cinq mil personnes de ceste ville ont faict le semblable, car il n'y a que ce seul moyen pour se garantir et sauver sa vie et son bien. Croyez-moy et faictes ce que je vous mande, car je says, de vray et suis bien assuré que tous ceulx qui vouldront faire autrement seront mis à mort, leurs biens perdus et toute leur famille destruite de fond en comble.' Charles Pradel, 'Un marchand de Paris', p. 422. *See also* the letter of Beza quoted at the beginning of this section.

[1] Two hundred and ninety-six of the 309 Huguenot 'reconcilations' occurred between Sept. 22 and 26. A.D.S.M., E, St. François-du-Havre and Notre-Dame-du-Havre, 1572. On the tension in Amiens: B.N., MS Français 15555, fo. 99, Leonor d'Orleans (?) to Longueville, Sept. 23, 1572.

[2] About 10 per cent of the men whose names appear in the acts in the Catholic parish registers noting the rebaptism of their children later reappear in the Huguenot baptismal registers, either as parents or godparents. Slightly under a quarter of the emigrés recorded in the census made at Rye in 1572 show up in these Huguenot registers. The permanence of most of the conversions or flights is evident.

[3] *Briefve et Chrestienne remonstrance à ceux qui pour eviter la persecution esmeue en France, principalement depuis le 24 d'Aoust 1572, ont abiuré la vraye Religion* (n.p., 1574), p. 36. In his history of the Reformed Church of Troyes, Nicholas Pithou cites the case of Symon Hagerit, a Protestant merchant from Chaumont-en-Bassigny married to one of the leading Huguenot *bourgeoises* of Troyes. Hagerit initially retired to Montbéliard after the massacre along with many of Troyes' Calvinists but then decided to convert while abroad. He returned to Chaumont. On his wife's death he married the daughter of one of Troyes' most violent Catholics, and for the rest of his life he continued to profess that faith, declares Pithou, without the least sign of remorse or repentance. B.N., MS Dupuy 698, fo. 397.

decisions originally made in panic either to convert or to emigrate permanently.

To understand what these considerations might have been, we must reconstruct the experience of Protestants living in predominantly Catholic cities such as Rouen over the preceding decade. 'We are today absolutely hated and odious to our fellow men', the minister of Orleans wrote Calvin late in 1563.[1] His comment applied perfectly to the situation in Rouen as well. The Huguenots were regarded almost as a cancer within the body social. Continuous popular hostility, frequent violent attacks, and intermittent periods of proscription and governmental persecution had all been their fate throughout the years from 1563 through 1572. Their lives had been affected in a number of ways.

For many of the more committed Protestants, the constant alternation of war and peace, tolerance and proscription had brought a life of constant uprooting. Some – by no means all – of the peregrinations of the Rouen-born minister Guillaume Feugeray are known, and his case provides a perfect example. After serving as a pastor in the region of Rouen during the early years of the Religious Wars, Feugeray was forced to flee to London after St Bartholomew's Day. Soon thereafter he moved to Leiden, where he taught theology. In 1583 he returned to Rouen, but only for two years before he was again forced to leave in 1585. He is known to have been in Dieppe, which was loyal to Henry of Navarre, from 1590 to 1594, and finally came home for good following Rouen's capitulation to the king.[2] In similar fashion, the artisan Nicolas Vancel lived in Normandy, Geneva, Lausanne, Payerne (Switzerland), and London, all between 1550 and 1564.[3] Surviving diaries of Protestants from other predominantly Catholic cities reveal equally peripatetic lives.[4]

The consistory records of the French Church of London indicate some of the consequences of this uprooting. The religious divisions of the period often broke up families, as did the decision of whether or not to leave for exile in times of persecution. This was not always a tragedy. Exile could prove a welcome substitute form of divorce, as it apparently did for Jean de Planches, admonished by the consistory for remarrying in England while his wife was still alive in Rouen, or Clement Papillon, chastised for refusing either to return to Normandy and live with his wife there or to pay for her to come over to London.[5] (She was a Papist, he claimed, had an income

[1] Quoted in Bernard de Lacombe, *Les débuts des guerres de religion (Orléans, 1559–1564): Cathérine de Médicis entre Guise et Condé* (Paris, 1899), p. 405.

[2] Daval, *Histoire de la Réformation à Dieppe*, pp. 149, 250.

[3] *Actes du consistoire*, Vol. 1, pp. 7–8.

[4] A. Crottet, ed., *Diaire ou journal du ministre Merlin, pasteur de l'église de La Rochelle au XVI siècle* (Geneva, 1855), pp. 11–22; Paul-F. Geisendorf, *Histoire d'une famille du Réfuge française: Les Des Gouttes de Saint-Symphorien-le-Châtel en Lyonnais et de Genève* (Geneva, 1943), ch. 4.

[5] *Actes du consistoire*, Vol. 2, pp. 80, 84.

of her own, and was perfectly content without him.) For most, however, the consequences of separation were more painful. Two Rouennais had to do public penance before the London congregation for having attended Mass while back in Rouen trying desperately but unsuccessfully to convince their families to follow them to England, while the wife and children of Jehan Prevost were said to have been reduced to beggary when he abandoned them to live in London.[1]

Exile not only broke up old families; it also affected the way in which new ones were formed. The 'parish' registers of the congregation of Rouen lack a complete list of marriages performed in the church, but simply from the fragments inserted in the back of the register of 1574–85 and 1594–1604 containing announcements of just 22 marriages it is clear that Huguenots married outside the city far more frequently than did Catholics. At least 12 of these 22 marriages involved one partner from outside Rouen, with the spouses hailing from as far away as England and Holland. The contrast with Catholic behavior could not be more striking, for only a minority of Rouen's Catholics looked so far as the next parish for a spouse; marriage outside the city was extremely rare except in the *faubourgs*, with their important populations of recent immigrants and agricultural laborers.[2] This specifically Protestant pattern of marriage was obviously the result of the wide geographical range of contacts which resulted from the Huguenots' forced mobility, and perhaps, too, of a conscious strategy of seeking family alliances with residents of other areas to whom one could turn for shelter in case of future persecution or violence. A high rate of exogamy also characterized other urban Protestant communities in this period and continued to do so in many cases right on through the seventeenth century.[3]

[1] *Ibid.*, Vol. 2, pp. 163, 198, 201.

[2] A sampling of three Catholic parishes for which the registers of marriages list both spouses' parish of residence shows a remarkably high level of parochial endogamy, even though there was a clear increase in marriage outside the parish during the period of the civil wars, which brought greater population mobility to Catholics as well as Protestants. It should be stressed that these figures refer to parish of residence, not parish of birth. They are derived from the incomplete parish registers of the A.D.S.M., which explains why it was impossible to obtain figures from the same time periods for each of the three parishes.

Residence of Catholic marriage partners in three parishes

1. both partners from same parish
2. one partner from other parish within Rouen
3. one partner from outside city and *faubourgs*

	St Vivien		St Nicaise			St Sever	
	1554–8	1573–4	1549–60	1563–6	1581–5	1547–58	1570–79
1	77%	57%	90%	70%	64%	63%	57%
2	20%	35%	9%	21%	31%	21%	21%
3	3%	8%	1%	9%	5%	16%	22%

[3] The same pattern emerges from the published registers of the sixteenth century for the congregation of Loudun, where many spouses come from as far away as Troyes, La Rochelle, Le Mans and Dinan.

Economic hardship had been another consequence of the uprooting and insecurity that had become the Protestants' lot. There were three reasons for this. First, those who left for exile could not always take all of their property with them, and at each outbreak of civil war royal letters-patent ordered the seizure of all goods left behind by those who had left their homes.[1] This was probably the least important cause of economic distress, since many departing Huguenots circumvented these decrees by selling their property before leaving town or ceding it to relatives, while others sought to hide their valuables.[2] A fascinating document from Montpellier recording the efforts of that city's officials to collect a special tax levied on its Huguenots in 1569 shows that those who fled rarely left much property behind to be seized. In case after case the sergeants report that they have gone to the house of an assessed Huguenot only to find it boarded up and vacant or else leased by a Catholic family. The few objects they were able to seize were virtually without value.[3] Nevertheless, the evasive tactics open to the Huguenots were not entirely foolproof. Those leaving for exile are rarely able to sell their belongings at full market value, so many of the Huguenots who sought to dispose of their valuables must have had to settle for prices below what their goods were worth. The potential dangers of hiding one's property are revealed by the case before the London consistory of one Jacques Cossart, who had to turn to the services of a cunning man after the valuables he had hidden had vanished in his absence.[4] Property that could not be hidden or transferred and was consequently seized by the authorities was always ordered restored to its original owners by the

Unfortunately, as with Rouen, the notation of place of residence is carelessly maintained, so no precise percentages of marriage outside the city can be calculated. C. E. Lart, ed., *Registers of the Protestant Church at Loudun 1566–1582* (Lymington, 1905). For the seventeenth century, a brief sampling among the registers of marriages for Rouen reveals that 36 of 100 Protestant nuptials in the years 1669–72 involved one partner from outside the city and *faubourgs*. A.D.S.M., E, Protestants de Quévilly, Mariages 1669–85. Further evidence of the distinctive Protestant marriage pattern can be found in Marcel Couturier, *Recherches sur les structures sociales de Châteaudun, 1525–1789* (Paris, 1969), p. 212. One presumes that the rate of exogamy was less where a large Reformed community was located far from any other Protestant congregations or in regions where the Protestants formed the majority of the population.

1 *See above*, p. 119.

2 Huguenot attempts to circumvent these measures are clear from an edict of February 20, 1568 barring all people from buying any goods from members of the R.P.R. 'par ce que plusieurs de la R.P.R. vendent chacun secretement leur bien...pour...s'en aller joindre avec la compagnie du Prince de Condé'. British Museum, Add. MS 30600, fos. 58–61. A brief check of Rouen's notarial records during 1568, when Protestantism was proscribed, did not turn up any contracts concerning such sales, but this is presumably because such transactions were carried out *sous seing privé* to escape official detection. In 1585, when Protestantism was again outlawed but the Huguenots were given six months to leave the country, one does find contracts in the *tabellionage* indicating that they were selling their property before leaving. For evidence that some tried to hide their valuables, *see below*.

3 A. D. Hérault, B 22269.

4 *Actes du consistoire*, Vol. 2, p. 121. It is not clear whether the *devin* succeeded in locating the lost property.

terms of the edicts of pacification. Court cases suggest, however, that this was not always done promptly or fairly.[1] The royal edicts ordering the seizure of Huguenot property were thus not entirely without economic impact.

The second cause of economic hardship was the expense of exile itself. The disruption of normal business activities, the costs of a voyage to England or elsewhere, and the difficulties in finding employment in a strange city surely all took their toll on a Huguenot family's resources.

Finally, to the losses incurred during the periods in which Protestantism was legally proscribed must be added those which resulted from the extortion and looting which accompanied many of the anti-Protestant riots in times of theoretical peace. The redistribution of wealth which stemmed from these disorders was considerable; the Venetian ambassador estimated the value of the booty seized during the St Bartholomew's Day Massacres at 2,500,000 *écus* in Paris alone.[2]

The combined effect of these hardships on the fortunes of a wealthy Protestant merchant in a Catholic-controlled town can be seen from the case of Jacques Faure of Albi. During the Second and Third Civil Wars Faure left the city and apparently could not carry on his commerce. He was then imprisoned along with all of Albi's Protestants at the time of the St Bartholomew's Day Massacres and only managed to regain his freedom by paying a substantial ransom. While he was in prison his wife hid his merchandise lest it be seized; the people with whom she hid it demanded a share. Faure estimates his total losses from these events at fully 16,000 *livres*. His missives of 1573 are long pleas to his creditors for more time to pay off his debts. 'You tell me that my letter is full of moaning and groaning. I will tell you that greater houses than mine, once rich and opulent, have been ruined from top to bottom by these deplorable times.'[3] The example comes from the other end of France, but the situation in which Faure found himself was comparable to that of Rouen's Protestant merchants.

Of course, it had always been possible to avoid the economic and personal hardships that resulted from emigration by remaining in France, but those Huguenots who had chosen this option had faced other hardships. Close surveillance, special taxes, soldiers billetted in their homes, and perhaps even imprisonment had been their lot. Furthermore, these men had been confronted with the ticklish spiritual problem of just how fully they ought

[1] A.D.S.M., B, Parlement, Arrêts, Mars–Mai 1568, arrêt of May 4, 1568. Gascon cites the case of a Protestant merchant of Lyon still living in an inn a full year after he had returned home following an edict of pacification, while two Catholics continued to occupy his house. Gascon, *Grand commerce*, p. 526.

[2] Quoted in Estèbe, *Tocsin pour un massacre*, p. 136.

[3] Pradel, 'Un marchand de Paris', pp. 423–7, esp. p. 426.

to participate in Catholic religious life. During the Third Civil War the monarch ordered all newborn babies baptized in the Catholic Church but did not force Calvinists to violate their consciences by attending Mass.[1] This compromise seems to represent the solution adopted by most Huguenots during periods in which they were forbidden to hold services of their own, although a minority would have nothing to do with Catholic ceremonies and refused even to have their infants baptized in the Roman Church, preferring to run the risk of having them die unbaptized.[2] During the last years of the Religious Wars when the exercise of the Reformed faith was barred for almost a decade, this sort of rigor became impossible and the Protestants were forced to participate quite fully in Catholic services. Even the English merchants in the city, who were specifically exempted from all repressive legislation in matters of religion, were forced to attend Mass and kneel at the elevation of the Host.[3] By this time, many Calvinists must have become experts at dissimulating their true beliefs, like the anonymous merchant 'sometimes of the Religion, but [who] now goeth to the mass, but in heart a Protestant' who informed the English in 1586 of a rumored plot against Queen Elizabeth's life that he had learned of while speaking with several monks.[4]

The decade prior to 1572 had thus dealt harshly with the Protestants. Total allegiance to the cause had come to entail a migratory existence, economic hardship, and an ever-present risk of losing one's life or seeing one's family broken up. As for the 'floaters' who moved back and forth between the two confessions depending upon the legal situation, their behavior mitigated some of the risks and hardships, but at the cost of placing them in an uncomfortable middle ground which left them exposed to the scorn of the purer Calvinists as well as the anger of the Catholic mobs. And not only had the decade been one of ostracism and suffering; it had also been one of disillusionment. By 1572 it was clear to all that the high

[1] Charles de Robillard de Beaurepaire, ed., *Cahiers des Etats de Normandie sous le règne de Charles IX*, publications of the Société de l'Histoire de Normandie, xxv (Rouen, 1891), pp. 26–7.

[2] Since the Catholic parish registers in times of proscription between 1567 and 1570 contain many entries recording the baptism of children of Huguenot parents, we can deduce that the majority of Protestants had no strong objections to giving their children a Roman baptism when the Reformed Church was not assembling. This can also be deduced from the more complete Huguenot baptismal registers of cities such as Caen. When these resume in 1570 after a long period of proscription, they do not reveal an exceptionally large number of baptisms in the first months, as one would expect had many parents refrained from baptizing their children until they could do so in the Reformed Church. For evidence that a few Protestants nonetheless avoided all Roman ceremonies, even baptism, *see* Robillard de Beaurepaire, *Cahiers des Etats sous Charles IX*, p. 26; B.N., MS Dupuy 698, fos. 353–4. That most avoided attending Mass insofar as possible is indicated by the efforts of Catholic vigilantes at several points to force them to do so; *see above*, Chapter 4, p. 119.

[3] Albert Sarrazin, ed., *Abrégé d'un journal historique de Rouen* (Rouen, 1872), pp. 29, 33; *Cal. S.P. For.* 1585–6, p. 300.

[4] *Cal. S.P. For.* 1585–6, p. 556.

hopes of the exhilarating years between 1560 and 1562 when it had looked as though Protestantism might sweep all before it had been greatly exaggerated. Calvinism's numerical growth had been checked. Defeats at Dreux and Jarnac had shown the limitations of the Protestant military strength. Now, with the massacre, their last, best hope was gone. Coligny had been murdered, and with him the possibility that had still been alive on the eve of his assassination that the court might be persuaded to back the Protestant cause. After a decade of struggle, of disappointment, of hardship, now that their papist neighbors had shown themselves capable of excesses on the horrendous scale of the massacres, why continue to live in danger among them in the service of a lost cause? It was better to conform or, since many Protestants had lived and even had relatives elsewhere, to emigrate. These were the counsels of despair which made the decline in Protestant strength so sharp and so long-lasting after 1572.

For many in this age quick to see the hand of providence in affairs, the despair may also have been intensified by a bitter sense of divine betrayal. 'Where is your God now?', the Catholics mockingly asked the Protestants as they went on their murderous rounds during the St Bartholomew's Day Massacres or encountered them in the streets in the subsequent weeks.[1] Many Huguenots could not find an answer. 'I began to consider it [the massacre] to be an expression of God's indignation, as though he had declared by this means that he detested and condemned the profession and exercise of our Religion', stated the Calvinist minister Hugues Sureau by way of explanation for his apostasy in 1572.[2] He was surely not the only one to feel such sentiments in the days of utter disheartenment of the late summer and autumn of that year.

If the St Bartholomew's Day Massacre had only been the blow which capped Protestantism's remarkable numerical decline, that alone would have qualified it as the crucial turning point in the history of French Protestantism in a city like Rouen. But it was more. It was also an event which altered the attitudes and behavior of those who remained faithful to the cause in a way that was to prove remarkably enduring.

Throughout the 1560s, we have seen, the Huguenots continued to be in many ways quite militant. Far from being a docile minority patiently suffering the slings and arrows of outraged neighbors, they still entertained hopes of regaining control of the city government, actively sought new converts and on occasion fought quite fiercely, as during the Massacre of Bondeville. In their own eyes they represented the majority of the

[1] *Mémoires de l'estat*, Vol. 1, p. 344; *Mémoires d'un calviniste de Millau*, p. 243; Jacques Gaches, *Mémoires sur les guerres de religion à Castres et dans le Languedoc* (Paris, 1879), p. 121.
[2] Quoted in Kingdon, *Geneva and the Consolidation*, p. 117n.

'honorable, ancient, and peaceful houses' in the city; to Catholic eyes they appeared arrogant. If anything, the Second and Third Civil Wars only reinforced many Protestants' confidence, for was not their constancy in the face of repression and exile yet another proof of their moral strength and firm devotion to God's cause?

It was precisely this maddening sense of superiority, this much-proclaimed dedication to obeying the word of God above all else, that the Catholics took a particular glee in seeing broken following the St Bartholomew's Day Massacre. The satisfaction is evident in the gloating account of the aftermath of the massacre written by Claude Haton, the curé of Provins whose diary is perhaps the most detailed and revealing guide to the opinions of a confirmed but unexceptional Catholic to have come down to us:

> The Huguenots who remained after the seditions, both in Paris and in the rest of France, except for those of La Rochelle, Sancerre and Montauban, all went to mass, without being compelled or ordered to go, even though they swore when they renounced the Catholic Church that they would never go there no matter what commandment was given them and even if they were to be burned alive; and it seemed as though they had never left or been separated, so cheerfully did they behave, going not by ones or twos but in large groups to sing in the churches. This clearly revealed their inconstancy and fickleness of spirit, for in the time of their prosperity they boasted aloud in any gathering that they would sooner be thrown in a burning pyre of a thousand faggots than go alive to mass...[1]

Even among those Huguenots who did not themselves give in and attend Mass, the spectacle of so many of their co-religionists doing so must have long haunted them. 'Stupor and lethargy' characterized many Reformed congregations in the wake of the massacre according to Beza, who was himself near despair.[2] The event also revealed to the Protestants as no other episode before it just how exposed and powerless they were amid a vastly larger enemy. The trauma of the event marked all of the subsequent behavior. No longer does one find references to their menacing behavior after 1572. No longer do the streets ring to the sound of psalms being sung in public. In 1576 the cardinal of Bourbon appeared at the recently reopened Reformed temple to urge the Huguenots to return to Roman Catholicism; the first reaction of the congregation when they spotted him coming was to flee, not to fight.[3] The Rouennais, and the Normans in

[1] *Mémoires de Claude Haton*, Vol. 2, p. 689.

[2] Theodore Beza, *Epistolarum theologicarum Theodori Bezae Vezelii liber unus* (Geneva, 1573), p. 327; Paul-F. Geisendorf, *Théodore de Bèze* (Geneva, 1949), p. 308.

[3] The best accounts of this incident are Pommeraye, *Histoire des Archevesques de Rouen* (Rouen, 1667), p. 618, and *Histoire de l'Eglise Cathédrale*, p. 150.

general, played virtually no role in the nationwide Huguenot political assemblies which began to be held regularly after 1572,[1] while the iconoclastic attacks of 1564 were the last ever committed in Rouen by Protestants. The promulgation of the edict of Nantes in 1598 provoked a brief resurgence of bravado. A few hearty souls dared sing psalms openly once again; a Catholic preacher was contradicted from the audience.[2] But such demonstrations were short-lived, and for most of the seventeenth century a timid conservatism, born of fear, continued to characterize the political behavior of Rouen's Huguenots. They resolutely refused to become involved in the struggles of the reign of Louis XIII between the crown and their co-religionists in the Midi, and their persistent desire to prove themselves more royalist than the king reached its crowning moment in 1649, when one of the church's pastors wrote a tract denouncing the execution of Charles I by the English Puritans – Calvinist brothers in theology, after all – as the most atrocious crime committed since the crucifixion.[3] In a very different context, Emmanuel Le Roy Ladurie has spoken of '*événements créateurs de structures*' – events so dramatic and powerful in their consequences that they shape behavior for years and even generations to come. Insofar as the political behavior of Rouen's Protestants was concerned, the St Bartholomew's Day Massacre seems to have been such an event. In the Protestant stronghold communities of the Midi and Center-West it may have driven the Huguenots into a more forthright and open stance of resistance than ever before. In Rouen, and presumably also other cities like it, it forged a reflexive conservatism that was to last through the seventeenth century.

Even in their choice of names for their children after 1572 one can see a greater desire on the part of Rouen's Protestants not to stand out from their neighbors, a declining willingness to testify publicly to their faith. Between 1565 and 1576–85 the percentage of Old Testament names bestowed on Huguenot children fell from 51 per cent to 36 per cent. Over the same period, the distinctively Calvinist Abraham and Isaac gave way in order of popularity to the religiously neutral Pierre and Jacques in the list of the most commonly chosen Protestant names. (See Table 10.) A slight decline in the frequency of Old Testament names seems to have taken place over these years even in major Huguenot strongholds such as La Rochelle, presumably the result of a general slackening of zeal for the cause once the

[1] Léonce Anquez, *Histoire des assemblées politiques des Réformés de France (1573–1622)* (Paris, 1859), passim. The only assembly of the period of the Wars of Religion for which there is any evidence of even a single Norman delegate attending is that of 1584, even though the assemblies were supposedly national and had royal approval throughout the early 1580s.

[2] Amable Floquet, *Histoire du Parlement de Normandie* (Rouen, 1840–42), Vol. 4, pp. 247–8.

[3] Philippe Joutard et al., *La Saint-Barthélemy, ou les résonances d'un massacre* (Neuchâtel, 1976), p. 80.

Table 10. *The most popular Protestant names, 1565–1602*

1565		1576–85		1595–1602	
		Boys			
Jean	46	Jean	72	Jean	50
Abraham	42	Pierre	54	Pierre	38
Isaac	41	Jacques	45	Jacques	36
Pierre	36	David	24	Abraham	27
Daniel	33	Isaac	17	Isaac	24
		Girls			
Marie	113	Marie	83	Marie	88
Judith	38	Judith	39	Madeleine	39
Sara	31	Anne	25	Susanne	35
Susanne	27	Susanne	23	Elisabeth	33
Anne	17	Ester	21	Anne	33

first great flush of enthusiasm began to wane.[1] Nevertheless, the decline was not nearly so marked in La Rochelle as in Rouen. More so than their co-religionists in cities where Calvinism was dominant, Rouen's Protestants were, it would seem, trying to assume a lower profile after 1572.

[1] In La Rochelle, the percentage of Old Testament names declines from 36 per cent in 1563–5 to 30 per cent in 1579–80. A. D. Charente-Maritime, I 3 and I 18.

6

Interlude

Precisely because it was so much larger in scale and more devastating in impact than any of the smaller religious riots which had preceded it, the St Bartholomew's Day Massacre also proved to be the last such riot to trouble the city until the crisis of the League reawakened religious militancy of a somewhat different sort in the later 1580s. By provoking the final and most dramatic act in the numerical collapse of the Protestant community and a radical change in the political behavior of those few men who remained faithful in it, the massacre lowered the temperature of religious antagonism within the city. As the chastened Protestants ceased to appear a threat to the Catholic majority, the violent anti-Huguenot sentiments shared by so many Catholics declined accordingly. For a city whose residents had once been called the kingdom's most difficult, Rouen became remarkably tranquil for the next dozen years. Between 1573 and 1584 not a single incident of confessional rioting took place; such national events as the formation of the first nationwide Catholic League in 1576 had only the faintest of local repercussions; and indeed any sort of organized Catholic militancy appears to have been non-existent.

With the thunder of the Religious Wars now increasingly remote, the city's commerce was also able to flow unhindered throughout these years and even to profit from Rouen's new position as a haven from the religio-political rivalries of the age. The years from 1573 through 1584 became ones of prosperity as well as tranquility – a development which in turn probably contributed further to the stability of the city. Only the occasional passage of a company of horse through the region, the relentless demands of the king for higher taxes, and his constant invention of new venal offices to peddle in the city were reminders that the civil wars continued to be fought elsewhere in France.

All Catholic hostility toward Protestantism did not disappear after 1572. The utter depravity of the Calvinists and the consequent desirability of their eradication were themes that continued to be sounded from the pulpit and in Catholic writings with little apparent diminution in frequency. The city's magistrates had already felt compelled to chastise preachers for the inflammatory nature of their sermons on three occasions – in 1552, 1561, and 1570.[1] They had to do so again in 1573, when the words of an unnamed preacher at the cathedral stirred fears of new violence against the erstwhile Huguenots, still apparently regarded with suspicion.[2] Nor had anti-Huguenot sentiments subsided any further within certain breasts when an anonymous author, probably a mendicant friar, sat down in 1582 to pen his 'Relation of the Troubles Excited by the Calvinists in the City of Rouen'. The work, frequently cited in the preceding pages, breathes a hatred of Protestantism as fierce and uncompromising as anything written in the earlier years of the Religious Wars.[3] A similar spirit infused the 1585 sermon of an unnamed Franciscan who told his audience that the holy feast of St Bartholomew ought to be celebrated six times a year.[4] Zealots among the Catholic clergy continued to chant their litany of hatred without interruption.

But the response from the congregation ceased to be as eager as it had been prior to 1572. The fullest guides to the grievances agitating Normandy's inhabitants in this period are the *cahiers de doléances* drawn up at the annual meetings of the provincial estates. These show a significant decline in concern with the threat posed by Protestantism in the years after 1572. Four *cahiers* have survived from the earlier period of the Religious Wars, covering the years 1567 through 1570. Anti-Protestant feelings find expression in at least one article in each *cahier*; often there are several. In 1569 fully six *doléances* entreat the king to force the Calvinists to participate in all Catholic rites, to prohibit them from practicing such sensitive occupations as weapons-maker, doctor, or inn-keeper, and to compel them to pay for the reconstruction of all churches damaged over the preceding years.[5] No *cahiers* have survived from the years between 1571 and 1578, but among the grievances expressed at the nine subsequent meetings of the provincial estates (1579 through 1587), anti-Protestant articles appear only

[1] A.D.S.M., B, Parlement, Registres Secrets, Chambre des Vacations 1549–56, entry of Nov. 7, 1552; B.M.R., MS Y 214 (5), entries of Aug. 5, 1562 and May 4, 1570.

[2] A.C.R., A 19, entry of March 3, 1573.

[3] *Relation des troubles excités par les calvinistes dans la ville de Rouen depuis l'an 1537 jusqu'en l'an 1582*, publication of *La Revue de Rouen et de la Normandie* (Rouen, 1837), passim. While this work is undated, most of it was clearly written in 1582 for the body of the work carries the narrative down to 'this present year 1582'. Some additional paragraphs are then tacked on at the end relating events in 1583. Suspicion that the author was a mendicant friar is aroused by the general zeal the work breathes; the broad range of reading, particularly in the church fathers, it suggests; its hints of millenarianism; and its thundering denunciations of society's general depravity and the special cupidity of the wealthy and powerful.

[4] *Cal. S.P. For.*, 1584–5, pp. 524–5.

[5] Charles de Robillard de Beaurepaire, ed., *Cahiers des Etats de Normandie sous le règne de Charles IX*, publications of the Société de l'Histoire de Normandie XXV (Rouen, 1888), pp. 6, 21, 39–41, 43, 58, 66–7. *See* Table 12 below, p. 162, for a complete breakdown of the *doléances* by topic between 1567 and 1587.

rarely. Only four such *doléances* were expressed, and all four came after 1585, when the threat of Henry of Navarre's accession to the throne had suddenly raised once more the specter of Huguenot domination.[1] Although certain Catholic ideologues continued to denounce the Huguenots as a dangerous, polluting force within the body social well after they had ceased to pose a serious threat within Rouen, the great bulk of the Catholic population thus seems to have been far less concerned with the problem after 1572 than before. A change in the perception of the Huguenot menace paralleled the changes which had occurred within the Protestant community.

These changes explain the city's new tranquility after 1572. The authorities did have a few brief alarms between 1573 and 1584, but none ever escalated into major threats to public order as the religious rioting so often had prior to 1572. The bad harvest of 1573 produced several minor scenes of disorder at the city's markets, but the *cinquantaine* was called out, the distribution of free bread was initiated, and the authorities averted a serious grain riot, which could easily have taken on anti-Huguenot overtones as well.[2] The formation of the Catholic League created another potentially dangerous situation in 1576. Reports that bands of horsemen were gathering in the area led to the reinforcement of the night watch on several occasions, but rumored attempts to seize the city never materialized. It was only after Henry III proclaimed himself the head of the association and instructed Carrouges to organize a local branch in Normandy that any efforts are known to have been made to enroll the Rouennais themselves in the cause. As seems to have been the case in most cities, these attempts evoked little enthusiasm; the League was apparently seen as merely a new ruse on the king's part to extract money on the pretext of a crusade against the Huguenots. The members of the cathedral chapter procrastinated for a month before finally voting to heed the appeal of the archbishop, join the cause, and pledge a tenth of their income to it. As for the Council of Twenty-Four, as far as can be told from its records, it never acted at all on a similar appeal made by Carrouges.[3]

[1] Charles de Robillard de Beaurepaire, ed., *Cahiers des Etats de Normandie sous le règne de Henri III*, publications of the Société de l'Histoire de Normandie xx (Rouen, 1888), Vol. 2, passim, esp. pp. 108, 126–7, and 204.

[2] A.D.S.M., B, Parlement, Registres Secrets, entries of May 20 and 27, June 2, 1573.

[3] A.C.R., A 19, entry of Aug. 10, 1576; B 3, entries of Aug. 9 and Oct. 23, 1576, June 12, 1577 (the meeting at which Carrouges proposed that the city join the League; the proposal is never mentioned again in either the *journal des échevins* or the registers of the deliberations of the Council of Twenty-Four); A.D.S.M., G 2171, entries of Jan. 4, 5, 12, 25, 26, Feb. 5, 1577 (all deliberations of the cathedral chapter about whether or not to join the League). The parlement also balked at joining the League. *See* Jonathan S. Dewald, *The Formation of a Provincial Nobility: The Magistrates of the Parlement of Rouen, 1499–1610* (Princeton, 1980), p. 48n. There are good discussions of the general suspicion of most cities about this first League and their reluctance to become involved in it in Ouvré's

Rouen remained equally unmoved two years later when a new 'league' of a different stripe was formed elsewhere in the province to protest the growing burden of royal taxation. Protestants and Catholics alike formed this association, which sent a letter to Rouen's *conseillers-échevins* in March 1579 detailing the outrages of 'those hateful financiers' and concluding with the ringing words: '*Messieurs nos concitoyens*, if you do not come to our aid you cannot be called Frenchmen but slaves.'[1] Most Rouennais were apparently content to be called slaves. The city did not stir, although three leading bourgeois were arrested later in the year for joining an alleged conspiracy against the king which may have been related to the activities of this association.[2]

As the disappearance of the religious violence was linked to the declining threat posed by the local Protestant community, so this refusal to become involved in the anti-tax league of 1578 may have been related to the commercial boom which Rouen was enjoying by that date. The growing remoteness of all fighting had enabled trade to pick up, and Rouen's inhabitants may not have wanted to jeopardize their renewed prosperity by becoming involved in an uprising against the king, nor perhaps were they as angered by the higher taxes as those elsewhere in the province because of their prosperity.

The Fourth Civil War, which had followed on the heels of the St Bartholomew's Day Massacre, had provoked renewed English and Rochelais piracy in the Channel and another rupture of trading relations with the British Isles in 1573–4, but this was the last of the civil wars to affect Rouennais commerce directly for fifteen years. Where the fighting had interrupted trade three times between 1562 and 1574, it was not to do so again until the combats associated with the second Catholic League flared up in 1589. Meanwhile, the great confrontation of the age between Catholic and Protestant had come to engulf the Low Countries as well as France, wreaking havoc on the trade of Europe's greatest port, Antwerp. Rouen was a safe neutral harbor in the conflict between Spain and the rebellious Low Countries, and as Antwerp's merchant community began to decompose under the successive blows of the blockade of the Scheldt in 1572, the

fine 'Essai sur l'histoire de la Ligue à Poitiers', *Mémoires de la Société des Antiquaires de l'Ouest* (1854), pp. 109–10; and Henri Drouot's often overlooked *Notes sur la Bourgogne et son esprit public au début du règne de Henri III, 1574–1579* (Dijon, 1937), ch. 3.

[1] A.C.R., Chartrier, tiroir 400 (2). The agitation of 1578–9 in Normandy desperately needs further study, but certain details about the unrest can be gleaned from Adrien Miton, 'Mémoire...sur l'histoire de cette ville et des environs depuis 1520 jusqu'en 1640', F. Bouquet, ed., *Documents concernant l'histoire de Neufchâtel-en-Bray et des environs* (Rouen, 1884), p. 26; Pierre de L'Estoile, *Mémoires-Journaux*, ed. Brunet, Champollion et al. (Paris, 1875–96), Vol. 1, pp. 275–6; and Madeleine Foisil, 'Harangue et rapport d'Antoine Séguier Commissaire pour le Roi en Basse-Normandie (1579–1580)', *Annales de Normandie*, XXVI (1976), pp. 25–40.

[2] A.C.R., A 20, entry of Aug. 22, 1579.

'Spanish Fury' of 1576, and the capture of the city by the prince of Orange in 1577, a number of its traders transferred their operations to Normandy's capital. Some 22 Spaniards, most of them refugees from the Low Countries, received letters of naturalization in Rouen in the years after 1580, and by 1585 the already considerable Castilian colony had grown to the point where it included 80 men able to bear arms. Other merchants who remained in the Low Countries began to send merchandise destined for Spain overland to Rouen and then by sea from there as a means of circumventing the stranglehold of the Sea Beggars over the mouth of the Scheldt. Often these merchants also began to purchase considerable quantities of linen and canvas in Normandy, their traditional Flemish sources of supply having been badly disturbed by the fighting. Combined with the stimulus provided Rouen's trade by the steadily expanding volume of Spanish exchanges with the Indies, these developments raised Rouen's commerce to a level of activity that was probably unmatched at any other point in the century. The Ruiz letters suggest a booming trade with Spain, while commerce with England also flourished and native Rouennais merchants even managed to oust the Genoese from their traditional domination of the alum trade.[1]

As Rouen's trade intensified, its industries were also stimulated. Not only did the region's linen trade prosper; the secular trend of decline in the city's woolen industry was momentarily halted,[2] while the production of silken fabrics developed into a major industry in this period. In 1581 a spokesman for the city's *tissotiers de soie* claimed that fully 2,500 workers were employed in Rouen, turning raw silk from Tours into satins, taffetas, and damasks for the Spanish and English markets.[3] To judge by a significant increase in the size of the goldsmiths' guild, the city's luxury trades also seem to have thrived.[4] Indeed, the air of prosperity seems general. The overall movement of baptisms in the city suggests a modestly increasing population between 1574 and 1583, while house rents doubled over the same period, a clear indication of the new wealth shared by many Rouennais.[5]

Rouen's docks and market-places bustled with activity in the later 1570s and early 1580s; tranquility reigned in place of the violence which had been so intense prior to 1572; but beneath the placid surface of a busy port, an undercurrent of discontent was growing. The deliberations of the Council

[1] For this entire paragraph, *see* Philip Benedict, 'Rouen's Foreign Trade During the Era of the Religious Wars (1560–1600)', forthcoming.

[2] The number of new master weavers in St Vivien increased from 180 between 1562 and 1572 to 186 between 1572 and 1582. A.D.S.M., G 7754–77.

[3] A.D.S.M., 5 E 589.

[4] A.D.S.M., 5 E 609, a list of those received as masters into the city's goldsmiths' guild reveals the following evolution: 1550–9, 54 new masters; 1560–9, 59; 1570–9, 70; 1580–9, 78; 1590–9, 29; 1600–9, 41.

[5] *See* Appendixes 3 and 4.

of Twenty-Four in these years reveal an almost complete absence of pressing political issues – with two signal exceptions. Royal tax demands were multiplying, as were schemes to create new venal offices, and the Council's minutes consequently contain virtually nothing of import other than announcements of these new measures for raising revenue, instructions given by the *échevins* to the delegations of protest routinely sent to Paris in response, reports from the delegates in Paris, further instructions to stand firm, and so forth. The discontent produced by the king's incessant money-raising measures was initially moderate – certainly not serious enough to prod the Rouennais into joining the anti-tax agitation of 1578. As the years passed and the king's demands grew, however, the discontent grew apace.

The evolution of taxation during the period of the Wars of Religion is currently an open question in the literature. J.-J. Clamageran's century-old but still unsurpassed history of French taxation suggests a tightening of the fiscal screw after 1576. According to the estimates of royal revenue upon which he relies, the tax burden on the French king's subjects increased only modestly in nominal value and actually declined significantly in real terms between 1549 and 1576, then doubled over the course of the last dozen years of Henry III's reign.[1] Clamageran's figures have recently been subjected to telling criticism by Martin Wolfe. As Wolfe points out, the key documents which Clamageran used do not actually date from the period of the Wars of Religion; they were drawn up after the close of the wars by Henry IV's fiscal officials, who were trying to estimate how much money had been raised by taxation in the past so that they could calculate what present tax assessments ought to be. Obviously there is reason to be suspicious of the accuracy of such estimates, especially since they betray absolutely no indication of the very significant disruption of the crown's tax-collecting machinery in those areas controlled by the Huguenots throughout the 1570s and 1580s.[2]

If, as Wolfe suggests, the entire problem needs to be approached anew, the most fruitful method of tracing the evolution of royal tax revenues over the course of the Wars of Religion may well lie in renouncing the use of the surviving national summaries of revenue. However tantalyzing their appearance of completeness may make them, these summaries nonetheless seem unreliable and, indeed, mutually contradictory.[3] The movement of

[1] J.-J. Clamageran, *Histoire de l'impôt en France* (Paris, 1868), Vol. 2, pp. 197, 229, 244–5.

[2] Martin Wolfe, *The Fiscal System of Renaissance France* (New Haven, 1972), pp. 205–12.

[3] B.N., MS Nouvelles Acquisitions Françaises 2043, fos. 291–343, is another set of royal accounts from 1581 which Clamageran does not appear to have consulted and which reveals a very different pattern from that suggested by his sources. It shows a significant *decline* in royal revenue between 1559 and 1581. The document was probably drawn up for the benefit of the Assembly of Notables of 1583

taxation can be reconstructed far more accurately from local records. Le Roy Ladurie has already studied the accounts of the *taille* for the city of Montpellier. His examination corroborates the pattern suggested by Clamageran; the sharpest tax increases of the Wars of Religion appear unmistakably between 1576 and 1590.[1] A similar investigation is possible in Rouen. Like many major northern French cities, Rouen was exempt from the *taille*, but this by no means meant that it escaped taxation altogether. Goods entering and leaving the city were subject to a variety of import and export duties that represented a considerable financial burden in a major commercial city; the king regularly turned to his *villes closes* in times of war for imposts known as the *solde pour les gens de guerre*; and the city could also expect to be assessed other extraordinary levies whenever pressing need arose. Although account books which would reveal the amounts actually raised by all of these taxes have not survived, it is possible to gain a fairly clear idea of the tax demands made on the city from the municipal registers of deliberations, which note any major new tax proposed by the crown.[2]

Table 11 presents the major royal tax demands revealed by the municipal registers of deliberations. It confirms, first of all, the relative mildness of the tax burden during Charles IX's reign. The typical amount which he demanded of the city in *rentes* and the *solde pour les gens de guerre* averages out to 76,864 *livres* per year, a modest nominal increase from the 69,986 *livres* which was raised each year under Henry II and in fact a significant decrease in real terms when inflation and currency devaluation are taken into account. An increasing reliance on *rentes* (government annuities paid back out of future customs duties) is also visible in these years – a sign of the growing weakness of the crown, which was now forced to bargain away future revenues rather than extract money through direct taxes. At first glance, the movement of taxation under Henry III suggests an even greater erosion of royal power. Not only did he continue the trend toward reducing direct taxes in favor of *rentes*;[3] he also gave in to the city's pleas for tax reductions far more often than did any of his immediate predecessors. Between 1574 and 1585 the total sums he demanded each year in *rentes*

in order to convince the members of the king's dire need for more money. If its provenance therefore renders it highly suspect, the same could be said about the documents upon which Clamageran relies. The point is that none of the documents in the B.N. appear thoroughly reliable.

[1] Le Roy Ladurie, *Paysans de Languedoc*, p. 1,026, graph 41.

[2] The registers of deliberations pose a few difficulties for the historian trying to estimate the level of taxation. At times the city petitioned the king for a reduction in the level of its taxes and it is unclear whether or not it won gain of cause. Occasional references also suggest that the city was not always able to raise promptly the sums demanded and fell into arrears for a while. Finally, some minor excise taxes seem not to be mentioned in the registers of deliberations at all. Thus, the registers cannot be relied upon to provide a precise accounting of the amounts actually raised from the city each year. They do nonetheless provide a clear idea of the general evolution of royal tax demands.

[3] The public debt grew from 43 million *livres* in 1561 to 133 million in 1588. J-J. Clamageran, *Histoire de l'impôt en France* (Paris, 1868), Vol. 2, pp. 202, 246.

Table 11. *The fiscal demands of the crown, 1550–1588*

The following table notes the major royal demands for new or special taxes recorded in the registers of deliberations of the Council of Twenty-Four. It does not purport to reveal the entire tax burden actually borne by the city each year, for there are no surviving records noting the annual returns from the numerous ongoing import and export duties levied on the city's trade, nor can one always be sure that the entire sums demanded by the king were actually raised.

1550	32,000 *l.**	*solde pour les gens de guerre*
1551	—	
1552	96,000 *l.*	*solde*
1553	6,000 *l.*	in *rentes*
	96,000 *l.*	*solde*
1554	100,500 *l.*	*solde*
1555	96,000 *l.*	*solde* – subsequently reduced to 36,000 *l.*
1556	51,680 *l.*	*solde*
1557	51,680 *l.*	*solde*
	100,000 *l.*	emergency *solde* and loan raised in the wake of the defeat at Saint-Quentin
	50,000 *l.*	*solde*
1558	—	
1559	50,000 *l.*	*solde*
	30,000 *l.*	*solde*
	— gap in municipal registers of deliberations —	
1563	12,000 *l.*	forced loan
	16,000 *l.*	*solde*
	16,500 *l.*	*solde*
1564	1,000 *l.*	in *rentes*
1565	150,000 *l.*	in *rentes*
1566	50,000 *l.*	in *rentes*
1567	—	
1568	160,000 *l.*	in *rentes*
	100,000 *l.*	*solde* – reduced to 60,000 *l.* in *rentes*
	100,000 *l.*	*solde*
1569	30,000 *l.*	*solde*
1570	30,000 *l.*	*solde*
1571	200,000 *l.*	*solde*
1572	—	
1573	15,000 *l.*	in *rentes* – subsequently reduced to 10,000 *l.*
	10,000 *l.*	for the voyage of Henry of Anjou to Poland
1574	60,000 *l.*	*solde* – subsequently combined with following year's demand and changed to 120,000 *l.* in *rentes*
1575	12,000 *l.*	in *rentes*
	45,000 *l.*	*solde* – subsequently combined with previous year's demand and changed to 120,000 l. in *rentes*
1576	36,750 *l.*	*solde* – subsequently reduced to 25,000 *l.* in *rentes*
	10,000 *l.*	for fortifications
	100,000 *l.*	forced loan – reduced to 60,000 *l.*
1577	80,000 *l.*	in *rentes* – reduced to 55,000 *l.*
		unspecified new duties on linen, grain, and wine
1578	90,000 *l.*	in *rentes*
	50,000 *l.*	in capitation – subsequently reduced to 30,000 *l.*
1579	210,000 *l.*	in *rentes* – subsequently reduced to 130,000 *l.*
1580	60,000 *l.*	*solde* – changed to *rentes*
1581	9,000 *l.*	in *rentes*

Table 11 *cont.*

	new duty of 20 *s.* per *muid* of wine entering city – subsequently reduced by half
	15,000 *l.* in *rentes*
1582	new duty of 5 per cent on cloth
	80,000 *l.* *solde* – subsequently reduced by one third – city ultimately entirely discharged from raising tax
1583	67,500 *l.* *solde* – subsequently reduced to 60,000 *l.*
1584	90,000 *l.* in *rentes*
1585	60,000 *l.* *solde*
	30,000 *l.* in *rentes*
1586	60,000 *l.* *solde* – changed to *rentes*
	new duty of 5 per cent on linen and canvas
	new duty on playing cards
1587	new duty of 3 per cent on flax
1588	3,600 *l.* *solde*
	tax of 5 per cent on linen and canvas revoked
	74,000 *l.* *solde* – subsequently entirely revoked

* *l.* represents *livres.*

Source: A.C.R., A 16–20

and the *solde* amounted to just 71,333 *livres*, a decline even in nominal terms by contrast with the preceding period. But this figure is misleading, for the new indirect taxes which Henry III levied were considerable. New excise duties on wine, cloth, and linen at least doubled the weight of taxation by 1587.[1] The tax burden thus did increase under Henry III, and the pattern suggested by Clamageran receives further corroboration.

In his quest for revenue, Henry III also relied heavily on the expedient of creating and selling royal offices. This was already a time-honored fiscal practice, but the last of the Valois pushed it to new heights. His zeal to turn appointive offices into venal ones and to create two judgeships where one had previously sufficed extended all the way down to the humblest inspectorships in Rouen's markets. In 1577 even the position of herring inspector became a venal office.[2] Meanwhile, the rather more prestigious places within the sovereign courts underwent a significant increase during

[1] An old duty of 5 *sous* per *muid* of wine entering the city was farmed out in 1580 for 20,000 *livres* per year. (A.D.S.M., C 1272, fo. 35.) The new tariff of 10 *sous* per *muid* added in 1581 thus could be expected to provide nearly 40,000 *livres* per year to the king's coffers. Similarly, the 5 per cent duty on cloth imposed in 1582 probably yielded at least 30,000 *livres* per year; about 36,000 pieces of cloth were imported each year from England alone, and their selling price had been about 17 *livres* per piece around mid-century. (*See here* P.R.O., S.P. 12186, no. 40; W. Brulez, 'The Balance of Trade of the Netherlands in the Middle of the 16th Century', *Acta Historiae Neerlandica*, IV (1970), p. 31.) These two taxes alone represent nearly a doubling of the revenue from *rentes* and the *solde*, and this is not even taking into account what was surely the most onerous tax of all, the impost on linen and canvas of 1586. The linen trade was the largest single element in Rouen's commerce, worth several million *livres* each year.

[1] A.C.R., A 19, entries of Sept. 7 and 17, 1577.

Henry III's reign. Although the precise rhythm of new creations cannot always be followed, it can be ascertained that the parlement grew from a body of 66 men in 1554 to one of 83 by 1600. At the same time the sale of offices took on a far more business-like character than before. Consideration of a candidate's merit ceased to play a major role in his selection and the fiction was abandoned that the purchaser was merely making the king a loan in return for his office after having been chosen for his competence. The highest bidder now got the office with few questions asked.[1] Any and all ruses became permissible. Often Henry used the threat of changing an appointed office into a venal one simply as a lever to pry money from the city government, which frequently thought it cheaper in the long run to buy the office itself and then let it stand empty or appoint a man of its own rather than have the town burdened with yet another officious inspector or unsupervised tax collector. In 1581 the Council of Twenty-Four paid no less than 15,700 *livres* to repurchase the position of *receveur des deniers communs* (city treasurer), thereby preventing a post whose potential for peculation was enormous from escaping the Council's zealous auditorship.[2] Yet even reacquiring a proposed office or tribunal proved no guarantee to the city that it would not subsequently be resurrected. In 1580 Henry III created a local *chambre des comptes* despite the fact that the Council of Twenty-Four had already bought up all the offices in such a court once, in 1543, to prevent the establishment of a tribunal which the *conseillers-échevins* feared would be Normandy's 'total destruction'.[3] Once created, the new court grew at a dizzying pace. It was divided into two semesters a year after its establishment. Ten additional councillors were added in 1586. In less than a decade it grew from its original 31 members to a corporation of 66.[4]

Both the multiplication of venal offices and the increase in taxation provoked considerable resentment. Outrage over the growth of venal offices was far greater than it would be in later centuries when the practice had come to seem inevitable, for never before had offices been put up for sale in such large numbers and with so little attention paid to past promises on the score.[5] Virtually nobody approved of the system except those who actually purchased offices. Public opinion placed much of the blame for the slowness and high cost of justice on the proliferation of official positions. Those who lost out in the scramble for place bitterly resented a system

[1] Dewald, *Formation of a Provincial Nobility*, pp. 69, 136–41.

[2] A.C.R., A 20, entries of Nov. 14 and Dec. 27, 1581.

[3] *Inv/Sommaire*, entry of Nov. 12, 1543; François Farin, *Histoire de la ville de Rouen*, Vol. 1 (Rouen, 1668), pp. 220–21.

[4] B.M.R., MS Y 55, pp. 59, 63, 258–65.

[5] The unprecedented scale of the sale of offices nationwide is confirmed by Martin Wolfe, *The Fiscal System of Renaissance France* (New Haven, 1972), p. 130; and Roland Mousnier, *La vénalité des offices sous Henri IV et Louis XIII* (Rouen, 1945), pp. 22, 26.

which sacrificed merit to wealth. Long-time members of the royal courts were unhappy that their prestige – and *épices* – were diluted among a flood of *parvenus*. As for the growth of taxation, it was beginning to have an adverse effect on the city's economy by the early 1580s. The 5 per cent surtax on cloth imposed in 1582 – a 'miserable cruel extortion' in the words of the English merchants trading with Rouen – was followed by a sharp and lasting drop in the number of new masters entering the weavers' guild.[1] The new taxes levied in 1586 on paper and playing cards were so steep that they provoked the emigration of many of the city's card and tarot manufacturers.[2] 'They are levying new taxes every day on every thing here', one of Simon Ruiz's correspondents wrote him in 1587. 'If Flanders were even the least bit safe, I would send a large part of the merchandise I have in this house there.'[3] A dip in the number of baptisms and levelling off of the sharp rise in house rents after 1583 suggest that the prosperity of the preceding years may have been seriously tarnished by the growing burden of taxation. For those with money to invest, the massive creation of *rentes* offered an alternative to trade and thus cushioned the impact of the higher duties on the leading articles of the city's commerce, albeit at the cost of accelerating the evolution from capitalist to *rentier* that is so enduring a theme in the history of the old regime's bourgeoisie. For those who worked with their hands, there was no such compensation. Furthermore, resentment about taxation was intensified by the very tranquility of the region in this period. Had the Protestants still represented a serious political threat within the city, or had they been at the gates outside, the need for higher taxes to combat the threat would have been clear. Instead, the fighting of the civil wars was now distant. For what was the city constantly being saddled with new excise duties and superfluous royal officials? The answer, it seemed, was simply to subsidize Anjou's foolhardy intervention in the Low Countries, to pay for fruitless crusades against the Huguenot strongholds in the Midi, and to support Henry III's *mignons* and his lap dogs.

The mounting anger about these developments shows up in the *cahiers de doléances*, first those drawn up by the Rouennais themselves for the Estates-General of 1576, then those surviving ones of the entire province adopted at the annual meetings of the provincial estates between 1579 and 1587. Most of the *doléances* compiled for the 1576 Estates-General from the grievances which all of the city's inhabitants were invited to present to the town scribe do not suggest a sorely discontented community. Calls

[1] *Cal. S.P. For.*, 1582/341. The number of *lettres de draperie* issued in St Vivien fell from 115 between 1577 and 1582 to 37 between 1582 and 1587. A.D.S.M., G 7754–77.

[2] A complaint to this effect in *Cahiers des Etats sous Henri III*, Vol. 2, p. 157, can be confirmed by B.M.R., MS Y 218, fo. 4, the *livre de raison* of a *cartier* who emigrated to Middleburg because of this tax.

[3] Ruiz, caja 122, 31, Jos Cunet to Simon Ruiz, Oct. 30, 1587.

Table 12. *Subjects of complaint in the* cahiers de doléances *of the estates of Normandy*

Subject of complaint	Number of *doléances* per year												
	1567	1568	1569	1570	1579	1580	1581	1582	1583	1584	1585	1586	1587
Burdensome taxation	6	1	6	13	4	12	14	8	11	10	7	15	14
Abuses of judicial system	4	—	5	9	6	9	16	1	8	6	12	8	9
Commercial problems	2	—	4	3	—	—	2	4	5	4	4	5	—
Misdeeds of soldiery and vagabonds	2	1	3	1	2	4	2	2	1	—	4	2	2
Violations of local privileges	2	—	6	4	—	—	3	1	4	2	1	2	2
Need for measures against Protestants	1	2	6	2	—	—	—	—	—	—	3	—	1
Need for improvement in Catholic religious life	1	3	6	2	4	—	1	—	2	2	4	2	4
Miscellaneous complaints*	1	—	5	1	5	5	1	4	1	5	8	10	8

* The most common *doléances* in this category involved appeals to improve the province's roads and bridges, to prevent the usurpation of titles of nobility, and to end the alienation of common lands. Other problems denounced ranged from blasphemy to fraud by the province's millers.

to improve the quality of the clergy, establish schools throughout the diocese, improve the sadly deteriorated university at Caen, crack down on the *assassinats* said to have become common throughout the realm, and take stronger measures against piracy suggest concern for the quality of Catholic religious life and alarm at a breakdown in law and order which apparently accompanied the civil wars, but hardly an enraged populace. Two issues, however, provoked a flood of complaints: the proliferation of venal offices and spiralling costs of justice. Eight different articles denounced abuses in these areas, with appeals being made to end all venality, reduce the excessive number of legal officials with which the city was burdened, and prevent men from gaining offices within the law courts before they reached the required minimum age of thirty or on the basis of *parentelles et alliances*.[1] The same appeals recur prominently in the *cahiers de doléances* of the provincial estates (see Table 12), which also reveal a growing volume of complaint about taxation. This takes on a note of real alarm and bitterness from 1582 onward. The provincial estates of 1582 complained of the 'infinite vexations and nearly insupportable *tailles*' levied on the province, because of which 'the poor populace, unable to continue its normal manufactures, is on the brink of despair, the old reduced to beggary, the young to brigandage...by which the country is filled with tears, desolation, and ruin'.[2] The tone of desperation only increases in the years which follow.

While Normandy may have escaped the direct impact of civil war between 1572 and the later 1580s, the indirect burdens placed on the province thus increased, and with them popular discontent. Popular songs were calling Henry a 'new Florentine tyrant' because of his burdensome 'inventions' in matters fiscal long before the crisis of the League.[3] When the new governor, Joyeuse, visited Rouen for the first time in 1583, the banner which greeted him over the city gate expressed the hope that 'afflicted Normandy' might be able to breathe again.[4] When Anjou's death the following year suddenly rekindled fears of Protestant domination, the resulting combination of reawakened religious passion with the growing socio-economic grievances would end the calm of the later 1570s and early 1580s and provoke a crisis more prolonged and disruptive than any other single conflict the city had previously experienced during the Religious Wars.

1 The *doléances* for the Estates-General of Blois are recorded in A.C.R., A 19, entry of Nov. 8, 1576. The appeal to all inhabitants to bring their grievances to the town scribe is in A.C.R., A 19, entry of Oct. 12.

2 *Cahiers des Etats sous Henri III*, Vol. 2, pp. 7–9.

3 Clamageran, *Impôt*, Vol. 2, p. 186, quoting a song of 1576.

4 Respire maintenant Normandie affligée
Ton Roy à ceste foys te veult voir de plus prez
Qui t'envoye aujourd'huy l'un de ses yeux exprez
Pour cognoistre tes maux et t'en rendre alegée

A.C.R., A 20, entry of March 25, 1583.

PART III

The crisis of the League, 1585–1594

The Chapter of Rouen representing the pastoral authority, the archiepiscopal see being vacant – to all faithful Catholics of the city of Rouen, greetings and peace in our Lord! The necessity of the affairs of the Church and the situation of France is at the present so great and urgent as all can readily see that we must seek through all means possible the goodness and mercy of almighty God, whose singular providence we have recognized over the past two or three years in the events which have, despite all of the ruses and inventions of the devil and his legions and against all hope and likelihood, succeeded one another to the advantage of the Catholics and the confusion of the enemies of the Church... In the present situation, our Catholic and Christian duty urges and even constrains us to praise and exalt above all of the armies of this world that divine providence and to rest the anchor of all of our hopes on the firm rock of that providence, forcing ourselves in total humility to prostrate ourselves before it to beg for pardon and remission for all of the sins we have committed against his divine Majesty, so that we may be rendered all the more deserving of being answered in the prayers which we make to him both for the preservation of the city of Paris and for the victory which we hope for over the heretics and their supporters. In order that, while Joshua and his Catholic army battles with Amalech and his army of heretics, we may like Moses assist our human forces with spiritual ones, it is most necessary that all good and zealous Catholics united in heart and will arm themselves incessantly with prayers and orisons, accompanied by contrition and repentance for having offended God, the amendment of evil ways, and a vow to serve and honor Him better in the future, without which the above-mentioned prayers cannot be agreeable to him... [Therefore,] Sunday after confession everybody will take and receive the precious body of our Lord, and all are exhorted to appease God's wrath by a true penitence and amendment of their ways, each according to his estate and vocation, that is to say that ecclesiastics shall give themselves over principally to exercising their sacred ministry with attention, reverence and devotion accompanied by exemplary living, laymen carrying arms shall abstain from pillaging, violence and blasphemy, and all shall be moved by the zeal which we owe to the defense of our religion to place nothing ahead of this cause, not our goods, not even our own lives.

Handbill posted around Rouen in
1591 by the cathedral chapter
(A.D.S.M., G.2476)

7

The *Sainte-Union* comes to power

The death in June 1584 of Henry III's younger brother, the duke of Anjou, dramatically altered France's political situation. There was little hope that Henry would ever beget an heir; special prayers for divine assistance in this matter had even been inserted into the liturgy at Rouen cathedral for an entire year, from 1581 through 1582, to no avail.[1] Anjou's death thus left as heir-apparent none other than Henry of Navarre, the political and military leader of the Protestants. Suddenly, the Huguenots appeared likely to gain through the vagaries of dynastic succession what they had never been able to achieve through persuasion or force of arms: domination of all France.

It was an alarming prospect for the country's Catholics, and especially so in a city such as Rouen which had already suffered a period of Huguenot domination and where English Catholic refugees telling tales of the recently intensified persecution in that country were frequent visitors. Although Navarre tried to reassure Catholic opinion with promises of toleration should he become king, experience and the English example both suggested that the abolition of the Mass and strong measures of persecution would follow a Protestant's accession. The possibility of Protestant domination had been remote for Rouen's Catholics since 1572. Suddenly it was a serious danger once more. But it was a danger of a different sort from the Protestant challenge of the 1560s. The threat did not come from within the city's walls, but from without, and the sporadic and disorganized mob violence which had been the core of the Catholics' response to the first Protestant challenge would no longer be adequate to meet the danger. Other means were needed if Navarre's accession was to be averted. Two soon emerged. Firstly, many of Rouen's inhabitants rallied to the political activism of the *Sainte-Union*, or Catholic League, which was quickly reconstituted in 1584, this time with a strong urban component, to provide Catholicism with the disciplined nationwide movement needed to meet the new political threat to the faith. Secondly, the city's Catholics threw themselves into a series of new processional and devotional activities which were introduced into the city

[1] A.D.S.M., G 2174, entry of Nov. 7, 1581. These prayers were requested by the king.

from 1588 onward. A striking revival of piety resulted, motivated clearly by a desire to deflect God's wrath by acts of contrition and thus spare the city the scourge of a heretic king. The next two chapters will examine each of these reactions in turn.

Our view of most of the major revolutionary upheavals in French history has tended to be the view from Paris, and of few has this been more true than the Catholic League. The early years of the movement in particular are known to us almost entirely from Parisian sources, for several exceptional participant accounts happen to lift the veil of secrecy that everywhere surrounded the organization's foundation high enough to reveal the clandestine activities of the initial knot of Parisian *ligueurs*, the Sixteen. From these we know that, not content to organize several thousand Parisian militants into neighborhood cells organized by *quartier* and *cinquantaine*, the Sixteen also sought to establish a network of like-minded groups throughout France. Delegates were dispatched to all leading provincial cities to urge Catholic zealots in each to create clandestine groups of their own, each of which was to be headed by a secret council of six men in regular correspondence with Paris. The League seems from the Parisian documents to have been the very prototype of a modern revolutionary party organized on a national scale.[1]

But how far did such a highly centralized party structure actually come to extend throughout the provinces? This is very difficult to know. Secret opposition parties which ultimately fail and are discredited rarely leave behind many documents which might compromise those involved in them. The scarcity of information is compounded in the case of the League because special efforts seem to have been taken to destroy all its papers.[2] The initial foundation, organization, and recruitment of the movement in the provinces consequently remains shrouded in mystery. In Rouen

[1] The clandestine activity of the Paris Sixteen is revealed by the *Dialogue d'entre le maheustre et le manant* (Paris, 1594) and the 'procez-verbal' of the king's spy Nicolas Poulain, printed in M. L. Cimber and F. Danjou, *Archives curieuses de l'histoire de France* (Paris, 1836), Vol. 11, pp. 289–323. There are numerous studies of the Paris League, of which the best are Paul Robiquet, *Paris et la Ligue* (Paris, 1886); DeLamar Jensen, *Diplomacy and Dogmatism: Bernardino de Mendoza and the Holy League* (Cambridge, Mass., 1964); and Peter M. Ascoli, 'The "Sixteen" and the Paris League, 1585–1591' (unpub. Ph.D. diss., University of California at Berkeley, 1971). H. G. Koenigsberger, 'The Organization of Revolutionary Parties in France and The Netherlands during the Sixteenth Century', *Journal of Modern History*, XXVII (1955), pp. 346–51, is the best discussion of the parallels between League organization and that of modern revolutionary parties, although the tradition of likening the League to modern revolutionary movements goes back at least to Alfred Maury, 'La Commune de Paris de 1588', *Revue des Deux Mondes*, XCV (1871), pp. 132–75.

[2] Sensing the decline of the League, members of the movement were taking steps as early as 1593 to prevent its papers from falling into hostile hands. A.D.S.M., B, Parlement, Registres Secrets – Rouen, entry of July 19, 1593. Following the fall of the League in Paris, all surviving pieces of League propaganda were ordered destroyed. Pierre de L'Estoile, *Mémoires-Journaux*, ed. Brunet, Champollion et al. (Paris, 1875–96), Vol. 4, p. vi.

virtually nothing can be ascertained about the League prior to its seizure of power in February 1589. We know that the Sixteen's envoy to Normandy, the lawyer Ameline, left Paris early in 1585.[1] He may have been one of the two men about whom Walsingham received word in England in May who had recently been expelled from Rouen for hatching plots for the 'holy and diabolic League'. (Dismayingly, Walsingham's informant, part of his extensive network of spies on the continent, entrusted the names of the two men to the bearer of his letter rather than committing them to paper.)[2] Whether or not Ameline succeeded in establishing a local League cell before leaving town remains unclear, however, as does the identity of most of those who might have joined such an association. Only one hint survives indicating that some sort of *Sainte-Union* grouping emerged in these early years of clandestinity, the comment of a member of the parlement justifying his behavior before the *ligueur* half of the court in 1593 in these terms: 'When the time came that there was a great risk and danger that the Catholic faith would suffer a great alteration by the negligence or malice of the late king Henry, I was one of the first to enter *the party of those who had united and come together for the defense of the faith*.'[3] This 'party...for the defense of the faith' may have had the tight structure and mass membership of the Paris League, but it is equally possible that it was simply a small, informal network of like-minded souls.

Whatever the constitution of this group, there can be no doubt that pro-League sentiment quickly became widespread in Rouen. The questions facing people in 1585 were largely ones of perception and trust. Navarre issued statements which sought to assure Catholics that he was not ill-disposed toward them, but could a Protestant ruler be expected not to harm the Catholic Church? Henry III was soon prompted into proclaiming his renewed desire to eliminate Calvinism, but could he be counted on to do so before Navarre succeeded to the throne? The answers men gave these questions determined in large measure how serious a threat to Catholicism they considered the possible accession of a Protestant king, and thus

[1] 'Procez-verbal de Poulain', p. 295.

[2] *Cal. S.P. For.*, 1584–5, p. 436. Walsingham's informant was François de Civille. One suspects that one of the two men, identified only by de Civille as being among Walsingham's 'greatest enemies', was the English Jesuit Robert Parsons, who was in Rouen in the early spring of 1585. *See here*, L. Hicks, ed., *Letters and Memorials of Father Robert Persons, S.J.*, Vol. 1, *to 1585*, Catholic Record Society Publication XXXIX (London, 1942), pp. lxvii–lxx.

[3] A.D.S.M., B, Parlement, Registres Secrets – Rouen, entry of June 19, 1593 (italics mine). In his study of the League in Burgundy, Henri Drouot also discusses the problems of determining whether or not local 'bureaus' of the League were established in the chief provincial cities during these years when the movement was first beginning to organize. Drouot was able to find evidence of one such group in Auxerre, which kept a role of adherents and corresponded regularly with Paris, and he is convinced that some sort of organization, formal or informal, was also established in other cities such as Dijon where there is no conclusive evidence of their existence. Henri Drouot, *Mayenne et la Bourgogne: Etude sur la Ligue en Bourgogne, 1587–1596* (Paris, 1937), pp. 134–6.

whether or not they thought it warranted to endanger the bonds holding society together by supporting a sworn association that might one day call upon them to defy their sovereign. For several reasons Rouen's Catholics were particularly predisposed to be fearful of a heretic king.

The propaganda of the *Sainte-Union* indicates the fears and grievances which contributed to the growth of *ligueur* sentiment. First, the fate of England's recusants was constantly cited as a warning. At precisely this time Elizabeth was stepping up her persecution of English Catholicism (the Act Against Jesuits and Seminary Priests dates from 1585); numerous works of *ligueur* propaganda stress that this is what could be expected from any Protestant ruler.[1] Several documents also indicate that France's Catholics feared that, once in power, the Huguenots would seek revenge for earlier atrocities such as the St Bartholomew's Day Massacre.[2] Finally, grievances over high taxes and the venality of office contributed to the movement's growth. The propaganda stressed that Henry III's past policies and behavior, particularly his fiscal measures and his ineffectual earlier wars against the Huguenots, had already shown him to be untrustworthy and tyrannical.[3] If this last argument was likely to meet with assent wherever people were feeling the pinch of taxation, the first two were particularly likely to appeal to a town such as Rouen. The intensity of the conflicts provoked locally in the 1560s and early 1570s meant that, even though anti-Huguenot sentiments may have lain dormant since then, they could easily be revived. As one of the provincial cities in which a local St Bartholomew's Day Massacre had occurred, fears of Huguenot revenge were naturally also particularly strong. Furthermore, from 1580 on, Rouen had become something of a center for English Catholic printing and plotting. Quite a few refugee Catholics had settled in the city, including an entire convent of nuns of the order of St Bridget; such tracts as Parson's *De Persecutione Anglicana* were printed in Rouen and then shipped to England via a highly organized smuggling network; and the presence of

[1] Louis Dorleans' pamphlet, *Advertissement des catholiques anglois aux catholiques françois du danger où ils sont de perdre leur religion et d'experimenter, comme en Angleterre, la cruauté des ministres, s'ils reçoivent à la couronne un Roy qui soit heretique* (Paris, 1586), reprinted in Cimber and Danjou, *Archives curieuses*, 1st ser., Vol. 11, is the most famous, but by no means the only, *ligueur* tract which cites the English example as a dire warning. The sufferings of England's Catholics were depicted in paintings and popular prints as well. *See here*, John Bossy, 'Elizabethan Catholicism: The Link with France' (unpub. Ph.D. diss., Cambridge University, 1960), pp. 176–90.

[2] On Catholic fears of a new St Bartholomew, *see* Frederic J. Baumgartner, *Radical Reactionaries: The Political Thought of the French Catholic League* (Geneva, 1975), p. 27; and F. Joüon des Longrais, ed. 'Information du Sénéchal de Rennes contre les Ligueurs 1589', *Bulletin et Mémoires de la Société Archéologique du Département d'Ille-et-Vilaine*, XLI (1911), p. 22, where it is clear that the *ligueurs* used warnings of Huguenot plans to massacre all the Catholics in their beds to foment the League uprising in Rennes.

[3] For the exploitation of grievances over taxation and venality of office in League propaganda, *see* Baumgartner, *Radical Reactionaries*, pp. 30–33. L'Estoile, *Mémoires-Journaux*, Vol. 2, p. 392, particularly stresses the importance of these issues in the growth of *ligueur* sentiment.

the refugees had led the local church authorities to organize several public processions to pray for the suffering brethren in England.[1] Few Rouennais could thus have escaped hearing about the persecution in England and drawing the appropriate lessons from it, especially as the persecution was presented in the most lurid terms. The combination of these factors was a potent one. The 'greatest part' of the populace was overtly pro-League by April 1585, according to a memorandum sent Henry III by Carrouges.[2]

The lieutenant-general's memorandum also provides a breakdown of *ligueur* sentiment among the different groups within the city. The clergy was highly suspect, Carrouges reported, and the large Spanish colony bore close watching. Particularly interesting is his analysis of the situation among the town's authorities. The parlement contained many who leaned toward the League, Carrouges warned. The Council of Twenty-Four, on the other hand, was more kindly disposed toward the king, even though it too was not entirely above suspicion. The parlement was a greater center of *ligueur* sentiment than the city council.

In reaction to the formation of the *Sainte-Union*, the crown and its agents took strong steps to guard its leading cities against attempts to surprise them. Within Rouen, Carrouges' first thought was to expel all Spaniards from the city. A measure to this effect was rescinded after the merchants convinced him of their lack of involvement in the city's internal affairs and their importance to the region's economy, but, not taking any chances, the lieutenant-general then imposed a 6 p.m. curfew on all non-residents and naturalized Frenchmen.[3] The night watch was also reinforced and all incoming ships subjected to a thorough search for hidden weapons.[4] To gain an even surer hold over the city, Henry III decided to dispatch to Rouen a substantial garrison commanded by the recently named new governor of Normandy, the royal favorite Joyeuse. Like most of Henry's stabs at ruling decisively, the idea was a poor one. Fear of an unruly company of royal troops within the city sparked predictable consternation. The Council of Twenty-Four showered the king with pleas against the garrison, and the irresolute monarch finally backed down from the scheme, a step interpreted by foreign observers at court as a serious defeat.[5] The king and governor both sent the city hasty letters assuring it that they would

1 A.D.S.M., G 2174, entry of Nov. 3, 1581; Hicks, ed., *Letters and Memorials of Persons*, p. 236; Bossy, 'Elizabethan Catholicism: The Link with France', pp. 78–91; Patrick McGrath, *Papists and Puritans under Elizabeth I* (London, 1967), pp. 188, 259; *Dictionary of National Biography* (Oxford, 1917–), Vol. 11, pp. 972–8, article 'John Leslie'.

2 B.N., MS Français 3358, fo. 42v. This memorandum is undated but the summary of it (B.N., MS Français 3358, fo. 78) reveals that it was written in early April 1585.

3 Ruiz, caja 104, 108, Francisco de Fontenada and Juan Pasqual to Simon Ruiz, May 6, 1585.

4 A.C.R., B 4, entries of April 23, 24, and 26, May 15, 1585.

5 A.C.R., A 20, entries of April 29 and May 23, 1585; René de Lucinge, *Lettres sur les débuts de la Ligue (1585)*, ed. Alain Dufour (Geneva–Paris, 1964), p. 73; Abel Desjardins, ed. *Négociations diplomatiques de la France avec la Toscane* (Paris, 1859–76), Vol. 4, p. 568.

never dream of doubting its loyalty or burdening it with soldiers. Joyeuse came to the city alone.[1]

The strength of the League gave Henry no choice but to make concessions to it. His retreat on the garrison issue was one indication of this; the edict of Nemours announced in July 1585 was further proof. By its terms Navarre was formally excluded from the line of succession to the throne, a new campaign was announced against the Huguenot strongholds in the Midi, and the exercise of the Reformed religion was outlawed throughout the country. Given six months in which to convert or to emigrate, most of the members of Rouen's now-small Reformed Church chose to go to England or Zeeland.[2] Fireworks helped celebrate the edict of Nemours in Normandy's capital, and one observer reported the city's Catholics to be 'very happy and content' at the subsequent departure of the Protestants.[3]

But the enthusiasm provoked by Henry III's new policy soon faded as the campaign against the Protestants bogged down into the usual wearying skirmishing that produced little in the way of tangible results other than higher taxes. New levies imposed in 1586 to pay for the renewed warfare were so numerous that the provincial estates protested that the only thing left untaxed was the air people breathed.[4] Throughout much of the province the tax collectors had to resort to force to raise the sums demanded.[5] In Lower Normandy, an important anti-fiscal, anti-war peasant uprising flared up, the revolt of the *gautiers*.

A concatenation of economic difficulties made the higher taxes of these years even harder to bear. The reopening of hostilities in France and Philip II's seizure of all English ships in Spain brought the pirates of La Rochelle and Plymouth back into the Channel in force in 1585. Before the year was out 120 privateering vessels were reportedly preying on French and Spanish shipping, creating fears among the Iberian merchants in Rouen that the entire trade of the Indies would be ruined. When a fleet of ships specially outfitted by Normandy's merchants to deal with the problem failed to make the seas any safer, the king had to resort once again to the tactic of seizing

[1] A.C.R., A 20, entries of May 5 and June 1, 1585; A.C.R., Chartrier, tiroir 400 (1), Henry III to *échevins*, May 25, 1585; tiroir 400 (2), Joyeuse to *échevins*, May 30, 1585. After Joyeuse's arrival a special *assemblée générale* was held in which the windows of the Hôtel de Ville were flung open so that the crowd in the courtyard could hear the duke personally report that the king had never so much as thought of sending a garrison to the city. This was merely a rumor concocted to stir up trouble, the duke asserted.

[2] Ruiz, caja 104, 113, Francisco de Fontaneda and Juan Pasqual to Simon Ruiz, Nov. 10, 1585, a report worthy of considerable credence since these merchants had frequent business dealings with the local Protestants.

[3] A.C.R., A 20, entry of July 23, 1585; Ruiz, caja 104, 110, Fontaneda and Pasqual to Ruiz, Aug. 2, 1585.

[4] Charles de Robillard de Beaurepaire, ed., *Cahiers des Etats de Normandie sous le règne d'Henry III*, publications of the Société de l'Histoire de Normandie XX (Rouen, 1888), Vol. 2, p. 159.

[5] *Ibid.*, p. 186; Bouquet, ed. *Documents concernant Neufchâtel-en-Bray*, p. 55.

all English ships in French harbors and staying trade with the British Isles.[1] An extremely tight money market also impeded commerce throughout these years. Worst of all, the harvest failed twice consecutively in 1585 and 1586. Grain prices skyrocketed to the highest levels in living memory, and efforts to alleviate the shortage by importing Baltic rye were hampered by the English privateering. Britain, too, had felt the effects of the bad weather, and in such periods of dearth it was every nation for itself; at least 16 ships laden with Danzig rye destined for Rouen were intercepted and taken to England, where the grain was seized and sold.[2] A mortality crisis as grave as the dreadful famine of 1522 resulted. An English ship captain returning from the city in August 1587 reported: '. . . they dye in evrie streete and at evrie gate, morning and eveninge, by viii or xii in a place, so that the like hath not byne hearde of. And the poore doth not onely die so in the streete, but the riche also in their bedde by 10 or 12 in a daye.'[3] Parish account books show that Rouen's gravediggers had to work at more than twice their normal pace in 1586–7.[4] As always happened, the subsistence crisis also provoked a slump in the demand for manufactured goods; so much of an average artisan's income went solely to buy food that nothing remained for clothing or other less immediately essential items. Cloth manufacturing consequently was reported to have virtually ceased throughout the *généralité* in 1587.[5] Nearly a fifth of the city's population was on the relief rolls at the height of the crisis.

The famine probably had the effect of intensifying dissatisfaction with

[1] Philip Benedict, 'Rouen's Foreign Trade During the Era of the Religious Wars (1560–1600)', forthcoming.

[2] B.N., MS Français 3358, fos. 50, 52, and 57, Carrouges to Henry III, June 17 and 25 and July 31, 1587. *See also* R. C. Anderson, ed., *Letters of the Fifteenth and Sixteenth Centuries from the Archives of Southampton*, publication of the Southampton Record Society (Southampton, 1921), p. 117. The movement of grain prices throughout these years is charted anxiously in the anonymous manuscript journal, B.M.R., MS M 41. The price rose rapidly from about 5 *écus* per *mine* to 16 or 18 *écus* within the month of April 1586. Thereafter it fluctuated between 10 and 18 *écus* for over a year depending upon the success of the authorities in requisitioning grain from the surrounding countryside and of the ship captains in evading the English privateers.

[3] S. P. Dom. 12/203, no. 12.

[4] Many parish account books note the number of burials in the parish each year. In the seven parishes for which good records exist at this time, there were 365 burials in 1587. The average over the preceding six years had been 162 burials per year. A.D.S.M., G 6245 (St André-de-la-Ville); 6341–2 (St Cande-le-Vieil); 6616–18 (St Godard); 6727–9 (St Jean); 6800–6802 (St Laurent); 7166–9 (St Michel); 7373–4 (Notre-Dame-de-la-Ronde); 7754–94 (St Vivien). Guy Bois, *Crise du féodalisme: économie rurale et démographie en Normandie orientale du début du 14e siècle au milieu du 16e siècle* (Paris, 1976), p. 335, provides a graph of the number of burials in St Michel for the entire period 1495–1590 which underlines the exceptional severity of the crisis of 1522. Unfortunately, this parish's records contain a gap precisely in 1587, so the gravity of the crisis at the two dates cannot be compared. The records for St Laurent, which also contain an uninterrupted series of accounts stretching back to 1520, reveal 63 burials in 1587–8. Again 1522 emerges as the worst previous crisis, but in this parish at least the earlier crisis was not so severe. Forty-five burials are recorded. No other mortality crisis in the intervening years compares in seriousness.

[5] H. Saint-Denis, *Histoire d'Elbeuf* (Elbeuf, 1894), Vol. 2, p. 317.

Henry III. At least one *ligueur* pamphlet blamed the disaster on the continued presence of heretics in France.[1] The worst of the economic crisis was nonetheless over before the first great political crisis of the League arrived. A good harvest in 1587 and the arrival of ships laden with Baltic grain returned prices to pre-crisis levels by August 1587. The trade dispute with England was patched over at about the same time.[2] The long and anxious lines in the Halles and the hordes of unemployed people working on the *fossés* were thus gone when the news suddenly came from Paris that the inhabitants of the capital had taken to the barricades and driven out the king and the Swiss guards he had unexpectedly stationed there on the night of May 12, 1588.

Would Rouen open its gates to the refugee king? The first moment of choice between commitment to the League and fidelity to the crown had come. Both Henry III and the rebellious Parisians hastened to send the other cities of the realm their versions of what had transpired on the 'Day of the Barricades'. Even before trouble had begun Henry had prudently dispatched one set of letters to the Rouennais explaining why he had been compelled to introduce troops into Paris; now he sent several *commissaires* to Normandy (among them Jacques-Auguste de Thou) to try to reassure his subjects further of the benevolence of his intentions.[3] The Parisians set out their side of the story in a long letter written by the *bureau de ville*, freshly purged of all royalists. The king's pernicious counsellors, they explained, had slipped troops into the city, intending to put it to sack. Divine intervention had saved the capital. Reminding the Rouennais of the close commercial links which bound their cities, the Parisians urged them not to endanger these bonds by siding with the king.[4]

Rouen's authorities reacted initially with caution, neither aligning the city openly with the *ligueurs* in Paris nor protesting overmuch their devotion to their king. The monarch, who first retired to Chartres, realized that swift action was needed if he was to keep the allegiance of his cities. Because of its strategic position midway between the capital and the English Channel, soon to be filling up with the galleons of the Invincible Armada, Rouen became the special object of his attentions. On May 26 Henry wrote to assure the city that he was favorably inclined toward its recent petition urging the suppression of several prospective new offices in the *vicomté de l'eau*.[5] Two weeks later he repealed several taxes, including the onerous

[1] Baumgartner, *Radical Reactionaries*, p. 32.

[2] B.M.R., MS M 41; *Cal. S.P. For.*, 1586–8, p. 329.

[3] A.C.R., Chartrier, tiroir 400 (1), Henry III to *échevins*, May 12, 1588; A.D.S.M., G 3718, Henry to cathedral chapter, May 26, 1588; G 2176, entry of June 4, 1588; Jacques-Auguste de Thou, *Histoire universelle* (The Hague, 1740), Vol. 7, pp. 223–5.

[4] François Bonnardot, ed. *Registres des délibérations du Bureau de la Ville de Paris* (Paris, 1902), Vol. 9, pp. 139–40.

[5] A.C.R., Chartrier, tiroir 400 (1), Henry III to *échevins*, May 26, 1588.

duty recently imposed on linen and canvas, and ordered the prompt payment of all *rentes*, which in some cases were years overdue.[1] In the meantime, the king's friends within the city, notably Carrouges and the first president of the parlement, Claude Groulart, worked patiently to convince the Council of Twenty-Four to side openly with the crown. Their efforts were successful; on June 10 Rouen sent a deputation to the king thanking him for his generosity toward the city and inviting him to visit it.[2] Henry entered Rouen three days later. Enthusiastic crowds lined the streets to greet him with cries of '*Vive le roi!*'[3]

Henry III's month-long sojourn in the Norman capital provided the occasion for both monarch and city to make ostentatious gestures of devotion to one another. The city entertained Henry sumptuously with a dinner to which '*les plus signalles damoiselles*' were invited '*pour dresser le bal*'. Mock naval battles were staged on the Seine for his amusement.[4] In return Henry showered favors on those of Rouen's inhabitants whose allegiance might be critical if push came to shove, granting a raise in the salary and perquisites of the members of the city's privileged militia companies and several *conseillers-échevins*.[5] So that the populace might remark on his devotion to Catholicism, he also made it his practice to go on foot to Mass at different churches throughout the city.[6] Hopes that an open confrontation might yet be averted were apparently still stronger within the Rouennais' breasts than scepticism about the king's motives, for all available sources stress the warmth with which the monarch was received.[7] Despite the heavy taxation of the past years and the uncertainty about the succession question, there was still a divinity about the king that

[1] A.C.R., A 20, entry of June 9, 1588.

[2] A.C.R., A 20, entry of June 10, 1588. Groulart attempts to claim all of the credit for himself for persuading the city to invite Henry to visit it and accuses Carrouges of working to discourage the king from coming. Claude Groulart, *Mémoires*, Michaud and Poujoulat, Vol. 11, p. 554. His memoirs are, however, often distorted and always self-serving; they cannot be trusted. Etienne Pasquier gives the credit for opening Rouen to the king entirely to Carrouges. Etienne Pasquier, *Lettres historiques pour les années 1556–1594*, ed., D. Thickett (Geneva, 1966), p. 317. The truth is probably that both Carrouges and Groulart were championing the king's cause.

[3] Charles de Robillard de Beaurepaire, ed., *Séjour de Henri III à Rouen* (Rouen, 1870), p. 5.

[4] A.C.R., A 20, entry of June 20, 1588; Jean de Seuille, *Brief discours sur la bonne et joyeuse reception faicte à la majesté du Roy par ses très-fidelles et obeissants sujects de la ville de Rouen* (Rouen, 1588), reprinted in Robillard de Beaurepaire, ed., *Séjour de Henri III*, passim; de Thou, *Histoire universelle*, Vol. 7, pp. 236–7.

[5] A.D.S.M., B, Cour des Aides, Mémorial no. 9, fos. 94–5; A.D.S.M., 5 E 117, fos. 31ff; Lebeurier, *Etat des anoblis*, pp. xiv, 116.

[6] De Thou, *Histoire universelle*, Vol. 7, pp. 236–7.

[7] In addition to de Seuille's perhaps propagandistic *Discours sur la bonne et joyeuse reception faicte à la majesté du Roy*, we have the comment of an anonymous memoirist that the king 'fut reçu avec joie et allégresse par les eschevins et bourgeois, ensemble de tout le clergé et de la judicature'. 'Journal historique de Rouen, extrait d'un manuscrit de la bibliothèque de l'abbé De la Rue', *Revue de Rouen* (1840), p. 254. The king himself wrote the duke of Nevers, 'Je suis à Roan, ou je été tres bien receu et veu de tous mes subjets d'icelle ville.' Robillard de Beaurepaire, ed., *Séjour de Henri III*, p. 6.

awakened the loyalty of his subjects in the provinces when he showed himself to them in person.

Henry spent the most important part of his time in Rouen negotiating with the League and its leaders. The upshot of these negotiations was the edict of Union of July. Henry vowed never to allow a heretic to succeed to the throne, to pardon all participants in the Day of the Barricades, to step up the military campaign against the Protestants, and to grant the League the cities of Orleans and Bourges as *places de sûreté*. In return, Paris vowed submission to his authority and all changes which had taken place in the municipal government of the rebellious city following the Day of the Barricades were annulled.[1] On July 21 the king left Rouen to return to the Louvre, once again his.[2]

The subsequent months saw the election of delegates and the drawing up of *cahiers* for the Estates-General called at Blois. Politics seemed to be moving along constitutional avenues once again as the assembly opened in October and Rouen's delegates presented their complaints about venal offices and heavy taxation, and urged that the duty of the king to maintain the Catholic faith be recognized as a fundamental law of the kingdom.[3] Then came the event which revealed with shocking swiftness that all of the eagerly received promises which Henry had made, first in Rouen and subsequently in the early weeks of the Estates-General – to defend the Catholic faith, to reduce taxes, to suppress superfluous offices, to see that the Council of Trent was published in France – were just so many hypocritical maneuvers 'to have the end of *messieurs de Guise*'.[4] The king had decided that the only way to shake off the tutelage of the duke of Guise, which was growing stronger with each passing day of the Estates, was to arrange for his assassination. Royal guards surprised and killed the duke on December 23, and his brother the cardinal of Guise met the same fate the next day. The cardinal of Bourbon, Rouen's archbishop and the man proclaimed heir-apparent by the League, was imprisoned. Henry exulted at the death of the 'king of Paris', but not for long. Far more than the Day of the Barricades, the assassination of the Guises was the signal for general revolt throughout France.

The mask had been torn off. Henry's ill-will toward the League was visible for all to see. No longer were the king's evil counsellors the target

1 *Edict du Roy pour l'establissement d'un asseuré repos au faict de la Religion Catholique...et union de ses sujects catholiques avec sa Majeste pour l'extirpation des scismes et hérésies par tout son Royaume*...(Rouen, 1588) (Printed handbill inserted in A.C.R., A 20); de Thou, *Histoire universelle*, Vol. 7, p. 238.

2 A.C.R., A 20, entry of July 21, 1588.

3 For Rouen's *doléances*, see *Harangue faicte au Roy par un depputé particulier de la Ville de Rouen dans son cabinet à Bloys, le 27 Octobre 1588* (Paris, 1588), passim.

4 The quotation is from a Rouennais journal, B.M.R., MS M 41.

of League pamphleteers; now it became the 'tyrant' himself who was attacked. Word of the murders at Blois led at once to a municipal revolution in Paris far more thorough and radical than that which followed the Day of the Barricades. Other towns soon followed: Amiens, Reims, Dijon, Orleans, Toulouse, Marseille in the first weeks, many others in subsequent months. The doctors of the Sorbonne met in solemn conclave and unanimously declared the king guilty of violating the public trust in a manner which endangered the true religion, the edict of Union, and the natural liberties of those who participated in the Estates-General. The people were therefore declared released from the duty of obedience.[1] Certain pamphleteers went even further in their attacks on 'Henry de Valois', as the king was now simply called by those to whom he was ex-king. 'He is unworthy not only of the crown, but unworthy of life', cried one.[2]

When the news of the assassinations at Blois first reached Rouen, it provoked 'great crying and lamentation among the people'.[3] But Carrouges' prompt action prevented any initial stirrings of revolt. The lieutenant-general quickly stationed men throughout the city to inform him at the first hint of unrest, exiled or disarmed all leading ex-Huguenots to reassure Catholic opinion, forbade preachers to mention the recent assassinations from the pulpit, and ordered the cathedral chapter to cancel a procession it had planned to pray for the release of its archbishop lest the procession overly inflame popular opinion against the king.[4] Rouen again adopted a position of neutrality, neither declaring itself for the League nor allowing royal troops into the city.

This posture was maintained for over a month, but with each passing week it became less and less tenable. As in the wake of the Day of the Barricades, both sides again rushed to inform the Rouennais of events as they saw them. The king wrote that time and again his clemency had led him to overlook the duke of Guise's evil designs against him; finally, however, these had grown so bold that he had been compelled to punish the duke. Henry urged that the *conseillers-échevins* ensure that nothing be done to the prejudice of the obedience owed him.[5] The *ligueur échevins* of both Paris and Amiens meanwhile wrote to denounce the murders at Blois as the most monstrous of all of Henry's repeated violations of his promises

[1] 'Advis et résolution de la Faculté de Théologie de Paris', L. Cimber and F. Danjou, eds., *Archives curieuses de l'histoire de France*, 1st ser. (Paris, 1834–7), Vol. 12, pp. 349–53.

[2] Anon., 'Exhortation à la Saincte-Union des Catholiques de France', *Mémoires de la Ligue sous Henry III et Henry IIII rois de France* (n.p., 1602), Vol. 3, p. 538.

[3] 'Journal historique de Rouen', p. 256.

[4] A.C.R., A 20, entry of Dec. 29, 1588; A.D.S.M., G 2176, entry of Dec. 30, 1588; *Cal.S.P.For.*, 1589, p. 114; Archives of the English College of Valladolid, Serie 2, L 5, 13, Elizabeth Sanders to Sir Francis Englefield, 'A Note of such Accidents as hath befell us in Fraunce'; B.N., MS Français 23295 ('Histoire de la Ligue'), fo. 473.

[5] A.C.R., A 20, entry of Dec. 29, 1588.

to defend the Catholic faith, entreating Rouen to join them in their attempt to avert the ruin of the Church, 'which can plainly be seen to be coming at full gallop'.[1] Naturally there might be those who balked at taking up arms against their legitimate sovereign; to assuage their consciences, the Parisians sent along a copy of the Sorbonne resolution.[2]

The exhortations of *ligueurs* outside the city were reinforced by the preaching of the Catholic clergy within Rouen. The silence which Carrouges attempted to impose on the pulpit following the events at Blois did not last. Two Jesuit fathers had been in Rouen since August, when they had been sent from Paris by Michel de Monchy, the dean of the cathedral and future chief of the League's *Conseil de l'Union* of Normandy. At that time moderation still prevailed within the cathedral chapter and the Jesuits had been forbidden to preach.[3] Now it was one of these Jesuits, Jacques Commolet, who first dared to defy the ban on mentioning the martyred Catholic champions from the pulpit. Appropriately, he chose to do so on St Thomas of Canterbury's day (December 29). The emotion which the assassination of the two Guise princes had aroused is clear from the account of his sermon left us by one of the refugee English nuns of the order of St Bridget:

> ...when he came into the pulpytt, all eyeis and mowthes gapying upon hym, the good man was in such a passyion that he seemyd lyke to burst and could scars bryng out hys words for weepyng, the passyon of that tyme had so alteryd hys voyce. Hys matter was of blessyd St Thomas, declaryng to the people the cause of hys martirdome in the behalfe of Chrystes churche, and of the quarrel betwyxt hym and the kyng, and how hys braynes were stroke out uppon the pavement before ye alter. Thys thyng was so apt for hys purpose that the people could by and by apply ytt that the preacher had no soner named the slaughter of theyr 2 prynces but thatt all fell out into weepyng, and the preacher ther sobyng allowde could saye no more. Butt after a preatty space, stryving with himself to speake, he clappyng of hys hands cryed aloude, o pover eglese galicane, and so came downe, the people and all so movyd as we never have seene nor shall see ye lyke.[4]

Commolet does not appear to have been punished for this sermon, and in the ensuing weeks numerous other sermons and processions were held, fanning Catholic emotion even higher.[5] Furthermore, with Paris upstream and Le Havre downstream already controlled by the League, sentiment in favor of the *Sainte-Union* was also growing for purely pragmatic reasons of trade and safety. Commerce had virtually come to a

[1] A.D.S.M., G 3716, *échevins* of Amiens to cathedral chapter of Rouen, Feb. 4, 1589; A.C.R., Chartrier, tiroir 400 (2), *échevins* of Paris to *échevins* of Rouen, Jan. 16, 1589.

[2] Bonnardot, ed., *Registres des délibérations de Paris*, Vol. 9, p. 273.

[3] A.D.S.M., G 2176, entry of August 13, 1588.

[4] Archives of the English College of Valladolid, Serie 2, L 5, 13.

[5] 'Journal historique de Rouen', p. 257.

standstill since the killings at Blois, and many of the city's merchants began to feel that declaring the city openly for the League was the only way ships could begin to move up and down the Seine again.[1] The League was growing stronger with each passing day.

The coup which finally swept the *Sainte-Union* into power indicates a degree of organization within the movement and thus reinforces suspicion that a clandestine bureau of the League had been in existence in the city since 1585. According to the sympathetic manuscript history of the League now in the Bibliothèque Nationale, the sequence of events leading up to Rouen's Day of the Barricades was initiated when letters written by Carrouges and a royalist member of the *chambre des comptes* urging the king quickly to send troops fell into the hands of the prior of the Carmelites.[2] He relayed these to Richard Regnault, seigneur du Pont, a member of the parlement and one of the men subsequently to head the *ligueur* governments within the city. Du Pont in turn met with several of the principal *ligueurs*. Together they decided that prompt action of their own was needed to prevent the city from falling into the king's hands. A degree of scepticism about this account is certainly justified; there may have been no intercepted letter, for, as de Thou remarks, rumors of an imminent royalist or even Huguenot attempt to seize the city were 'everywhere the signal for revolt'.[3] Accurate or not, however, reports that troops were advancing on the city certainly were effective in stirring the populace to act. On February 4 *ligueur* partisans ran through the streets spreading word that royal soldiers were approaching and calling the people to arms. Barricades quickly went up throughout town. On the following day, a Sunday, a large religious procession was staged. As it wound its way toward the Franciscan monastery in the heart of the city, the procession suddenly metamorphosed into a rebellion. The participating harquebusiers and militia members rushed to the Hôtel de Ville, located just a block from the monastery, seized control of it, and obtained the keys to the city gates and the municipal munitions supply. Once the militia had secured the strategic points within the city, the League leaders moved quickly to consolidate their victory before matters got out of hand and looting began. Du Pont went to the abbey of St Ouen, where Carrouges was installed with thirty of his men,

[1] B.N., MS Français 23295 ('Histoire de la Ligue'), fo. 475; Ruiz, caja 136, 233, Francisco de Fontaneda and Juan Pasqual to Simon Ruiz, Jan. 27, 1589; caja 129, 56, same, March 13, 1589; Benedict, 'Rouen's Foreign Trade', forthcoming.

[2] B.N., MS Français 23295, fos. 473–4. This anonymous work, one of the best sources available on the League in the provinces, comes originally from the library of the Oratorians in Paris, a religious order whose ranks included a number of descendants of the leading Paris *ligueurs*. Its author is clearly a devoted Catholic who was pro-League. Sections of the work have been printed in an excellent edition by Charles Valois, *Histoire de la Ligue, oeuvre inédite d'un contemporain* (Paris, 1914), but unfortunately the parts of the work concerning the movement in the provinces are omitted.

[3] De Thou, *Histoire universelle*, Vol. 7, p. 403.

to negotiate with the lieutenant-governor. In the ensuing parley between 'those who simply wanted to assure their safety [Carrouges and his men] and those who wanted after dissipating the volatile unrest of the people, to remain the masters [du Pont and the other leaders of the League]',[1] Carrouges was persuaded to relinquish control of the two royal strongholds. Just hours later, the militia marched into the Château and Vieux Palais in full parade order, banners flying.[2] Henry III's attempt to buy their loyalty had failed. For the second time in the Wars of Religion, Rouen had risen in revolt and driven out the king's lieutenant.

Who were the men behind this uprising? The identity of the local pillars of the League is finally revealed for the first time by the account of a special assembly held on February 7 to pack an enlarged city council with men loyal to the *Sainte-Union.* The town scribe's account of this gathering conveys his alarm and bewilderment at the unwonted events of the day.[3] Summoned unexpectedly from his house, he was surprised to find on arriving at a crowded Hôtel de Ville that the *échevins* were not seated at their desks as usual, but were instead on the bench of the former *conseillers.* A list of men said to have been nominated by the four quarters of the city to govern it in conjunction with the 6 *conseillers-échevins* then in office was thrust into his hands, and he was ordered to read it aloud. On the list were 4 representatives each of the church, the city's judicial officials, and the bourgeois:

for the church:

Pierre Sécard, curé of St Maclou

Claude Sécard, his brother, canon of the cathedral

Michel de Monchy, dean of the cathedral and *conseiller-clerc* in the parlement

Jean Dadré, *théologal* and penitentiary of the cathedral[4]

for *la justice*:

Jean de Bauquemare, seigneur de Bourdeny, *maître des requêtes*

Jacques de Bauquemare, seigneur de Mesnil-Vitot, his brother, *président aux requêtes*

[1] B.N., MS Français, 23295, fo. 474.

[2] The account of Rouen's Day of the Barricades is based above all on *Ibid.*, fos. 473–5; and Albert Sarrazin, ed., *Abrégé d'un journal historique de Rouen* (Rouen, 1872), pp. 33–4. A rather detailed account of the uprising may also be found in the contemporary pamphlet, *Les connivences de Henry de Valois avec Monsieur de Charouges Gouverneur de la ville de Rouen* (Paris, 1589), but this work, which probably was written as well as published in Paris, is so unreliable that it does not even provide the correct date of the uprising. It seems to be this pamphlet which is the source for Floquet's assertion that the barricades were followed by a massacre of several Protestants, an assertion for which I have found no supporting evidence. Amable Floquet, *Histoire du Parlement de Normandie* (Rouen, 1840–42), Vol. 3, p. 289.

[3] A.C.R., A 20, entry of Feb. 7, 1589.

[4] Dadré shared this position with the provincial of the Carmelite order.

Richard Regnault, seigneur du Pont, *conseiller* in the parlement
Jean du Perron, seigneur de Benesville, *conseiller* in the parlement

for the bourgeois:

Jean Voison, seigneur de Guenouville, *secrétaire du roi* and ex-*conseiller moderne*
M. Gueroult, *secrétaire du roi*
Etienne de la Val, ex-*conseiller moderne*
M. de Bornes.

After these names were read aloud the men were all confirmed in office by general acclamation.

Further changes were made in the personnel of the city government two weeks later at a second assembly.[1] One of the 6 *conseillers-échevins* in place, Bigot d'Esteville, had refused to participate in the original assembly on February 7 and had subsequently been 'revoked by the people'. De Mesnil-Vitot, one of the representatives of the judicial officials, had fallen ill. A militia captain had left town. Replacements were thus needed to fill three positions. Those initially elected were, as Bigot's replacement, Jehan Puchot, seigneur de la Pommeraye, an ex-*conseiller moderne*; as de Mesnil-Vitot's replacement, Despinez, seigneur de Canteleu, *conseiller aux requêtes*; and as militia captain, Guillaume Mautalent. But Mautalent's election was rescinded 'at the clamor of the people', and Jehan de la Haye was named in his stead. The doctrine of popular sovereignty which was used to justify the revolt against Henry III was also a useful tool when the League needed to replace officials hostile to it. The 'people', however, may not have had an absolutely free rein to name whomever they pleased to office. As the meeting drew to a close, a *priseur de vin* named Robert Heultes had the courage to point out that the hall was lined with armed men. If the inhabitants had been allowed to choose their representatives in free parish assemblies as they normally did, he claimed, other individuals would have been selected. Heultes was quickly hustled out of the room and the assembly voted a disavowal of his claim that it was being intimidated, 'recognizing the members of the council to be *fort gens de bien*'. The disavowal notwithstanding, the incident suggests a pattern familiar to twentieth-century eyes. A revolutionary party which had taken power in the name of popular sovereignty was now, once in power, dictating to the people the terms of their sovereignty.

The radicalism of League political theory and of the movement in Paris has often blinded historians to the eminent notability of the League's leaders in many provincial cities.[2] The men swept into power in Rouen's

[1] A.C.R., A 20, entry of Feb. 23, 1589.

[2] Thus, Howell A. Lloyd has written in his recent account of the League's takeover in Rouen that the actions taken in the wake of the uprising 'struck at the oligarchic character of [the] governmental

municipal revolution were hardly newcomers to the positions of authority. Unlike in Paris, where only one of the eight men brought into the *bureau de ville* by the League was a member of a sovereign court and most were mere *procureurs* or merchants of the second rank,[1] Rouen's new rulers were drawn almost exclusively from the very highest strata of society. Most had already exercised a measure of political responsibility within the city. Three were full-fledged *parlementaires*, two more were members of the court's *chambre des requêtes*, and yet three others had already been *conseillers-échevins* at some time in the past. Two bore the title of *secrétaire du roi*, one was a *maître des requêtes*, and seven owned a *seigneurie* and the title that went with it. The clerics were all officials of the cathedral chapter or, in one case, the parish priest of the city's largest parish. Of all the members of the new city council only the mysterious Monsieur de Bornes is not immediately identifiable as already part of Rouen's power elite. This was no group of outsiders catapulted into power by the *Sainte-Union*. The same pattern seems common to many provincial cities which passed over to the side of the League at this time: rather than being the uprising of 'outs' frustrated by the closure of access to the sovereign courts and their growing power over municipal affairs that Drouot describes in his classic study of Burgundy, the League takeover represented the triumph of one faction of 'ins' over another.[2]

structure'. Howell A. Lloyd, *The Rouen Campaign, 1590–1592: Politics, Warfare, and the Early-Modern State* (Oxford, 1973), p. 128. As we shall see, they did nothing of the sort. In general, Lloyd's account of events within Rouen must be used with some caution. His study provides an excellent view of the international context and diplomatic and military aspects of the Rouen campaign from 1590 to 1592, but his grip on the local scene is often less sure. For instance, the representatives of *la justice* named to the council were hardly, as he asserts, 'lawyers'; Rouen's parlement was not yet a 'rump *parlement*' in February and March; the Monchy family came from Artois, not Normandy; the '*établissements de Rouen*' did not govern the structure of municipal government.

[1] The men chosen as Paris' *échevins* either following the Day of the Barricades or after the assassination of the Guises included four merchants, two *procureurs*, a *général des monnaies*, and a *maître des comptes*. J. H. M. Salmon, 'The Paris Sixteen, 1584–94: The Social Analysis of a Revolutionary Movement', *Journal of Modern History*, XLIV (1972), 548–54. Salmon identifies the merchants as being 'of wealth and status', but the more detailed research of Denis Richet shows that few of the merchants in the League leadership came from the aristocracy of commerce. Denis Richet, 'Aspects socio-culturels des conflits religieux à Paris dans la seconde moitié du XVIe siècle', *Annales: E.S.C.*, XXXII (1977), p. 779 and personal communication.

[2] The explanation of the social tensions underlying the League provided by Henri Drouot over forty years ago in one of the first of the great French local histories, *Mayenne et la Bourgogne*, remains to this day the most compelling social explanation of the movement. Essentially Drouot's thesis is this. Toward the end of the sixteenth century access to the parlements became steadily more difficult due to the growing practice of passing offices down within the court from father to son. A main avenue of social advancement was thus blocked just at the moment when the economic difficulties caused by the Wars of Religion were prompting more and more families to direct their sons away from trade and toward careers in law. Aspirations for social mobility were frustrated, breeding a revolutionary situation which expressed itself in the wake of the League's triumph in an attack on the powers of the parlements and a reassertion of the authority of the municipal governments that had been steadily usurped by the sovereign courts over the course of the century. (Drouot, *Mayenne et la Bourgogne*, pp. 43–55, 334–43.)

Three identifiable characteristics distinguished the *ligueurs* within Rouen's governing elite from their royalist counterparts.[1] The first, hardly surprisingly, was a strong commitment to Roman Catholicism in its most uncompromising form. Most of the men brought into the city government by the League remain shadowy figures about whom very little is known, but all who have left additional traces in the surviving records appear to

Dijon provided Drouot's field of observation, and his thesis has since received corroboration from the research on Paris carried out by Richet and Salmon. Such authors as Roland Mousnier and Salvo Mastellone seem to accept Drouot's view without question. (Roland Mousnier, *La vénalité des offices sous Henri IV et Louis XIII* (Rouen, 1945), pp. 544–8; Salvo Mastellone, *Venalità e machiavellismo in Francia (1572–1610): All'origine della mentalità politica borghese* (Florence, 1972), pp. 148–9.) But Drouot's model does not fit the facts of the case in Rouen. Not only was the League led by men already in positions of power rather than those on the fringes of power like the Paris Sixteen; there had also occurred no closing of access to offices in the province's high courts in the decades prior to the League. As the table below shows, over two-thirds of the *conseillers* entering the parlement of Normandy in the years 1581–90 still came from families not previously represented on the tribunal, and the percentage of those who inherited a position had risen but little since the 1520s.

New *conseillers* accepted into the parlement of Rouen, 1511–90

1. Member of a family new to the parlement.
2. Office inherited.
3. Member of a family already represented in the court, although not inheriting the position.

	1	*2*	*3*		*1*	*2*	*3*		*1*	*2*	*3*
1511–20	20	1	1	1541–50	28	3	4	1571–80	33	4	2
1521–30	24	3	2	1551–60	19	3	1	1581–90	22	4	4
1531–40	12	2	2	1561–70	29	2	2				

It was the half-century *following* the League which witnessed the closure of access to the court in Normandy; between 1594 and 1640 only 67 of 163 new *conseillers* came from families not already represented within the court. (Henri de Frondeville, *Les conseillers du Parlement de Normandie: Recueil généalogique* (Paris–Rouen, 1960–64), Vol. 2, passim, and Vol. 3, p. v.) Finally, as we shall see in Chapter 9, the period of the League did not witness an increase in the power of Rouen's municipal government at the expense of the parlement. If anything, the opposite occurred. There are many other cities as well where the League seems to have remained controlled by urban notables throughout the period of *Sainte-Union* domination and where the social tensions discussed by Drouot never seem to have appeared, e.g., Lyon, Poitiers, Abbeville, and the short-lived case of Rennes. *See here* André Latreille et al., *Histoire de Lyon et du Lyonnais* (Toulouse, 1975), p. 195; Henri Ouvré, 'Essai sur l'histoire de la Ligue à Poitiers', *Mémoires de la Société des Antiquaires de l'Ouest* (1854), passim; Ernest Prarond, *La Ligue à Abbeville, 1576–1594* (Paris, 1868–73), Vol. 2, passim; F. Joüon des Longrais, ed., 'Information du Sénéchal de Rennes contre les Ligueurs 1589', *Bulletin et Mémoires de la Société Archéologique du Département d'Ille-et-Vilaine*, XLI (1911), pp. 9–10; and now Robert R. Harding, *Anatomy of a Power Elite: The Provincial Governors of Early Modern France* (New Haven, 1978), pp. 93–4.

[1] In the analysis that follows of the factors underlying the division between *ligueur* and royalist, it has been possible to investigate only a few of the characteristics which may have predisposed men to support either the *Sainte-Union* or the king. For want of evidence such potentially crucial factors as wealth and clientage relations have had to go uninvestigated. Furthermore, the only members of the League whose identities are revealed by the surviving documents are a score of the movement's leaders and the less than three dozen members of the sovereign courts who remained in Rouen and supported the cause. We desperately need a good social analysis of the rank-and-file of League membership, but Rouen's archives do not provide the materials necessary for such an analysis. The limited nature of the evidence must be kept in mind in evaluating the material presented in the following paragraphs.

have been exceptional in their zeal for the church. Monchy, the dean of the archiepiscopal see, was declared to be 'assuredly a man of God and full of zeal for the cause of Catholicity' by no less an authority on such matters than the English Jesuit Parsons.[1] Jean Dadré's exceptional commitment to a church unsullied by heresy is apparent from his will. Where most of his fellow canons whose wills have survived begin their testaments with a perfunctory invocation of a few saints, Dadré opens his with a long statement of his attachment to the true faith.[2] As for the two Sécard brothers, devotion to hard-line Catholicism ran deep in their family; we have already met their uncle Adam, who preceded Pierre as curé of St Maclou (Claude was in turn to succeed Pierre), one of the most violent anti-Protestant preachers of the early years of the Religious Wars.[3] Finally, the *conseiller au parlement* Regnault du Pont was such a diehard opponent of the Prince of Navarre that he was to choose exile after Rouen's ultimate capitulation to the king in 1594 rather than recognize Navarre as monarch. Du Pont subsequently assisted the Spanish in their surprise of Amiens in 1596 and ultimately died a refugee in the southern Netherlands of the Archdukes.[4]

The split which took place within the sovereign courts in the months following the *Sainte-Union* takeover reveals other factors dividing royalist from *ligueur*: length of time in office, and, very possibly, age. Like all the parlements except that of Bordeaux, Rouen's parlement divided into two halves in the early months of 1589 following the king's edict of Blois, which ordered all royal courts transferred out of those cities held by the League and deprived of their offices those court members who defied this order. The magistrates were thus faced with a particularly clear choice: either they supported the king and left Rouen for Caen, where Henry had ordered the royalist parlement to meet, or else by remaining in Rouen they cast their lot unmistakably with the League. One by one, the magistrates loyal to the king began to slip out of Rouen. Some were administered a none too gentle

[1] Hicks, *Letters and Memorials of Persons*, pp. 107–8.

[2] 'Je...rends graces à dieu immortel de ce que je garde jusques icy la foy pure et entiere que j'ay receue aux sainct fonds de baptesme et en laquelle je desire par la grace dieu perseverer jusques à la mort, je luy rends graces ausy de ce que je n'ay jamais adheré ny consenti à aulcun schisme qui ayt esté en l'eglise catholique. Quand à la charité divine et chrestienne je confesse y avoir insignement prevariqué. Je prie le bon dieu me vouloir pardonner mes offenses par la mort et passion de nostre sauveur Jesus Christ avant que ma pauvre ame soit presentée devant sa saincte face et au cas qu'il le voulust punir selon ces demerites au feu cretien du purgatoire je prie toute la court celeste et principalement la sacrée Vierge Marie, les sainctes, prophetes, apostres, martyres et confesseurs afin que par leur priere la peine soit du tout remisse ou diminué.' A.D.S.M., G 3428. The contrast between this will and those of the other canons strikes one immediately when one reads through the collection of wills of canons in the series G.

[3] On the Sécard family, *see* L. Prévost, *Histoire de la paroisse et des curés de Saint-Maclou depuis la fondation jusqu'à nos jours* (Rouen, 1970), p. 37. On Adam Sécard's sermons, *see above*, p. 67.

[4] Frondeville, *Conseillers du Parlement de Normandie*, Vol. 2, p. 487.

Table 13. Parlementaire *allegiance and length of time in office*[1]

Date of reception in Parlement	Royalist	*Ligueur*	Unknown or neutral
Received before 1574	8	19	2
Received 1574–88	23	6	5

shove toward Caen; in May the *Sainte-Union* authorities arrested and temporarily detained six *parlementaires* on suspicion of the sympathy with the king.[2] (This was not, as might be thought, an expression of hostility toward the court's stature of a piece with the Paris Sixteen's famous arrest and execution of the first president Barnabé Brisson; the men behind the arrests seem to have been themselves the *parlementaires* within the League *Conseil de l'Union*.) Ultimately, 33 members of the court gathered at Caen. Twenty-seven chose to remain in Rouen, while a few retired prudently to their estates.[3] As Table 13 reveals, the choice of sides correlates strikingly with the length of time the magistrates had been in office. The median length of service of the royalist *parlementaires* who gathered in Caen was just four years, while the comparable figure for those who remained in Rouen and supported the League was eighteen.[4] The same pattern can be discerned in the behavior of the members of the *chambre des comptes*. Since this court had only been created in 1580, all of its members were naturally relative newcomers to office. All but one fled to Caen.[5]

[1] This table is taken from Jonathan S. Dewald, 'Office Prices and Social Tensions in Sixteenth-Century Rouen', unpublished paper. I would like to thank the author for permission to use this material. The figures have been reworked slightly on the basis of the lists in the Registres Secrets and Frondeville's genealogies. The column totals fall slightly short of the full number of *parlementaires* in Caen and Rouen respectively because of gaps in Frondeville's genealogies.

[2] A.D.S.M., B, Parlement, Registres Secrets – Rouen, entry of May 12, 1589. *See also* entry of June 18, 1593 for the animosity which subsequently troubled the court as a result of these arrests.

[3] These figures, it must be confessed, oversimplify a fluid reality. The number of *parlementaires* who joined the court at Caen grew over the course of 1589 and 1590, as can be seen by comparing the various lists of members in the Registres Secrets. By September 1590 the court had 34 members, of whom 2 were new magistrates appointed by Navarre. A list of those still in Rouen in November 1591 reveals 27 names, but 5 of these men were absent from the city for reasons of health or personal or official business. Lists from subsequent years show 29 and 28 members respectively, with several new creations counterbalancing the losses due to death or defection from the cause. That certain court members chose neutrality can be deduced by comparing the lists of those magistrates reported to have fled Rouen by May 24, 1589 (Registres Secrets – Rouen) with the subsequent lists of those present at Caen.

[4] Figures calculated from Frondeville, *Conseillers au Parlement*. The author occasionally errs in his identifications of men as either royalists or *ligueurs*; I have corrected his work on the basis of the Registres Secrets.

[5] Among the 'Remonstrances de la cour de Parlement à Monseigneur le Duc de Mayenne' (A.D.S.M., B, Parlement, Registres Secrets – Rouen, sheet inserted between fos. 162–3 of the register for the years 1592–3) is the request that, since all but one of the *maîtres des comptes* have left Rouen, the *chambre des comptes* should be suppressed.

This pattern – which, incidentally, does not seem to have characterized the division of the Paris parlement[1] – must be related first and foremost to the League's often stated desire to roll back the size of a bureaucracy bloated by the proliferation of venal offices. The long-time members of the courts particularly resented the multiplication of their once select numbers and thus were more prone to oppose the king, while those who had purchased their positions more recently were obviously those who stood to lose should the *Sainte-Union* make good on its promises to cut back the size of the courts. They had excellent reasons to support Henry III.

It is tempting to hypothesize that age was also a factor. The division along lines of seniority is so clear that it would seem that a split between the generations must have been involved. Such a split would not be surprising. The older magistrates represented a cohort which had come of age in or before the critical years of religious polarization of the early 1560s, had experienced the full passion of these years, and could still remember the events of 1562 and the period of Protestant domination vividly. Most of the younger *officiers*, on the other hand, would have been too young at the time to have absorbed the religious hatreds of these early years. They matured instead amid repeated civil wars which may have bred in them an abhorrence of religious extremism and a recognition that the state needed a single strong source of authority if chaos was to be averted. Like the English Revolution, Rouen's revolt of the League could have been an uprising led by the old.[2] In an age when rebels protested violations of the *ancient* constitution and usually justified their cause by harking back to the good old days, such a pattern would not be as surprising as it appears today.

While one striking aspect of the new League government formed in the wake of Rouen's Day of the Barricades was the experience and social prominence of those within it, another was the presence of four clerics among the twelve men chosen to rule. Here was something for which no precedent could be cited. The members of the first estate had played no

[1] A comparison of the Parisian *parlementaires* who remained in the capital for the entire period of the League with the hard-core royalist members of the court (i.e., those who fled quickly from Paris and had gathered at Tours by the court's second session there) reveals a median term of service of 14 years for the royalists as against just 10 for the *ligueurs*. Calculation based on Edouard Maugis, *Histoire du parlement de Paris de l'avènement des rois Valois à la mort d'Henri IV* (Paris, 1916), Vol. 3, passim, esp. pp. 275–87. This contrast makes it clear once again that very different forces were at work in Rouen and Paris. Drouot suggests briefly that in Dijon the most recently received *parlementaires* were the most ardent royalists. Drouot, *Mayenne et la Bourgogne*, p. 160.

[2] The wording of this assertion must remain tentative. Because Frondeville's genealogies provide no information on date of birth and I have been unable through other sources to identify the ages of a large sample of Rouen's *ligueurs*, the evidence needed to provide full corroboration of an age split is lacking. Perhaps the hypothesis can be tested more fully elsewhere. It would seem probable that it would not apply to those cities where resentment over blocked upward mobility was a powerful force behind the growth of the League, since here one would expect the young to have been heavily involved in the movement.

role in municipal government, so far as I can tell, since the formation of the commune in the late twelfth century; they certainly had not participated in the deliberations of the city council at any point earlier in the sixteenth century. Their sudden inclusion in government now was the first example of what was to become a characteristic of the entire period of League domination: the tendency to abolish divisions between cleric and layman, the secular realm and the sacred, so that priests became magistrates and magistrates sanctified their power by priestly rite. This was a *Holy* League which now ruled. Its sacred mission to save the realm for Catholicism was what gave legitimacy to a form of government unsanctioned by law or precedent and which dared to repudiate the authority of the king, God's anointed representative on earth. The actions taken by the *Sainte-Union*'s leaders in the weeks following the creation of the new city government show a persistent inclination to involve the first estate in politics, to link the governing institutions to symbols of religious power, and to create political rituals of a quasi-religious nature so that the holiness of the League would be stressed.

One of the *ligueurs*' first acts was to have Rouen's inhabitants swear the oath of the Union. Having dissolved the traditional bonds of political society, new ones had to be forged, and the mechanism used was that of a sacred oath by which all the city's inhabitants pledged 'by God, his glorious mother, and the angels and saints of paradise' to defend the Catholic religion and the security of the city to their last drop of blood.[1] The oath was first presented to the populace at a mass gathering held in the Hôtel de Ville on February 10, at which deputies were dispatched to all of the important judicial and ecclesiastical bodies in the city urging them to sign. Several institutions, most notably the parlement, which still contained the royalists who were later to flee to Caen and which considered itself the guarantor of approved legal precedent, balked at the demand. Under pressure, however, all ultimately pledged their support for the cause. Once signed, the sworn copies of the oath were kept – significantly – at the Carmelite monastery.[2]

Three weeks later, when the duke of Guise's brother and successor as League chieftain, the duke of Mayenne, came to Rouen for several days, the ceremony which greeted him revealed the same concern to sanctify political life. The contrast between this ceremonial entry and the royal entry of 1550 could not have been any more pronounced. For four hours, 'the bulk of the populace both great and small' filed barefoot through the street carrying burning tapers. They snaked their way from the cathedral, the chief holy place in the city, through the Vieux Marché, the hub of everyday

[1] A.C.R., A 20, fo. 406 contains a copy of the oath of the League.
[2] A.C.R., A 20, entries of Feb. 10 and 23, 1589; A.D.S.M., G 2176, entry of March 30, 1589.

life, past the Palais de Justice and Hôtel de Ville, the chief shrines of government, and back to the abbey of St Ouen, another holy place which was soon to be made the seat of the *Conseil de l'Union*. At St Ouen the consecrated Host was displayed in great splendor on the high altar. The place of honor in the ceremony went to Rouen's recently formed companies of Penitents in *cagoules* of red, white, and black, who bore banners depicting the murders of the duke and cardinal of Guise and the face of the cardinal of Bourbon peering forlornly out of the window of his prison cell.[1]

During his stay in Rouen, Mayenne supervised the creation of a new administrative body for Normandy created by the League, the *Conseil de l'Union*. This was the Norman analogue of the governing councils set up throughout *ligueur*-controlled territories to control government activity and coordinate fiscal and military affairs with Paris until such time as the Estates-General could be called.[2] The twelve men added to the city government on February 7 comprised the core of this council, but as he had done in Paris, Mayenne also added a few moderate *ligueurs* loyal to him so that he might have more control over it.[3] Again clerics were liberally represented (five of seventeen members).[4] The council held its thrice-weekly meetings in the abbey of St Ouen.

By the time Mayenne departed early in March 1589, important changes had thus been made in the structure of political authority. Although the precise balance of power between the new ruling body created by the League, the *Conseil de l'Union*, and the older authorities like the governor and the parlement remained to be worked out and would only become clear after several tests of strength between them, a militant group had seized control of the city, reorganized its administration, and above all redefined the proper nature of political authority. What had occurred had been something less than a full-fledged revolution in the personnel of local government, for the city's new rulers were drawn overwhelmingly from the ranks of the old elite. What had changed, however, was the justification of their rule. In place of men whose power was legitimized by custom and

[1] Descriptions of this ceremony are provided by A.D.S.M., G 2176, entry of Feb. 22, 1589, and the letter printed in the appendix to Eugène Saulnier, *Le rôle politique du Cardinal de Bourbon (Charles X), 1523–1590* (Paris, 1912), pp. 300–301.

[2] Henri Drouot, 'Les conseils provinciaux de la Sainte-Union (1589–1595): Notes et questions', *Annales du Midi*, LXV (1953), pp. 415–33.

[3] Those added to the council were Nicolas Rassent, sieur d'Archelles and Jacques le Chandelier, sieur de Chantelou, both lay members of the parlement; Guillaume Pericard, a canon and *conseiller-clerc* of the parlement; the curé of St Vivien; and two noblemen, de Veraines and de la Londe. The lieutenant-general and two *échevins* were also allowed to participate in the council sessions when needed. A.D.S.M., B, Parlement, Arrêts – Rouen, Février–Juin 1589, arrêt of March 4, 1589.

[4] This was common in these councils. *See* Drouot, 'Conseils provinciaux', p. 426; A. Dubois, ed., *La Ligue: Documents rélatifs à la Picardie d'après les registres de l'échevinage d'Amiens* (Amiens, 1859), p. 31; Harding, *Power Elite*, p. 93.

precedent and derived ultimately from a king who in turn received his power from God, there now ruled men whose authority was sanctioned by the people and sanctified by commitment to a holy crusade. These changes were just part of the larger attempt at communal sanctification and purification which we shall see in the next chapter to have been fundamental to the period of the League.

8

Penitents as well as militants

The registers of the cathedral chapter from the months following the duke of Mayenne's departure reveal exceptional doings. On March 30, Michel de Monchy, one of the leading members of the *Conseil de l'Union*, presented a request to his fellow canons of the cathedral chapter that the companies of Penitents which had marched in the ceremony greeting Mayenne be allowed to stage regular processions within the cathedral by night. Four days later Monchy was back, this time to upbraid certain of his fellows for provoking scandal by keeping mistresses in their lodgings. After due investigation, two canons were found guilty as charged and were fined and imprisoned, the first time any concrete action had been taken against members of the chapter guilty of this oft-denounced but never previously punished offense. Ten days after this episode the chapter was busy organizing a procession to accompany the Corpus Domini to the parish church of St Vivien, where the *oratoire* was established for the week. 'Little children went there dressed in white, some with bare feet, others not, and women and young maidens, and others of the populace...with more devotion than it was possible to say.'[1] At the parish church, as was becoming customary, the Host was exposed for a week on an altar draped with tapestries. Men stood guard day and night, an organist played regularly, and several sermons were preached in the course of the week. The faithful who came to pray dropped over 48 *livres* into the collection plate placed nearby, more than was normally amassed in the church's collection basins in a full six months.[2] And two days after the procession to St Vivien the canons were making preparations for the upcoming sermons to be delivered by the general of the Capuchin order. Large crowds were expected, even though he would be preaching in Italian.[3]

Life was jolted out of its normal rhythms in many ways during the period

[1] 'Journal historique de Rouen, extrait d'un manuscrit de la bibliothèque de l'abbé De la Rue', *Revue de Rouen* (1840), p. 258.

[2] A.D.S.M., G 7767, compte de fabrique de St Vivien. The account book notes payments for the construction of '*pyramides*' alone with disbursements for the tapestries, organist, sermons, etc.

[3] A.D.S.M., G 2176, entries of March 30, April 3, 13, and 15, 1589. The unprecedented nature of the punishments given those who kept concubines emerges from a comparison with the earlier volumes of the chapter's deliberations.

of League domination. These five years were years of heroism, in which the common artisans of the town's privileged militia companies marched out to battle for one of the last times in the history of these organizations which were becoming increasingly ceremonial in nature, many of the militia members giving their lives for the cause. They were years of lawlessness, in which the city's streets were given over by night to marauding gangs of soldiers and civilians. And they were years of ever-intensifying economic hardship, the worst and most prolonged economic crisis which the city experienced between the close of the Hundred Year's War and the last terrible years of the reign of Louis XIV. Yet of all the extraordinary aspects of these years, none was more striking and more important than the dramatic religious fervor which is evident simply from the deliberations of the cathedral chapter for one month in 1589. Beginning in 1588, even before the *Sainte-Union* came to power, and continuing, albeit with slackening enthusiasm, down to the very end of the period of League rule, a series of new forms of devotion, new confraternities, and new religious orders were all introduced into the city. All touched a deep chord of common concern. The result was a veritable explosion of popular devotional activity which is all the more striking when it is contrasted with the general inertia which had characterized Catholic religious life for the earlier decades of the Religious Wars.

This upsurge of penitential piety accompanying the League has not received very sympathetic or extensive treatment in the historical literature. Certain manifestations of *ligueur* spirituality, notably the dramatic processions staged in many cities, were so spectacular that historians have been unable to overlook them. Most students of the League, however, pass these off with brief comments about popular fanaticism before examining with far greater attention and sympathy these aspects of these years which seem particularly intriguing to modern eyes, usually because they prefigure later revolutionary movements: its doctrine of popular sovereignty and its elements of popular radicalism. For most church historians, meanwhile, little connection has seemed possible between the great reforming impulses of the 'century of the saints' and the violent, indeed seditious, upheavals of the preceding period of the Religious Wars. The later sixteenth century has consequently been all but neglected by students of Catholic religious life. Both the political historians of the League and the church historians studying the Counter-Reformation may be distorting the picture of the phenomena which interest them by neglecting these religious activities of the period of the League. The League itself certainly cannot be understood fully unless the perhaps somewhat medieval impulse toward communal purification that is manifested so clearly in the religiosity of the period is set alongside the aspects of the *Sainte-Union* that prefigure modern revolutionary parties. The deeply rooted tendency of men in this period to see misfortune as punishment for sin and the performance of works of contrition and piety as ways to deflect God's wrath inevitably made the *ligueurs*, to borrow Denis Pallier's apt phrase, 'penitents at the same time as militants'.[1] Yet the upsurge of pious foundations and religious devotions also represents more than just the mass breast-beating in the face of calamity so deeply ingrained in the religious mentality of the era. The first important flickers of the spirit of the Counter-Reformation in Rouen can also be discerned among the activities of the League. By jolting the Catholic Church out of its inertia, the political crisis may well have provided the initial push that was needed for the Counter-Reformation to get underway.

The early decades of the Wars of Religion certainly had seen few signs of a reforming spirit within local Catholicism.[2] Attempts to revivify local religious life or to reform the abuses which Catholic as well as Protestant authors agreed riddled the Roman Church were rare. As we have seen, the initial reaction of the local ecclesiastical hierarchy to the growth of Protestantism was to mobilize the propaganda resources of the church, notably the sermon and the procession, and to use them to denounce heresy violently. A few efforts to rekindle devotion to certain aspects of Catholic doctrine attacked by the Calvinists began to appear on the eve of the First Civil War, notably the foundation of the General Confraternity of the Holy Sacrament. One might have expected that Protestantism's success in attracting converts and the threat it seemed to pose to the Catholic Church would have stimulated further such attempts throughout the tense first decade of the civil wars. Instead, massive indifference characterized the attitude of the local authorities to the tasks of improving the quality of the local clergy or stepping up popular religious instruction so as to reduce Protestantism's appeal and bind the great mass of the Catholic faithful more closely to the church.

Since Rouen's archbishop, the cardinal of Bourbon, was usually to be found at court, the canons of the cathedral chapter were the true administrators of the archdiocese. Despite their power, the registers of their deliberations are strikingly devoid of any major attempts to combat Protestantism by means other than staging an occasional procession or dispatching delegations to court to protest the measures of toleration granted the Calvinists at each edict of pacification. As for the parish priests,

[1] Denis Pallier, *Recherches sur l'imprimerie à Paris pendant la Ligue (1585–1594)* (Geneva, 1975), p. 173.

[2] The paragraphs which follow on the period 1562–88 summarize material presented in greater detail in my article, 'The Catholic Response to Protestantism, Church Activity and Popular Piety in Rouen, 1560–1600', *Religion and the People, 800–1700*, ed. James Obelkevich (Chapel Hill, 1979), pp. 173–8. Full references may be found there.

if they took any measures whatsoever to counter the growth of Protestantism, these have left no traces in the surviving records.

Such few signs of ambitious or innovative attempts to improve the state of Catholic religious life as one does find came from outsiders to the city, the archbishop and especially the members of the new religious orders which he sought to introduce to the city. Even these proved to be decidedly limited in their success. The cardinal of Bourbon convened an archdiocesan council in 1581 to deliberate how to put into practice the decrees of the Council of Trent, the first such local council in France, but the reforming articles which this assembly promulgated remained little more than pious statements of good intentions. As the cathedral chapter itself admitted in 1591, none of the decrees was put into practice. Individual Jesuit fathers also made several visits to Rouen at the cardinal's behest between 1565 and 1583, preaching before large crowds, encouraging eucharistic devotion, organizing associations of pious ladies to visit the Hôtel-Dieu and tend to the sick, and attempting to found a regular program of catechitical instruction. The Jesuits made an undeniable impact on the city during their visits by the force of their personalities and the power of their preaching, but they failed in their chief objective: to establish a permanent Jesuit college so that their influence might be exerted continuously rather than sporadically during brief missions. The archbishop endowed the society with a *rente* of 2,000 *livres* for such a purpose in 1569, but the Jesuits found their way blocked by the combined opposition of the other religious orders in the city, the cathedral chapter, and the parlement. The four mendicant orders, encouraged by the cathedral chapter, initiated a suit against the proposed school on the grounds that it infringed upon their right to control all educational establishments within the city. Even though a Jesuit father, Antonio Possevino, had earned the parlement's gratitude during a stay in Rouen by helping pacify the mob which had been threatening violence against those Huguenots who refused to take Easter communion, the tribunal upheld the mendicant orders in their suit. A second attempt to establish a Jesuit college made in 1583 met with a similar lack of success when the general of the Jesuit order decreed that a new *rente* which the cardinal granted the society against the revenues of his abbey of St Ouen was insufficient to guarantee the college's financial security, since future abbots might contest this alienation of their revenues. In 1588 there was thus still no Jesuit college in Rouen.

Only one new religious order managed to establish itself in the city during the first decades of the Religious Wars, the Capuchins. Little is known about the activities of these strictly observant Franciscans in Rouen, although it can be established that their house opened in 1580 and that their popularity as preachers soon grew so great that their little chapel could not hold the crowds. The friars often had to preach from atop a nearby boulder so that all could hear. But however great the Capuchins' popularity and impact, the final balance sheet of changes in the Catholic Church during the first twenty-five years of the Religious Wars remains meager: just one new religious order founded, several inspiring but short visits by Jesuit preachers, and an archdiocesan council whose reforming decrees were ineffectual. The essence of the Catholic response to Protestantism's challenge in these years was almost wholly negative. Rather than attempting measures of internal reform or reinvigoration, the church hierarchy sought simply to denounce and destroy its new rival. As we have seen, it was not an unsuccessful policy. The anti-Huguenot violence which developed, largely at the incitation of the first estate, did deal Protestantism a nearly mortal blow. And as the Huguenot challenge faded in the 1570s, whatever sense of urgency the movement's initial success had given efforts to meet this challenge faded as well.

To jolt Catholicism into vigorous action beyond the simple vilification of Protestantism apparently required a truly alarming crisis which could not be resolved merely through violence against a local enemy. This is what the crisis of the League provided. Not only was this a threat to the faith that came from beyond the city walls; it was also one which strongly suggested God's warning hand. Just as kings could be *Dieudonné*, so presumably were heirs-apparent, and if the heir-apparent was now a Protestant, this was surely a warning of divine chastisement to come unless the Rouennais mended their wicked ways. The link between the political crisis and the religious activities of the period is clear in the public appeals posted around the city by the cathedral chapter at several moments during the years of League domination. 'The vessel of this Church...is in such perilous straits that we fear its imminent shipwreck', asserted one, 'unless by our fervent prayers and true penitence we awaken that great Pilot our Lord Jesus Christ, whom our sins now keep sleeping in a profound slumber.'[1] A sincere effort at moral reform, and above all else, frequent acts of penance were the remedies prescribed to meet the danger:

> Do penance. You are lost and damned forever if you do not do penance...Sparing nothing have recourse to the remedies which the goodness and mercy of our Lord gives us in his Church: the Sacrament of Penitence,...which transforms misery to happiness and changes us from children of wrath to beloved children of God, and in consequence renders us strong and powerful against our enemies.[2]

Not only was Rouen to be bound to the Holy League; it had to be transformed into a holy community. In Paris the zeal for moral reform was

[1] A.D.S.M., G 2476. *See also* the similar sentiments of the placard quoted at the beginning of this section.

[2] A.D.S.M., G 2476.

such that wool replaced silk and those who went out in public in too great finery ran the risk of having the ruffles torn from their clothes.[1] In Rouen the impulse toward reform and penitence found expression in four important religious initiatives: the introduction of the *oratoire*, the foundation of the confraternities of Penitents, the establishment of the Jesuit college, and an attempt to introduce the female order of the Carmelites into the city. There was also a striking increase in processional activity.

Among the religious activities of this period, the one which perhaps stands out the most is the establishment of the Jesuit college. It was no mere coincidence that the *Collège de Bourbon*, as the institution was ultimately named, finally opened in 1593 when the *ligueurs* ruled Rouen after having failed twice to do so in the preceding decades. The financial security of the institution was no more adequate than it had been in 1583. In fact, soon after the school opened the Jesuits had to be granted special subsidies by the city government to keep the college functioning.[2] The general of the order nonetheless relented in his opposition to establishing a college on unsteady financial foundations due to a radical change of attitude on the part of all of Rouen's authorities, judicial, ecclesiastical, and municipal. The cathedral chapter and the Council of Twenty-Four both wrote to the society in 1592 urging the establishment of a college; the city council granted the Jesuits a two-year pension; and the members of the parlement raised money among themselves to help finance the cost of setting up the institution.[3] The key to this change of attitude on the part of these corporations previously hostile to the Jesuits lies with the control now exercised by the *ligueur* elements within them. The Jesuits had been allied with the radical *ligueurs* within the city for quite some time. Long before the Jesuit Commolet arrived in Rouen in August 1588 to agitate for the League, the house of the future head of the *Conseil de l'Union*, Michel de Monchy, had been a center for the activities of the English Jesuits. Robert Parsons, who stayed with Monchy when he was in Rouen in 1581 supervising the publication of *De persecutione anglicana*, spoke warmly of him, calling him 'more than a most loving friend of our society'.[4] And pro-League sentiments were to die hard within the Collège de Bourbon once established; as late as 1630 its rector published a book that was burned by

[1] Marcel Poëte, *Une vie de cité: Paris de sa naissance à nos jours*, (Paris, 1931), Vol. 3, p. 233. For pamphlets calling the Parisians to this sort of moral reform, *see* the titles cited in Pallier, *Recherches sur l'imprimerie*, pp. 331, 404. Local evidence does not permit us to ascertain how fully this Catholic Puritanism took hold in Rouen.

[2] A.D.S.M., B, Parlement, Registres Secrets, entries of Jan. 27 and Feb. 5, 1594.

[3] A.C.R., A 21, entry of Sept. 17, 1592; A.D.S.M., G 2178, entry of Sept. 24, 1592; Henri Fouqueray, *Histoire de la compagnie de Jésus en France des origines à la suppression (1528–1762)* (Paris, 1910), Vol. 2, p. 315.

[4] L. Hicks, ed., *Letters and Memorials of Father Robert Persons, S.J.*, Vol. 1, *to 1585*, Catholic Record Society Publication XXXIX (London, 1942), p. 107.

the authorities as '*ligueur* and totally seditious'.[1] The charge of its enemies that the society as a whole was tied to the League has been effectively demolished by Roland Mousnier and now A. Lynn Martin; as a group the Jesuits were divided over the League and were no more strongly *ligueur* than the other major religious orders.[2] Nonetheless, the link between the society and the *ligueurs* in Rouen was clear and strong.

In the long run, the Collège de Bourbon was undoubtedly the most important of the institutions founded in Rouen during the period of the League. Within a decade of its creation some 1,800 students were enrolled, receiving the characteristic Jesuit education, at once theologically orthodox and pedagogically innovative, that shaped unmistakably the ideas and interests of generations of future Rouennais including Pierre Corneille and the Cavalier de La Salle.[3] In the short run, however, it is arguable that two other, closely interrelated practices of these years made a more dramatic impact on the city's inhabitants. These were the *oratoire*, known today as the perpetual devotion, and the processions which accompanied it.

The *oratoire* was introduced in Rouen early in 1588 and was the symbolic focal point for efforts to spur popular devotion. As such it seems to have been quite successful. The practice involved displaying the Holy Sacrament amid relics on a richly decorated altar for a week at a time in each parish church. Men stood guard before the altar in a full-time vigil, while special prayers and sermons were said in the church in which the *oratoire* was set up.[4] At the end of each week an elaborate public procession would accompany the Corpus Domini as it was moved to the next church. The already cited comment of one Rouennais journal that the *oratoire* and its accompanying processions stimulated 'more devotion than it was possible to describe' is confirmed both by Elizabeth Sanders, the refugee English nun, who speaks of the 'mervelous devotyon' of these years, and by the large sums of money collected in the basins placed alongside the altar on which the Host was displayed.[5] The *oratoire* also saw a great vogue

1 Michel Mollat, 'Collège de Bourbon et Lycée Corneille: Notes de bibliographie et d'histoire', *Bull. Soc. Emul. S-I.* (1940–41), p. 295.

2 Roland Mousnier, *L'assassinat d'Henry IV* (Paris, 1964), pp. 197–212; A. Lynn Martin, *Henry III and the Jesuit Politicians* (Geneva, 1973), passim, esp. p. 211.

3 Enrollment figures are from François de Dainville, 'Collèges et fréquentation scolaire au XVIIe siècle', *Population*, XII (1957), p. 467. On the college's curriculum and noteworthy alumni, *see* Mollat, 'Collège de Bourbon', passim.

4 The best description I have found of this practice is in Antoine Richart, *Mémoires sur la Ligue dans le Laonnois* (Laon, 1869), p. 222. The payments noted in the parish account books enable one to determine that the practice was essentially the same in Rouen and Laon, the main difference being that in Laon two-man teams of volunteers spent two-hour shifts praying before the *oratoire* and guarding it, while in Rouen special guards seem to have been paid to watch over it. The most detailed payments for the *oratoire* are recorded in A.D.S.M., G 6245, G 6341, G 7167, and G 7767.

5 Archives of the English College of Valladolid, Serie 2, L 5, no. 13; A.D.S.M., G 6245, G 6341, and G 7767.

elsewhere in France during these years of the League.[1] Nonetheless, the practice seems to have been discontinued after 1593. All mention of it disappears from the accounts of the parish treasuries. It was a practice strictly connected with the years of the League.

The processions which accompanied the *oratoire*, spectacular ceremonies in which much of each parish's population was invited to participate, were by no means the only special processions held during the period of League domination. Small ceremonies were staged regularly several times each week throughout the period of League domination (it was a sign of slackening zeal when the cathedral chapter decreed in 1591 that henceforward processions would be held only twice weekly),[2] and special, unusually elaborate commemorative rituals were added for signal events such as Henry III's death in August 1589 or the delivery of the city from royalist attack in the wars which soon were underway in the region. Although we are not nearly as well informed about the details of the processions in Rouen as we are about those in Paris, where Pierre de l'Estoile declared that the inhabitants were so 'heated up' (*eschauffé*) about these events that they would rouse their parish priests out of bed to lead them, the manuscript history of the League reports that the processions in Rouen were 'exemplary'.[3] With the prominent role given children and the gestures of mortification such as marching barefoot, the processions are among the clearest examples of the penitential thrust of so much of the spirituality of the time.

The two other important initiatives of this period were largely the work of one man, Jehan de Quintanadoines, seigneur de Brétigny. His fascinating biography deserves a brief excursus, for in it one can see the confessional struggle being played out within a single family.

Quintanadoines was descended from an important family of Burgos wool merchants, the Quintanadueñas, some of whose members emigrated around the turn of the century to a number of the major north European ports with which the family traded. One line of the family established itself in Rouen, and like many of the Spanish merchant families in Normandy, it was quickly assimilated into the city's leading circles.[4] One mark of the degree to which the Quintanadueñas – their name now frenchified to Quintanadoines – soon drifted away from their Spanish origins was the

[1] *See* Richart, *Laonnois*, p. 222; P. Richard, *La papauté et la Ligue française: Pierre d'Epinac, Archevêque de Lyon (1573–1599)* (Paris, 1901), pp. 452–3; Jean Pussot, 'Mémoires ou Journalier', ed. E. Henry, *Travaux de l'Académie Imperiale de Reims*, xxv (1857), p. 8.

[2] A.D.S.M., G 2177, entry of Jan. 11, 1591.

[3] B.N., MS Français 23295, fo. 499. On the atmosphere in Paris, *see* Pierre de L'Estoile, *Mémoires-Journaux*, ed. Brunet, Champollion et al. (Paris, 1875–96), Vol. 3, p. 247.

[4] On the Quintanadoines family and its early years in Rouen, *see* Michel Mollat, *Le commerce maritime normand à la fin du Moyen Age* (Paris, 1952), p. 512.

conversion of two members of the second generation to Protestantism. One was Fernande, seigneur de Brétigny, Jehan's father.[1]

Jehan himself was born in the quayside parish of St Etienne-des-Tonneliers in 1555. Sometime in 1562, he was – curiously – sent back to Spain, where he was to receive an extremely Catholic education from private tutors in his uncle's house in Seville.[2] Now it is highly improbable that a Protestant father would of his own volition choose to give his eldest son a strongly Catholic upbringing. The most plausible explanations of this peculiar action are either that pressure from the rest of the family was brought to bear on Fernande, or that he left the city briefly following the Catholic reconquest and that his son was sent away in his absence. It can be ascertained that there was another member of the Quintanadoines family in Rouen around 1562, a cousin Antoine, who was born in Burgos and who was to return there before marrying but who was nonetheless the head of the clan during his years in Rouen.[3] Antoine was a zealous Catholic, as is evident from the fact that he fled the city during the Huguenot occupation and had 10,889 *livres* worth of goods confiscated. (The Rouen-born brothers, even the Catholics among them, stayed in the city and had no property seized.)[4] Clearly the family was divided on religious grounds, and in the extended families characteristic of the leading merchant and *officier* circles it does not seem impossible that the leader of the clan might command the authority to determine the form of his cousin's education.[5]

[1] A.D.S.M., E, Protestants de Quévilly, Baptêmes, 1564–6, entry of Aug. 9, 1566; Christiane Douyère, 'Les marchands étrangers à Rouen au 16e siècle (vers 1520–vers 1580): Assimilation ou ségrégation?', unpub. thèse de l'Ecole Nationale des Chartes (1973), p. 242.

[2] P. de Beauvais, *La vie de Monsieur de Brétigny, prestre, fondateur des Carmélites de Sainte Thérèse en France et aux Pays-Bas* (Paris, 1747), p. 11; Pierre Serouet, ed., *Quintanadueñas: Lettres de Jean de Brétigny (1556–1634)* (Louvain, 1971), p. vii. Neither Serouet nor de Beauvais are aware of their hero's Protestant father and thus do not find Jehan's being sent to Spain unusual.

[3] It was he who carried on the family's business correspondence with Simon Ruiz. Ruiz, cajas 2–4. *See also* Serouet, ed., *Quintanadueñas*, p. 27n.

[4] A.D.S.M., B, Parlement, Arrêts, Novembre 1562–Mars 1563, arrêt of Feb. 27, 1563; A.D.S.M., G 2165, entries of April 17 to June 3, 1562.

[5] Studies of elite family structure are only beginning to suggest the strength of the extended family in sixteenth-century urban society. It was not uncommon for sons of both merchants and *officiers* in Rouen to live with their parents for a number of years after marriage, a pattern which is parallelled by the upper strata in other French cities as well. A.D.S.M., Tabellionage, Meubles 2e série, contract of March 10, 1568; Jonathan S. Dewald, *The Formation of a Provincial Nobility: The Magistrates of the Parlement of Rouen, 1499–1610* (Princeton, 1980), p. 276; Etienne Trocmé, 'La Rochelle de 1560 à 1628: Tableau d'une société réformée au temps des guerres de religion', unpub. thèse de théologie protestante (Paris, 1950), p. 128; Natalie Zemon Davis, 'Ghosts, Kin, and Progeny: Some Features of Family Life in Early Modern France', *Daedalus*, CVI (1977), p. 101; Pierre Goubert, 'Famille et province: Contribution à la connaissance des structures familiales dans l'ancienne France', paper presented to the Davis Center, Oct. 22, 1976, p. 13. In Parisian robe circles, the work of Denis Richet will show, careers could be launched for young men not by their father but by their uncle, and some exceedingly unusual family patterns could develop. The young Robert Arnauld d'Andilly spent half of each day at his father's house, half at his uncle's.

The suspicion that young Jehan was sent away to remove him from his father's heretical influence is strengthened by the fact that Fernande reconverted to Catholicism in 1569 and Jehan returned home the following year.

The relations between father and son in the ensuing years were ambivalent, to say the least. The elder Quintanadoines wanted his son to marry and continue as a merchant. Jehan, already deeply pious but also very timid, wanted to enter holy orders but also to obey his father's wishes. Twice marriage arrangements were on the brink of being concluded. Twice Jehan fell mysteriously ill. During his second illness, as he hovered near death, his father agreed to allow him to become a cleric. A miraculous recovery ensued.[1]

The long family drama affected Jehan profoundly. He grew up to be extremely afraid of speaking in public, and once was struck dumb in the pulpit when forced by his superior to preach. In his later years, he often suffered from attacks of extreme scruples, so much so that he would on occasion refuse to say Mass without a confessor nearby lest he sin on the way to the altar.[2] A remarkable spiritual dialogue between himself and God which he wrote in 1610 shows that he had a sense of being virtually paralyzed by guilt and the feeling that he had wasted the few moments given him on earth. In it he echoes the Prodigal Son: 'Father, I have sinned against heaven and before you; I am no longer worthy to be called your son.'[3]

Despite his timidity and sense of personal unworthiness, Quintanadoines' accomplishments during the period of the League and shortly thereafter were far from negligible. The most important of these was the role he played in the establishment of the female order of the Carmelites in France. It is well known that the Carmelites were first introduced to France in 1603 thanks to the influence of the circle in Paris around Mme Acarie and Bérulle. Less well known is the history of the first attempt to establish this Spanish order in France made in Rouen during the period of the League.[4] After Quintanadoines' first betrothal-induced illness, he was sent to Spain. There he was introduced to, and greatly impressed by, the spiritual activities of the Carmelite disciples of St Theresa. It became his goal to

1 De Beauvais, *Vie de Monsieur de Brétigny*, pp. 36, 140; Paul Baudry, *Les religieuses carmélites à Rouen* (Rouen, 1875), p. 25. One of Quintanadoines' letters of 1580 strongly suggests that his illness of that year was psychosomatic. Serouet, ed., *Quintanadueñas*, p. 1.

2 Baudry, *Les religieuses carmélites à Rouen*, pp. 29, 68–71.

3 *Ibid.*, p. 69; Serouet, ed., *Quintanadueñas*, p. 335.

4 Accounts of this attempt may be found in de Beauvais, *Vie de Monsieur de Brétigny*, pp. 117ff; Baudry, *Les religieuses carmélites à Rouen*, pp. 16ff; Henri Brémond, *Histoire littéraire du sentiment religieux en France depuis la fin des guerres de religion* (Paris, 1932), Vol. 2, pp. 275–82; and Serouet, ed., *Quintanadueñas*, pp. xiv–xv.

carry the Carmelite rule back to France with him. The opportunity to realize this goal seemed to present itself during the years of the League. To fulfill a vow of thanksgiving made when the siege of Rouen of 1591–2 was raised, Quintanadoines undertook with the encouragement of the widow of the duke of Joyeuse (who was also the protectoress of the violently *ligueur* Capuchins of Caen)[1] to convince Rouen's cathedral chapter and the duke of Mayenne to back his project. In this he was successful, but his subsequent voyage to the Escorial to persuade Philip II to permit the transfer of several Carmelite sisters to France failed for reasons which are not clear. The enterprise had to be abandoned for a time. On Quintanadoines' return from Spain, though, he translated from Spanish to French a biography of St Theresa, and it was this work that caught the attention of Mme Acarie and led her to support the project. One can see quite clearly here a link between these religious activities of the years of the League and those of the *dévot* circles of the early seventeenth century – the same kind of link that can also be found in the biographies of many of the leading Parisian *dévots* including Mme Acarie herself.[2]

A few years before his attempted foundation of a Carmelite convent in Rouen, Quintanadoines was instrumental in establishing a confraternity about whose activities in the city very little can be discovered, but which is of great interest because of its role in recent historiography: the Penitents. The number, size, and importance of the companies of Penitents in the Midi throughout the Ancien Régime have recently been revealed by the studies of Pecquet, Venard, and Agulhon.[3] What these authors do not note is that the Penitents expanded into northern France as well during the period of the League.[4] Confraternities were founded in the second-level cities of Abbeville and Laon as well as in Paris and Rouen, and traces of other groups could probably be found elsewhere in northern France during this period if one searched diligently.[5]

Because Rouen's Penitents disappeared with the fall of the League

1 Godefroy de Paris, *Les Frères-Mineurs Capucins en France: Histoire de la Province de Paris* (Paris, 1937–9), Vol. 1, fasc. 2, pp. 107–8.

2 Monsieur Acarie earned the title 'the valet of the League' for his role in the movement; his wife received her initiation into mysticism during the years of the League from the *ligueur* Bernard de Mont-Gaillard. These and other links between the League and the *dévots* are suggested by Marguerite Pecquet, 'Des compagnies de Pénitents à la Compagnie du Saint-Sacrement', *XVIIe Siècle*, 69 (1965), pp. 3–36.

3 *Ibid.*, Marc Venard, 'Les confréries de pénitents au XVIe siècle dans la province ecclésiastique d'Avignon', *Mémoires de l'Académie du Vaucluse*, 6th ser., 1 (1967), pp. 55–79; Maurice Agulhon, *Pénitents et francs-maçons de l'ancienne Provence* (Paris, 1968), passim.

4 The fact is noted, however, by Louis Guibert in his still fundamental, if occasionally unreliable, 'Les confréries de Penitents en France et notamment dans le diocèse de Limoges', *Bulletin de la Société Archéologique et Historique du Limousin*, XXVII (1879), pp. 5–193.

5 The confraternities in Abbeville and Laon are mentioned in Ernest Prarond, *La Ligue à Abbeville, 1576–1594* (Paris, 1873), Vol. 1, p. 188; Richart, *Mémoires sur la Ligue dans le Laonnois*, p. 266.

leaving no documents, their activities and membership are only revealed by passing references in the journals of the time. They were founded in 1588 by Quintanadoines after Spanish models, their goal being, according to Elizabeth Sanders, 'to reforme the people'.[1] Their first meeting was held in the chapel of the English nuns of St Bridget, a center for *ligueur* spirituality, and their members were said to include 'a large number of people, even of distinguished birth'.[2] Although their statutes have not survived, from recent studies of the Penitents we can assume that, in addition to staging the spectacular torchlit processions within the cathedral for which they requested permission in March 1589, they also swore to perform a regular series of devotions, abstain from blasphemy and public immorality, and perhaps take frequent communion. What precise connections existed between them and the *ligueur* political activists within Rouen is unclear. Elsewhere, however, the ties were strong, so strong in fact that the parlement of Paris abolished the confraternities following the fall of the *Sainte-Union.*[3] It is tempting to hypothesize that one reason why the Penitents were found exclusively in the South in the seventeenth and eighteenth centuries is that these groups had become popular there several decades before the period of the League. They consequently were not associated too closely with the movement and did not suffer from the opprobrium which fell after 1594 on all things *ligueur* and which explains the disappearance of the Penitents in the North after that date.

The Penitents, like the *oratoire*, may have disappeared from Rouen with the fall of the League, but while both lasted they provided perfect forms of expression for the anguished piety of this period of political crisis. That both of these institutions were not confined to Rouen but were common to many northern French strongholds of the League only underscores the close link between the political situation and these forms of religious devotion. During the League, the streets of cities like Rouen became theaters in which the inhabitants could act out their contrition as a way to avert political calamity. In such a situation, it is worth pointing out, even such political reforms proposed by the League as abolishing the sale of office were essentially part of the penitential thrust of these years. Trying to set right a judicial system whose proper functioning had been upset by a system of venality that rewarded wealth instead of virtue was little different from attempting to stamp out simony or concubinage within the church or such manifestations of moral decay among the mass of the population as indecent dress or excessive luxury. In every case, vice had sapped the proper order

[1] Archives of the English College of Valladolid, Serie 2, L 5, no. 13.

[2] De Beauvais, *Vie de Monsieur de Brétigny*, p. 89.

[3] Pecquet, 'Des compagnies de Pénitents à la Compagnie du Saint-Sacrement', pp. 26–7; Guibert, 'Confréries de Penitents', pp. 30–32; Richart, *Mémoires sur la Ligue dans le Laonnois*, pp. 333–40.

of society. The community had to be cleansed of such sinfulness if it was to survive the crisis it faced.

While the political and the religious activism of this period both sprang from similar impulses, not every penitent was necessarily a *ligueur* militant. For certain men the devotional and political activities were but two aspects of one struggle. This was true, for example, for Michel de Monchy, the nephew of the cardinal of Pellevé whose name appears everywhere in the documents of the period. He directed the provincial *Conseil de l'Union* for much of its existence; sat in the parlement until his militancy ran him afoul of the governor, Villars, and provoked his banishment from the city in 1593; and toured the parishes under his charge in his role as archdeacon of the cathedral 'accompanied by personages of rare doctrine and piety in order to confute the heretics, instruct the people, and correct the clergy'.[1] We have already met Monchy as a host and associate of the English Jesuit Parsons and as the man who upbraided his *concubinaire* fellow canons in 1589. He was also apparently somehow linked to the Penitents, since it was he who announced to the other canons when the confraternity wished to hold one of its processions in the cathedral. Finally, it was he who invited Commolet to Rouen in the wake of the Parisian Day of the Barricades.[2] Monchy was at once a religious reformer and a political militant. Others, however, neglected political activity so that they would give themselves over more completely to a life of religious service. This was the case for Jehan de Quintanadoines, who, for all his importance on the religious scene, never crops up once in the political or administrative documents of the time. The contrast between the two leading figures on Rouen's religious scene in this period was a contrast typical of the Catholicism of the time – between religious currents which encouraged activism in this world and ones which subordinated political concern to works of charity, prayer, and mystical contemplation. (In this regard Monchy's close ties to the Jesuits and Quintanadoines' with the Carmelites of St Theresa were undoubtedly more than fortuitous.) Following the defeat of the League the latter of these two paths was to know an increasing vogue. While the fear of a Huguenot king which provoked the League also heightened religious concern among the strongly Catholic members of the urban elite, the subsequent chaos of the League was to serve to discredit mass politics among this group and promote a retreat toward, on the one hand, mysticism, and, on the other, secret underground pressure groups such as the *Compagnie du Saint-Sacrement*.

In any account of devotional activity of the sort so far examined in this chapter, one question inevitably arises: Did these ceremonies truly

[1] A.D.S.M., B, Parlement, Registres Secrets – Rouen, entry of June 19, 1593.

[2] A.D.S.M., G 2176, entry of Aug. 13, 1588.

reflect the sentiments of the great bulk of the population? Only a handful of people within the church hierarchy or among the elite of pious laymen are required to launch a new religious order or confraternity, and it is dangerous to assert without supporting evidence that their actions reflect feelings stirring among the mass of people living at the time. Processions obviously indicate more about that elusive entity, popular piety, for a large segment of the community takes part in them. In their case, however, doubts always remain about the meaning of an individual's participation in such a ceremony, and such doubts are especially warranted in a case such as the one we are studying here where the local government was controlled by a party of religious zealots who frequently harrassed those whom they considered insufficiently attached to the cause. Did those who marched in the processions of the League do so because they believed that it was important for the community that they do so, because somebody in a position of religious authority had told them it was important that they do so, or simply because it was the obviously prudent thing to do? One cannot be sure. Of course, certain indications have already been encountered that suggest that the religious enthusiasm of this period cut quite deep: the comments of eyewitnesses about the 'mervelous devotyon' of the people and the large numbers who joined the confraternities of Penitents; the substantial sums deposited in the collection plates set up alongside the *oratoire*; the indications from Paris, presumably paralleled in Rouen as well, that laymen did not merely participate dutifully in the processions of the time but often took the initiative in organizing them. Nonetheless, the reliability of each of these indicators could be questioned. To verify the pattern of a striking upsurge in Catholic piety during the period of the League following decades of relative inertia, it seems prudent to employ quantitative tests of religious practice.

In the four decades since the pioneering works of Gabriel Le Bras began to appear, French historians and sociologists of religion have come to recognize that traditional forms of documentation are often unreliable as guides to the religious opinions of the mass of the population. A great deal of effort has consequently been devoted to devising quantitative measures that detect reliably changes in the degree of popular fervor.[1] Although sources from this period of Rouen's history are lacking for many of the

[1] The most important of Gabriel LeBras' extremely influential articles have been collected and published as *Etudes de sociologie religieuse* (Paris, 1956). Major recent historical works which employ quantitative tests of religious practice include Louis Perouas, *Le diocèse de La Rochelle de 1648 à 1724: Sociologie et pastorale* (Paris, 1964); Michel Vovelle, *Piété baroque et déchristianisation en Provence au XVIIIe siècle: Les attitudes devant la mort d'après les clauses des testaments* (Paris, 1973); and *idem.*, 'Analyse spectrale d'un diocèse méridional au XVIIIe siècle: Aix-en-Provence', *Provence Historique*, XXII (1972), pp. 352–449. This last article is particularly valuable methodologically. Jacques Toussaert, *Le sentiment religieux en Flandre à la fin du Moyen-Age* (Paris, 1963) is a somewhat less successful attempt at quantification.

indices recently developed – the degree of abstention from Easter communion, for example, or the frequency with which testators left money for Masses for the souls in purgatory – it remains possible to calculate two measures of popular attachment to Catholic religious practices. These allow insight into the evolution of popular Catholic piety during these years that can supplement the material from more traditional sources.

The first test is a relatively crude one, but one which seems particularly apt for present purposes since it enables us to discover the degree to which Rouen's inhabitants shared in the privacy of their own houses – of their beds, in fact – the impulse toward penitence and purification which the public religious ceremonies of the period paraded so ostentatiously through the streets. This involves examining the extent of sexual abstinence during Lent. During the early Middle Ages the church rigorously forbade intercourse between husband and wife during Lent. This requirement gradually softened into a pious recommendation over the course of the later Middle Ages, but confessors nonetheless continued to urge it on the faithful through the sixteenth century and even beyond. The techniques of historical demography make it a relatively easy matter to discover whether or not these counsels were heeded in any given area, for where they were a dip in conceptions during March appears clearly on the graphs of baptisms per month.[1] By using Rouen's Catholic parish registers to calculate the seasonal movement of baptisms, the prevalence of this practice among the Norman capital's inhabitants can thus be determined.

Figure 4 sets forth the results obtained from such a calculation for the periods 1563–77 and 1580–94 for two contrasting groups of parishes: five small, relatively well-to-do parishes in the central and western sections of the city, and the two large popular parishes in the east of town, St Maclou and St Vivien. (The index must be calculated for intervals of at least fifteen years to eliminate the influence of random annual fluctuations in the pattern of births.) The graphs suggest that abstinence during Lent was widespread throughout this period in the wealthier parishes but only spread to the city's poorer parishes in the later years of the civil war, around the period of the League. The curves of the five western and central parishes show a drop in March conceptions that is equally deep in each of the fifteen-year

[1] The fullest discussions of the belief in continence during Lent and its relation to monthly fluctuations in the number of conceptions are Roger Mols, *Introduction à la démographie historique des villes d'Europe du XIVe au XVIIIe siècle*, Vol. 3 (Louvain, 1956), pp. 298–9; and Etienne Hélin, 'Opinions de quelques casuistes de la Contre-Réforme sur l'avortement, la contraception et la continence dans le mariage', Hélène Bergues et al., *La prévention des naissances dans la famille, ses origines dans les temps modernes* (Paris, 1960), pp. 247–9. François Lebrun, 'Démographie et mentalités: Le mouvement des conceptions sous l'Ancien Régime', *Annales de Démographie Historique* (1974), pp. 45–50, expresses some reservations about the link between the March dip in conceptions and Lenten sexual abstinence, but his arguments fail to account for much of the evidence which exists in support of the connection.

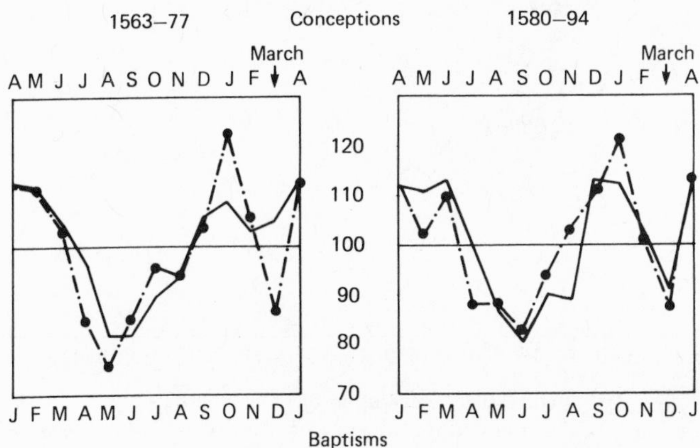

Figure 4. The monthly movement of conceptions
(The movement of conceptions is calculated by extrapolating backward nine months from the movement of baptisms.)

periods, suggesting that an equally large percentage of the population of these parishes practiced sexual abstinence during Lent throughout the years of the Wars of Religion. In St Maclou and St Vivien, on the other hand, the March trough does not appear at all in the first period but is quite marked in the second.

Because the first measure must be calculated in fifteen-year segments, it does not permit a close analysis of changes in popular fervor, although it does suggest a certain growth in religious concern around the period of the League. The second index permits finer discrimination. This is based on the sums collected in the basins which were placed in each parish church to receive the offerings of the faithful. Each church had several basins, most commonly one dedicated to the Virgin and one, the '*bassin de l'oeuvre*', for the upkeep of the church. A few parishes also maintained a basin of the relics. The sums collected annually in these receptacles are noted in the accounts of the parish treasuries. Relatively complete sets of these accounts have survived from thirteen parishes scattered about the entire city, permitting a study of the movement of pious offerings in a representative sample of the city's parishes.[1]

Since the adoration of the Virgin was one of the most violently contested

[1] *Comptes de fabrique* from the sixteenth century are A.D.S.M., G 6245 (St André-de-la-Ville); G 6300–6302 (St Cande-le-Jeune); G 6341–2 (St Cande-le-Vieil); G 6583–5 (St Gervais); G 6616–18 (St Godard); G 6727–9 (St Jean); G 6800–6802 (St Laurent); G 6885–907 (St Maclou); G 7166–9 (St Michel); G 7228–33 (St Nicaise); G 7329–30 (St Nicolas); G 7373–4 (Notre-Dame-de-la-Ronde); and G 7754–75 (St Vivien). I am indebted to David Nicholls for calling my attention to these accounts and generously passing along his figures for the years prior to 1562.

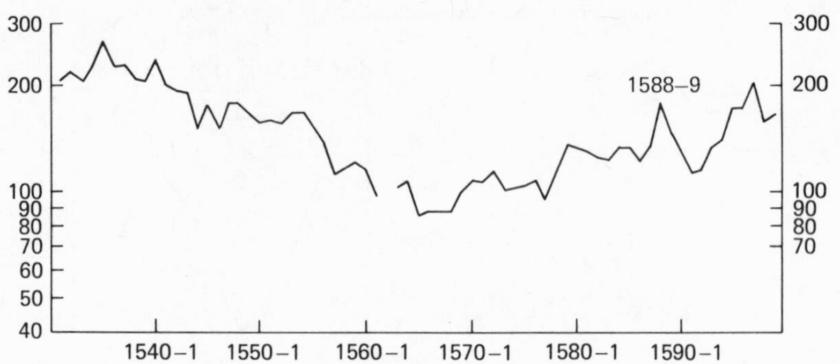

Figure 5. The evolution of pious offerings.
(Cumulative index of donations to the *bassins de la Vierge, de l'oeuvre, et des reliques*, 13 parishes.)

Catholic practices, the evolution of donations to the basin of the Virgin would appear to be an excellent test of the popular response first to Protestant attacks on the cult, then to Catholic attempts to reinvigorate traditional forms of devotion. The significance of gifts to the *bassin de l'oeuvre* is harder to interpret, but such donations probably reflected above all an interest in the physical adornment of the parish church, again a point of contention between Catholics and Protestants. In any case, the curves of the *bassin de l'oeuvre* parallel almost exactly those of the basin of the Virgin in those parishes where donations to each were recorded separately in the account books.[1] Similar impulses apparently motivated donations to each one.

Figure 5 is a cumulative index which reflects the movement of donations to all of the basins in the thirteen parishes for which the accounts survive. Examining briefly the movement of donations in the earlier part of the century, it is clear first of all that, as would be expected, a marked drop occurred in the level of pious offerings in the decades prior to the outbreak of the Wars of Religion. The decline is evident from 1535 on and is particularly dramatic in the period 1555–61. Whatever economic difficulties the city might have experienced in this period certainly cannot explain a fall in donations of over 60 per cent: clearly it is the diffusion of Protestant ideas which is reflected here. Significantly, two parishes were exceptions to this general trend of declining donations: the semi-agricultural *faubourg* St Gervais and the poor cloth-working parish of St Nicaise. That the Protestant movement largely bypassed the poorest and least educated sections of the city is confirmed once again.

[1] Individual graphs for each basin and each parish may be found in Appendix v of my dissertation.

The subsequent evolution of donations during the first twenty-five years of the Religious Wars is highly ambiguous. Following the gap in the curve caused by the interruption of Catholic worship in 1562, the cumulative index fell to its lowest point of the century in the later 1560s, then rose slowly for the next two decades. While this increase might reflect slowly reawakening Catholic piety, it should also be remembered that these decades were ones of rampant inflation. Grain prices almost doubled in Paris between the five-year periods 1563–7 and 1583–7,[1] and only in the parishes of St Godard, St Gervais, and St Nicolas did pious offerings rise as rapidly. But the effect which inflation might be expected to have on the level of offerings is by no means clear. On the one hand, people had more spending money in their pockets which they might have been tempted to place in the church basins. On the other hand, somebody who was used to giving four *sous* to the Virgin every Easter would not necessarily have felt that a larger gift was necessary to gain her patronage simply because the cost of living was rising. Because of this uncertainty, no confident assertions can be made as to whether the rise in giving in these years ought to be considered the product of inflation or the reflection of a gradual reawakening of Marian devotion. All that can be said for sure about the period 1562–87 is that the movement of donations revealed no dramatic trend in any direction.

The jump in donations which coincided with the early years of the League is subject to no such ambiguities, for the level of offerings in the year 1588–9 stands out as a sharp peak in the graph. In nine of the twelve parishes for which the account books exist for this period, the amounts collected in the church basins reached their highest level of the entire period of the Religious Wars between 1587 and 1591. In three, the amounts collected in these years more than doubled the sums amassed in the years immediately preceding them. The account books suggest strongly that the dramatic public manifestations of religious fervor were just part of a deeper upsurge of concern during these troubled years.

They also suggest that a drop in donations followed quickly, a drop that must be attributed primarily to the severe economic crisis which, as we shall see in the next chapter, accompanied the later years of League domination. Growing disaffection with the movement probably also contributed to this decline, but it is striking that the decline was quickly followed by a new upsurge in offerings with the return of peace and prosperity under Henry IV. Brief soundings in two parishes suggest that this rise then continued strongly until at least the middle of the seventeenth century, at which point the parish accounts began to be maintained differently, making further

[1] Micheline Baulant and Jean Meuvret, *Prix des céréales extraits de la mercuriale de Paris (1520–1698)* (Paris, 1960), Vol. 1, p. 243.

comparison impossible.[1] Here we see the 'take-off' of the Counter-Reformation, a development also reflected by the extraordinary spate of new religious foundations in these years in which seventeen new convents and monasteries were created within a span of fifty years.[2]

The two quantitative indicators of Catholic fervor thus seem clearly to confirm the pattern of change already suggested by more traditional documents. After twenty-five years during which violence against the Protestants had bulked far larger than attempts to reinvigorate Catholic religious life among those committed to the Roman Church, the crisis of the League stimulated a rash of new forms of devotional activity which aimed to rekindle mass religious fervor and express the contrition for the city's sinful ways considered necessary to deflect the wrath of an angry God. Of course, not every Rouennais was caught up in the religious fervor of the period; like Paris, the Norman capital surely had its Pierre de l'Estoiles, looking on at the fevered activity of their neighbors with a mixture of bemusement and contempt. There were also undoubtedly those who were following the dictates of prudence rather than the promptings of conscience when they participated in the *ligueur* processions or prayed before the *oratoire*.[3] But men are only forced to become hypocrites when other men are aroused about an issue, and the degree to which Rouen's Catholics became aroused about the crisis which faced their religion and gave vent to their anxieties in spectacular forms of devotion is surely one of the most striking aspects of this period. That the French Counter-Reformation may owe some of its origins to these years when Catholicism's fate seemed to hang precariously in the balance only adds to the fascination of the Catholic activities of these years.

[1] I examined the records of St Cande-le-Vieil (A.D.S.M., G 6342–3), where gifts to the Virgin rose by 70 per cent between the five-year periods 1595–1600 and 1632–37, and St Gervais (A.D.S.M., G 6585), where the increase between 1599–1600 and 1654–5 was 133 per cent.

[2] *See* François Farin, *Histoire de la ville de Rouen* (Rouen, 1833), Vol. 3, for a full list of the religious houses in the city with their dates of foundation.

[3] Antoine Richart tells us that in Laon those suspected of being royalists were unfailingly the first to turn out for processions and the last to return home from church. Richart, *Mémoires sur la Ligue dans le Laonnois*, p. 92.

9

Sacrifice and disaffection

Although the period of the League witnessed a flowering of dramatic religious ceremonies, enthusiasm for them waned as the years passed. Pious offerings showed a regular decline from 1590 onward, and by 1593 the *oratoire* had ceased and processions were becoming rarer. The fate of the religious enthusiasm provides a parable for the larger fate of the *Sainte-Union*. Its seizure of power was followed by a burst of measures designed to put its platform into effect and increase popular support, but its failure to secure all of the surrounding areas of Normandy meant that the region soon filled up with the rival troops of king and League. The civil war which ensued proved a standoff. As the war dragged on from year to year showing no signs of resolution, and as the economic crisis which it provoked deepened, support for the League steadily waned.

The initial actions taken by Rouen's new *Sainte-Union* masters attacked the issues of high taxation and venal office that had helped fuel the movement. By a series of letters-patent issued by Mayenne and registered by the parlement in May, taxes were ordered reduced and all superfluous offices were suppressed as soon as they became vacant through the death or resignation of their incumbents.[1] Those who have tended to see in the League a movement of would-be *officiers* trying to break down the barriers which increasingly kept *procureurs* and *avocats* from joining the sovereign courts have generally regarded the latter decrees as empty promises which the *ligueurs* never intended to fulfill. In fact, although the duke of Mayenne frequently succumbed to the temptation to overlook these edicts so that he might use vacant offices as a means of rewarding loyal supporters, Rouen's parlement resisted many of his attempts to name new men to offices, allowing them instead to lapse. On several occasions the court refused to register letters of appointment granted by the duke.[2] It also revived the once-traditional requirement, abandoned in 1554 because of the

[1] A.D.S.M., B, Parlement, Arrêts, Février–Juin 1589, arrêt of May 15, 1589.

[2] A.D.S.M., B, Parlement, Registres Secrets – Rouen, entries of Oct. 22, 1591, June 25, 1592, Aug. 16 and 17, 1593; Arrêts, Avril–Août 1591 (Rouen), arrêt of Aug. 7, 1591; B.N., MS Français 22454, fo. 244.

growing frankness of the sale of offices, by which all new *officiers* had to swear that they had not paid money to obtain their letters of appointment.[1] The concern about excessive taxation and venal office which had fueled the League's growth was translated into action once the movement came to power.

Other actions taken by the *Conseil de l'Union* in the wake of Rouen's Day of the Barricades sought to ensure the League's control over the city. English merchants, tepid *officiers*, and, more generally, all those suspected of hostility toward the League soon found themselves targets of surveillance and harassment. So many were rounded up and imprisoned that, in May, 5 or 6 people were reportedly packed into even the smallest cells in the *conciergerie*.[2] Security precautions had to be tightened further in June after a plot to turn the city over to the king, the plot of the Three Saucers (so-called after the inn in which it was planned), was detected and foiled. The usual restrictions governing the use of torture in interrogations were even suspended by the parlement for the trials of those arrested in connection with the plot.[3] Most of those imprisoned in these early months of the League were finally released and allowed to leave the city, but only on payment of substantial ransoms.[4]

While instituting close surveillance over those suspected of royalist sentiments within Rouen, the *Conseil de l'Union* also sought to extend its control over the rest of Normandy. Its success was mixed. Letters were dispatched to the other cities of the province urging them to join the cause of the League.[5] While many did, including Lisieux, Evreux, Caudebec, Neufchâtel, Honfleur, Le Havre, and Avranches, others remained royalist, notably the province's second and third largest cities, Caen and Dieppe. The nobility of the region also split into two camps, with most of the leading seigneurs choosing to side against the League, which some saw as an attempt 'to efface the prerogatives and dignity of all the nobles of the kingdom'.[6]

The League's leaders had initially hoped that uprisings throughout Normandy might bring about a province-wide repudiation of the faithless Henry III, enable taxes to be rolled back to the level which prevailed in

[1] A.D.S.M., B, Parlement, Registres Secrets – Rouen, entry of Aug. 14, 1592. On the suppression of the traditional oath, *see* B.N., MS Français 22454, fos. 78–9.

[2] A.D.S.M., B, Parlement, Registres Secrets – Rouen, entry of May 15, 1589.

[3] A.D.S.M., B, Parlement, Arrêts, Février–Juin 1589, arrêt of June 6, 1589. The plot is described in *La thraison descouverte des Politiques de la ville de Rouen* (Paris, n.d. [1589]).

[4] A.D.S.M., B, Parlement, Registres Secrets – Rouen, entries of May 12 and 15, 1589; Arrêts, Juin 1593–Avril 1594 (Rouen), arrêt of April 30, 1594; *Cal. S.P. For.*, 1589, pp. 153, 228, 343; Amable Floquet, *Histoire du Parlement de Normandie* (Rouen, 1840–42), Vol. 3, pp. 333–5.

[5] C. R. H. L. d'Estaintot, *La Ligue en Normandie 1588–1594* (Paris, 1862), p. 12.

[6] The words are those of the duke of Montpensier, quoted in *ibid.*, p. 20.

the good old days of Charles IX, and lead to the convocation of a new meeting of the Estates-General, an assembly of the entire kingdom that could resolve such still outstanding questions as how the deposed king was to be replaced. Their failure to secure full control of the region introduced an unsettling factor into their calculations. Fighting soon broke out between soldiers raised by the League and troops still loyal to Henry III garrisoned at Pont-de-l'Arche, Dieppe, and the château of Blainville. The fighting then intensified following Henry III's assassination on August 1, 1589 by the young Dominican monk Jacques Clément. Paris had been under attack by the combined royal and Huguenot forces at the time of Henry's fatal stabbing, but after his death many who had initially supported the king now chose to go over to the side of the League rather than fight for the heretic Navarre, whom Henry had named as his successor shortly after the termination of the Estates of Blois. The erosion of support forced Navarre, now Henry IV, to fall back from Paris. He headed into Normandy, attempting en route to Dieppe a brief surprise attack on Rouen which was beaten back easily.[1] For the next three years Upper Normandy became the chief battlefield of the realm, scene of many of the most critical episodes in the struggle between Navarre and Mayenne for control of France, notably the battles of Arques and Ivry. The campaigns which criss-crossed the region between 1589 and 1592 were crucial in determining the subsequent evolution of the League in Rouen, for they guaranteed that the movement would develop amid an atmosphere of constant warfare.

The fighting had four major consequences for the League's development. First of all, the fighting quickly ruptured the regional network of production and exchange which fueled so much of Rouen's trade, disrupting commerce. The local Day of the Barricades had provoked optimism within the city's merchant community, since now the city was aligned on the same side as Le Havre and Paris. 'Business will become more secure', Simon Ruiz's factors wrote him hopefully on March 13.[2] Their optimism soon turned to gloom. Within three months royalist troops under the duke of Montpensier had captured the major linen markets of Bernay and Beaumont-le-Roger, seizing in the process large quantities of cloth belonging to Rouennais merchants. Quillebeuf and Honfleur, both ports near the mouth of the Seine, were also taken by the royalists, and henceforward ships could only move up and down the river in armed convoys.[3] Upper Normandy

[1] The brevity of this siege did not prevent the *ligueurs* from claiming a major victory when Henry retired. *See* the *Vray discours et defence des Catholiques de la ville de Rouen*... (Paris, 1589), reprinted in C. R. H. L. d'Estaintot, ed., *La première campagne de Henri IV en Normandie, Août–Octobre 1589*, publication of the Société des Bibliophiles Normands XXXII (Rouen, 1878).

[2] Ruiz, caja 129, 56, Francisco de Fontaneda and Juan Pasqual to Simon Ruiz, March 13, 1589.

[3] Ruiz, caja 136, 214, Jos Cunet to Ruiz, June 18, 1589.

became, in the words of one merchant, 'so disturbed...and with the partisans of the Bearnais and of the Catholic union so intermingled that there is no corner where anything is secure'.[1] Many of Rouen's merchants became convinced that they would be better off transferring their operations elsewhere.

Since Englishmen who happened to be in the city were particular targets of the new *ligueur* authorities, they were the first to depart. By May virtually all had left town, and one Briton still languishing in prison moaned in a letter to the Privy Council that there was not a soul remaining from whom he could borrow the ransom he needed to gain his freedom.[2] Merchants of other nationalities departed only slightly less hastily than the English. Simon Ruiz's two main factors had moved to Lille by June 1589, and in the course of the following year four more of his Rouennais correspondents slipped out of town.[3] These men appear to have been typical of the Spanish merchants in the city. The growth in the size of Rouen's foreign merchant colonies that had been prompted by the decline of Antwerp in the 1570s and early 1580s was thus wiped out when Normandy, too, became a center of conflict.

The interruption of normal economic relations provoked by the campaigning made the second consequence of the fighting particularly grave. This was the abandonment, under the pressure of war, of all attempts to reduce taxes. Despite the *ligueurs*' initial efforts at rolling back taxation, an ineluctable pattern common to many early modern revolts soon manifested itself. Although a rising burden of taxation had helped to create a revolutionary situation, once the revolution came it provoked a costly civil war which compelled the new rulers to demand sums of money from the taxpayers as great as or greater than the amounts exacted by the old authorities. Between 1589 and 1591 no less than nine new levies had to be imposed to raise the money needed to carry on the struggle against the royalist forces nearby.[4] A complete set of municipal accounts has survived for 1592, showing that direct taxes of 63,000 *livres* and indirect levies amounting to an additional 41,000 *livres* more were raised from the city. Even this fell far short of paying for the troops needed to defend the city, and a further 50,892 *livres* had to be raised through loans from those

[1] Ruiz, caja 143, 100, Pedro de Alava to Ruiz, May 25, 1590.

[2] *Cal. S.P. For.*, 1589, p. 228.

[3] V. Vazquez de Prada, ed., *Lettres marchandes d'Anvers* (Paris, n.d.), Vol. 4, p. 350. From the summer of 1590 onward only the Lucchese merchant Pandolfo Cenami remained in Rouen out of the seven men with whom Ruiz had been doing business in the city. Cenami was more a banker than a trader in commodities, and for the rest of the period of the League the few letters arriving in Medina del Campo from Rouen concerned only minor financial transactions.

[4] A.C.R., A 20, entries of Dec. 30, 1589, Feb. 28, 1590, April 5, 1591; A 21, entries of Aug. 28, Oct. 30, and Dec. 20, 1591; A.D.S.M., B, Parlement, Arrêts, Janvier–Avril 1591 (Rouen), arrêts of Jan. 24, Feb. 6 and Feb. 11, 1591; Registres Secrets – Rouen, entry of April 26, 1591.

inhabitants particularly commited to the *ligueur* cause.[1] This unusual expedient had become necessary because, as might be expected, considerable opposition had developed over the course of the preceding year to any additional taxes. The Rouennais had expected the League's triumph to mean an end to the constant fiscal burden and were ill-disposed to the new taxes demanded by the movement's authorities. A special assembly of the city called in December 1589 to deliberate about the best means of raising money had dissolved into a shouting match, and when order had been restored and the delegates of each quarter of the city called upon to speak in turn, the representatives of St Hilaire and Cauchoise had refused to say anything at all, while those of Beauvoisine would only opine, 'Taxes, they didn't want any.'[2] Refusal to pay the tax imposed by the authorities in spite of these protests had been widespread,[3] and in the subsequent years tax resistance had only grown. New levies on wine and salt instituted in 1591 produced so much hostility that they were finally reduced after one tax-collector barely escaped being thrown into the Seine and others reported that they had encountered widespread non-compliance.[4]

The resistance to the new taxes levied by the *ligueur* authorities was only part of a larger breakdown in public order which followed the *Sainte-Union*

[1] A.D.S.M., C 2314, 'Registre et controole de la recepte generalle de Rouen pour l'annee 1592' provides what is virtually a complete budget for the year. It reveals a sizable deficit that breaks down as follows (all figures in *livres tournois*):

Revenue		Expenditures	
direct taxes on city		payment of soldiers	327,846
nouveau subside pour les gens de guerre	33,820	*gages* of *officiers*	28,578
		payment of *rentes*	1,083
cotisation	29,847	repayment of loans	2,580
indirect taxes on city		miscellaneous	4,599
aides	22,560		
5 *sous* per *muid* of wine	4,196	total	364,686
Romaine	15,185		
direct taxes on countryside			
taille	65,282		
indirect taxes on entire region			
gabelle	38,738		
miscellaneous			
loans	50,892		
revenue of absentees	12,926		
décimes	2,529		
other miscellaneous	4,363		
total	280,338		

Nearly all of those to whom *rentes* were paid are identified as being either poor or else members of the sovereign courts; the normal payment of *rentes* was apparently suspended, and only those with influence or those who absolutely depended on this income were paid their dividends.

[2] A.C.R., A 20, entry of Dec. 26, 1589.

[3] A.D.S.M., B, Parlement, Arrêts, Février–Juillet 1590 (Rouen), arrêt of March 28, 1590.

[4] A.D.S.M., B, Parlement, Registres Secrets – Rouen, entries of April 30, and May 3, 1591.

takeover. This was the third consequence of the fighting in the region. For every true believer moved to take up arms for the League even prior to its takeover there was soon a soldier of fortune for whom the subsequent fighting promised booty in a period when it was hard to make one's living any other way. By the end of 1589 alarming signs of anarchy were beginning to preoccupy the city's authorities. Marauding bands of both soldiers and civilians roamed the city by night. The courtyard of the Palais de Justice was occupied and threats were uttered against the parlement. Men tangled with the night watch in the Vieux Marché and hurled imprecations against the *Conseil de l'Union*.[1] No single political line governed the actions of these groups, although at times they engaged in what was clearly vigilante action against those thought insufficiently committed to the League, as when the châteaux of several *parlementaires* who had retired to their estates were attacked by mounted raiders, attired in black masks embroidered with crosses and white tears.[2] A similar motivation may have been at work when, within the city, a group of armed men forced its way into the house of a nobleman detected cooking meat during Lent, smashed his furniture, and climaxed the raid with a gesture of derision that may seem profoundly unsettling today when natural bodily functions are so rigidly secret but was perhaps less so among men less repressed on this score – defecating in the middle of his kitchen.[3] But much of the disorder involved little more than classic soldierly misbehavior: the seizure of grain and livestock from the peasantry of the surrounding countryside, the extortion of money from those city dwellers in whose houses the soldiers were billetted, and so forth.[4] Some of the violence thus appears to have been brigandage with an ideological justification, some simple brigandage. The parlement issued repeated *arrêts* expelling all noblemen and soldiers unattached to any company and forbidding all '*pilleries, oppressions, volleries et molestes au pauvre peuple*', with little apparent success.[5] Even while certain of Rouen's inhabitants were engaged in spectacular demonstrations of penitence, others were heightening the anxieties of the pious with their violent and disorderly conduct.

The disorder which characterized the first years of the period of League rule gradually died down as Rouen increasingly fell under the iron hand

1 A.D.S.M., B, Parlement, Registres Secrets – Rouen, entry of Aug. 9, 1590; Arrêts, Février–Juillet 1590 (Rouen), arrêt of July 27, 1590.

2 A.D.S.M., B, Parlement, Arrêts, Juillet 1589–Février 1590 (Rouen), arrêt of Nov. 3, 1589; Février–Juillet 1590 (Rouen), arrêt of July 30, 1590.

3 A.D.S.M., B, Parlement, Registres Secrets – Rouen, entry of April 12, 1591.

4 A.D.S.M., B, Parlement, Registres Secrets – Rouen, entries of Jan. 14, 1591 and Jan. 23, 1592; Arrêts, Février–Juillet 1590 (Rouen), arrêt of March 6, 1590.

5 A.D.S.M., B, Parlement, Arrêts, Février–Juillet 1590 (Rouen), arrêts of Feb. 8, March 6, 1590; Août–Décembre 1590 (Rouen), arrêt of Dec. 12, 1590; Janvier–Avril 1591 (Rouen), arrêt of Jan. 16, 1591.

of its successive military governors. Here was the last and perhaps most important consequence of the constant fighting of the period 1589–92 – the shifts it produced in the balance of power between the city's different governing authorities. From the start the League was an alliance between two groups: disgruntled, ambitious noblemen and zealously Catholic urban ideologues. In the months immediately following Rouen's Day of the Barricades this latter group, represented by the *Conseil de l'Union*, became the dominant one within the city, dictating to the parlement and Council of Twenty-Four the campaign of repression against its enemies that was launched.[1] But the constant compaigning in Normandy had the effect of strengthening the authority of the chief military commander within Rouen, the governor. As time passed the *Conseil de l'Union* became steadily more subservient to him. When the *Conseil* attempted in 1591 to punish the families of those royalists who had left town, its measures were successfully countermanded by the parlement.[2] By 1593 the council had disappeared from the political scene altogether, and the governor had forced its leader, Michel de Monchy, into exile.[3] The governor was by now virtually the unchallenged ruler of the city. He had effective control of all disbursements, determined the form which was to be followed for election to the Estates-General of 1593, and refused to allow the city council to hold any general assemblies without his permission.[4] It was thus the chief representative of the noble wing of the League who profited the most from the movement in the long run.

A number of men held the governorship over the course of the League. The king's longstanding lieutenant-general, the sieur de Carrouges, initially attempted to keep this position for himself, announcing his resignation as royal lieutenant shortly after the local Day of the Barricades and declaring himself now to be the head of the League.[5] His conversion came too late to convince anybody. He was quickly replaced by a series of interim lieutenants, first the duke of Aumale, then the duke of La Mailleraye. But

[1] Although the *Conseil*'s deliberations have not survived, its power and certain of its actions can be deduced from the records of the parlement and the Council of Twenty-Four.

[2] A.D.S.M., B, Parlement, Registres Secrets – Rouen, entry of April 26, 1591.

[3] An entry in the Registre Secret of the parlement for July 19, 1593 refers to the *Conseil de l'Union* 'estably *lors* en ceste ville'. (Italics mine.) On the governor's expulsion of Monchy *see* A.D.S.M., B, Parlement, Registres Secrets – Rouen, entries of June 18, 19, 21, and 26, 1593.

[4] A.D.S.M., B, Registres Secrets – Rouen, entries of Oct. 14, 1592, June 15, 1593; A.C.R., A 21, entry of Jan. 9, 1593. The tendency for the *Conseil de l'Union*'s power to decline and the governor's authority to grow with time appears to have been the norm in cities controlled by the League, although it was occasionally resisted. *See* Henri Drouot, 'Les conseils provinciaux de la Sainte-Union (1589–1595): Notes et questions', *Annales du Midi*, LXV (1953), p. 433; Robert R. Harding, *Anatomy of a Power Elite: The Provincial Governors of Early Modern France* (New Haven, 1978), p. 98; Peter M. Ascoli, 'French Provincial Cities and the Catholic League', *Occasional Papers of the American Society for Reformation Research*, I (1977), pp. 21–7.

[5] A.C.R., A 20, entry of Feb. 10, 1589.

because of Rouen's strategic importance, Mayenne felt that ultimately the city had to be placed under as important a nobleman as possible. Early in 1590 he therefore replaced La Mailleraye with Jean de Saulx-Tavanes, son of the famous military captain and governor of Burgundy, Gaspard de Saulx-Tavanes. Tavanes quickly set about aggrandizing his authority within Rouen, overturning the results of the municipal election of July 1590 and replacing the duly-elected *échevins* with his own men, using the pretext that those elected were 'disagreeable to the people'.[1] But it was not Tavanes who was destined to be the city's final governor. He was notoriously vain and unpredictable and soon alienated many of those in positions of influence within Rouen. His high-handed behavior ultimately provoked his downfall when, during a joint military expedition against the royalist-controlled château of Blainville, his attempt to seize the lion's share of the credit and booty for himself and his men aroused the anger of an ally and rival far cleverer than himself, the duke of Villars, governor of Le Havre.[2]

Villars was one of those noblemen for whom the League was less a religious crusade than a vehicle for self-advancement. Originally attached to the cause by a bribe of 30,000 *écus* from the Paris Sixteen, he showed little concern for the ideological aspects of the struggle, not hesitating to accept into his retinue a man who had been involved in the royalist plot of the Three Saucers.[3] By 1590 he had added the governorship of the Pays de Caux to that of Le Havre, and after his quarrel with Tavanes in the following year he saw an opportunity to extend his empire farther. On the occasion of a visit to Rouen by the duke of Mayenne, he camped himself outside the city with 15 ships and 1,500 men, threatening to take them over to the royalist side if Tavanes were not unseated as governor of Normandy. Mayenne preferred offending Tavanes to losing Villars and Le Havre and so forced Tavanes to accept a new position with the army in Picardy. Mayenne then appointed his own son as governor of Normandy, with Villars to be his lieutenant with full powers until the young boy came of age.[4] Villars was henceforward the dominant figure within the city.

1 A.C.R., A 20, entries of March 21, July 10, 1590.

2 A.C.R., A 20, entries of March 1 and April 23, 1591; A.D.S.M., B, Parlement, Registres Secrets (Rouen), entry of April 20, 1591. According to Villars, Tavanes had consistently mistreated his men before Blainville. He had fed them spoiled bread, underpaid them, and then, when the castle was captured, deprived them of their rightful share of the booty by keeping them confined in the courtyard while his own troops sacked the château.

3 Jacques-Auguste de Thou, *Histoire universelle*, (The Hague, 1740), Vol. 7, p. 226; *Mémoires de Pierre Thomas, Sieur du Fossé*, ed. F. Bouquet, (Rouen, 1876), Vol. 1, pp. 6–7. Another of Villars' retainers who again demonstrates his lack of ideological fussiness was Etienne de la Fond, a once and future *fidèle* of the Protestant Sully. Bernard Barbiche, *Sully* (Paris, 1978), p. 57.

4 B.M.R., MS Y 214 (7), entry of July 20, 1591; Jacques Lavaud, *Un poète de cour au temps des derniers Valois: Philippe Desportes (1546–1606)* (Paris, 1936), p. 351. Desportes was one of Villars' chief advisors; Lavaud's solidly researched thesis thus contains much information concerning Rouen during the period of Villars' lieutenant-governorship.

Two other bodies also shared political power in Rouen, the parlement and the Council of Twenty-Four. Their relative power underwent a somewhat surprising transformation over the course of the five years of League domination. Unlike their counterparts in many League cities who sought vigorously to reassert communal power, Rouen's Council of Twenty-Four went into eclipse in these years. It rarely assembled except when summoned by the parlement, carried out little besides routine administrative chores assigned it by the other pillars of authority in the city, and often had difficulty obtaining the quorum needed to meet at all. Those *parlementaires* who remained in Rouen meanwhile managed to extend their influence into spheres previously controlled entirely by the Council of Twenty-Four. Members of the court began to preside over council meetings, something never done before, and the court assumed for the first time the right to oversee municipal finances.[1] Rouen's parlement weathered the storm of the League quite successfully.

While fighting swirled constantly around Rouen throughout the period of League rule, for the first two years none of the campaigning touched the city directly except the brief, half-hearted siege mounted by Navarre in 1589. The city authorities devoted most of their attention during these years to keeping order and raising the taxes demanded by the crisis, while the soldiers garrisoned in the Norman capital, when not plaguing the local populace, directed their energies toward the siege and demolition of the heavily fortified castle of Blainville, which was a constant royalist thorn in the side of the city's supply routes until finally taken in March 1591. But in the summer of 1591 Rouen suddenly became the focal point of the international politics of western Europe. Henry of Navarre was running desperately short of money, while Queen Elizabeth was eager to see him concentrate his military efforts in Normandy so that the Channel coastline might not fall under the domination of the allied League and Spanish forces. In July 1591 the two therefore signed an agreement to mount a joint expedition against Rouen.[2]

Within the city the threat of a direct attack generated fevered activity.

[1] The increase in the parlement's authority *vis à vis* the Council of Twenty-Four emerges from the Registres Secrets and the municipal registers of deliberations. On the reassertion of communal power elsewhere, *see* Jean H. Mariéjol, *La Réforme et la Ligue*, Vol. 6[1] of Ernest Lavisse, *Histoire de France* (Paris, 1904), pp. 342–3; Henri Ouvré, 'Essai sur l'histoire de la Ligue à Poitiers', p. 192; Fernand Braudel, *La Méditerranée et le monde méditerranéen à l'époque de Philippe II* (1st ed., Paris, 1949), pp. 1066–7; Henri Drouot, *Mayenne et la Bourgogne: Etude sur la Ligue en Bourgogne, 1587–1596* (Paris, 1937), Vol. 1, pp. 410–13; Ascoli, '"The Sixteen" and the Paris League', p. 28.

[2] An excellent analysis of the foreign policy considerations which moved Elizabeth to intervene in the war in Normandy is R. B. Wernham's old article 'Queen Elizabeth and the Siege of Rouen, 1591', *Transactions of the Royal Historical Society*, 3rd ser., IX (1932), pp. 65–76. Howell A. Lloyd, *The Rouen Campaign, 1590–1592: Politics, Warfare and the Early Modern State* (Oxford, 1973), now also provides a fine narrative of the events in Normandy. The background of the English intervention is discussed in Chapters 1–4.

All residents were set to work on the fortifications one day per week. Grain was commandeered from the peasants of the surrounding countryside. New taxes were introduced to pay for the improvements on the city walls. Finally, when the joint English and royalist force appeared on the horizon, the order was given to set afire and raze the *faubourgs* so as to deprive the attackers of cover.[1] The dismayed residents sought to resist, but with little success. Similar orders had been given in 1562 but the *faubourgs* had not suffered a major decline in population as a result. This time the order was carried out ruthlessly. Parish registers show that the areas outside the walls were entirely abandoned from October 1591 through July 1593 and were only slowly repopulated thereafter, not even reattaining half of their pre-destruction population until 1603.[2]

The second major siege which Rouen underwent in the course of the Religious Wars began on November 11, 1591. As in 1562, the rebellious city faced a royal army commanded by the king of Navarre, but this time the Rouennais rebels were Catholic, not Protestant, while the king of Navarre, Henry not Anthony, also claimed to be king of France. English troops were again involved, but they were attacking, not defending, the city. And unlike the first siege, the attacking forces lacked a decisive advantage in manpower or artillery. A rapid victory such as that of 1562 was impossible, the more so since the attackers were also hampered by poor coordination between the English and French troops.[3] The siege opened with the sort of chivalric gesture which still was made on Europe's battlefields thanks to the 'imaginative refeudalization of society' promoted by pageant and poetry even though feudal warfare itself had long since fallen before the combined power of gunpowder and the professional mercenary. The earl of Essex, commander of the English forces, challenged the duke of Villars to meet him in individual combat, maintaining that 'the king's cause is more just than the League's, I am better than you, and my mistress is more beautiful'. Rouen's governor declined the invitation, claiming that his responsibilities within the city were too great to allow him to risk his life at the moment. (He would be glad to fight Essex later, he declared.) In his reply, he gave the lie to all of Essex's claims:

> You lie and will lie every time that you maintain it [that you are better than me], just as you lie when you maintain that the cause I undertake in defense of my religion is not better than that of those who seek to destroy it. And as for the comparison of your mistress to mine, I would like to think you are not more correct

[1] A.C.R., A 21, entry of July 30, 1591; R.P. 445, entry of Nov. 18, 1591; Guillaume Valdory, *Discours du siège de la ville de Rouen au mois de Novembre mil cinq cens quatre vingts onze* (Rouen, 1592), pp. 4, 6.

[2] Philip Benedict, 'Catholics and Huguenots in Sixteenth-Century Rouen: The Demographic Effects of the Religious Wars', *French Historical Studies*, IX (1975), pp. 215–17.

[3] Lloyd, *Rouen Campaign*, p. 151.

'The Siege of Rouen 1591–92'

Source: engraving by Franz Harenberg, from the author's collection.

in this matter than in the others, although it is not something which concerns me much at present.[1]

This exchange of gallantries finished, the siege then settled down into the long, slow, brutal attempt to starve Rouen into submission that had become the standard, all-too-prosaic reality of sixteenth-century warfare.

Within Rouen, an elaborate system was introduced to ensure the equitable distribution of the city's supplies of bread.[2] Processions wound their way regularly through the city to implore divine protection, while fortuitous escapes from danger were given wide publicity as proof that that protection was indeed forthcoming.[3] From the cathedral pulpit, the penitentiary Dadré reminded the inhabitants of St Paul's denunciations of all dealings with false apostles.[4] All of these measures served to bolster the city's resolve. Common citizens went into battle with a crusading zeal (the curé Hesbert was credited with killing no less than 19 attackers), and many members of the militia and privileged military companies gave their lives for the cause.[5]

As the siege wore on, however, even the measures taken to ensure the equitable distribution of bread could not prevent that precious commodity from running short. By early February the number of loaves on sale at the Halles was enough to satisfy only half the customers.[6] The city implored Mayenne to come to its aid. Supplies were dwindling fast, the parlement wrote him on January 20; the city could not hold out much longer.[7] But the duke dared not advance on the large English–royalist army until he received reinforcements from the duke of Parma's *tercios* in the Low

[1] I quote from Guillaume Valdory, *Discours du siège de la ville de Rouen au mois de Novembre mil cinq cens quatre vingts onze*, ed. E. Gosselin (Rouen, 1871), p. 16. The incident is mentioned in many of the histories of the period, e.g., P. V. Palma Cayet, *Chronologie Novenaire*, Petitot, 1st ser., Vol. 40, pp. 355–7; and B.N., MS Français 23296 ('Histoire de la Ligue'), fos. 479–81. The author of the latter work judges the exchange of letters 'fort galant', but Queen Elizabeth reprimanded Essex for having issued the challenge on the grounds that it was improper for 'a noble man and a peer of this realm by birth' to make such a challenge to 'a mere rebel'. Lloyd, *Rouen Campaign*, p. 154n. On the larger revival of chivalric forms of which this episode is a part, there are excellent analyses in Frances A. Yates, 'Elizabethan Chivalry: The Romance of the Accession Day Tilts', *Journal of the Warburg and Courtauld Institutes*, XX (1957), pp. 4–25; and Roy Strong, *Splendor at Court: Renaissance Spectacle and the Theater of Power* (Boston, 1973), pp. 37ff.

[2] A.D.S.M., B, Parlement, Registres Secrets – Rouen, entry of Dec. 7, 1591; Enrico Davila, *The Historie of the Civill Warres of France*, trans. W. Aylesbury (London, 1647–8), p. 1054; Lavaud, *Desportes*, p. 356; Lloyd, *Rouen Campaign*, pp. 143–5.

[3] A.D.S.M., B, Parlement, Registres Secrets – Rouen, entry of Nov. 12, 1591; A.D.S.M., G 2177, entry of Feb. 11, 1592; Valdory, *Discours du siège*, pp. 57–60 and passim.

[4] De Thou, *Histoire universelle*, Vol. 8, p. 51.

[5] Valdory, *Discours du siège*, pp. 46–7; A.D.S.M., 5 E 117.

[6] A.D.S.M., B, Parlement, Registres Secrets – Rouen, entry of Feb. 1, 1592.

[7] A.D.S.M., B, Parlement, Registres Secrets – Rouen, entries of Jan. 24, and 30, 1592.

Countries – a fact which did not stop him from responding with continual letters assuring Rouen that he was on his way.[1] He would be there within six days, he wrote on February 19. Four weeks later he still had not arrived. Crowds gathered around the bakeries day and night, and all vagabonds or relatives of absent royalists were expelled from town to reduce the number of mouths to feed.[2] A month later the siege was still continuing, and still Mayenne had not appeared. The situation was so dire that soldiers were stealing the bread intended for the poor.[3] Rouen held out heroically. Finally, desperate and disaffected, a group of rioters crying '*du paix ou du pain*' invaded the Palais de Justice on April 16 and assaulted a number of Villar's lieutenants.[4] Just as the city's resolve seemed to be tottering, the *tercios* of the duke of Parma appeared on the horizon. On April 21, after more than five months, Navarre and Essex were forced to lift the siege.

Rouen had been saved, but famine and disease remained even after the attacking troops withdrew. A number of authors have suggested that the measures taken to ensure the distribution of supplies prevented any serious shortages.[5] The city's parish registers tell a different story. The siege provoked a mortality crisis even more terrible than that of 1586–7, one which began during the fighting itself but then lasted until the end of 1592. As the complete graph of baptisms, marriages and burials for the parish of St Martin-sur-Renelle shows, the death rate rose dramatically during the siege and continued to mount even after the attacking forces had withdrawn. The surrounding countryside had been stripped bare by the besiegers, making provisions nearly unobtainable until the new harvest.[6] As often happened, the troops had also brought infectious disease with them, and they left it behind them after they withdrew. In October the municipal authorities were still battling the 'contagion'.[7] Deaths did not fall below conceptions until the first quarter of 1593. By then, according to the parish account books, nearly three times as many people had been

1 A.D.S.M., B, Parlement, Registres Secrets – Rouen, entries of Jan. 21, Feb. 20, March 3, 6, and 17, 1592.

2 A.D.S.M., B, Parlement, Registres Secrets – Rouen, entries of Feb. 20, March 17 and 18, 1592.

3 A.D.S.M., B, Parlement, Registres Secrets – Rouen, entry of April 11, 1592.

4 A.D.S.M., B, Parlement, Registres Secrets – Rouen, entry of April 16, 1592; B.N., MS Français 23296, fo. 496; Valdory, *Discours du siège*, pp. 65–6.

5 Valdory, *Discours du siège*, p. 69; Davila, *Historie of the Civill Warres*, p. 1054; Lavaud, *Desportes*, p. 356.

6 By the end of the siege, the attacking forces had been ranging far afield scavenging for provisions and even so had been running short. Lloyd, *Rouen Campaign*, pp. 98–9. After the siege was raised efforts were made to alleviate the shortages by importing grain from Abbeville. Prarond, *Ligue à Abbeville*, Vol. 2, pp. 391–2.

7 Lloyd, *Rouen Campaign*, p. 166; A.D.S.M., B, Parlement, Registres Secrets – Rouen, entries of Aug. 11, Oct. 30 and 31, 1592. The entry of Oct. 30 outlines detailed measures which the Council of Twenty-Four was to take to combat this *peste*.

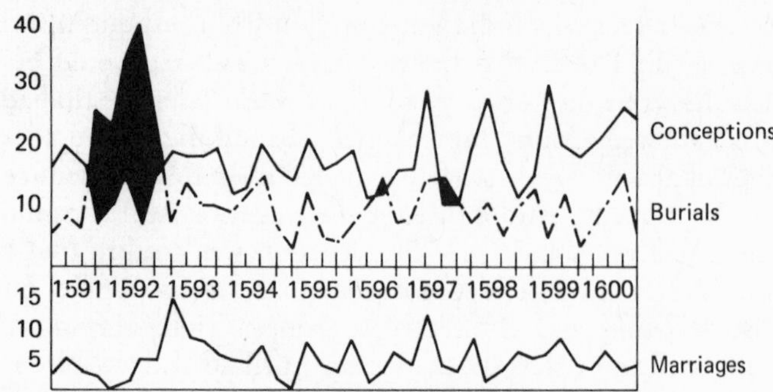

Figure 6. Trimestrial movement of conceptions, marriages, and burials, St Martin-sur-Renelle, 1591–1600

The graph reveals the classic symptoms of a mortality crisis in this far from poor tanners' parish: a soaring death rate, a decline in conceptions, and a drop in the number of marriages followed by a sharp rise once the crisis had passed.

buried as in a normal year.[1] Virtually all were casualties not of the fighting but of the famine and plague provoked by the siege.[2]

The heroic resistance to the siege represented the League's last hurrah, for the severe mortality crisis which resulted was the crowning blow in four years of economic hardship. Ever since the outbreak of fighting, the volume of traffic entering and leaving the city had been merely 15–35 per cent of pre-1588 levels. In the first quarter of 1591, for example, linen exports had been just a third of what they had been in the mid-1570s; in 1592 the tax on wine entering the city had yielded barely a fifth of what tax farmers had considered normal in a year between 1580 and 1585.[3] The decline in trade had also brought hardship to the city's artisans. Unprecedented cuts had to be made in the taxes levied on certain of the city's products 'given the necessities and calamities of the time', while the number of new masters received into the weavers' and goldsmiths' guilds fell to their lowest points of the entire seventy-five years from 1550 through 1625.[4]

[1] In the seven parishes for which the *comptes de fabrique* are available, there were 440 burials in 1592, as opposed to 365 during the crisis of 1587 and approximately 160 in a normal year. On this source, *see* Chapter 7, p. 173.

[2] Of 72 people buried in the parishes of St Lô and St Martin-sur-Renelle during the siege, only 7 were direct casualties of the fighting, 6 soldiers and 1 '*povre*' shot '*alant faucher*'. A.C.R., R.P.'s 288 and 445.

[3] Philip Benedict, 'Rouen's Foreign Trade During the Era of the Religious Wars (1560–1600)', forthcoming.

[4] A.D.S.M., B, Parlement, Arrêts, Avril–Août 1591, arrêts of May 17 and 18, June 18, 1591; B.M.R., MS Y 214 (7), entry of Sept. 3, 1590. Where roughly 25 new masters had been admitted to the weavers' guild every year over the preceding decade, only 16 new masters received their *lettres de draperie* in the parishes of St Vivien and St Nicaise during the entire four-year stretch from 1589 to 1593 (after which the number of *lettres de draperie* was suddenly swelled by a mass of refugees from Darnétal forced by a 1593 court decision to join the guild). Similarly, only 16 new master

The crisis cast much of the region's population adrift. Inhabitants of the surrounding areas flooded into Rouen seeking refuge behind its walls. As early as March 1590 the inhabitants of nearby Boisguillaume complained that:

As a result of the destruction of houses, exactions, ravages, pillaging, theft, ransomings, and other acts of hostility which have been and still are daily committed against the aforesaid inhabitants by soldiers, both those who claim to hold to the party of the *Sainte-Union* and those of the opposite party but especially those lodged in the *faubourgs* of Rouen, the aforesaid inhabitants have been forced for the past two months to leave and abandon their houses and farms and take refuge in this city of Rouen, where they still are at present and to which they have also brought what little livestock they could save...[1]

The number of refugees subsequently increased as the fighting in the vicinity intensified. Darnétal's 5,000 inhabitants all abandoned that nearby *bourg* when Henry of Navarre made it his headquarters during the siege, and most headed to Rouen and remained there for the rest of the period of the League.[2] So too did the *laboureurs* of nearby rural parishes, whose livestock grazing in the unbuilt spaces of St Vivien and St Nicaise became a common sight.[3] Yet despite this influx of refugees, the number of baptisms recorded in the city's parish registers declined by 15 per cent between the eight-year periods 1579–86 and 1587–94.[4] The decline suggests the severity of the mortality crises of 1586–7 and 1592 – and that a counter-movement of out-migration must also have accompanied the League. Although emigration is always the most difficult of demographic phenomena to measure, scattered references confirm that this was a major factor in the decline in baptisms. Not only did foreign merchants and royalist officials leave Rouen; apprentices broke their contracts to flee abroad in search of work, while established artisans moved to nearby cities

goldsmiths were received into the *orfèvres*' guild during the 5 years of League rule where 72 new masters had entered the guild in the decade prior to the League. A.D.S.M., G 7231–2, 7754–77; 5 E 609. The slump in the number of men entering the guilds which accompanied the League can also be deduced from a list of masters of the brass- and pewter-founders' guild made in 1602. (A.D.S.M., 5 E 465.) It includes just 4 men who had become masters during the period of the League as opposed to 11 received into the guild between 1583 and 1588, even though under normal circumstances one would expect that more masters admitted in the former period would still be alive in 1602 than admitted in the latter period.

1 A.D.S.M., B, Parlement, Arrêts, Février–Juillet 1590 (Rouen), arrêt of March 6, 1590.

2 Philip Benedict, 'Heurs et malheurs d'un gros bourg drapant: Note sur la population de Darnétal aux 16e et 17e siècles', *Annales de Normandie*, XXVIII (1978), p. 201.

3 A *laboureur* of St Hilaire, a village in Rouen's *banlieue* that was burned to the ground during the siege, reported in 1593 that that village's inhabitants had all moved to Rouen, A.D.S.M., G 3621. It is also possible to find references to refugees from Bernay, Elbeuf, and Biennetz (?). A.D.S.M., B, Parlement, Arrêts, Avril–Août 1591 (Rouen), arrêt of Aug. 30, 1591; Septembre 1591–Août 1592 (Rouen), arrêt of Aug. 11, 1592; Avril–Juillet 1594, arrêt of May 14, 1594.

4 Benedict, 'Catholics and Huguenots', p. 232.

so that they could ply their trades in peace.[1] The number of those who left the city must have been considerable, for the movement of house rents suggests a shrinking city. Rents fell in nominal as well as real terms for the first and only time in the half-century between 1550 and 1600, while several of the houses whose history can be traced through the ecclesiastical account books stood empty.[2]

In the surrounding countryside, the economic crisis was yet worse. The extended royalist and English campaigns, not to mention the multitude of smaller offensives and counter-offensives launched by the local garrisons, had made it virtually impossible for the peasantry to cultivate the land. Case after case before the parlement between 1590 and 1594 involved *fermiers* forced to sue for a reduction in their rent or villages for a diminution of the *taille* because their crops and livestock had been requisitioned, their houses burned to the ground, or their money extorted by the bands of soldiers which criss-crossed the province.[3] The court issued stern orders against such depredations and attempted to work out truces around harvest time for the '*repos des laboureurs*' – but with little success.[4] The English intervention in the campaign against Rouen in 1591 proved particularly devastating, for the soldiers brought along no supplies and were given virtually free rein by their commander to plunder the countryside.[5]

A detailed inquiry by the *bailliage* officials into the condition of those villages whose curés owed clerical tithes to the cathedral chapter reveals the extent of damage done to the surrounding countryside by August 1593. In Etreville, near Quillebeuf, the officials reported: 'There remain in the village only a very few farmers, some having died in prison, others of poverty, and others of disease... The land for the most part is uncultivated

[1] A.D.S.M., 5 E 599–600.

[2] *See* Appendix 4. In the 32 houses which formed the basis of my examination of house rents, there were only occasional, short vacancies in the early decades of the Religious Wars. One dwelling stood empty for six months in 1562–3, another for three months in 1568–9, and a third for six months in 1581. By contrast, in the early 1590s one house was unoccupied for nine months in 1592–3 and two stood empty for a full year in 1593–4.

[3] A.D.S.M., B, Parlement, Arrêts, Janvier–Avril 1591 (Rouen), arrêts of March 6, April 5, 26, and 29, 1591; Avril–Août 1591 (Rouen), arrêts of May 2, 10, 14, 18, 21, and 31, June 10, 12, 18, 21, 22, and 25, July 2, 4, 5, and 29, 1591; Septembre 1591–Août 1592 (Rouen), arrêt of Oct. 5, 1591; Septembre 1592–Juin 1593 (Rouen), arrêts of April 29 and June 26, 1593. Excellent general discussions of the effects of warfare on rural society may be found in Gustave Fagniez, *L'économie sociale de la France sous Henri IV, 1589–1610* (Paris, 1897), pp. 5–6; J. Jacquart, 'La Fronde des Princes dans la région parisienne et ses conséquences matérielles', *Revue d'Histoire Moderne et Contemporaine*, VII (1960), pp. 257–90; and the same author's *La crise rurale en Ile-de-France, 1550–1670* (Paris, 1974), pp. 194–9.

[4] A.D.S.M., B, Parlement, Arrêts, Août–Décembre 1590 (Rouen), arrêt of Nov. 11, 1590, reveals an early effort to work out a truce for the '*repos des laboureurs*'. The attempt was not subsequently repeated until 1593, presumably because of its lack of success.

[5] A.D.S.M., B, Parlement, Arrêts, Août–Décembre 1590 (Rouen), arrêt of Nov. 9, 1590; Janvier–Avril 1591 (Rouen), arrêt of Jan. 16, 1591; Lloyd, *Rouen Campaign*, pp. 97–100.

and there is but little livestock.' Notre-Dame-de-Franqueville, just southeast of Rouen, had been the scene of daily raids by the rival garrisons of Château-Gaillard and Pont-de-l'Arche throughout 1589 and 1590. The presbytery and granges had been burned to the ground and the trees of the village cut down for firewood during the siege of Rouen. Church services had not been held for four years, most of the population was dead, and the bulk of the land was uncultivated. In Barneville, three buckles of the Seine downriver from Rouen, 'not even the eighth part' of the land was being worked. Eight horses and eight cows remained in the village. The *bailliage* officials visited or heard testimony concerning twenty-seven villages in all, scattered throughout the Seine valley, Pays de Caux, and Pays de Bray. In all they found variations on the same tragic theme.[1]

The crisis of agricultural production in turn added to the difficulties experienced by the city itself. While city and countryside may have been worlds apart in Ancien Régime France in terms of social structure and levels of culture, they remained economically interdependent. Urban ecclesiastical institutions had extensive rural holdings upon which they depended for the bulk of their income. By the later sixteenth century many private individuals among the urban elites also owned land. The extension of bourgeois control over rural property in the countryside surrounding major cities had been one of the major social changes of the century, and the region around Rouen had been no exception to this nationwide trend. By 1594 72 of the 142 fiefs recorded in the rolls of the *ban* and *arrière-ban* of the *vicomté* of Rouen belonged to bourgeois of the city.[2] The destruction wrought by the soldiery therefore provoked a significant drop in the income of both the city's ecclesiastical institutions and its elite of *officiers* and merchants, with all of the attendant consequences for the artisans and service personnel who catered to these groups.[3] The nuns of Ste Catherine-de-Grandmont and Bonnes Nouvelles even had to petition the parlement

[1] A.D.S.M., G 3621.

[2] G.-A. Prévost, ed., 'Documents sur le ban et l'arrière-ban, et les fiefs de la vicomté de Rouen en 1594 et 1560, et sur la noblesse du bailliage de Gisors en 1703', *Mélanges de la Société de l'Histoire de Normandie*, 3e série (1895), pp. 231–423. The growing extent of bourgeois landownership in the sixteenth century was first diagnosed by Marc Bloch in his classic *Les caractères originaux de l'histoire rurale française* (Paris, 1951), Vol. 1, pp. 129–31. It has been amply documented by Emmanuel Le Roy Ladurie, 'Sur Montpellier et sa campagne aux XVIe et XVIIe siècles', *Annales: E.S.C.*, XII (1957), pp. 223–30; P. de Saint-Jacob, 'Mutations économiques et sociales dans les campagnes bourguignonnes à la fin du XVIe siècle', *Etudes Rurales*, I (1961), p. 43; Jacquart, *Crise rurale en Ile-de-France*, pp. 241–53; and Richard Gascon, *Grand commerce et vie urbaine au XVIe siècle: Lyon et ses marchands (vers 1520–vers 1580)* (Paris–The Hague, 1971), Vol. 2, pp. 811–72.

[3] Jonathan S. Dewald, *The Formation of a Provincial Nobility: The Magistrates of the Parlement of Rouen, 1499–1610* (Princeton, 1980), p. 212–15, demonstrates the declining revenue of the *parlementaires*. The serious economic difficulties of the city's ecclesiastical institutions can be seen from the financial crisis of the Hôtel-Dieu, reflected in A.D.S.M., B, Parlement, Arrêts, Août–Décembre 1590 (Rouen), arrêt of Nov. 19, 1590; Juin 1593–Avril 1594 (Rouen), arrêt of June 26, 1593; Archives Hospitalières, 1 E 237, entries of Aug. 2 and Oct. 8, 1597, Jan. 10, 1598.

for special pensions, so meager was their income in this period of agricultural disruption.[1] Rouen's grain supply was also affected by the devastation of the surrounding countryside. Agricultural production fell so sharply and was so slow to recover that the city had to import Baltic grain to meet its needs for four years after the civil wars came to an end.[2] Grain prices remained at abnormally high levels throughout the five years of League rule.[3]

By the time of the siege matters had thus become little short of desperate for many Rouennais. Far from improving the economic situation of a city burdened by taxation, the League had provoked the most prolonged and severe economic crisis of the entire period of the Wars of Religion – at the same time that the demands of war had prevented the *ligueur* authorities from lowering taxes as they would have liked. Trade and industry slumped even while both taxes and the price of grain rose. The desperate measures to which many inhabitants were reduced as a result are shown by the frequent complaints of the officials of the *eaux et forêts* that the nearby woods were being overrun with town-dwellers foraging for the firewood they could no longer afford to purchase.[4] The economic crisis also added to the ranks of the brigands-cum-soldiers, said to be swelling daily with new '*manants*, *pillards*...and vagabonds'.[5] And the ultimate effect of the crisis was to weaken enthusiasm for the League. Longing for a man who could restore order began to take precedence over all other considerations.

Other developments were also undermining support for the League. In November 1591 the Paris Sixteen set up a special revolutionary tribunal that condemned and executed the president of the parlement of Paris, Barnabé Brisson. Among the upper classes already alarmed by the actions

[1] A.D.S.M., B, Parlement, Arrêts, Février–Juillet 1590 (Rouen), arrêts of March 16 and April 6, 1590.

[2] A.C.R., B 5 contains numerous *congés* recording the importation of grain by merchants from Hamburg, Amsterdam, Flanders, Calais, and also Nogent-le-Roy between 1594 and 1598. Such imports had not been necessary in most years prior to the period of the League.

[3] Entries in the *journal des échevins* occasionally note the price of grain. Between 1589 and 1594 the prices recorded never fell below 6 *livres* per *mine*. By contrast, prices had varied from 3 to 5 *livres* per *mine* in non-crisis years during the decade preceding the *Sainte-Union* takeover. *See also*, Micheline Baulant and Jean Meuvret, *Prix des céréales extraits de la mercuriale de Paris* (*1520–1698*) (Paris, 1960), Vol. 1, pp. 61–71.

[4] On at least four occasions the officials of the *eaux et forêts* had to appear before the parlement to try to put an end to the 'grandes ruynes, degast, et depopullation des boys des forestz, lequel est abattu et emporté par le commun peuple tant de ceste ville et faulxbourgs que des environs'. A.D.S.M., B, Parlement, Registres Secrets – Rouen, entry of Oct. 17, 1591; Arrêts, Février–Juillet 1590 (Rouen), arrêt of April 6, 1590; Août–Décembre 1590 (Rouen), arrêt of Oct. 24, 1590; Septembre 1592–Juin 1593, arrêt of Feb. 10, 1593. These were not the first complaints on this score heard by the parlement in the sixteenth century, but such complaints were far more frequent during the League than at any previous period. *See also here* Michel Devèze, *La vie de la forêt française au XVIe siècle* (Paris, 1961), Vol. 2, p. 234.

[5] A.D.S.M., B, Parlement, Arrêts, Janvier–Avril 1591 (Rouen), arrêt of Jan. 16, 1591.

of the marauding bands of soldiers and civilians, this increasingly radical behavior drove many into opposition. Furthermore, those who remained faithful to the League had become split into a number of rival factions. The cardinal of Bourbon, whom the League had proclaimed king on Henry III's death, had never been able to escape his prison cell and had died in 1590. Partisans of Mayenne, the Spanish Infanta, and a host of lesser pretenders struggled bitterly over the right to succeed him. These divisions diminished any hopes the League's supporters might have had that the movement would be capable of restoring the order for which people now longed.

Henry IV realized that time was on his side. Following the Rouen campaign he dismissed many of his soldiers, ceased his military offensive, and agreed to a series of truces.[1] The *Sainte-Union* further weakened itself in internecine struggles during the inconclusive Estates-General of 1593. Then, in July of that year, Navarre removed the major obstacle to reconciliation by abjuring Calvinism and returning to the Roman Church. The conversion was denounced by the more radical *ligueurs* as the ruse of a relapsed heretic, but it sparked many defections. Several *parlementaires* and other judicial officials abandoned Rouen for Caen. The cathedral chapter began secret negotiations with the new royalist archbishop it had previously refused to recognize, the cardinal of Vendôme, Bourbon's nephew.[2] The original spark of crusading zeal was now all but gone from the League, and Villars ruled a sullen populace as a virtual dictator. The League was disintegrating from month to month. Only Villars' strong hand kept Rouen in the party's camp at all.

Henry IV's ultimate triumph over the League, in Rouen as in so many other regions of France, was not secured on the battlefield. It was purchased. The ever-opportunistic Villars could hardly fail to see which way the wind was blowing and how he might profit from his control over such a rich and strategic region. In February 1594 he began secret negotiations with the crown over the terms of a possible capitulation. A month later matters had proceeded to the point where the king's envoy, Rosny, could dare enter the city publicly. The population greeted him with enthusiasm and applause, the future duke of Sully was pleased to note; even if Rouen witnessed none of the pro-Henry IV rioting that preceded the fall of the League in other cities, it was nonetheless ready to welcome Navarre as king.[3] A sizable pension, the offices of admiral of France and lieutenant-

[1] A.D.S.M., B, Parlement, Registres Secrets – Caen, entry of Aug. 11, 1593, a copy of the truce signed between Navarre and Mayenne for a period of three months. It was subsequently extended on Oct. 19 and Nov. 4, 1593.

[2] A.D.S.M., G 3716; d'Estaintot, *La Ligue en Normandie*, pp. 313–14.

[3] Rosny was greeted on his arrival 'avec un grand aplaudissement du simple peuple qui commenceoit à se lasser infiniment des incommoditez de la guerre'. *Les Oeconomies royales de Sully*, ed. D. Buisseret and B. Barbiche (Paris, 1970), Vol. 1, p. 407. *See also*, pp. 391–2. Roland Mousnier, *La*

general of Normandy, and a passel of the province's richest abbeys finally sufficed to bring Villars into the royal camp.[1] Troops loyal to the king were secretly introduced into the city, and the duke then revealed his intentions to the parlement and the Council of Twenty-Four. On March 30 Rouen declared its allegiance to Henry IV. A *Te Deum* at the cathedral commemorated the city's reunion with the crown.[2]

The Wars of Religion were over, but a series of problems bequeathed by the conflicts remained. Royalist had to be reconciled with *ligueur* and Catholic made to live in peace with Protestant. The shattered regional economy needed reconstruction. Henry IV wanted to reverse the trend toward the decentralization of political power that had developed during the Wars of Religion.

Following Rouen's reduction, Henry IV addressed himself immediately to these tasks. He began with that of reconciling the two sides in the past civil war. By royal letters-patent of April 1594, he ordered the memory of all actions taken by both sides during the past five years to be legally expunged; no lawsuits concerning any of these actions were permitted. All confiscations of property by both sides were annulled and the confiscated goods ordered returned to their original owners. New taxes imposed since 1589 were repealed. Appointments made by Mayenne to vacant offices in the course of the League were confirmed, as were all judicial decisions in cases involving two individuals of the same party. As Villars had demanded before his capitulation, no religion but the Catholic was permitted within the *vicomté* of Rouen. Finally, those unwilling to recognize Henry IV as king and live under his authority were to be granted passports to whatever destination they chose.[3]

In general, these provisions seem to have been carried out with little difficulty. Of Rouen's *ligueurs*, only the ever-zealous Regnault du Pont seems to have availed himself of the offer of a passport to leave the city. A number of lawsuits resulted from situations where both Mayenne and

vénalité des offices sous Henri IV et Louis XIII (Rouen, 1945), p. 547, declares that Sully was greeted particularly warmly by the city's *officiers*, but Sully's memoirs do not seem to support this contention. Popular demonstrations in support of Henry IV elsewhere are mentioned in Drouot, *Mayenne et la Bourgogne*, Vol. 2, pp. 285–8, 296; A. Dubois, ed., *La Ligue: Documents relatifs à la Picardie d'après les registres de l'échevinage d'Amiens* (Amiens, 1859), p. 100.

[1] 'Et est M. de Villars celui de tous les chefs de la Ligue qui s'est fait le mieux payer.' Pierre de l'Estoile, *Journal pour le règne de Henri IV*, ed. L.-R. Lefevre (Paris, 1948), Vol. 1, p. 400. According to both l'Estoile and Rosny Villars received a pension of 60,000 *livres* per annum and the abbeys of Jumièges, Tiron, Bonport, Vallasse, and St Taurin. Claude Groulart, *Mémoires*, Michaud and Poujoulat, Vol. 11, pp. 568–9, sets Villars' pension at 715,430 *écus*.

[2] *Oeconomies royales*, Vol. 1, pp. 437–46; A.C.R., A 21, entry of March 30, 1594.

[3] *Lettres patentes en forme d'edict du Roy sur la reduction des villes de Rouen, Le Havre, Harfleu, Montivillier, Ponteaudemer et Verneuil en son obeissance* (Rouen, 1594). A copy of these letters patent may be found in B.N., MS Français 3989, fos. 279–88.

Navarre had appointed officials to fill the same vacancy or where the League had ousted one man from a municipal position and appointed another. These were generally resolved by allowing both men to continue in office until one died.[1] Only one clause in these letters-patent was consistently disobeyed, and this with the king's tacit approval: the ban on Protestant worship. Henry IV was indebted too strongly to his ex-co-religionists to enforce the clause in Villars' capitulation banning Protestantism in Rouen. Although the Reformed Church was not legally allowed to hold services until a royal brevet of August 1599 granted the congregation the right to gather for worship at Dieppedalle, in fact the group began meeting as early as September 1594.[2] When the parlement attempted to crack down on these semi-secret meetings in 1597, delegates of the court were summoned to Paris for a royal tongue-lashing.[3] After nine years of banishment, the Reformed Church was thus able to re-establish itself in Rouen thanks to Henry's protection. It had survived the flood; fittingly, it now chose as its emblem the image of the ark. The church even managed a modest growth in size after the royal brevets of 1599 were issued, attracting new converts as well as welcoming back homecoming exiles and old members who had converted to Catholicism in 1572 or 1585.[4] By the first decade of the seventeenth century, the revived congregation contained some 5,000 or so worshippers, roughly 7 per cent of the population.

The task of reviving the economy also preoccupied Henry IV. He

[1] A.C.R., A 21, entry of June 6, 1594; A.D.S.M., B, Parlement, Registres Secrets, entry of Aug. 21, 1595.

[2] As can be inferred from the congregation's baptismal registers, which recommence in this month.

[3] *Plainctes des Eglises Réformées de France, sur les violences et injustices qui leur sont faites en plusieurs endroits du Royaume* (n.p., 1597), p. 92.

[4] *See above*, p. 133. In the years from 1594 to 1598 the number of baptisms was well below that of the early 1580s, as many Protestants apparently hesitated to participate fully in church activities so long as the faith remained outlawed. To cite just one particularly noteworthy example which can be deduced from the parish registers of the two faiths, Lucas Legendre, patriarch of what was to become one of the leading families of the 'Protestant bank', prudently had several of his children baptized in the parish church of St Etienne-des-Tonneliers between 1594 and 1599 even though he had participated in Protestant baptisms while a refugee in Caen prior to 1594 and was to have all of his children born after 1599 baptized in the Reformed temple of Quévilly. (Legendre's appearance in the baptismal register of the congregation at Caen – A. D. Calvados, C 1571, entry of Jan. 16, 1594 – incidentally disproves the contention of Georges Vanier that Legendre did not convert to Protestantism until 1602 and then only to facilitate his trade with England and Holland, Georges Vanier, 'Une famille de grands marchands rouennais aux XVIe et XVIIe siècles: Les Legendre', *Bull. Soc. Emul. S.-I.* (1946–7), pp. 74, 115–16.) The subsequent wave of adhesions to the Reformed Church was primarily composed of ex-Protestants returning to the fold after having lived as Catholics since 1572 or 1585. For example, the parish register of St André-de-la-Ville records the relapse of three men who had lived as Catholics 'avec une insigne et damnable hippochrisye' since St Bartholomew's Day, one of whom had even served as parish treasurer in the interim. A.C.R., R.P. 12. That some of the increase was, however, produced by people converting to Protestantism for the first time is shown by Henri Labrosse, ed., 'Livre de Raison de la famille LeCourt de Rouen (XVIe–XVIIe siècle)', *Bull. Soc. Emul. S.-I.* (1937), pp. 121–54, the diary of a family of goldsmiths and stained-glass-workers which converted to Calvinism early in the seventeenth century.

Seal of the Reformed Church of Rouen
Source: *B.S.H.P.F.*, II (1854), p. 233.

granted special privileges to entice foreign merchants to introduce new techniques of linen and woolen manufacturing and the cultivation of silkworms to Rouen. While on a visit to the city in 1596, he even spoke vaguely of constructing a major new town just across the river. None of these enterprises proved very successful – the mulberry trees for the silkworms soon succumbed to Normandy's chill and damp, the new town never got beyond the planning stage, and the fate of the linen and cloth manufactories is unknown, which suggests that they did not become major employers – but such projects nonetheless demonstrated the king's concern for the city's welfare.[1] Under the climate of security and royal benevolence which Henry was able to create, a spontaneous economic recovery took place. The population losses of the period of the League were rapidly made good, so that by 1600 the level of baptisms of 1585 had already been regained.[2] Trade revived, and the old colonies of foreign merchants re-established themselves in the city, now joined by two new groups, the Portuguese Marranos and a colony of North Germans.[3] An increase in the number of new masters entering Rouen's guilds suggests that industrial production also picked up.[4] The adverse economic effects of the Wars of Religion were not all erased in these few years. It would be some time before the peak levels of trade or industrial production attained in the sixteenth century were equalled in the seventeenth, and certain oppor-

[1] A.C.R., A 21, entry of Nov. 7, 1596; A.D.S.M., 5 E 605; E. Gosselin, ed., *Documents authentiques et inédits pour servir à l'histoire de la marine normande et du commerce rouennais pendant les XVIe et XVIIe siècles* (Rouen, 1876), p. 139; Fagniez, *Economie sociale*, pp. 116–17, 139–41, 161.

[2] *See* Appendix 3, p. 263; Benedict, 'Catholics and Huguenots', pp. 218, 232.

[3] A.C.R., B 5, entry of Dec. 23, 1596; J. Mathorez, *Les étrangers en France sous l'Ancien Régime* (Paris, 1919–21), Vol. 2, pp. 160–61; Cecil Roth, 'Les Marranes à Rouen, un chapitre ignoré de l'histoire des Juifs de France', *Revue des Etudes Juives*, LXXXVIII (1929), p. 116; I. S. Révah, 'Le premier éstablissement des Marranes portugais à Rouen (1603–1607)', *Mélanges Isidore Lévy* (Brussels, 1955), pp. 539–52; Ivan Cloulas, 'Les Ibériques dans la société rouennaise des XVIe et XVIIe siècles', *Revue des Sociétés Savantes de Haute Normandie*, 61 (1971), pp. 19–21.

[4] The number of *lettres de draperie* issued rose to 137 in the decade 1595–1605 and continued to mount steadily until approximately 1630 before slumping sharply. Similarly, the number of new master goldsmiths increased from 29 to 41 between the 1590s and the first decade of the seventeenth century.

tunities for economic growth may have been lost forever as a result of the fighting of the League, notably the chance to inherit some of the trade diverted from Antwerp.[1] Nevertheless, after the extreme disruption of the last years of the civil wars, the steady economic recovery which marked the reign of *le roi de la poule au pot* must have made these years appear to Rouen's inhabitants as a new golden age.

The final preoccupation visible in Henry IV's actions in the years following his reduction of Rouen was his desire to restore some of the power and prestige of the Council of Twenty-Four. The *conseillers-échevins* had emerged from the period of the League with their prerogatives sorely diminished as a result of the parlement's extension of its authority during the years of *Sainte-Union* domination. In a series of royal decisions, Henry IV returned to the municipal government a number of minor perquisites of office which the parlement had taken away from it in 1593.[2] Likewise, and more importantly, the monarch reaffirmed the Council of Twenty-Four's complete control of municipal finances, putting an end to the high court's supervision of the city's accounts.[3] Finally, he blocked an attempt by the parlement to demote the *conseillers-échevins* to a position below all of the royal courts in the order of precedence to be followed for the royal entry staged in 1596, ordering instead that they be allowed to march in their accustomed place just behind the most important sovereign courts.[4]

This desire on the king's part to restore to Rouen's municipal authorities their old power and status might seem puzzling at first glance, given Henry's well-known policy of reducing the autonomy of most city governments.[5] In fact, it was less municipal authority which Henry worked consistently to weaken than local autonomy in whatever form it might take, and in Rouen the parlement, not the city council, had emerged from the period of the League as the local or regional institution wielding the most power and independence. Henry therefore was bolstering what had become by now

[1] We have as yet few reliable studies of the Rouennais economy in the first half of the seventeenth century. The general impression one gains from the work carried out to date suggests that the population levels of the sixteenth century were regained about 1615, with growth continuing to about 1635. *See especially here* the population curves in Jean-Pierre Bardet, 'Rouen et les Rouennais au XVIIIe siècle', *Etudes Normandes*, XXIII (1974), pp. 18–20. The foundations of this growth are unclear. The cloth industry never quite regained its sixteenth-century peaks to judge from the number of *lettres de draperie*.

[2] A.C.R., Chartrier, tiroir 40.

[3] A.C.R., Chartrier, tiroir 72; A.C.R., A 21, entries of Jan. 25, 1595 and April 3, 1596.

[4] A.C.R., A 21, entries of Sept. 27 and Oct. 12, 1596.

[5] 'The crown had a clear policy of reducing municipal independence.' J. H. M. Salmon, *Society in Crisis: France in the Sixteenth Century* (New York, 1975), p. 301. This policy is analyzed generally in Charles Petit-Dutaillis, *Les communes françaises: Caractères et évolution des origines au XVIIIe siècle* (Paris, 1947), pp. 223–6, while some examples of the policy at work in nearby provinces may be found in Jean Lestocquoy, *Histoire de la Picardie* (2nd ed., Paris, 1970), pp. 80–81; and Charles Laronze, *Essai sur le régime municipal en Bretagne pendant les guerres de religion* (Paris, 1890), pp. 28, 34–5.

only a minor threat to his authority, the Council of Twenty-Four, in order to counterbalance the body which was emerging as the chief obstacle to royal power, the parlement. It was not a policy which pleased the grave magistrates of the court, and they made their displeasure known by refusing to register several royal edicts, most notably the edict of Nantes. (The parlement of Rouen was the last of France's parlements to register the edict, procrastinating until 1609 before approving the full text of the document.) Even as the wounds of the past half-century of religious conflict were being healed, the struggle which was to dominate Rouen's political history for the next fifty years, that between the centralizing monarchy and the parlement, was being engaged.[1]

[1] An important article by Jonathan Dewald analyzes the background to this new hostility between crown and parlement around 1600: 'Magistracy and Political Opposition at Rouen: A Social Context', *Sixteenth Century Journal*, v (1974), pp. 66–78.

10

Conclusion: the Wars of Religion and the people of France

In August 1561, as religious agitation was intensifying throughout France, the Spanish ambassador in Paris wrote to Philip II that the situation in Normandy looked particularly alarming. A majority of Rouen's parlement was tainted with heresy, he reported, and he attributed this infection to the influence wielded within the province by the admiral Coligny.[1] The ambassador was misinforming his sovereign. Very few members of Rouen's parlement ever became Protestant. But his error is highly revealing, for it reflects a view of the political forces at work in sixteenth-century France that was second nature to most observers at the time and has continued to affect the judgments of historians to this day – a view in which a relative handful of elite actors was credited with a preponderant influence over the course of events.

It is obvious why contemporaries tended to analyze politics as if *les grands* were the only men who mattered. Normal politics in the Ancien Régime *was* the affair of a small elite of courtiers, great noblemen, and state servants. If the voice of the mass of the king's subjects was heard at all, it was usually in reaction against the decisions of these men, as with the numerous peasant revolts of the 1630s and 1640s sparked by the higher taxes and imposition of absolutist state structures that accompanied France's entry into the Thirty Years' War. But the Wars of Religion were not episodes in normal politics. The religious divisions cut deep into society, provoking bitter conflicts in provincial cities such as Rouen. The religious parties had an existence at the local level that was substantially independent of the actions of the court elites. Their fate was determined as much or more by the play of local forces as it was by events in Paris. Observers such as the Spanish ambassador consequently misperceived the reality of the times when they continued to analyze affairs as if the influence of the great nobility could explain all developments – just as Charles IX and Henry III both misjudged the depth of the forces at work in their kingdom when they imagined that

[1] *Archivo documental español: Negociaciones con Francia* (Madrid, 1950–59), Vol. 2, p. 317.

first the assassination of Coligny and then that of the Guises might bring an end respectively to the Protestant movement and the challenge of the League.

This study has sought to elucidate the course and nature of the conflicts agitating one major provincial town during the years from 1560 through 1594, as well as to describe the influence of these events on both the city's economic life and its religious evolution. Any study of a single community, however, inevitably begs one great question: to what extent was that community typical of the larger society of which it was a part? Was the experience of most other French cities comparable to Rouen's during these years? Can the same three phases visible in Rouen's history be discerned more generally in the Religious Wars? And if they can, were the major turning points brought about by forces similar to those at work in Rouen's history, or did different factors determine the religious and political evolution of each community? Definitive answers to these questions must await further studies of other provincial communities, but this conclusion will attempt to suggest at least some tentative answers on the basis of the existing local histories and published memoirs. The attempt, it is hoped, will not only enable us to place Rouen's fate in comparative perspective; it should also help us to understand more clearly the nature of the Religious Wars and the ways they affected local communities throughout France.

Confessional violence began to trouble Rouen seriously in 1560, shortly after Protestantism entered a period of rapid growth. Was the city's experience unique? Anything but. A dramatic increase in Protestant numbers was practically universal throughout France between 1559 and 1562, and it was quickly followed almost everywhere by open clashes between Huguenot and Catholic.

Protestantism's initial growth had been slow and irregular. Luther's works were on sale in Paris within two years of the posting of his ninety-five theses, and his ideas and those of the other reformers were subsequently disseminated across the length and breadth of the kingdom by wandering preachers, through surreptitiously distributed books, or by heretical schoolmasters who had become converted to the new doctrines and then used their classrooms as a forum to spread them further. But the new doctrines remained outlawed as heresy; the few attempts made at the local level over the period 1520–55 to bind the scattered Protestant converts into formal, organized congregations were usually detected by the authorities and defeated; and the number of those attracted to the new ideas never exceeded a small percentage of any city's population. When the first formal

Reformed congregations were founded by ministers from Geneva in the later 1550s, they were quite small.[1]

It was in the period following the peace of Cateau-Cambrésis that Calvinism became a true mass movement in France. The rare Protestant baptismal registers stretching back to the years prior to the outbreak of the civil wars indicate the speed of the new faith's growth. In the Reformed Church of St Lô, founded in 1555, only 16 baptisms were celebrated in 1557. The number had risen to 88 by 1560 and reached 130 in the following year.[2] At the other end of France, in Montpellier, the growth in these later years was even more rapid; the number of baptisms per month tripled over the course of the twelve months following September 1560, then doubled again in the succeeding five months.[3] Literary sources indicate that these cases were anything but unique. Memoirs from almost every corner of France comment in similar terms that Calvinism was 'growing from day to day', 'augmenting miraculously', 'becoming strong'.[4] Only the distant reaches of Brittany and Auvergne, where Protestant ideas never penetrated deeply, seem to have been exempt from the rapid spread of the new faith.

[1] The fullest account of the early history of French Protestantism remains P. Imbart de la Tour, *Les origines de la Réforme* (Paris, 1905–35). The halting pace of the new faith's growth also emerges from such contemporary histories as Crespin's book of martyrs, the *Histoire ecclésiastique des églises réformées au royaume de France*, ed. G. Baum, E. Cunitz, and R. Reuss (Paris, 1883–9), Vol. 1, and local chronicles like 'Une chronique de l'établissement de la Réforme à Saint-Seurin-d'Uzet en Saintonge: Le registre de baptêmes de Jean Frèrejean (1541–1564)', *B.S.H.P.F.*, L (1901), pp. 135–57. Only in Lyon was a Protestant assembly that endured founded prior to 1555. Tracing Protestantism's growth on a year-by-year basis with numerical precision is thus impossible during these early decades, for it is only when a formal church exists that one can obtain a precise idea of just how many people subscribe to the faith's tenets, participation in the church being the critical touchstone of commitment. The best guide to Protestantism's early numerical strength thus has to be the first Reformed baptismal registers from the years after 1555, for the number of baptisms in the first months of the churches' existence presumably reflects with some accuracy the number of people secretly won over to Protestant ideas prior to the congregations' establishment. One additional indication of Protestantism's numerical strength prior to 1555 has also survived, this for Meaux, where in 1546 a short-lived congregation was formed modelled on the French church of Strasbourg. The *Histoire ecclésiastique* tells us (V. 1, pp. 67–70) that when this assembly was discovered and dispersed later in the year, it contained 300 to 400 members. Assuming that this figure is accurate, such totals would indicate that between 3 and 8 per cent of the city's population had been won over to the cause. (In 1713 Meaux contained 1,034 *feux*, and like most towns in the region around Paris it had probably been substantially larger in the sixteenth century.) These percentages cannot be considered typical. Meaux was one of the leading centers of early French Protestantism. Instead, the figure of 3 to 8 per cent probably represents an upper limit, the maximum level of strength achieved by Protestantism in the 1540s in one of its foremost citadels.

[2] *See* Appendix 1, p. 254.

[3] A. C. Montpellier, GG 314. Similar growth can be seen in the small church of Vitré, where the number of recorded baptisms quintupled between the second half of 1560 and the first half of 1562. A. D. Ille-et-Vilaine, Etat Civil Protestant de Vitré.

[4] 'L'Eglise de Vitry-le-François en Août 1561 et les de Vassan', *B.S.H.P.F.*, XL (1891), p. 478; Achille Gamon, *Mémoires*, Petitot, 1st ser., Vol. 34, p. 305; Jean Philippi, *Mémoires*, Petitot, 1st ser., Vol. 34, p. 341; Amos Barbot, *Histoire de La Rochelle* (Paris–Saintes, 1886–90), Vol. 2, p. 163.

As soon as Calvinism became a mass movement, collective violence quickly followed virtually everywhere, for intolerance was deeply rooted in the religious outlook of both sides, whether it be Calvinist intolerance of idolatrous rituals that polluted the true church or Catholic intolerance of heretics who desecrated sacred objects and thus endangered the community.

The teachings of the reformers struck at a whole series of beliefs around which men had long organized their vision of the world and of the proper route within it to salvation. For those who accepted the new doctrines, the traditional beliefs and the devotional practices which they engendered suddenly appeared in a new light, their true light the converts were convinced. They were superstitious accretions that perverted the gospel, perhaps even deliberate hoaxes perpetrated by a bloated and corrupt First Estate to line its coffers. The converts felt outrage at the way in which they had been misled in the past. They were dismayed that others continued to be duped in the present. Once they grew strong enough in number to dare to do so, they attempted to put an end to the traditional Catholic practices, disregarding in the process the urging of their ministers and consistories that they remain calm. The same high hopes of the Reformation's imminent triumph and the same impatient iconoclasm which we have seen in Rouen in these years were characteristic throughout France. To anyone reading through the local chronicles of these years, in fact, the accounts of statues defaced, processions disrupted, and preachers interrupted soon become so familiar as to seem virtually predictable.

Equally predictable is the outraged Catholic reaction. The Protestants were desecrating objects which that fraction of the Catholic population still deeply committed to traditional beliefs considered sacred. They were questioning beliefs that were central to all true hopes for salvation. They were, in short, luxury-loving apostates, enemies of God and the true religion, threats to social peace. In most areas the Catholic reaction took the form of spontaneous acts of violence in response to specific Protestant outrages. In some cities confraternities were founded dedicated to reaffirming doctrines attacked by the Protestants – or, as with the Confraternity of St Gunstan in Dieppe and the 'Syndicate' in Bordeaux, to exterminating the heretics.[1] A fatal cycle of violence was initiated. As the Catholic attacks on Protestant assemblies grew more frequent, the Protestants responded by recruiting their own armies and placing themselves in a state of readiness for war, this months or even years before Beza and

[1] Guillaume and Jean Daval, *Histoire de la Réformation à Dieppe* (Rouen, 1878), Vol. 1, p. 19; Robert Boutruche et al., *Bordeaux de 1453 à 1715* (Bordeaux, 1966), p. 219.

Condé sent out their nationwide appeals to the Calvinist churches to muster men and money for the cause in March 1562.[1] France was tearing apart community by community.

Contemporaries were struck by the rapid spread of Calvinism and society's consequent polarization in the years around 1560, but they were generally at a loss to explain these phenomena except as proof, depending upon their religious convictions, that wickedness was growing or God was hastening the triumph of the pure gospel. Modern historians have not always fared better in accounting for Protestantism's sudden expansion. Some have seen a link with the increasing resentment against tithes that manifested itself in a spreading refusal to pay this hated form of clerical expropriation. The argument would be more persuasive, however, had anti-tithe strikes not been common in parts of northeastern France that remained staunchly Catholic as well as in much of the heavily Protestant Midi. Furthermore, Calvinism was a predominantly urban movement, and much of its greatest success in the countryside was achieved among rural artisans, hardly the pattern one would expect if anti-tithe feelings were an important cause of its success.[2]

For many historians, a fractious, warlike nobility was the chief catalyst of both Protestantism's rapid growth and the subsequent slide toward civil war. A striking influx of noblemen into the Protestant movement is known to have taken place in the years following the close of the Italian Wars, and scholars have often followed such contemporary observers as the Spanish ambassador in crediting these converts with stimulating in turn the conversion of many tenants, clients, and retainers. There undoubtedly were regions of 'manorial Protestantism' where the religious choice of the local seigneur determined the conversion of a village, but we must beware of overestimating the influence which the nobility could exercise over the religious behavior of the mass of the population. David Nicholls' recent study of the growth of Protestantism in Normandy suggests a view of the forces behind the faith's growth that seems to accord well with what is known about the movement throughout France: the protection of noble converts determined the faith's implantation in a few isolated regions of

[1] A. H. Guggenheim, 'Beza, Viret, and the Church of Nimes: National Leadership and Local Iniatitive in the Outbreak of the Religious Wars', *Bibliothèque d'Humanisme et Renaissance*, XXXVII (1975), pp. 33–48, is a good study of one community which shows how events at the local level often outran those at court.

[2] The case for a link between the growth of Protestantism and resentment against the tithe is argued by Emmanuel Le Roy Ladurie, *Les paysans de Languedoc* (Paris, 1966), pp. 380–82, and Denis Richet, *La France moderne: L'esprit des institutions* (Paris, 1973), p. 109. The best introduction to the anti-tithe agitation and its geographic spread is Victor Carrière, *Introduction aux études d'histoire ecclésiastique locale* (Paris, 1936), Vol. 3, pp. 319–52.

Lower Normandy, but the amount and kind of rural industry and the nature of contacts with the world beyond the village were far more important determinants of Protestantism's growth in those rural regions of the province where the religion struck its deepest roots.[1] In the cities, where Protestantism enjoyed its greatest successes, the great noble families naturally had even less sway. A family of Catholic champions such as the Guises might be able to keep a lid on Protestantism's growth in a few towns such as Reims where they enjoyed particularly extensive powers of patronage, and the conversion of men such as the prince of Condé might lead a few of his clients within the urban magistracy to follow his example, but most town-dwellers made their choices in matters of religion subject to little pressure from the nobility. Furthermore, not only is there limited support for the claim that France's great noblemen exerted a determining influence on the conversion of the great bulk of Protestants who flooded into the movement in the years 1559–62; in some areas it was very clearly the members of the third estate who first converted *en masse* and then drew the nobility into the movement in their wake. The memoirs of Blaise de Monluc reveal that in Guyenne many noblemen were attracted into the Protestant camp by pensions offered them by congregations in need of protection against the growing Catholic violence. The Huguenots paid particular attention to wooing those military noblemen thrown out of work by the end of the Italian Wars and known to be badly in debt, and their recruiting campaign met with considerable success.[2] Here at least the growing religious violence brought about the influx of noblemen into the cause rather than the other way around.

As the first modern historian to emphasize the degree to which the rise of Protestantism was a truly popular movement, Henri Hauser deserves a special place in French Reformation historiography. His theory that the growth of the new faith represented a crusade for social justice on the part of an artisan class slowly being proletarianized by the growth of capitalism and ever-higher barriers to master's status nonetheless appears today also

[1] David J. Nicholls, 'The Origins of Protestantism in Normandy: A Social Study' (unpub. Ph.D. dissertation, University of Birmingham, 1977), passim, esp. ch. 6. Dr Nicholls also shows that in certain regions the peasantry turned violently against their local seigneurs if these last manifested too great an attachment to Protestantism. The inhabitants of a village might stand on the other side of the religious divide from the local nobleman. It should be noted too that Protestantism did not strike deep roots in those regions of Normandy such as the Roumois and Lieuvin which were centers of the linen industry. The mere presence of rural industry was not by itself sufficient to guarantee the implantation of heretical ideas; the nature of the rural industry was also important. Just what in the structure of the linen industry made those engaged in it less likely to be won over to the new ideas than other rural artisans is a question that needs clarification.

[2] Blaise de Monluc, *Commentaires*, ed. Paul Courteault (Paris, 1964), pp. 477–9, 510. *See also* the comments of Joyeuse cited in Robert R. Harding, *Anatomy of a Power Elite: The Provincial Governors of Early Modern France* (New Haven, 1978), p. 49.

to be inadequate to explain the movement's expansion.[1] What we have learned about the social composition of Rouen's Reformed congregation belies his contention that the workingman's cause and the cause of the reform were one and the same; no clear class lines divided Catholic from Protestant, and the more proletarianized workers, notably those in the weaving industry, were if anything less likely to embrace Calvinism than those with a measure of independence. The evidence from other cities seems to provide equally little support for his theory. Insofar as social differences can be discerned between the members of the two confessions, they are generally subtle ones, matters of small variations in the percentage of artisans of different types attracted to one faith or the other. Such social or psychological factors as literacy or degree of personal independence seem to be critical in explaining these differences.

Of course, skilled, self-reliant, semi-educated artisans of the type to which Calvinism seems especially to have appealed were to be found in France long before 1560. As the subsequent contraction of Protestantism was to make abundantly clear, an opposition religion needs more than potential converts. It also needs a certain amount of growing space. Here the unsettled political situation which followed Henry II's accidental death was of the utmost importance. His apparently providential death, the equally providential one of his son Francis II a year later, and the subsequent uncertainties over the constitution of a regency government all weakened the crown and gave encouragement to the Protestants. For want of direction at the center, the authorities in the provinces were often unclear about how to deal with the increasingly audacious Protestant measures of proselytization. The repression which had kept the movement in check was weakened. Many who might previously have hesitated before joining an outlawed movement now rushed to do so as it seemed that even the crown itself might espouse the cause. Many others were exposed to a heady dose of Calvinist propaganda for the first time. For the Protestant cause, it was one of those exhilirating springtimes that social movements occasionally enjoy when they are first able to emerge from clandestinity and suddenly appear to be about to sweep the old order away before them. As Monluc wrote about the faith in these years: 'Every good mother's son wanted a taste.'[2]

If it was the polarization of communities throughout France around two radically hostile sets of religious symbols that largely provoked the country's slide into civil war, the civil wars, once underway, in turn aggravated the polarization further. We have seen how the events of the

[1] Henri Hauser, 'La Réforme et les classes populaires', *Revue d'Histoire Moderne et Contemporaine*, I (1899–1900), passim.

[2] Monluc, *Commentaires*, p. 481.

First Civil War added new venom to the already bitter feelings dividing the two faiths in Rouen, begetting a situation in which religious riots of escalating intensity punctured the city's peace almost annually for the next decade. Rouen's fate in these years was not typical of most French communities; in few other towns did the First Civil War produce so disastrous a dénouement as the siege and sacking of Rouen, and in few, if any, cities were the subsequent scenes of unrest so numerous. But if not typical, the pattern of violence could be considered archetypal. The years from 1562 through 1572 were the golden age of the religious riot throughout France. All of the major, widely publicized incidents of religious violence that were to form the stuff of both Protestant and Catholic martyrologies occurred in these years: the massacres of Vassy and Sens, the *Michelade* of Nimes, the incident of the Croix de Gastines in Paris, the St Bartholomew's Day Massacres. Few towns of any importance escaped at least a minor *émeute* or imbroglio.[1] Communities throughout the country were bitterly divided over the religious issues.

They did not remain so forever, however. As the civil wars continued, a significant shift occurred in the predominant forms of collective violence. As in Rouen, the religious rioting that was so common up to 1572 all but ceased throughout France in the subsequent years. Where local annals record countless clashes between members of the rival faiths up through the St Bartholomew's Day Massacres, I have found evidence of only three such incidents in the fifteen years between 1573 and 1588, all minor.[2] Instead, the peasant revolt emerged as the most common form of popular unrest. We have already seen the agitation which twice troubled the Norman countryside in these years: the anti-tax 'league' of 1578–9 and the revolt of the *gautiers* in 1587. The first was part of a larger movement that threatened to become a generalized tax strike throughout nearly all of northern France, while other major peasant revolts occurred in Gascony, the Agenais, Quercy, and Perigord in 1576, in Provence in 1578, and along the Rhone valley in 1579–80. The revolts were directed primarily against that traditional target of popular violence, the tax collector, but often included forays against the local seigneur or passing contingents of troops as well. In some regions peasants of both religions joined together to drive

[1] Episodes of confessional violence may be found in virtually any local history or memoir of this period, but there were a few towns which escaped conflict. Rennes, for instance, appears to have remained calm despite the presence of a not insignificant Protestant minority, while Reims, a town where Calvinism was virtually nonexistent, was also tranquil. Jean Meyer et al., *Histoire de Rennes* (Toulouse, 1972), p. 200; E. Henry, *La Réforme et la Ligue en Champagne et à Reims* (St Nicolas, 1867), p. 40.

[2] Pierre de L'Estoile, *Mémoires-Journaux*, ed. Brunet, Champollion et al. (Paris, 1875–90), Vol. 1, p. 157, records a minor incident in Paris in 1576, while Philippi, *Mémoires*, p. 389, reports two more serious clashes in Béziers and Montpellier in 1577. I am not counting here those cases where troops belonging to one faith captured a city controlled by the other and put it to sack.

out soldiers devastating their fields, then turned their anger against the local noblemen who were supposed to protect them.[1]

It has been a fundamental axiom of this study that incidents of collective violence provide one of the best guides to the issues and grievances agitating the great mass of the population that was otherwise cut off from participation in the political system of the Ancien Régime. The change in the major form of collective violence after 1572 suggests a significant shift in those issues and in the nature of the civil wars. The religious riots of the early years reflected conflicts dividing community after community throughout France. These anti-tax, anti-war uprisings suggest a spreading revulsion *against* the continuing warfare, from which the elements of eager popular participation and deep-seated religious passion had now disappeared.

What explains this shift? As in Rouen, the key to the changing pattern of violence would seem to lie with changes taking place around the same time in the relative numerical strength of the two confessions.

Throughout the mid-1560s, the Huguenots remained at least a substantial minority in nearly every major city about which evidence is available. The First Civil War braked the rapid growth which the faith had been experiencing on the eve of the hostilities, and the terms of the peace of Amboise permitting Reformed worship in only one town per *bailliage* and on the lands of noblemen possessing *plein fief de haubert* led to the disappearance of certain smaller congregations, but the surviving Protestant baptismal registers indicate that most larger congregations did not suffer any decline in size as a result of the initial civil war. Many may even have grown slightly in size between 1563 and 1568 by comparison with their pre-civil-war strength.[2] While the exact percentage of Huguenots can be computed only in a few cases, these known cases varied from 13 per cent of the population in Amiens to 21 per cent in Rouen to over 50 per cent in such strongholds as La Rochelle, Montauban, and Caen.[3] More

[1] L'Estoile, *Mémoires-Journaux*, Vol. 1, pp. 275–6; Henri Drouot, *Notes sur la Bourgogne et son esprit public au début du règne de Henri III, 1574–1579* (Dijon, 1937), pp. 137–48; Le Roy Ladurie, *Paysans de Languedoc*, pp. 294, 400; Liewain Van Doren, 'Revolt and Reaction in the City of Romans, Dauphiné, 1579–1580', *The Sixteenth Century Journal*, v (1974), pp. 71–100; J. H. M. Salmon, *Society in Crisis: France in the Sixteenth Century* (New York, 1975), pp. 280ff. Daniel Hickey, 'The Socio-Economic Context of the French Wars of Religion: A Case Study, Valentinois-Diois' (unpub. Ph.D. dissertation, McGill Univ., 1973), pp. 123–70 sets the peasant unrest particularly well in its social and political context.

[2] *See here* Appendix 1, p. 254. Most monographic studies of individual Protestant congregations in this period suggest the same pattern, although the recent article by Joan Davies, 'Persecution and Protestantism: Toulouse, 1562–1575', *The Historical Journal*, XXII (1979), pp. 34–5, indicates that in this city where the Huguenots were the object of particularly savage repression following their nearly successful attempt to seize the city at the outbreak of the First Civil War, the turning point came in 1562–3.

[3] On Amiens: A. D. Somme, I 2; Edouard Maugis, *Recherches sur les transformations du régime politique et social de la ville d'Amiens des origines de la commune à la fin du XVIe siècle* (Paris, 1906), Appendix 4. On Rouen: Philip Benedict, 'Catholics and Huguenots in Sixteenth-Century Rouen', p. 224. The

cities were like Amiens or Rouen than La Rochelle or Caen, but given the religious indifference of a sizeable, if unknowable, fraction of the nominally Catholic population, even the smaller percentages were sufficient to produce an uneasy balance between the two confessions. The religious fate of most communities could still appear uncertain. Either confession might hope to seize power with a well-timed coup. In such a situation, violence between the two faiths boiled easily to the surface.

By the aftermath of St Bartholomew's Day, the tense balance generally prevailing between the two confessions resolved itself nearly everywhere in favor of one party or the other. In most regions, the Protestant movement collapsed, as both the repressive edicts of 1567–8 and the 1572 massacres provoked significant movements of emigration and conversion. The chronology of the decline was not always the same as in Rouen; towns such as Caen or Montpellier witnessed more defections in 1568–70 than in 1572. But the massacres of 1572 everywhere cemented the process of change already begun in 1568. By their aftermath the Protestants had been reduced to a far smaller and more politically docile group than had been the case in the mid-1560s. Just the opposite evolution occurred in a few regions. In communities such as La Rochelle and Montauban, generally located far from Paris in terrain that was easy to defend and where the Huguenots had risen to the majority position by the mid-1560s, the Protestant party was able to seize control at the oubreak of both the Second and the Third Civil Wars and withstand royal efforts to force them back into the Roman fold. The royal edicts of persecution and the popular violence of the massacres only bred a determined policy of resistance in these areas, leading the Huguenots to institutionalize their domination. The Catholics who remained were cowed into submission. There were thus two contrasting patterns of development, but in either case, whether it was the Protestants or the Catholics who had cemented their domination by 1573, the religious struggle was essentially settled on the local level.

Yet the civil wars continued. Many parts of southern France now resembled a mosaic of interlocking Protestant and Catholic areas. Bands of soldiers recruited by the local nobility staged regular raids back and forth, and a guerrilla-like warfare, '*la picorée*', became endemic in much of Dauphiné, Languedoc, and Gascony. On a national level, the Fifth, Sixth, and Seventh Civil Wars all came and went, products of the unstable

total population of La Rochelle, Montauban, and Caen is unknown for this period, making the precise percentage of Protestants in these towns impossible to calculate, but the number of Huguenots suggested by the level of baptisms in each town (roughly 440 apiece, indicating a total Huguenot population of about 11,000) suggests that the Protestants were in the majority. None of these towns was likely to have had a total population of over 20,000 inhabitants.

situation at court where the Guises, the Montmorencys, and the duke of Anjou were all pursuing their ambitious designs. 'Nobody even thought of speaking of religion', Claude Haton wrote about these civil wars,[1] and indeed they had lost most of the confessional passion which had fired the earlier conflict. Where the first four civil wars all resulted from mounting suspicion and hostility between the members of the two confessions, these later civil wars were little more than the work of a military nobility which had found warfare to be an excellent means of boosting its sagging fortunes. A rising volume of complaint about the nobility consequently accompanied these later civil wars. The *gentilhommerie* had become a *gens-pille-hommerie*, deliberately prolonging the warfare the better to shear the peasantry, people charged. The charges had foundation. In Dauphiné, one of the regions where combats between rival noble bands became virtually constant, a recent study has shown a significant transfer of land from the peasantry to the nobility and the bourgeois of the region's small towns, who often fought in wars alongside the nobility.[2] Meanwhile, the examples of both Rouen and Languedoc suggest that taxes were rapidly rising to pay for the wars, whose necessity surely escaped the inhabitants of most communities. This is the background to the growing tide of peasant unrest and its often anti-seigneurial, as well as anti-fiscal, character.

The element of confessional passion thus largely disappeared from the civil wars for fifteen years after the St Bartholomew's Day Massacres and their aftermath cemented the local domination of one party or the other. But why did Protestant numbers diminish so markedly in so many communities? Richard Gascon has recently argued that the faith's decline in Lyon was the product of a 'veritable reconquest of souls' carried out by certain elements within the Catholic Church, most notably the Jesuits, who launched a sustained campaign of preaching, debate, and religious instruction in these years.[3] Gascon's discovery of the intense Jesuit activity in Lyon is extremely important, for it demonstrates that inertia was not everywhere the rule within the Gallican Church at this time. In attributing

[1] Claude Haton, *Mémoires de Claude Haton contenant le récit des événements accomplis de 1553 à 1582, principalement dans la Champagne et la Brie*, ed. Félix Bourquelot (Paris, 1857), Vol. 2, p. 77. The Venetian ambassador also wrote of the Fifth Civil War, 'They speak but little of religion, which only plays a secondary role'. M. N. Tommaseo, ed., *Relations des ambassadeurs vénitiens sur les affaires de France au XVIe siècle* (Paris, 1838), Vol. 2, p. 227. A similar judgment may be found in James Westfall Thompson, *The Wars of Religion in France 1559–1576: The Huguenots, Catherine de Medici and Philip II* (Chicago, 1909), p. 493.

[2] Hickey, 'Socio-Economic Context', pp. 168–70. Cf. the quite different fate of the nobility in the generally peaceful Hurepoix: Jean Jacquart, *La crise rurale en Ile-de-France, 1550–1670* (Paris, 1974), pp. 223–7.

[3] Richard Gascon, *Grand commerce et vie urbaine au XVIe siècle: Lyon et ses marchands (vers 1520–vers 1580)* (Paris–The Hague, 1971), Vol. 2, pp. 511–15.

the Protestant reconversions to this activity, however, he may be falling into the error of explaining developments common to many cities by causes unique to a few. Many Huguenots were also 'reduced' to Catholicism in cities such as Rouen where signs of renewal within the local church are scarce. A Jesuit in Paris admitted in a letter written soon after the St Bartholomew's Day Massacre there: 'With this "catechism" [i.e. the massacre] our king has converted more souls to Christ than all the preachers and catechists together in the past twenty years.'[1]

It would be equally misleading to attribute the numerous Protestant reconversions to internal tensions within the Reformed movement between the strict morality enforced by the consistory and the more relaxed recreational and associational patterns dear to the artisan classes. Such an explanation is suggested by Natalie Davis' brilliant study of one group, the Protestant printing workers of Lyon.[2] The temptation to extend her explanation beyond the fate of this one group must be resisted, however, for the fact that Huguenot numbers declined sharply in some cities while holding firm in others suggests that external pressures varying from region to region were more important causes of the movement's decline than internal tensions which are likely to have been universal within it. Above all it appears to have been the pressure of popular intolerance and governmental proscription which was critical in provoking the movement's collapse in those communities where it lacked either the safety of numbers and power or the protection of a nearby Huguenot stronghold to which believers could retire in times of danger.

The confessional passions which largely disappeared from the civil wars between 1573 and 1585 re-emerged during their last phase, that of the League. The death of the duke of Anjou revived the threat of Protestant domination that had seemed distant in most communities since 1572, while discontent over rising taxes and the multiplication of venal offices had already sapped much of Henry III's prestige. The response was the Catholic League, formed late in 1584 and soon a formidable threat to the crown. When the unfortunate Henry tried to rid himself of this threat by arranging the assassination of its aristocratic leaders, a wave of uprisings swept the country in reaction, carrying the League into power in city after city.

There is a mild paradox about the League uprisings of 1588–9. The founders of the movement had sought, with some success it would appear, to create a nationwide organization that could act in concert, yet it is harder

[1] Austin Lynn Martin, ed., 'Jesuits and the Massacre of St. Bartholomew's Day', *Archivum Historicum Societatis Iesu*, XLIII (1974), p. 113.

[2] Natalie Zemon Davis, 'Strikes and Salvation', *Society and Culture in Early Modern France: Eight Essays* (Stanford, 1975), pp. 1–16.

to generalize about the nature of the League and the causes of its uprisings than about any of the other upheavals of the Religious Wars. A blend of religious, political, and social grievances fueled the movement, and the precise mixture of these ingredients varied considerably from region to region.

In Rouen memories of the 1562 Huguenot takeover and the presence of many refugee English Catholics made fear of a Protestant king especially strong, while the openness of access to the parlement muted resentment against that body. The League was led by a fraction of the city's governing elite and supported overwhelmingly by the older, long-established members of the sovereign courts. Even after the League came to power, the parlement continued to play an important role in city government and no revival of communal power occurred. There appear to have been many other provincial cities where the League movement also never escaped the control of the urban elites. In Lyon the urban aristocracy of merchants and *officiers* dominated the party. The small nucleus of active *ligueurs* in Rennes was composed almost entirely of members of the parlement. Abbeville and Reims were just two of the many cities where the triumph of the League was accompanied by no popular agitation whatsoever; a simple majority vote of the town council sufficed to take each of these cities over to the side of the League.[1] In Dijon and Paris, on the other hand, resentment against the exclusiveness of the sovereign courts was strong. Here the League became a movement of protest against the new aristocracy of the robe. The *ligueurs* in these towns were drawn heavily from the ranks of the lawyers, lesser merchants, and lower clergy. Once in power, they sought energetically to revive the dwindling powers of the city government and reduce the prerogatives of the sovereign courts.[2] An impulse toward communal independence also fueled the movement in certain cities, although it must be said that the well-known cases of St Malo and Marseilles – both of which became virtually autonomous republics under *ligueur* domination – have often led historians to overestimate this factor's importance.[3]

[1] André Latreille et al., *Histoire de Lyon et du Lyonnais* (Toulouse, 1975), p. 195; F. Joüon des Longrais, ed., 'Information du Sénéchal de Rennes contre les Ligueurs 1589', *Bulletin et Mémoires de la Société Archéologique du Département d'Ille-et-Vilaine*, XLI (1911), pp. 9–10; Ernest Prarond, *La Ligue à Abbeville, 1576–1594* (Paris, 1873), Vol. 2, pp. 1–120; Henry, *Réforme et Ligue en Champagne*, ch. 5.

[2] Henri Drouot, *Mayenne et la Bourgogne: Etude sur la Ligue en Bourgogne, 1587–1596* (Paris, 1937), pp. 43–55, 334–43; J. H. M. Salmon, 'The Paris Sixteen 1584–94: The Social Analysis of a Revolutionary Movement', *Journal of Modern History*, XLIV (1972), passim; Denis Richet, 'Aspects socio-culturels des conflits religieux à Paris dans la seconde moitié du XVIe siècle', *Annales: E.S.C.*, XXXII (1977), p. 779.

[3] A recent account of events in St Malo and Marseilles may be found in Peter M. Ascoli, 'French Provincial Cities and the Catholic League', *Occasional Papers of the American Society for Reformation Research*, I (1977), pp. 22–5. As both he and Robert R. Harding point out *contra* Braudel, these cities were far from typical. In most towns the League cannot be said to have been 'above all...a return

Finally, in certain particularly isolated regions, the religious anxieties or social resentments that contributed to the movement throughout most of France took a back seat to purely local rivalries. According to a detailed memorandum about the League in Auvergne written by the president of the *cour des aides* of Montferrand, the town of Riom passed into the camp of the *Sainte-Union* largely out of resentment against the king for recently having located Auvergne's *siège présidial* in rival Clermont. Clermont, on the other hand, sided with the crown because of the momentary ascendancy within the city of the powerful Enjobert family, supporters of Henry III because their bitter foes, the Maugins, happened to support the local *ligueur* chieftain de Randan. The author of this memorandum reports on the situation in all of the province's cities, and only in the case of Aurillac does he mention religious passion as being of the least importance.[1] As for the other cities among that minority of towns which like Clermont remained loyal to the king, two common characteristics can be discerned. Many were cities which sheltered a large number of Protestants or erstwhile Protestants, e.g. the two leading royalist cities in Normandy, Caen and Dieppe. Others such as Bordeaux, Angers, or Blois, were kept loyal to the crown by an energetic governor ensconced in an impregnable castle within the city walls. This task was not always easy, for the governor often had to face fiery preaching by the local clergy and considerable agitation on the part of the Catholic populace.[2]

Although the nature and motivation of the League movement may have varied considerably from city to city, certain of the patterns visible in Rouen's history during this period were more widespread. First of all, the ferment of penitential activity and of new forms of religious devotion visible in Rouen seems to have been echoed in many other *ligueur* cities in the years immediately following the *Sainte-Union's* triumph. For the clergy, an effort of personal and communal reform was the necessary accompaniment to the League's defense of the true faith. Their appeals to the faithful bore fruit in a number of new confraternities or novel devotional forms in many cities. Paris and Orleans witnessed the foundation of the Confraternity of the

to an age of urban independence, the age of the city-state'. *Ibid.*, pp. 27–8; Harding, *Power Elite*, p. 98.

[1] Jehan de Vernyes, *Mémoires 1589–1593* (Clermont–Ferrand, 1838). Inter-urban rivalries such as those between Riom and Clermont were also important in pushing Poitiers into the League camp. *See* Henri Ouvré, 'Essai sur l'histoire de la Ligue à Poitiers', *Mémoires de la Société des Antiquaires de l'Ouest* (1854), pp. 170, 186.

[2] B.N., MS Français 23295, fos. 484–6; Ernest Mourin, *La Réforme et la Ligue en Anjou* (Paris–Angers, 1856), pp. 214–63; Boutruche et al., *Bordeaux*, pp. 311–12. Châlons-sur-Marne, one of the rare cities to support the king in strongly *guisard* Champagne, provides a striking reversal of the pattern of a royalist governor preserving a city for the king despite considerable sentiment for the League among the populace at large. There the royalist city council moved quickly to expel the *guisard* governor as soon as news arrived of the uprisings elsewhere in France, securing the city for the king. Henry, *Réforme et Ligue en Champagne*, pp. 135–8.

Name of Jesus, whose members pledged themselves to undergo a daily examination of conscience, take frequent communion, participate in special processions, and fight to the last drop of blood against Navarre and the '*faux politiques*'.[1] Lyon and Reims witnessed the establishment of the *oratoire*.[2] A particularly good example of how political activism and religious innovation could be intertwined in these years comes from Laon, where a Jesuit father of singular oratorical power, Antoine Tholozan, settled in town at the request of the *ligueur* municipal government and soon became the League's outstanding spokesman. Not only were Tholozan's sermons ardent defenses of the *Sainte-Union*; while in Laon he also introduced the *oratoire* and founded a company of Penitents. The association soon included the better part of the city's inhabitants and became an essential element in Tholozan's efforts to keep the League in power during the declining years of the movement, for it was Tholozan's practice to have all of the *confrères* of the association confess to him at least once a month, and he then reportedly threatened those whose zeal for the League began to slacken with revealing the secrets confided to him in confession.[3] The history of Catholic religious life in the later sixteenth century remains obscure, and until a good deal more research is carried out in this area it is difficult to know the precise extent of the religious ferment of the period of the League and the role it played in the broader development of a reforming spirit within French Catholicism. But the depth of the ferment in such towns as Paris and Rouen is clear, and it does seem to set this period off as a special phase in the history of Catholic religious life, one that provides an important window into the depth of popular anxiety about the threat of a Huguenot king and may well have been a critical step in the development of the French Counter-Reformation.

While the spectacular processions and wave of religious foundations accompanying the early years of the League in many towns testify to the degree of mass concern about the perilous situation in which the Catholic Church found itself in 1588–9, the zeal of the urban masses tended to decline as the years progressed. There were several reasons for this. First, the movement tended to become more and more subservient to the great nobility. The extended civil war which followed quick upon the League uprisings in the aftermath of Blois provided the chief military commanders in every region with numerous opportunities to extend their power over the cities they were defending. Many governors seized these opportunities

1 B.N., MS Français 23296, fo. 365; Marcel Poëte, *Une vie de cité: Paris de sa naissance à nos jours* (Paris, 1931), Vol. 3, pp. 241–5.

2 P. Richard, *La papauté et la Ligue française: Pierre d'Epinac, Archevêque de Lyon (1573–1599)* (Paris, 1901), pp. 452–3; Jean Pussot, 'Mémoires ou Journalier', ed. E. Henry, *Travaux de l'Académie Impériale de Reims*, Vol. XXV (1857), p. 8.

3 Antoine Richart, *Mémoires sur la Ligue dans le Laonnois* (Laon, 1869), pp. 333–40.

to whittle away at the authority of the town councils or *Conseils de l'Union* and to capture near-dictatorial powers for themselves.[1] Furthermore, many of these *ligueur* chieftains seemed to the Catholic masses to betray the cause. Those noblemen claiming the right to succeed to the cardinal of Bourbon's mantle as pretender feuded among one another so bitterly that effective military action against Navarre was often impeded.[2] Personal ambition seemed to shoulder aside commitment to the defense of the faith. Finally, it quickly became apparent to the urban population that, far from improving their economic condition as people had hoped a League takeover might be able to do, the urban uprisings had only led to deterioration. Taxes could not be reduced as had been promised, while the fighting provoked a dreadful economic crisis.

Enough local studies have now accumulated to give us a fairly clear picture of the fate of the French economy over the course of the Religious Wars, and it is evident that the country as a whole suffered hardships during the League that were unparallelled for extent and degree during any of the preceding civil wars. The amount of disruption varied widely during the first decades of the civil wars depending upon the chronology and intensity of the fighting in any given area. If Rouen experienced intermittent disruption of its trade between 1562 and 1574 followed by recuperation and even growth for the next decade, vast regions of Languedoc where the fighting was endemic in the 1570s and early 1580s saw agricultural productivity dip to its nadir in these years, while the population grew without interruption between 1562 and 1585 in parts of Brittany and Anjou skirted altogether by the campaigning of these decades.[3] The fighting of the League, however, touched virtually every corner of France, and so did the economic crisis that accompanied it. Across the northern half of the kingdom from Picardy to Poitou and Brittany to Burgundy, the devastation

[1] As Robert R. Harding has recently written, 'apart from the remarkable popular juntas and dictatorships of the 1590s – Marseille, Abbeville, St Malo, and a few others – most towns escaped the direct control of the central government only to slide deeper under the control of provincial governors and the hundreds of new town governors'. Harding, *Power Elite*, p. 98. Poitiers was another exception; its *échevins* refused to allow the troops of the provincial governor into their city and ignored all orders coming from *Conseils de l'Union* beyond the city walls.

[2] The relief of Rouen in 1591–2 was slowed by such rivalries. Howell A. Lloyd, *The Rouen Campaign, 1590–1592: Politics, Warfare and the Early-Modern State* (Oxford, 1973), pp. 175–80.

[3] Emmanuel Le Roy Ladurie and Joseph Goy, 'Première esquisse d'une conjoncture du produit décimal et domanial, fin du Moyen Age-XVIIIe siècle', Goy and Le Roy Ladurie, eds., *Les fluctuations du produit de la dîme: Conjoncture décimale et domaniale de la fin du Moyen Age au XVIIIe siècle* (Paris–The Hague, 1972), p. 354; Pierre Goubert, 'Registres paroissiaux et démographie dans la France du XVIe siècle', *Annales de Démographie Historique* (1965), pp. 43–8. For additional evidence on the pattern of economic disruption during these decades, *see* Jacquart, *Crise rurale en Ile-de-France*, chs, 5–6; Gascon, *Grand commerce*, part 2, ch. 3; Alain Croix, *Nantes et le Pays nantais au XVIe siecle: Etude démographique* (Paris, 1974), pp. 79–94; and Fernand Braudel and Ernest Labrousse, eds., *Histoire économique et sociale de la France* (Paris, 1977), Vol. 1, part 2, p. 711.

of these years was by far the worst of the entire period.[1] Those regions of the Midi which had already suffered severe hardships prior to 1588 experienced continued economic disruption only slightly less severe after that date.[2] Of all the towns or regions whose fate is known, only St Malo and La Rochelle enjoyed a measure of prosperity during the years of the League, and these well-fortified, resolutely independent, and geographically isolated ports were the exceptions that prove the rule. They owed their exceptional activity to trade diverted from other ports whose hinterlands were too troubled to allow much traffic to pass through them.[3]

Amid this deepening economic crisis and the growing disillusionment with the League, the last years of the movement witnessed a new surge of anti-war, anti-seigneurial peasant unrest. A virtual class war enflamed parts of Brittany, while the rising of the *Croquants* and *Tard-Avisés* set bands of peasants marching against the warring armies throughout the southwest from Poitou to Quercy. This inchoate peace movement spilled over into the cities in 1593–4, when uprisings or demonstrations against League garrisons and in favor of Henry IV occurred in Dijon, Amiens, and Reims.[4] The ultimate reduction of most *ligueur* cities was purchased through lavish pensions offered their governors, but the consummation of these deals was made easier by the groundswell of popular opinion in favor of Henry IV. Even in selling their cities, the *ligueur* sultans were operating within parameters of action set by the great mass of city-dwellers.

For all the undeniable importance of regional diversity, many of the same patterns which can be seen in Rouen's history thus were also characteristic

[1] Local studies which demonstrate the exceptional gravity of the economic crisis accompanying the League include, on Amiens and its region: Pierre Deyon, 'Variations de la production textile aux XVIe et XVIIe siècles: Sources et premiers résultats', *Annales: E.S.C.*, XVIII (1963), pp. 948–9, and *Contribution à l'étude des revenus fonciers en Picardie, les fermages de l'Hôtel-Dieu d'Amiens et leurs variations de 1515 à 1789* (Lille, n.d.), pp. 23–5, 73; on Paris and its region, Denis Pallier, *Recherches sur l'imprimerie à Paris pendant la Ligue (1585–1594)* (Geneva, 1975), pp. 16, 121ff, and Jacquart, *Crise rurale en Ile-de-France*, pp. 179ff; on Reims, Jean-Louis Bourgeon, *Les Colbert avant Colbert: Destin d'une famille marchande* (Paris, 1973), p. 166; on Burgundy, Albert Silbert, 'La production des cé réals à Beaune d'après les dîmes, XVIe–XVIIIe siècles', in Goy and Le Roy Ladurie, eds., *Produit de la dîme*, pp. 146–7; on Lyon, F. Bayard, 'Les Bonvisi, marchands banquiers à Lyon, 1575–1629', *Annales: E.S.C.*, XXVI (1971), pp. 1,255–6, 1,268–9; on Nantes and its region, Croix, *Nantes et le Pays nantais*, pp. 149–50, 163–5; on Poitou, Louis Merle, *La métairie et l'évolution agraire de la Gâtine poitevine de la fin du Moyen Age à la Revolution* (Paris, 1958), pp. 179–80.

[2] Le Roy Ladurie and Goy, 'Première esquisse', p. 354.

[3] *See here* Charles Laronze, *Essai sur le régime municipal en Bretagne pendant les guerres de religion* (Paris, 1890), p. 231; Croix, *Nantes et le Pays nantais*, p. 158; and Etienne Trocmé and Marcel Delafosse, *Le commerce rochelais de la fin du XVe siècle au début du XVIIe* (Paris, 1952), p. 198.

[4] Salmon, *Society in Crisis*, pp. 276–91; Le Roy Ladurie, *Paysans de Languedoc*, pp. 400–403; Corrado Vivanti, *Lotta politica e pace religiosa in Francia fra Cinque e Seicento* (Turin, 1963), pp. 27ff; Drouot, *Mayenne et la Bourgogne*, Vol. 2, pp. 285–8; A. Dubois, ed., *La Ligue: Documents relatifs à la Picardie d'après les registres de l'échevinage d'Amiens* (Amiens, 1859), p. 100; Pussot, 'Mémoires', Vol. 25, p. 22.

of French society as a whole. The intensity of popular confessional violence over the dozen years from 1560 to 1572; the subsequent decline in religious rioting after 1572 as issues were settled within each community in favor of one faith or the other; the revival of religious concern during the period of the League; the severe economic difficulties provoked by this crisis – these and other patterns seem to have been anything but unique to Rouen. The country as a whole was divided by the crisis of the Religious Wars.

The country was also shaped by the crisis in enduring ways. A new religion that at one point had appeared as if it might be the wave of the future ultimately encountered such violent resistance that it found itself reduced in most of the realm to the status of a small and politically timid minority. An established church whose initial response to challenge was simply to denounce and seek to exterminate its critics ultimately found itself jolted into measures of innovation and internal reform as well. In the countryside the devastation of the wars forced many small peasant proprietors under, accelerating the transfer of property to the bourgeoisie and the spread of share-cropping,[1] while in the cities trade and industry was seriously disrupted, damaging badly the aspirations of the country's two commercial poles, Lyon and Rouen, to join the Antwerps, Venices, and Amsterdams in the very front rank of the European economy.

Finally, the wars bequeathed a series of problems to the new century dawning. The semi-independent administrative system which the Huguenots had imposed on the areas under their control after 1572 was permitted to continue by the secret articles of the edict of Nantes, posing a challenge to the growth of royal absolutism that was only liquidated in 1629 after a protracted conflict. The continuities between the religious activities of the period of the League and those of the *dévots* have already been suggested. Last of all, the confessional hatreds built up during the years of the Religious Wars continued to provoke scattered incidents of popular religious violence throughout the seventeenth century; in areas of the Midi where the violence of the civil wars burned itself particularly deeply into the inhabitants' memories, these hatreds even survived to influence the conflicts of the Revolution and Restoration.[2] The Religious Wars left an enduring legacy of popular passion.

[1] P. de Saint-Jacob, 'Mutations économiques et sociales dans les campagnes bourguignonnes à la fin du XVIe siècle', *Etudes Rurales*, 1 (1961), pp. 34–49; Jacquart, *Crise rurale en Ile-de-France*, pp. 213–30, 724–5.

[2] Burdette C. Poland, *French Protestantism and the French Revolution: A Study in Church and State, Thought and Religion, 1685–1815* (Princeton, 1957), pp. 112–40; Gwynn Lewis, 'The White Terror of 1815 in the Department of the Gard: Counter-Revolution, Continuity, and the Individual', *Past and Present*, 58 (1973), pp. 108–35, esp. p. 117.

APPENDIX 1

The evolution of Protestant strength, 1557–1600: a comparative look at eight congregations

Historical demographers have long recognized that changes in the number of births in a given community provide a reliable, if crude, indication of larger trends in its population. In the pre-birth-control era, it is safe to assume that a significantly increasing number of baptisms indicates a growing community, a declining number of baptisms a shrinking community. Students of the Wars of Religion have always wanted to know just how many Protestants there were at any given time, but it is a mark of the neglect of this period by social historians, as well as of the lack of familiarity with newer methodologies on the part of those historians who have examined the era, that no previous attempt has been made to seek out the surviving Reformed baptismal registers from these years in order to clarify the faith's numerical evolution.

The Protestant baptismal registers which served as the basis for this study's comparative examination of Huguenot strength were scattered across France in many different kinds of archives – national, departmental and municipal. I sought to locate all those communities within France's sixteenth-century boundaries for which good sets of Protestant 'parish' registers date back to the first decade of the Religious Wars.[1] The partial listings in B. Faucher, 'Les registres de l'état civil protestant en France depuis le XVIᵉ siècle jusqu'à nos jours', *Bibliothèque de l'Ecole des Chartes*, LXXXIV (1923), pp. 304–46, and Paul-F. Geisendorf, 'Les registres d'état civil protestant des XVIᵉ et XVIIᵉ siècles conservés dans la série TT des Archives Nationales', *Mélanges Charles Braibant* (Paris, 1959), pp. 153–62, provided initial indications. These were supplemented with letters to all departmental archives in regions where Protestant churches are known to have existed in the sixteenth century inquiring whether or not they had any Huguenot registers amid their holdings. The search unearthed fifteen sets of registers in addition to Rouen's. The use of certain of these (the

[1] The unique case of Metz, a city for which excellent Protestant registers have survived, was eliminated from consideration. Its special status as a part of the Holy Roman Empire under French 'protection' meant that in certain regards it was outside the boundaries of sixteenth-century France. Its experience over the course of the civil wars was somewhat different from those cities legally part of the kingdom of France.

registers of Nimes, Vitré, and all those listed by Geisendorf from the series TT not to be found in Table 9) ultimately had to be renounced because the records proved so badly scrambled at certain points or indicated such utterly improbable fluctuations in the number of baptisms that they did not appear reliable. In three other cases, those of Loudun, Saintes, and La Baume-Cornillan, the registers proved extremely fragmentary. They did provide enough information to permit comparison of Protestantism's strength before and after 1572 and thus are included in Table 9 and Map 8. (*See* above, pp. 136–9.) They are not included in the following table because they cover just a few years of the period. Presented below are the annual figures from the eight remaining Protestant congregations for which longer series of reliable baptismal registers have survived. Naturally my search may not have located all such registers. Additional ones may yet turn up in municipal archives or private repositories.

Chapters 5 and 10 discuss the most important revelations yielded by these figures: the dramatic increase after modest beginnings shown by the few registers which date back to the years prior to 1562; the lack of evidence of significant decline between 1562 and the mid-1560s; and the sharp contrasts which emerge after 1568 between the stronghold Protestant communities where Huguenot numbers held stable or even increased and the more fragile congregations whose ranks tumbled dramatically in 1568 and/or 1572. La Rochelle, Montauban, Monoblet, and Verteuil-Ruffec are clear examples of stronghold congregations. All held steady or grew in size between the 1560s and the end of the civil wars. The church of Caen meanwhile declined by 65 per cent between 1565 and 1580, while Gien's congregation lost 46 per cent of its members over the same period and St Lô's dwindled by 60 per cent over the longer period 1564–1600. Rouen's church, of course, declined by 87 per cent between 1565 and 1580. A few additional points deserve brief mention here. First of all, it should be recalled that records are far more likely to have survived for those congregations whose meetings were rarely or never interrupted than for those whose assemblies ceased with each outbreak of fighting. The percentage of congregations whose numbers held firm or increased after 1572 is thus much higher among the examples below than among the total universe of sixteenth-century Protestant congregations, many of which in fact disappeared entirely during the course of the civil wars.

The gaps in the registers are often as significant as the entries they contain. The lacuna in Monoblet's records between 1587 and 1591 was produced when the pastor left town following an unspecified '*insolence*' committed against him by the village's youth. In all other cases, except where registers are noted as missing, the gaps correspond to periods when

Protestantism was legally outlawed. It is thus clear that the royal edicts banning Protestant worship at the beginning of each civil war between 1567 and 1577 were effectively enforced in many communities but were flouted by the Protestants in regions where they were in control (i.e., La Rochelle, Monoblet, Montauban). Montpellier represents a rather unusual case. Its Reformed church ceased to assemble during the Third Civil War and again in 1572, but from 1574 onward the *politique* governor Montmorency-Damville chose to ignore further royal edicts outlawing the faith. Control of the city council was divided between the Catholics and Protestants, and over the subsequent years the Reformed church made a modest comeback.[1] Striking differences appear among the congregations at the time of the League. The edict wrung from the king in 1585 outlawing Protestantism was ignored in Verteuil, as it was in Huguenot strongholds such as La Rochelle and Montauban. In Caen and Gien, on the other hand, as in Rouen, services ceased. Unlike Rouen, these towns remained royalist after 1588. Once Henry of Navarre came to the throne, their Reformed churches began to assemble again. The communities became modest meccas for Protestant refugees from other nearby cities now returning from exile. (One encounters, for example, numerous Rouennais Protestants in Caen's baptismal registers from 1592 onward.) The number of baptisms therefore attained peaks during these last years of the League. In Verteuil and Gien the number of baptisms then declined again as these refugees left following the collapse of the League. Caen, on the other hand, saw the number of baptisms remain at higher levels under Henry IV than had been the case in the middle years of the Religious Wars. Here, as in Rouen, the new reign of tolerance brought about a modest recovery in the size of the Protestant community.

Finally, major increases in the number of baptisms appear in the records of La Rochelle and Montauban during almost every major period of civil war, with certain minor differences in timing between the two communities that probably reflect the differing chronology and intensity of the conflicts locally. The increases are the product primarily of the waves of refugees that poured into these cities at each outbreak of fighting. The local Catholic population was also constrained to participate in Reformed services during these years.[2]

[1] Jean Philippi, *Mémoires*, Petitot, 1st ser., vol. 34, p. 384; Louise Guiraud, *Etudes sur la Réforme à Montpellier* (1918), Vol. 1, pp. 427ff.

[2] This was the case, at least, in La Rochelle. Etienne Trocmé, 'L'Eglise réformée de La Rochelle jusqu'en 1628', *B.S.H.P.F.*, XCIX (1952), p. 138.

Appendix 1

Protestant baptisms per calendar year

	Caen	Gien	La Rochelle	Monoblet	Montauban	Montpellier	St Lô	Verteuil-Ruffec‡
1557	—	—	—	—	—	—	16	—
1558	—	—	—	—	—	—	28	—
1559	—	—	—	—	—	—	49	—
1560	—	—	—	—	—	21 (4)	88	—
1561	40*	—	—	—	—	199	130	—
1562	107*	—	—	40 (10)	—	520	99	—
1563	129 (9)*	37 (5)	—	32	—	335	157	—
1564	382	126	479	26	—	345	163	—
1565	491	105	448	33	466	416	—	—
1566	433	[register	497	34	464	369	—	—
1567	436	missing]	482	33	515	453	—	—
1568	298 (9)	—	828	19	586	283 (4)	—	—
1569	—	—	500	34	742	—	—	—
1570	53 (3)	16 (4)	[register	29	723	40 (3)	—	209 (10)
1571	258	66	missing]	27	435 (10)	221	—	241 (11)
1572	206 (8)	49 (8)	—	32	559	143 (8)	—	172 (7)
1573	—	—	—	18 (10)	428	—	—	—
1574	—	—	976	24	554	36 (2)	—	—
1575	—	—	1257	25	619	247	—	—
1576	106 (7)	34 (7)	796	27	526	206	—	100 (8)
1577	—	4 (3)	1179	32	863	334	—	108§
1578	93	46	776	26	712	221	—	172
1579	142	60	791	27	739	244	—	190
1580	192	58	715	42	817	120†	[register(s)	197
1581	145	70	712	26	644	254	missing]	209
1582	177	67	586	37	631	296	—	193
1583	166	71	571	25	634	286	—	213

1584	151	48	567	39	658	325	—	178
1585	58 (6)	22 (5)	597	36	725	318	—	139§
1586	—	—	891	18	712	310	—	73§
1587	—	—	703	15 (11)	552	336	—	154§
1588	—	—	887	—	680	300	—	223
1589	—	—	718	—	668	194	—	226
1590	33	12 (4)	733	—	546	338	—	226
1591	119	34	624	12 (3)	568	351	—	269
1592	196	90	760	31	515	319	36	279
1593	203	70	635	22	438	346	66	279
1594	229	68	733	35	656	388	63	136‖
1595	287	40	—	21	544	215 (7)	76	16 (2)‖
1596	247	60	—	30	686	—	58	89‖
1597	234	55	[register missing]	26	696	[register missing]	57	64‖
1598	181	47		16	554		17 (?)	74‖
1599	241	52	—	35	492	31 (1)	66	65‖
1600	195	55	—	38	642	419	62	79‖

* Based on a single register kept by one of the city's three pastors. The other two registers have been lost.

† The abnormally low total of this year was due to a severe plague.

‡ Prior to 1572 a single congregation at Verteuil served the Protestant population of a region encompassing Nanteuil, Salles, Lizent, Villegast, Aizecq, and Ruffec as well. After 1576 the region was divided into two congregations with the second located at Ruffec. Figures provided after that date represent the number of acts in both congregations added together.

§ Irregular gaps in the two registers.

‖ Figures for Verteuil only. Since the congregations of Ruffec and Verteuil were almost identical in size, these figures represent a decline from the preceding years.

Sources: Caen – A.D. Calvados, C 1565–74. La Rochelle – A.D. Charente-Maritime, I 1–18. Gien – Bibliothèque de la Société de l'Histoire du Protestantisme Français, MS 1082 (1); A.N., TT 244 (15). Verteuil-Ruffec – A.N., TT 264 (159–60), 275 (10–15). Montauban – A.C. Montauban, 12 GG 1–8. Monoblet – A.D. Gard, 5 E 169 (2). Montpellier – A.C. Montpellier, GG 314–20. St Lô – R. Leclerc, *Le Protestantisme à St Lô* (St Lô, 1926), part II, pp. 35–6. Loudun – C.E. Lart, ed. *The Registers of the Protestant Church at Loudun, 1566–1582* (Lymington, 1905). Saintes – A.D. Charente-Maritime, I 146–7; La Baume-Cornillan – A.N., TT 233 (19).

APPENDIX 2

Protestant names, Catholic names

Far more clearly than any summary table, the complete list of the names chosen by Rouen's Protestants for their children in 1565, 1576–85, and 1595–1602 – compared with a similarly sized sample of Catholic names – displays the contrasts between the two groups in their choice of names and the changes which occurred within the Reformed community over the course of the Wars of Religion. The saints' names attacked by Calvin were almost exclusively Catholic, although diminishing Protestant rigor allowed a few Guillaumes and Marguerites to slip back in in the later years. Old Testament names were preponderantly Protestant but declined in popularity over the course of the period. The names of the apostles or other New Testament figures cut across the confessional lines.

Among details worth noting, the fate of the name Elizabeth stands out. It was a name chosen only by Protestants, among whom its popularity grew markedly over the four decades as the bitter memories of the English queen's slowness to send aid in 1562 gave way to gratitude for the asylum England provided in subsequent times of persecution. An occasional classical name (e.g. Achilles, Hector) appears on the Catholic side of the list, perhaps the pale reflection of Renaissance influences. Such names violated church law, which stipulated that only the names of saints or biblical figures could be conferred at baptism. The Provincial Council of 1581 issued a warning against the choice of classical names.

The Catholic sample is drawn from the parish registers of St Maclou at the approximate mid-point of the Wars of Religion, 1578–9.

Protestant names, Catholic names

	Protestants			Catholics
	1565	1576–85	1595–1602	1578–9
Aaron	1	0	0	0
Abel	3	0	1	0
Achilles	0	0	0	1
Abraham	42	12	27	7
Adam	1	0	4	1
Adrien	0	0	0	1
Alexandre	0	0	0	2
Alexis	0	0	0	2
Albert	0	0	0	1
Alonze	0	1	0	0
André, Andrieu	3	9	3	0
Anselme	0	0	0	1
Antipos	0	1	0	0
Antoine	0	0	3	3
Balthazar	0	0	0	1
Bastien	0	0	0	1
Benjamin	0	3	1	0
Benoist	0	0	1	0
Bernard	0	0	0	1
Bonaventure	0	0	0	2
Charles	0	0	3	8
Christian	0	1	0	0
Christofle	0	0	0	1
Daniel	33	12	22	2
David	14	24	20	0
Denis	0	0	2	3
Edouard	0	0	1	0
Eléazar	0	0	2	0
Elizar	1	0	0	0
Elizée	0	0	2	1
Emmanuel	2	0	0	0
Esaye, Isaye	0	4	5	0
Etienne	6	7	5	2
Eustache	0	0	0	1
Ezechiel	1	0	0	0
François	0	0	0	10
Frémin	0	0	0	1
Ganseaulme	0	0	0	1
Geoffroy	0	0	0	2
Georges	0	0	0	3
Germain	0	0	1	0
Gilles	0	0	0	4
Goderne	1	0	0	0
Gregoire	0	0	0	1
Guillaume	0	0	5	30
Guillebert	0	0	0	1
Gynard	0	0	0	1

	Protestants			Catholics
	1565	1576–85	1595–1602	1578–9
Hilaire	0	0	0	1
Hector	0	0	0	1
Hellie, Helye	2	2	2	1
Henri	0	0	0	1
Isaac	41	17	24	3
Ismael	1	0	0	0
Israel	0	0	2	0
Jacob	5	7	10	0
Jacques	22	45	36	22
Jan	0	0	6	0
Jean, Jehan	46	72	50	70
Jean-Baptiste	0	0	0	1
Jérémie	5	1	4	0
Jérome	0	0	1	1
Jessé	0	0	0	5
Jonas	12	1	3	1
Jonathan	0	0	1	0
Josias	3	1	5	0
Joseph	1	0	0	0
Josué	3	0	0	0
Jude	1	0	0	0
Laurent	0	0	0	5
Lazare	0	1	1	1
Léonard	0	0	0	1
Louis	0	0	0	1
Lucas	0	0	2	0
Marc	1	0	2	1
Marin	1	0	0	4
Martin	0	0	0	2
Mathieu	1	3	1	4
Mathurin	0	0	1	1
Melchizadeh	1	0	0	0
Michel	0	5	1	5
Moïse	2	2	1	0
Nathaniel	1	1	1	0
Nicolas	0	2	3	26
Noäh	1	0	0	0
Noël	2	0	0	3
Ozaye, Ozée	0	0	2	0
Pacquet	0	0	0	1
Pan	0	1	0	0
Pascal	0	0	0	1
Paul	9	3	7	0
Philippe	1	3	3	6
Pierre	36	54	38	27

	Protestants			Catholics
	1565	1576–85	1595–1602	1578–9
Raoulin	0	0	0	2
Raphael	0	0	0	1
Regné, René	0	0	2	0
Richard	0	1	0	8
Robert	0	0	0	17
Roboam	0	0	1	0
Roger	0	0	0	1
Romain	0	0	0	3
Roquet	0	0	0	1
Sadoc	0	0	1	0
Salomon	5	3	8	0
Samson	0	2	0	0
Samuel	4	3	8	1
Simon	1	3	3	0
Théodore	0	0	1	0
Théophile	1	0	0	0
Thomas	1	4	3	5
Timothie	1	3	0	0
Tobie	0	1	1	0
Toussaint	0	0	0	2
Vincent	0	0	0	1
Zacharie	3	0	0	0
Total	322	315	343	334
Abigail	1	0	0	0
Alice, Alix	0	0	0	4
Angelique	0	0	0	1
Anne	17	25	33	26
Barbe	0	0	0	8
Blanche	0	0	0	1
Béatrix	0	0	1	0
Bonne	0	0	0	1
Catherine	0	0	1	41
Charlotte	0	0	0	2
Ciphague	0	0	0	1
Clare, Cler	0	0	1	1
Clemence	0	0	0	1
Colette	0	0	0	2
Elizabeth	11	16	33	0
Ester	15	21	27	2
Florence	0	0	0	3
Françoise	0	0	0	3
Geneviève	0	0	0	6

Appendix 2

	Protestants			Catholics
	1565	1576–85	1595–1602	1578–9
Guillaumette	0	0	0	5
Hélène	0	0	0	3
Huguette	0	0	0	1
Huittare (?)	0	0	0	1
Isabeau	0	0	1	14
Isabelle, Isabella	0	0	0	2
Jacqueline	0	0	0	10
Janine	0	0	2	0
Jeanne	8	13	10	28
Judith	38	39	14	2
Louise	0	0	0	5
Magdaleine	7	13	39	12
Marguerite	0	0	1	33
Marie	113	83	88	63
Marthe	10	7	2	2
Martine	0	0	0	2
Mathurine	0	0	0	1
Michelle	0	0	0	4
Nicolle	0	0	0	1
Noëmi	0	2	2	0
Perette	0	0	0	7
Rachel	11	11	9	0
Raouline	0	0	0	1
Rebecca	2	0	0	1
Remone	0	0	1	0
Renée	0	0	0	1
Rhode	1	0	0	0
Roberte	0	0	0	1
Robine	0	0	0	3
Sara	31	18	14	0
Suzanne	27	23	35	4
Symée	0	0	0	1
Symone	0	0	0	1
Thomasse	0	0	0	3
Toynette	0	0	0	3
Total	292	271	314	318

APPENDIX 3

An indication of population trends: the movement of baptisms

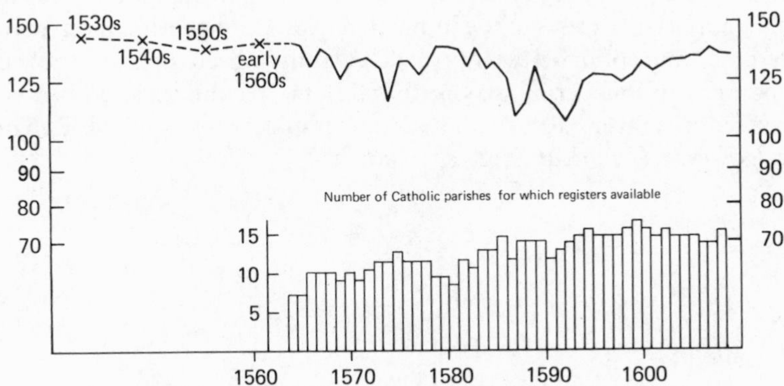

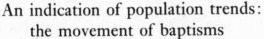

Figure 7. The movement of baptisms, 1530–1609

This graph indicates the fluctuations in the total number of baptisms in Rouen, Protestant and Catholic combined. It thus conveys a sense of the city's demographic evolution over the course of the later sixteenth century. The curve is a weighted index based on the surviving parish registers with 1599 taken as the base year for the Catholic population and the estimated percentage of Protestants then added for all years when services were held at the Reformed temple. For the years 1564, 1567–8, and 1570–72, when the Reformed baptismal registers have been lost, I have assumed a Protestant population that was stable between 1564 and 1568 and which then suffered one third of its subsequent decline in the years between 1568 and 1570. The extrapolated curve for the years prior to 1564 rests on fragmentary figures from just six parishes. Most of them are small, and they are not scattered randomly over the entire city, instead clustering in the center and west of town. They are a fragile reed on which to base any conclusions – *caveat lector*. The figures for the subsequent years can be accepted with greater confidence, for, although good parish registers may have come down to us for less than half of the city's parishes in these years, most of the surviving registers belong to the larger parishes. Picking a year at random, one finds in 1577 that the 11 parishes on which the curve is based were ones which witnessed fully 57 per cent of the city's baptisms in the period 1690–99. These parishes *are* well distributed across the city.

The period of the League emerges clearly from this graph as the most serious and prolonged period of population decline. The later 1560s and early 1570s also seem to have been a phase of mild decline, while the late 1570s and early 1580s appear as a period of increasing population. Henry IV's reign was clearly one of steady demographic recovery. The particularly pronounced dips in the curves in 1574, 1587–8, and 1592 are the result of the major mortality crises of the immediately preceding years, for in periods of famine conception was impeded. A fuller discussion of the city's demography in this period may be found in my 'Catholics and Huguenots in Sixteenth-Century Rouen: The Demographic Effects of the Religious Wars', *French Historical Studies*, IX (1975).

APPENDIX 4

The movement of house rents

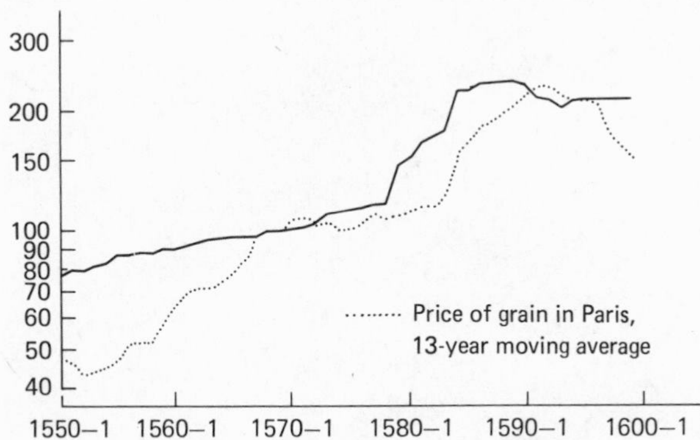

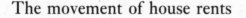

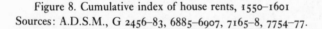

Figure 8. Cumulative index of house rents, 1550–1601
Sources: A.D.S.M., G 2456–83, 6885–6907, 7165–8, 7754–77.

The movement of house rents ranks among the best indicators of a sixteenth-century city's general state of prosperity. Although influenced to some degree by the general movement of prices, rents were determined first and foremost by changes in demand, hence by changes in the city's overall population and the disposable income of its inhabitants. (Changes in housing supply could also be of some importance, but in the case of later sixteenth-century Rouen this factor can be discounted, for it is known that very few houses were built in the city between 1550 and 1600.)[1] The figure above, tracing the evolution of house rents as compared with the movement of the largest single element in an average inhabitant's budget, bread, is based on the account books of the cathedral and of three parish churches. These ecclesiastical corporations owned modest quantities of urban real estate, which they rented out on the basis of three-, six-, or nine-year leases. Their account books enable one to follow for most of the half-century 1550–1600 the rental of 32 houses located in 9 widely scattered parishes. For the first three years of this period, the index is calculated on the basis

[1] Raymond Quenedey, *L'habitation rouennaise: Etude d'histoire, de géographie et d'archéologie urbaines* (Rouen, 1926), pp. 46–7.

of only 18 of these houses; thereafter the number of houses per year on which it is based oscillates between 27 and 32. The rents of virtually all houses examined evolved according to the same general pattern, suggesting that the sample provides an accurate reflection of the trends of the time.

The graph reveals three phases. Up to 1578–9 rents rose only slowly, lagging significantly behind the general inflationary trend characteristic of this century of the price revolution. A dramatic rise occurred over the next six years, with rents almost doubling. After 1584–5 they then levelled off again and even declined during the period of the League.

Bibliography

MANUSCRIPT SOURCES

The shape taken by any local study is invariably determined to a great degree by the nature of the locally available documentation. This study rests above all on the archival material concerning the later sixteenth century contained in Rouen's two major repositories, the Archives Communales de Rouen (housed in the Bibliothèque Municipale) and the Archives Départementales de la Seine-Maritime. Because of the peculiarities of the Norman custom and the vagaries of documentary survival, these have relatively few of the sorts of records – tax rolls, inventories after death, revealing marriage contracts – that could be used for a detailed quantitative reconstruction of the city's social structure such as that carried out by Richard Gascon for sixteenth-century Lyon. Other cities also provide better locales in which to study the economic history of the period or to attempt an in-depth portrait of either the local Protestant community or the rank-and-file of *ligueurs*. The great strength of Rouen's archives is that they contain a good deal of material about political developments within the city and happen to include several exceptional sources, notably the Protestant baptismal registers and the Catholic parish account books, that yield unusually good information about the evolution over time of both Protestant numerical strength and Catholic religious attitudes. The decision to chronicle the changes undergone by both religions and the interplay of *mentalités* and events over the full course of the Wars of Religion was thus dictated in large measure by the materials in Rouen's archives, which lend themselves better to a study of the broad sweep of the city's history over this period than to the microscopic analysis of any one aspect within it. The research for this book was not confined, however, to Rouennais archives; I also relied heavily on the manuscript collections of the Bibliothèque Nationale, while the comparative investigation of Protestantism's numerical evolution took me to a number of other provincial repositories. Scattered pieces of interest were also found in English, Spanish, and Swiss archives.

Archives Communales de Rouen

These archives contain the papers of the municipal government prior to 1789. Four series of records were of particular value. The municipal registers of deliberations, which form the series A, are invaluable for tracing the city's political and administrative history. Registers A 16–21 cover the years 1547–1602, with a gap between July 1559 and October 1562 caused by the loss or intentional destruction of one volume in the wake of the siege and sack of 1562. The information in these registers is usefully supplemented by the '*Journaux des Echevins*', forming the series B. (Volumes B 1–5 cover the years 1550–1600 without lacunae.) These provide information on the city's trade and the movement of grain prices as well as about political and administrative matters. The *chartrier*, or collection of other municipal records, proved disappointing. Its *tiroirs* contain none of the tax rolls or customs records which other municipal archives boast, but among them were to be found useful pieces on such matters as poor relief, the city militia, and the mechanics of municipal administration. *Tiroir* 400, containing copies of the city's correspondence with the king and important ministers, proved particularly valuable. Finally, the original copies of the city's parish registers are now in the Archives Communales. As with the *tiroirs* of the *chartrier*, I consulted all those from the sixteenth century.

Archives Départementales de la Seine-Maritime

Housed in a twenty-six story skyscraper that dominates Rouen's skyline, the papers in this collection form one of the richest provincial archives in France. Particularly important are the records of Normandy's administrative tribunals, contained in the series B, and the exceptionally complete church records contained in the series G, although these by no means exhaust the A.D.S.M.'s resources. In addition to the usual records one would expect to find in a past provincial capital, it also houses the dauntingly forbidding mass of Rouen's *tabellionage*, numerous registers about Rouen's guilds in the series 5 E, many sets of private papers in the series 16 J, and the separately catalogued Archives Hospitalières.

The series B was unclassified at the time I consulted it. It contains the records of Normandy's courts, among them the parlement's *registres secrets* and *arrêts*, both essential for reconstructing political events within the city. The *registres secrets* are fragmentary, covering only the years 1570–79, 1581, and 1589–1600, with partial registers for the period 1549–65 and 1569 and records for the parlements of both Rouen and Caen during the period of the League. Fortunately, some of the gaps in the *registres secrets* can be filled in on the basis of extracts made before the missing registers were lost: Bibliothèque Municipale de Rouen, MS Y 214. As for the *arrêts*, their very bulk (several enormous registers per year) discourages their use simply to seek out the occasional *arrêt de reglement*, but I did consult them for those periods which I considered to be particularly important or eventful – 1562–4, 1567–9, 1572–3, and 1588–94. One volume of the *arrêts* deserves particular mention, a special volume covering the period December 1568–June 1569 containing only cases arising out of the royal edict of 1568 which deprived all Protestant office-holders of their positions. The cases come from throughout the province, thus making the volume of interest to researchers working on the history of Protestantism anywhere in Normandy. The *mémoriaux* of the *cour des aides*, registers 3–13, also contained several entries of use.

The ecclesiastical records of the series G provide the basic information about the personnel and functioning of the local ecclesiastical hierarchy, as well as such evidence as survives about parish confraternities. The Registres Capitulaires

(G 2165–80 for the period 1562–1600) reveal the actions of the cathedral chapter and may be supplemented with the chapter's account books and correspondence (G 2546–83, 3620–21, 3716–21). Once again, the Bibliothèque Municipale also contains a multi-volume set of extracts from these registers (B.M.R., MS Y 102), which I consulted for the first six decades of the century. The lifestyle, libraries, and, to a lesser degree, religious attitudes of the chapter's canons and chaplains can be reconstructed from the exceptional collection of their wills and inventories after death (G 3424–42, 3464); these documents extend from the fifteenth to the eighteenth century and would undoubtedly repay extended analysis. G 9869–70 and 9878–80, the statutes, membership lists, and account books of the General Confraternity of the Holy Sacrament, provided the basis for my analysis of that group, while G 9894, 9896, and 9897 are lists of foundations for three parish churches that enabled me to gain some sense of religious attitudes as indicated by the movement of pious foundations. Finally, an excellent collection of parish account books provided an especially rich source whose potential value for both social and religious history has not been sufficiently recognized. Not only do these accounts note the amounts collected annually in the various parish basins, thus indicating changes in popular piety; they also provide through their disbursements a window into the religious activities of the parish. Entries reveal special celebrations, preachers hired, and so forth. Furthermore, the accounts contain a good deal of incidental information about social and economic conditions: material for the study of house rents, door-to-door collections which provide partial censuses of the parishes, occasional lists of Protestants 'reduced' to Catholicism, and even (a Rouennais peculiarity) the payments for *lettres de draperie* which are the best available source for studying the movement of the local cloth industry. The richness of these account books contrasts strikingly with the paucity of documentation concerning the deliberations of the parish *fabriques*. Registers of these deliberations are rare and unrevealing for this period.

Among the other series in the archives, the fiscal records of the Series C yielded two quite important documents: C 216, 'Cotisation sur les marchands', 1565; and C 2314, 'Registre et controole de la recepte generalle de Rouen, 1592', invaluable on taxation during the period of the League. The Series D provided useful information about the early history of the Jesuits in Rouen (D 26–8, 31–2) and the history of education generally (D 324, 329). Cataloguing of the Series E had only begun when I was in Rouen, but among its unclassified parish registers were those of the Reformed Church of Rouen/Quévilly, as well as numerous registers from Rouen's Catholic parishes, for the most part copies of the records in the Archives Communales. (These registers are generally less than complete and must be used with great caution. See here my discussion of the problem of duplicate parish registers in Philip Benedict, 'Catholics and Huguenots in Sixteenth-Century Rouen: The Demographic Effects of the Religious Wars', *French Historical Studies*, IX (1975), Appendix.) Most of the guild records in the Sub-Series 5 E date from the seventeenth or eighteenth century, but the records of the harquebusiers (5 E 116–20), *cinquantaine* (5 E 406), *fondeurs* (5 E 464–5), *merciers* (5 E 594–5, 599–602, 605), and *orfèvres* (5 E 609) did yield relevant information about these groups and the development of industry generally. In the unclassified series H a few pieces of interest were located on the social recruitment and history of the Franciscans and Carmelites, while sub-series 16 J yielded the records of the *bureau de police* for the period 1578–80 (16 J 188).

Bibliothèque Municipale de Rouen

In addition to the volumes of extracts from the parlement's *registres secrets* and the cathedral chapter's deliberations, the manuscript collection of this repository provided several unpublished or partially published local memoirs and *livres de raison:* MS M 41, 'Journal historique de Rouen' (parts of this journal have been published in the *Revue de Rouen*, 1840, and by Albert Sarrazin in 1872); MS Y 128, 'Livre de raison des familles LeCornu et Acart'; and MS Y 202, 'Notes et mémoires de Claude Groulart' (partially published in Michaud and Poujoulat, Vol. 11). The Fonds Leber also contains a rich collection of sixteenth-century books, pamphlets, and published edicts.

Bibliothèque Nationale (Paris)

France's provincial archives are rich, but no historian of any French community can afford to neglect the resources offered by the leading Parisian collections as well. The numerous '*recueils*' and '*mélanges*' of '*lettres*', '*dépêches*', and '*pièces originales*' in the Bibliothèque Nationale's manuscript room contain letters and administrative documents pertaining to every region of France, often revealing details about developments within a community that are not indicated in any local documents. I consulted:

Fonds Français

3155	'Mémoire du règne du roy Henri II'
3216	'Mémoire du règne du roy Charles IX'
3306, 3310	'Mémoire du règne du roy Henri III'
3358, 3389	*Idem.*
3394	*Idem.*
3891	'Mémoires de la Ligue'
3989	'Recueil de lettres et de pièces originales'
15534	'Mélange de pièces anciens'
15543–8	'Lettres servant à l'histoire de France'
15550–53	*Idem.*
15560	*Idem.*
15876	'Lettres et dépêches originales'
15878	*Idem.*
15905	'Lettres escrit à M. de Bellièvre'
15909	*Idem.*
17832	'Instructions aux ambassadeurs et autres pièces d'estat'
20647	'Lettres originales'
23191	*Idem.*
23193	*Idem.*

Nouvelles Acquisitions Françaises
2043 'Mélanges historiques des XVIe et XVIIe siècles'

Also of great value were Fonds Français 23295–6, the manuscript history of the League partially published by Charles Valois; Fonds Français 32318, 'Abrégé historique du Parlement de Rouen'; and Fonds Dupuy 333 and 698, pieces relating to the history of Protestantism in Troyes.

Other Archival Collections

For this period prior to the creation of absolutist administrative structures, the Archives Nationales are far less useful than the Bibliothèque Nationale. I found useful only the Protestant baptismal registers in the Series TT, which are cited above in Appendix 1 along with all of the other registers of the Protestant *état civil* consulted in various provincial archives. Three other Parisian libraries, the Bibliothèque de l'Institut, the Bibliothèque Mazarine, and the Bibliothèque de la Société de l'Histoire du Protestantisme Français, each yielded up a piece of two of minor interest about Rouen, while certain foreign repositories proved somewhat more revealing. The Public Record Office and British Museum each contained scattered pieces of interest. The Archives Tronchin in Geneva's Bibliothèque Publique et Universitaire provided the fascinating 'Remonstrance de ceux de l'église réformée de Rouen' (vol. 8, fos. 76–9) regarding the disputed municipal election of 1566. While in Geneva I was also able to consult the microfilm copies of the articles adopted at the provincial synods of Normandy's Reformed Churches in the Musée Historique de la Réformation. (The originals of these are in the library of the Remonstrant church in Rotterdam.) Finally, the voluminous 'correspondencia dirigida a Simon Ruiz' in the Archivo Histórico Provincial y Universitario de Valladolid turned out to include over 5000 letters dispatched from Rouen containing occasional pieces of information about political developments as well as a detailed view of the city's commerce with Spain. The Archives of the English College of Valladolid contain the vivid letter of Sister Elizabeth Sanders, 'A Note of such Accidents as hath befell us in Fraunce' (series 2, L 5, no. 13).

PRINTED SOURCES

Abrégé d'un journal historique de Rouen, ed. Albert Sarrazin. Rouen, 1872. Other extracts from this journal have been published under the title 'Journal historique de Rouen, extrait d'un manuscrit de la bibliothèque de l'abbé De la Rue', *Revue de Rouen*, 1840.

Actes du consistoire de l'église française de Threadneedle Street, Londres. Vol. 1 (1560–65), ed. Elsie Johnston. Publications of the Huguenot Society of London XXXVIII. Frome, 1937. Vol. 2 (1571–7), ed. Anne M. Oakley. Publications of the Huguenot Society of London XLVIII. London, 1969.

Anderson, R. C., ed. *Letters of the Fifteenth and Sixteenth Centuries from the Archives of Southampton*. Publications of the Southampton Record Society. Southampton, 1921.

Bibliography

Anquetil, Eugène, ed. *Abjurations de Protestants faites à Bayeux : Guerres de religion (1570–1573)*. Bayeux, n.d.

Apologie des ministres et anciens de l'église reformée en la ville de Rouen sur le brisement des images. N.p., 1562.

Archivo documental español: Negociaciones con Francia. 9 vols. Madrid, 1950–59.

Arrests de la court de Parlement et ordonnances faictes sur la police en ceste ville de Rouen. Rouen, 1587.

Beauxamis, Thomas. *Resolution sur certains pourtraictz et libelles intitulez du nom de Marmitte*. Paris, 1562.

La marmite renversée et fondue, de laquelle nostre Dieu parle par les saincts Prophètes. Paris, 1572.

Beza, Theodore. *Epistolarum theologicarum Theodori Bezae Vezelii liber unus*. Geneva, 1573.

'Deux lettres de Théodore de Bèze sur la Saint-Barthélemy', *B.S.H.P.F.*, VII (1858).

Correspondance, ed. H. Meylan et al. 5 vols. Geneva, 1960–.

Bigars, Antoine de, Sr. de la Londe. *Mémoires*, ed. A. Héron. *Société de l'Histoire de Normandie*, *Mélanges*, V.

Bonnardot, François, ed. *Registres des délibérations du Bureau de la Ville de Paris*. Vol. 9 (*1586–90*). Paris, 1902.

Bordier, Henri-Léonard, ed. *Le chansonnier huguenot du XVIe siècle*. Paris, 1870.

Bourgueville, Charles de. *Les recherches et antiquitez de la province de Neustrie, à présent Duché de Normandie*. Caen, 1833.

Bréard, Charles and Paul, eds., *Documents relatifs à la marine normande*. Rouen, 1889.

Briefve et Chrestienne remonstrance à ceux qui pour eviter la persecution esmeue en France, principalement depuis le 24 d'Aoust 1572, ont abiuré la vraye Religion. N.p., 1574.

Calendar of State Papers, Foreign Series, of the Reign of Elizabeth, ed. Joseph Stevenson et al. 23 vols. London, 1863–1950.

Calvin, John. *Institutes of the Christian Religion*. 2 vols. Philadelphia, 1960.

Catherine de Medici. *Lettres de Cathérine de Médicis*, ed. Hector de la Ferrière and Baguenault de Puchesse. 9 vols. Paris, 1880–99.

Cest la deduction du sumptueux ordre plaisantz spectacles et magnifiques theatres dressés et exhibés par les citoiens de Rouen. . . à la sacrée Majesté du Treschristian Roy de France Henry second. . . Rouen, 1551.

Chamberland, A., ed. 'Le commerce d'importation en France au milieu du XVIe siècle d'après un manuscrit de la Bibliothèque Nationale', *Revue de Géographie*, XXXI–XXXIII (1892–3).

Cimber, L. and Danjou, F., eds. *Archives curieuses de l'histoire de France*. 1st ser. 15 vols. Paris, 1834–7.

Les Connivences de Henry de Valois avec Monsieur de Charouges Gouverneur de la ville de Rouen. Paris, 1589.

Crespin, Jean. *Histoire des martyrs persecutez et mis a mort pour la verité de l'evangile, depuis le temps des apostres jusques a present (1619)*. Toulouse, 1889.

Daval, Guillaume and Jean. *Histoire de la Réformation à Dieppe*. Rouen, 1878.

Davila, Enrico. *The Historie of the Civill Warres of France*, trans. William Aylesbury. 2 vols. London, 1647–8.

Declaration du Roy pour le faict de ceulx de la nouvelle opinion qui se sont absentez depuis le XXIIIIe d'Aoust, 1572. Paris, 1572.

Desjardins, Abel, ed. *Négociations diplomatiques de la France avec la Toscane*. 6 vols. Paris, 1859–76.

d'Estaintot, C. R. H. L., ed. *La première campagne de Henri IV en Normandie, Août–Octobre 1589*. Publications of the Société des Bibliophiles Normands XXXII. Rouen, 1878.

De Thou, Jacques-Auguste. *Histoire universelle*. The Hague, 1740.

Dialogue d'entre le maheustre et le manant contenant les raisons de leurs debats et questions en ces presens troubles au Royaume de France. Paris, 1594.

'Discours abbregé et memoires d'aulcunes choses advenues tant en Normandye que en France depuis de commencement de l'an 1559, et principalement en la ville de Rouen', ed. A. Héron. *Deux chroniques de Rouen*. Rouen, 1900.

Dubois, A., ed. *La Ligue: Documents rélatifs à la Picardie d'après les registres de l'échevinage d'Amiens*. Amiens, 1859.

'Etat nominatif des Protestants de la Vicomté de Coutances en 1588', *B.S.H.P.F.*, XXXVI (1887).

Faurin, Jean. *Journal sur les guerres de Castres*, ed. M. de la Pijardière, *Pièces fugitives pour servir à l'histoire de France*. Montpellier, 1878.

Félix, J., ed. *Comptes-rendus des Echevins de Rouen, avec des documents relatifs à leur élection*. Vol. I (*1409–1620*). Rouen, 1890.

Fontanon, Antoine. *Les Edicts et Ordonnances des Roys de France depuis S. Loys jusques à present*. Paris, 1580.

Frederick the Pious. *Briefe Friedrich des Frommen Kurfürsten von der Pfalz*, ed. A. Kluckhohn. Braunschweig, 1872.

Gaches, Jacques. *Mémoires sur les guerres de religion à Castres et dans le Languedoc*. Paris, 1879.

Gamon, Achille. *Mémoires*. Petitot, 1st ser., Vol. 34.

Geisendorf, Paul-F., ed. *Livre des habitants de Genève*. 2 vols. Geneva, 1957–63.

Godfray, H. M., ed. *Registre de l'église wallonne de Southampton*. Publications of the Huguenot Society of London IV. Lymington, 1890.

Gonzaga, Francesco. *De origine Seraphicae Religionis Franciscanae eiusque progressibus*. Rome, 1587.

Gosselin, E. *Documents authentiques et inédits pour servir à l'histoire de la marine normande et du commerce rouennais pendant les XVIe et XVIIe siècles*. Rouen, 1876.

Gouberville, Gilles de. *Journal pour les années 1549, 1550, 1551, 1552*. *Mémoires de la Société des Antiquaires de Normandie*, 4th ser., II (1895).

[Goulard, Simon]. *Memoires de l'estat de France sous Charles IX*. Middleburg, 1578.

Memoires de la Ligue sous Henry III et Henry IIII Rois de France. 6 vols. N.p., 1602.

Groulart, Claude. *Mémoires.* Michaud and Poujoulat, Vol. 11.

Guicciardini, Giovani Battista. *Lettere di Giovani Battista Guicciardini a Cosimo e Francesco di Medici scritte dal Belgio dal 1559 al 1577*, ed. Mario Battistini. Brussels–Rome, 1949.

Harangue faicte au Roy par un depputé particulier de la ville de Rouen dans son cabinet à Bloys le 27 octobre 1588. Paris, 1588.

Haton, Claude. *Mémoires de Claude Haton contenant le récit des événements accomplis de 1553 à 1582, principalement dans la Champagne et la Brie*, ed. Félix Bourquelot. 2 vols. Paris, 1857.

Hervet, Gentian. *Discours de ce que les pilleurs, voleurs, & brusleurs d'eglises disent qu'ilz n'en veulent qu'aux moynes & aux prestres.* Reims, 1563.

Histoire ecclésiastique des églises réformées au royaume de France, eds. G. Baum, E. Cunitz, and R. Reuss. 3 vols. Paris, 1883–9.

L'Histoire et Cronique de Normendie. Rouen, 1578.

d'Huisseau, Isaac. *La discipline des Eglises Réformées de France.* N.p., 1656.

Isambert, Decrusy, and Taillandier. *Recueil général des anciennes lois françaises depuis l'an 420 jusqu'à la Révolution de 1789.* Paris, 1821.

Joüon des Longrais, F., ed. 'Information du Sénéchal de Rennes contre les Ligueurs 1589', *Bulletin et Mémoires de la Société Archéologique du Département d'Ille-et-Vilaine*, XLI (1911).

Journal d'un bourgeois de Rouen, mentionnant quelques événemens arrivés dans cette ville depuis l'an 1545 jusqu'à l'an 1564. Publication of *La Revue de Rouen et de la Normandie.* Rouen, 1837.

Labrosse, Henri, ed. 'Le Livre de Raison de la famille LeCourt de Rouen (XVIe–XVIIe siècle)', *Bull. Soc. Emul. S–I.*, 1937.

La Ligue renversée, ou response à la Ligue ressuscitée. Publications of the Société des Bibliophiles Normands XLIX. Rouen, 1896.

La Mothe-Fénélon, Bertrand de. *Correspondance diplomatique de Bertrand de Salignac de La Mothe-Fénélon, Ambassadeur de France en Angleterre de 1568 à 1575.* 5 vols. Paris–London, 1838–40.

La Popelinière, Lancelot Voysin, sieur de. *La vraye et entiere histoire des troubles...advenues...depuis l'an 1562.* La Rochelle, 1573.

Lart, C. E., ed. *The Registers of the Protestant Church at Loudun 1566–1582.* Lymington, 1905.

Legendre, Philippe. *Histoire de la persecution faicte à l'eglise de Rouen sur la fin du dernier siècle.* Rotterdam, 1704.

Le Laboureur, J. *Les mémoires de Messire Michel de Castelnau, seigneur de Mauvissière, illustrez et augmentez de plusieurs Commentaires et Manuscrits.* Paris, 1659.

Leroux, A., ed. *Nouveaux documents historiques sur la Marche et le Limousin.* Limoges, 1887.

Léry, Jean de. *Au lendemain de la Saint-Barthélemy, guerre civile et famine : Histoire mémorable du Siège de Sancerre (1573) de Jean de Léry*, ed. Geralde Nakam. Paris, 1975.

L'Estoile, Pierre de. *Mémoires-Journaux*, ed. Brunet, Champollion et al. 12 vols. Paris, 1875–96.

Lucinge, René de. *Lettres sur les débuts de la Ligue (1585)*, ed. Alain Dufour. Geneva–Paris, 1964.

Lettres sur la cour d'Henri III en 1586, ed. Alain Dufour. Geneva, 1966.

Martin, Austin Lynn, ed. 'Jesuits and the Massacre of St. Bartholomew's Day', *Archivum Historicum Societatis Iesu*, XLIII (1974).

Mémoires de Conté. London, 1743.

Mémoires d'un calviniste de Millau, ed. J. L. Rigal. Rodez, 1911.

Merlin, Jacques. *Diaire ou journal du ministre Merlin, pasteur de l'église de la Rochelle au XVI*[e] *siècle*, ed. A. Crottet. Geneva, 1855.

Miton, Adrien. 'Mémoire... sur l'histoire de cette ville et des environs depuis 1520 jusqu'en 1640', ed. F. Bouquet. *Documents concernant l'histoire de Neufchâtel-en-Bray et des environs*. Rouen, 1884.

Monluc, Blaise de. *Commentaires*, ed. Paul Courteault. Paris, 1964.

Montaiglon, Anatole de and Rothschild, James de, eds. *Recueil de poésies françoises des XV*[e] *et XVI*[e] *siècles*. 15 vols. Paris, 1855–78.

Ordonnances contre la peste faictes par la court de l'eschiquier. Rouen, 1513.

Ordonnances du roy Henry III...sur les plaintes et doleances faictes par les depputez des Estats de son Royaume convoquez et assemblez en la ville de Bloys. Rouen, 1587.

Palma Cayet, P. V. *Chronologie novenaire*. Petitot, 1st ser., Vol. 38.

Panel, G., ed. *Documents concernant les pauvres de Rouen*. 3 vols. Rouen, 1917–19.

Parsons, Robert. *Letters and Memorials of Father Robert Persons, S.J.* Vol. 1 (to 1588), ed. L. Hicks. Publications of the Catholic Record Society XXXIX. London, 1942.

Pasquier, Etienne. *Lettres historiques pour les années 1556–1594*, ed. D. Thickett. Geneva, 1966.

Pastor, Ludwig, ed. 'Die Reise des Kardinals Luigi d'Aragona durch Deutschland, die Niederlande, Frankreich und Oberitalien, 1517–1518, beschrieben von Antonio de Beatis', *Erläuterungen und Ergänzungen zu Janssens Geschichte des deutschen Volkes*, IV, 4, 3. Freiburg-im-Breisgau, 1905.

Philippi, Jean. *Mémories*. Petitot, 1st ser., Vol. 34.

Plainctes des églises reformées de France sur les violences et injustices qui leur sont faites en plusieurs endroits du Royaume. N.p., 1597.

Prévost, G-A., ed. 'Documents sur le ban et l'arrière-ban, et les fiefs de la vicomté de Rouen en 1594 et 1560, et sur la noblesse du bailliage de Gisors en 1703', *Mélanges de la Société de l'Histoire de Normandie*, 3rd ser. (1895).

Pussot, Jean. 'Mémoires ou Journalier', ed. E. Henry, *Travaux de l'Académie Impériale de Reims*, XXIII (1856) and XXV (1857).

Quintanadoines, Jehan de. *Quintanadueñas: Lettres de Jean de Brétigny (1556–1634)*, ed. Pierre Serouet. Louvain, 1971.

Read, Charles, ed. 'La Saint-Barthélemy à Orléans racontée par Joh.-Wilh. de Botzheim, étudiant allemand témoin occulaire', *B.S.H.P.F.*, XXI (1872).

Relation des troubles excités par les calvinistes dans la ville de Rouen depuis l'an 1537 jusqu'en l'an 1582. Publication of *La Revue de Rouen et de la Normandie*. Rouen, 1837.

Remonstrance chrestienne et salutaire aux François que se sont desvoyez de la vraye Religion et polluez es superstitions et idolatries de la Papauté. N.p., 1586.

Remonstrance des habitans de la ville de Rouen, addressée aux Presidents et Conseillers du Parlement, ayans abandonné le service de Dieu et du Roy pour tenir conventicule à Louviers. N.p., 1562.

Response à une lettre envoyée par un gentil-homme de basse Bretagne à un sien amy estant à la suitte de la Cour sur la misere de ce temps trouvée à Rouen à la porte de Martainville. Rouen, 1588.

Returns of Aliens Dwelling in the City and Suburbs of London from the Reign of Henry VIII to That of James I, eds. R. E. G. and E. F. Kirk. Publications of the Huguenot Society of London X. 2 vols. Aberdeen, 1900–1908.

Richart, Antoine. *Mémoires sur la Ligue dans le Laonnois*. Laon, 1869.

Robillard de Beaurepaire, Charles de, ed. *Séjour de Henri III à Rouen*. Publications of the Société des Bibliophiles Normands XXIV. Rouen, 1870.

Cahiers des Etats de Normandie sous le règne d'Henri IV. Vol. I (1589–1601). Publications of the Société de l'Histoire de Normandie XII. Rouen, 1880.

Inventaire–Sommaire des Archives Communales antérieures à 1790. Vol. I, *Délibérations*. Rouen, 1877.

Cahiers des Etats de Normandie sous le règne d'Henry III. Publications of the Société de l'Histoire de Normandie XX. 2 vols. Rouen, 1888.

Cahiers des Etats de Normandie sous le règne de Charles IX. Publications of the Société de l'Histoire de Normandie XXV. Rouen, 1891.

Sainctes, Claude de. *Le Concile provincial des diocèses de Normandie tenu à Rouen, l'an 1581*. Rouen, 1606.

'La Saint-Barthélemy à Meaux', *Bulletin de la Société de l'Histoire de France*, no. 4 (1838).

Seuille, Jean de. *Brief discours sur la bonne et joyeuse reception faicte à la majesté du Roy par ses très-fidelles et obeissants sujects de la ville de Rouen*. Rouen, 1588.

Sponde, Henry de. *Les Cimitieres Sacrez*. Bordeaux, 1597.

Suite des remonstrances et articles presentez au Roy depuis la derniere requeste de Messieurs les Cardinaux et Princes Catholiques. Rouen, 1588.

Sully, Maximilien de Béthune, Duc de. *Les Oeconomies Royales de Sully*, ed. David Buisseret and Bernard Barbiche. 2 vols. Paris, 1970.

Taillepied, F. N. *Recueil des antiquitez et singularitez de la ville de Rouen*. Rouen, 1587.

Tarbé, P., ed. *Recueil de poésies calvinistes (1550–1566)*. Reprint edition. Geneva, 1968.

Thomas, Pierre. *Mémoires de Pierre Thomas, Sieur du Fossé*, ed. F. Bouquet. Rouen, 1876.

La thraison descouverte des Politiques de la ville de Rouen. Paris, n.d. (1589).

Tommaseo, M. N., ed. *Relations des ambassadeurs vénitiens sur les affaires de France au XVIe siècle*. 2 vols. Paris, 1838.

Tougard, A., ed. *Les trois siècles palinodiques, ou histoire générale des Palinods de*

Rouen, Dieppe, etc. Publications of the Société de l'Histoire de Normandie XXXI. 3 vols. Rouen–Paris, 1898.

Les triomphes de l'Abbaye des Conards. Rouen, 1587.

'Une mission à la Foire de Guibray: lettre d'un ministre normand à Calvin', *B.S.H.P.F.*, XXVIII (1879).

Valdory, Guillaume. *Discours du siège de la ville de Rouen au mois de Novembre mil cinq cens quatre vingts onze*, ed. E. Gosselin. Rouen, 1871.

Valois, Charles, ed. *Histoire de la Ligue, oeuvre inédite d'un contemporain.* Paris, 1914.

Le Vary Pourtraict de la ville de Rouen assiegée et pris par le roy Charles 9. Paris, n.d.

Vazquez de Prada, V., ed. *Lettres marchandes d'Anvers.* 4 vols. Paris, n.d.

Vernyes, Jehan de. *Mémoires, 1589–1593.* Clermont–Ferrand, 1838.

Vielleville, François de Scépeaux, Sire de. *Mémoires.* Michaud and Poujoulat, 1st ser., Vol. 9.

Weiss, Nathaniel, ed. 'Un témoin de la Saint-Barthélemy à Rouen, 17–20 Septembre 1572', *B.S.H.P.F.*, L (1901).

SECONDARY WORKS

A. Rouen and Normandy

Bardet, Jean-Pierre. 'La maison rouennaise aux XVIIe et XVIIIe siècles: Economie et comportements', *Le bâtiment, enquête d'histoire économique XIVe–XIXe siècles*, Vol. 1, 'Maisons rurales et urbaines dans la France traditionnelle'. Paris–The Hague, 1971.

'Enfants abandonnés et enfants trouvés à Rouen dans la seconde moitié du XVIIIe siècle', *Sur la population française au XVIIIe et XIXe siècles: Hommage à Marcel Reinhard.* Paris, 1973.

'Rouen et les Rouennais au XVIIIe siècle', *Etudes Normandes*, XXIII (1974).

and Ricque, Marie-Paule. *Rouen vers 1770.* Caen, 1972.

Baudry, Paul. *L'église paroissiale de Saint-Vincent de Rouen.* Rouen, 1875.

Les religieuses carmélites à Rouen. Rouen, 1875.

Beaujour, Sophronyme. *Essai sur l'histoire de l'église réformée de Caen.* Caen, 1877.

Beauvais, P. de. *La vie de Monsieur de Brétigny, prestre, fondateur des Carmélites de Sainte Thérèse en France et aux Pays-Bas.* Paris, 1747.

Benedict, Philip. 'Catholics and Huguenots in Sixteenth-Century Rouen: The Demographic Effects of the Religious Wars', *French Historical Studies*, IX (1975).

'Heurs et malheurs d'un gros bourg drapant: Note sur la population de Darnétal aux 16e et 17e siècles', *Annales de Normandie*, XXVIII (1978).

'The Catholic Response to Protestantism: Church Activity and Popular Piety in Rouen, 1560–1600'. *Religion and the People, 800–1700*, ed. James Obelkevich. Chapel Hill, 1979.

'Rouen's Foreign Trade During the Era of the Religious Wars (1560–1600)', forthcoming.

Bois, Guy, *Crise du féodalisme: économie rurale et démographie en Normandie orientale du début du 14e siècle au milieu du 16e siècle*. Paris, 1976.

Bonnenfant, G. *Les séminaires normands du XVIe au XVIIIe siècle*. Paris, 1915.

Bost, Charles. *Récits d'histoire protestante régionale pour servir de complément à l'histoire des Protestants de France: Normandie*. Le Havre, 1926.

Bouard, Michel de et al. *Histoire de la Normandie*. Toulouse, 1970.

Bourienne-Savoye. 'Saint-Vincent de Rouen, une paroisse de marchands au XVe siècle', *Bulletin des Amis des Monuments Rouennais* (1958–70).

Cloulas, Ivan. 'Les Ibériques dans la société rouennaise des XVIe et XVIIe siècles', *Revenue des Sociétés Savantes de Haute Normandie*, 61 (1971).

Clutton, George. '"Abel Clemence" of "Rouen": A Sixteenth-Century Secret Press', *The Library*, 4th ser., XX (1939).

Corvisier, André. 'Quelques aspects sociaux des milices bourgeoises au XVIIIe siècle', *Annales de la Faculté des Lettres et Sciences Humaines de Nice*, 9–10 (1969).

Denis, Ferdinand. *Une fête brésilienne célébrée à Rouen en 1550*. Paris, 1851.

D'Estaintot, C. R. H. L. *La Ligue en Normandie 1588–1594*. Paris, 1862.

La Saint-Barthélemy à Rouen, 17–21 Septembre 1572. Rouen, 1877.

Dewald, Jonathan S. 'Magistracy and Political Opposition at Rouen: A Social Context', *The Sixteenth Century Journal*, V (1974).

'The "Perfect Magistrate": Parlementaires and Crime in Sixteenth-Century Rouen', *Archiv für Reformationsgeschichte*, LXVII (1976).

The Formation of a Provincial Nobility: The Magistrates of the Parlement of Rouen, 1499–1610. Princeton, 1980.

Douyère, Christiane. 'Les marchands étrangers à Rouen au 16e siècle (vers 1520–vers 1580): Assimilation ou segrégation?', unpub. thèse de l'Ecole Nationale des Chartes (1973).

Farin, François. *Histoire de la ville de Rouen*. 3 vols. Rouen, 1668.

Floquet, Amable. *Histoire du privilège de Saint-Romain*. 2 vols. Rouen, 1833.

'Histoire des Conards de Rouen', *Bibliothèque de l'Ecole des Chartes*, I (1839–40).

Histoire du Parlement de Normandie. 7 vols. Rouen, 1840–42.

Foisil, Madeleine. *La révolte des Nu-Pieds et les révoltes normandes de 1639*. Paris, 1970.

'Harangue et Rapport d'Antoine Séguier Commissaire pour le Roi en Basse Normandie (1579–1580)', *Annales de Normandie*, XXVI (1976).

Frondeville, Henri de. *Les presidents du Parlement de Normandie (1499–1790): Recueil généalogique*. Paris–Rouen, 1953.

Les conseillers du Parlement de Normandie au seizième siècle (1499–1594). Paris–Rouen, 1960.

Les conseillers du Parlement de Normandie sous Henri IV et sous Louis XIII (1594–1640). Paris–Rouen, 1964.

Glainville, L. de. *Histoire du Prieuré de Saint-Lô de Rouen*. Rouen, 1890.

Join-Lambert, M. 'La pratique religieuse dans le diocèse de Rouen sous Louis XIV', *Annales de Normandie*, III (1953).

'La pratique religieuse dans le diocèse de Rouen de 1707 à 1789', *Annales de Normandie*, V (1955).

La Fontaine-Verwey, H. de. 'Une presse secrète du XVIe siècle: Abel Clémence, imprimeur à Rouen', *Mélanges Frantz Callot*. Paris, 1960.

Lafosse, Henri. *La juridiction consulaire de Rouen, 1556–1791*. Rouen, 1922.

Lavaud, Jacques. *Un poète de cour au temps des derniers Valois: Philippe Desportes (1546–1606)*. Paris, 1936.

Lebeurier, P-F. *Etat des anoblis en Normandie de 1545 à 1661*. Evreux–Paris–Rouen, 1866.

Leclerc, R. *Le protestantisme à Saint-Lô*. Saint-Lô, 1926.

Lemarchand, Guy. 'Crises économiques et atmosphère sociale en milieu urbain sous Louis XIV', *Revue d'Histoire Moderne et Contemporaine*, XIV (1967).

Léonard, Emile-G. *Histoire de la Normandie*. 4th ed. Paris, 1972.

Le Parquier, E. *Contribution à l'histoire de Rouen: Une année de l'administration municipale au XVIe siècle (l'année 1515)*. Rouen, 1895.

Le siège de Rouen en 1562. Sotteville-lès-Rouen, 1907.

'Un chroniqueur rouennais à l'époque de la Réforme: Le chanoine Jean Nagerel', *Congrès du Millénaire de la Normandie (911–1911): Compte-Rendu des Travaux*. Rouen, 1912.

'Un episode de l'histoire de Rouen en 1564', *B.S.H.P.F.*, LXII (1913).

Les élections municipales à Rouen au XVIe siècle. Rouen, 1925.

Levainville, J. *Rouen: Etude d'une agglomération urbaine*. Paris, 1913.

Lloyd, Howell A. *The Rouen Campaign, 1590–1592: Politics, Warfare and the Early-Modern State*. Oxford, 1973.

Martin, L. *Répertoire des anciennes confréries et charités du diocèse de Rouen approuvées de 1434 à 1610*. Fécamp, 1936.

McGowan, Margaret M. *L'entrée de Henri II à Rouen 1550*. Amsterdam, n.d.

Mollat, Michel. 'Collège de Bourbon et Lycée Corneille: Notes de bibliographie et d'histoire', *Bull. Soc. Emul. S-I.*, 1940–41.

'Les hôtes et courtiers dans les ports normands à la fin du Moyen Age', *Revue Historique de Droit Français et Etranger*, 4th ser., XXIV (1946).

Le commerce maritime normand à la fin du Moyen Age. Paris, 1952.

Nicholls, David J. 'The Origins of Protestantism in Normandy: A Social Study'. Unpub. Ph.D dissertation, University of Birmingham (1977).

Osmont de Courtsigny, C. 'Jean LeHennuyer et les Huguenots de Lisieux en 1572', *B.S.H.P.F.*, XXVI (1877).

Ouin-Lacroix, Charles. *Histoire des anciennes corporations d'arts et métiers et des confréries religieuses de la capitale de la Normandie*. Rouen, 1850.

Oursel, M. C. 'Notes pour servir à l'histoire de la Réforme en Normandie au temps de François Ier, principalement dans le diocèse de Rouen', *Mémoires de l'Académie Nationale des Sciences, Arts et Belles-Lettres de Caen*, 1912.

Perrot, J-C. 'Note sur les contrats de mariage normands'. *Structures et relations sociales à Paris au milieu du XVIIIe siècle*, ed. A. Daumard and F. Furet. Paris, 1961.

Pommeraye, Dom J. T. *Histoire des Archevesques de Rouen*. Rouen, 1667.

Histoire de l'Eglise Cathédrale de Rouen. Rouen, 1686.

Prentout, Henri. *Les Etats Provinciaux de Normandie*. Caen, 1925.

Prévost, L. *Histoire de la paroisse et des curés de Saint-Maclou depuis la fondation jusqu'à nos jours*. Rouen, 1970.

Procacci, Giuliano. *Classi sociale e monarchia assoluta nella Francia della prima metà del secolo XVI*. Turin, 1955.

Quenedey, Raymond. *L'habitation rouennaise: Etude d'histoire, de géographie et d'archéologie urbaines*. Rouen, 1926.

Querière, E. de la. *Description historique, archéologique et artistique de l'église paroissiale de Saint-Vincent de Rouen*. Rouen, 1844.

Révah, I. S. 'Le premier établissement des Marranes portugais à Rouen (1603–1607)', *Mélanges Isidore Lévy*. Brussels, 1955.

Robillard de Beaurepaire, Charles de. *Recherches sur l'instruction publique dans le diocèse de Rouen avant 1789*. Evreux, 1872.

Notice sur la Compagnie des Arbalétriers autrement dite la Cinquantaine de Rouen. Rouen, 1885.

Roche, Louis-P. *Claude Chappuys (?–1575): Poète de la cour de François Ier*. Poitiers, 1929.

Roth, Cecil. 'Les Marranes à Rouen, un chapitre ignoré de l'histoire des Juifs de France', *Revue des Etudes Juives*, LXXXVIII (1929).

Rouault de la Vigne, René. 'Les Protestants de Rouen et de Quévilly sous l'Ancien Régime: Leurs registres de l'état civil, leurs cimetières', *Bull. Soc. Emul. S-I.* (1938).

Saint-Denis, H. *Histoire d'Elbeuf*. 2 vols. Elbeuf, 1894.

Sion, Jules. *Les paysans de la Normandie orientale (Pays de Caux, Bray, Vexin Normand, Vallée de la Seine): Etude géographique*. Paris, 1909.

Vanier, Georges. 'Une famille de grands marchands rouennais aux XVIe et XVIIe siècles: Les Legendre', *Bull. Soc. Emul. S-I.* (1946–7).

Veyrat, Maurice. *Essai chronologique et biographique sur les baillis de Rouen (1171–1790)*. Rouen, 1953.

'Les gouverneurs de Normandie du XVe siècle à la Révolution', *Etudes Normandes*, IX (1953).

Voiment, H. *Notes chronologiques sur l'ancien bourg de Darnétal (près Rouen), XIVe siècle–1805*. Evreux, 1900.

Weiss, Nathaniel. 'Note sommaire sur les débuts de la Réforme en Normandie (1523–1547)', *Congrès du Millénaire de la Normandie (911–1911): Compte-Rendu des Travaux*. Rouen, 1912.

Wernham, R. B. 'Queen Elizabeth and the Siege of Rouen, 1591', *Transactions of the Royal Historical Society*, 4th ser., XV (1932).

B. General and comparative

Agulhon, Maurice. *Pénitents et Francs-Maçons de l'ancienne Provence*. Paris, 1968.

Anquez, Léonce. *Histoire des assemblées politiques des Réformés de France (1573–1622)*. Paris, 1859.

Ascoli, Peter M. '"The Sixteen" and the Paris League', unpub. Ph.D. dissertation, University of California at Berkeley (1971).

'French Provincial Cities and the Catholic League', *Occasional Papers of the American Society for Reformation Research*, I (1977).

Barbot, Amos. *Histoire de La Rochelle*. 3 vols. Paris–Saintes, 1886–90.

Baulant, Micheline and Meuvret, Jean. *Prix des céréales extraits de la mercuriale de Paris (1520–1698)*. Paris, 1960.

Baumgartner, Frederic J. *Radical Reactionaries: The Political Thought of the French Catholic League*. Geneva, 1975.

Bayard, F. 'Les Bonvisi, marchands banquiers à Lyon, 1575–1629', *Annales: E.S.C.*, XXVI (1971).

Belle, Edmond. 'La Réforme à Dijon des origines à la fin de la lieutenance-générale de Gaspard de Saulx-Tavanes (1530–1570)', *Revue Bourguignonne*, XXI (1911).

Beloch, K. J. *Bevölkerungsgeschichte Italiens*. 2 vols. Berlin, 1940.

Benedict, Philip. 'The Saint Bartholomew's Massacres in the Provinces', *The Historical Journal*, XXI (1978).

Bennassar, Bartolomé. *Valladolid au siècle d'or, une ville de Castille et sa campagne au XVIe siècle*. Paris–The Hague, 1967.

Bernard, Leon. *The Emerging City: Paris in the Age of Louis XIV*. Durham, N.C., 1970.

Bloch, Marc. *Les caractères originaux de l'histoire rurale française*. 2 vols. Paris, 1951.

Bossy, John. 'Elizabethan Catholicism: The Link with France', unpub. Ph.D. dissertation, Cambridge University (1960).

The English Catholic Community, 1570–1850. Oxford, 1976.

'Review Article: Holiness and Society', *Past and Present*, 75 (1977).

Bourgeon, Jean-Louis. *Les Colbert avant Colbert: Destin d'une famille marchande*. Paris, 1973.

Boutruche, Robert et al. *Bordeaux de 1453 à 1715*. Bordeaux, 1966.

Braudel, Fernand. *La Méditerranée et le monde méditerranéen à l'époque de Philippe II*. 1st ed. Paris, 1949.

and Labrousse, Ernest, eds. *Histoire économique et sociale de la France*. Vol. I in 2 parts, *1450–1660*. Paris, 1977.

Brémond, Henri. *Histoire littéraire du sentiment religieux en France*. 11 vols. Paris, 1916–33.

Browe, Peter. *Die Verehrung der Eucharistie im Mittelalter*. Rome, 1967.

Bücher, Karl. *Die Bevölkerung von Frankfurt am Main im XIV and XV Jahrhundert*. Tubingen, 1886.

Carrière, Victor. *Introduction aux études d'histoire ecclésiastique locale*. 3 vols. Paris, 1936.

'Les lendemains de la Saint-Barthélemy en Languedoc', *Revue de l'Histoire de l'Eglise de France*, XXVII (1941).

Caswell, R. N. 'Calvin's View of Ecclesiastical Discipline', *John Calvin*, Courtenay Studies in Reformation Theology I. Appleford, Berks., 1966.

Chartrou, J. *Les entrées solennelles et triomphales à la Renaissance 1484–1551*. Paris, 1928.

Christian, William A. Jr. *Person and God in a Spanish Valley*. New York, 1972.

Clamageran, J-J. *Histoire de l'impôt en France*. 3 vols. Paris, 1868.

Clark, Peter and Slack, Paul. *English Towns in Transition 1485–1551*. Oxford, 1976.

Coornaert, Emile. *Les Français et le commerce international à Anvers*. 2 vols. Paris, 1961.

Couturier, Marcel. *Recherches sur les structures sociales de Châteaudun 1525–1789*. Paris, 1969.

Crew, Phyllis Mack. *Calvinist Preaching and Iconoclasm in the Netherlands, 1544–1569*. Cambridge, 1978.

Croix, Alain. *Nantes et le Pays nantais au XVIe siècle: Etude démographique*. Paris, 1974.

Dainville, François de. 'Collèges et fréquentation scolaire au XVIIe siècle', *Population*, XII (1957).

Davies, Joan. 'Persecution and Protestantism: Toulouse, 1562–1575', *The Historical Journal*, XXII (1979).

Davis, Natalie Zemon. 'The Protestant Printing Workers of Lyons in 1551', *Aspects de la propagande religieuse*. Geneva, 1957.

'Some Tasks and Themes in the Study of Popular Religion', *The Pursuit of Holiness in Late Medieval and Renaissance Religion*, ed. Charles Trinkaus and Heiko Oberman, Studies in Medieval and Reformation Thought X. Leiden, 1974.

Society and Culture in Early Modern France: Eight Essays. Stanford, 1975.

'Ghosts, Kin, and Progeny: Some Features of Family Life in Early Modern France', *Daedalus*, Spring 1977.

Delumeau, Jean. *Naissance et affirmation de la Réforme*. 3rd ed. Paris, 1973.

Le Catholicisme entre Luther et Voltaire. Paris, 1971.

deSchickler, F. *Les églises du Réfuge en Angleterre*. Paris, 1892.

Devèze, Michel. *La vie de la forêt française au XVIe siècle*. 2 vols. Paris, 1961.

Deyon, Pierre. 'Variations de la production textile aux XVIe et XVIIe siècles: Sources et premiers résultats', *Annales: E.S.C.*, XVIII (1963).

Etude sur la société urbaine au 17e siècle: Amiens, capitale provinciale. Paris, 1967.

Contribution à l'étude des revenus fonciers en Picardie: Les Fermages de l'Hôtel-Dieu d'Amiens et leurs variations de 1515 à 1789. Lille, n.d.

Dominguez Ortiz, Antonio. *Las clases privilegiadas en la España del Antiguo Regimen*. Madrid, 1973.

Doucet, Roger. *Les institutions de la France au XVIe siècle*. 2 vols. Paris, 1948.

Doumergue, Emile. *Jean Calvin, les hommes et les choses de son temps*. 7 vols. Lausanne, 1899–1927.

Drouot, Henri. *Mayenne et la Bourgogne: Etude sur la Ligue en Bourgogne, 1587–1596*. 2 vols. Paris, 1937.

Notes sur la Bourgogne et son esprit public au début du règne de Henri III, 1574–1579. Dijon, 1937.

'Les conseils provinciaux de la Sainte-Union (1589–1595): Notes et questions', *Annales du Midi*, LXV (1953).

Dumoutet, Edouard. *Le désir de voir l'hostie et les origines de la dévotion au Saint-Sacrement*. Paris, 1926.

DuPlessis, Robert. 'Urban Stability in the Netherlands Revolution: A Comparative

Study of Lille and Douai', unpub. Ph.D. dissertation, Columbia University (1973).
'L'église de Vitry-le-François en Août 1561 et les de Vassan', *B.S.H.P.F.*, XL (1891).
Esmein, A. *Cours élémentaire d'histoire du droit français*. Paris, 1921.
Estèbe, Janine. *Tocsin pour un massacre: La saison des Saint-Barthélemy*. Paris, 1968.
and Vogler, B. 'La genèse d'une société protestante: Etude comparée de quelques registres consistoriaux languedociens et palatins vers 1600', *Annales: E.S.C.*, XXXI (1976).
Fagniez, Gustave. *L'économie sociale de la France sous Henri IV 1589–1610*. Paris, 1897.
Faucher, B. 'Les registres d'état civil protestant en France depuis la XVIe siècle jusqu'à nos jours', *Bibliothèque de l'Ecole des Chartes*, LXXXIV (1923).
Febvre, Lucien. *Au coeur religieux du XVIe siècle*. Paris, 1959.
Fouqueray, Henri. *Histoire de la compagnie de Jésus en France des origines à la suppression (1528–1762)*. Paris, 1910.
Fossier, Robert et al. *Histoire de la Picardie*. Toulouse, 1974.
France, Peter. 'Les Protestants à Grenoble au XVIe siècle', *Cahiers d'Histoire*, VII (1962).
Galpern, A. N. *The Religions of the People in Sixteenth-Century Champagne*. Cambridge, Mass., 1976.
Garden, Maurice. *Lyon et les Lyonnais au XVIIIe siècle*. Paris, 1970.
Gascon, Richard. *Grand commerce et vie urbaine au XVIe siècle: Lyon et ses marchands (vers 1520–vers 1580)*. 2 vols. Paris–The Hague, 1971.
Geisendorf, Paul-F. *Histoire d'une famille du Réfuge français: Les Des Gouttes de Saint-Symphorien-le-Châtel en Lyonnais et de Genève*. Geneva, 1943.
Théodore de Bèze. Geneva, 1949.
'Les registres d'état civil protestant des XVIe et XVIIe siècles conservés dans la série TT des Archives Nationales', *Mélanges Charles Braibant*. Paris, 1959.
'Métiers et conditions sociales du premier Réfuge à Genève (1549–1587)', *Mélanges Antony Babel*, Vol. I. Geneva, 1963.
Girard, Albert. *Le commerce français à Séville et Cadix au temps des Habsbourg: Contribution à l'étude du commerce étranger en Espagne aux XVIe et XVIIe siècles*. Paris–Bordeaux, 1932.
Godefroy de Paris. *Les Frères-Mineurs Capucins en France: Histoire de la Province de Paris*. Vol. I. Paris, 1937–9.
Goubert, Pierre. 'Une fortune bourgeoise au XVIe siècle: Jehan Pocquelin, bisaïeul probable de Molière', *Revue d'Histoire Moderne et Contemporaine*, I (1954).
Beauvais et le Beauvaisis de 1600 à 1730, contribution à l'histoire sociale de la France du XVIIe siècle. Paris, 1960.
'Recent Themes and Research in French Population between 1500 and 1700', *Population in History: Essays in Historical Demography*, ed. D. V. Glass and D. E. C. Eversley. London, 1965.

'Registres paroissiaux et démographie dans la France du XVIe siècle', *Annales de Démographie Historique*, 1965.

'Famille et province: contribution à la connaissance des structures familiales dans l'ancienne France', paper presented to the Shelby Cullom Davis Center for Historical Studies, October 22, 1976.

Goy, Joseph and Le Roy Ladurie, Emmanuel. *Les fluctuations du produit de la dîme: Conjoncture décimale et domaniale de la fin du Moyen Age au XVIIIe siècle*. Paris–The Hague, 1972.

Gueneau, Yves. 'Les Protestants dans le Colloque de Sancerre de 1598 à 1685', *Cahiers d'Archéologie et d'Histoire du Berry*, 30–31 (1972).

Guenée, Bernard. *Tribunaux et gens de justice dans le bailliage de Senlis à la fin du Moyen Age (vers 1380–vers 1550)*. Paris, 1963.

Guggenheim, A. H. 'Beza, Viret, and the Church of Nîmes: National Leadership and Local Initiative in the Outbreak of the Religious Wars', *Bibliothèque d'Humanisme et Renaissance*, XXXVII (1975).

Guibert, Louis. 'Les confréries de Pénitents en France et notamment dans le diocèse de Limoges', *Bulletin de la Société Archéologique et Historique du Limousin*, XXVII (1979).

Guiraud, Louise. *Etudes sur la Réforme à Montpellier*. 2 vols. Montpellier, 1918.

Gutton, Jean-Pierre. *La société et les pauvres: L'exemple de la généralité de Lyon, 1534–1789*. Paris, 1971.

Halkin, Léon-E. 'Les martyrologes et la critique: contribution à l'étude du martyrologe protestant des Pays-Bas', *Mélanges Jean Meyhoffer*. Lausanne, 1952.

Harding, Robert R. *Anatomy of a Power Elite: The Provincial Governors of Early Modern France*. New Haven, 1978.

Hardy, W. J. 'Foreign Refugees at Rye', *Proceedings of the Huguenot Society of London*, II (1887–8).

Hauser, Henri. *Ouvriers du temps passé*. Paris, 1899.

'La Réforme et les classes populaires', *Revue d'Histoire Moderne et Contemporaine*, I (1899–1900).

Heawood, Edward. 'Sources of Early English Paper Supply, II – The Sixteenth Century', *The Library*, X (1929–30).

Hélin, Etienne. 'Opinions de quelques casuistes de la Contre-Réforme sur l'avortement, la contraception et la continence dans le mariage'. Hélène Bergues et al. *La prévention des naissances dans la famille, ses origines dans les temps modernes*. Paris, 1960.

Henry, E. *La Réforme et la Ligue en Champagne et à Reims*. St Nicolas, 1867.

Henry, Louis. *Manuel de démographie historique*. Geneva–Paris, 1967.

Hickey, Daniel. 'The Socio-Economic Context of the French Wars of Religion: A Case Study: Valentinois-Diois', unpub. Ph.D. dissertation, McGill University (1973).

Histoire des Protestants en France. Toulouse, 1977.

Huppert, George. *Les Bourgeois Gentilshommes: An Essay on the Definition of Elites in Renaissance France*. Chicago, 1977.

Imbart de la Tour, P. *Les origines de la Réforme*. 4 vols. Paris, 1905–35.

Jacquart, Jean. 'La Fronde des Princes dans la région parisienne et ses conséquences matérielles', *Revue d'Histoire Moderne et Contemporaine*, VII (1960).

La crise rurale en Ile-de-France, 1550–1670. Paris, 1974.

Jeannin, Pierre. *Les marchands au XVIe siècle*. Paris, 1957.

Jensen, De Lamar. *Diplomacy and Dogmatism: Bernardino de Mendoza and the French Catholic League*. Cambridge, Mass., 1964.

Joutard, Philippe et al. *La Saint-Barthélemy, ou les résonances d'un massacre*. Neuchâtel, 1976.

Julia, Dominique. 'Le prêtre au XVIIIe siècle, la théologie et les institutions', *Recherches de Sciences Religieuses*, LVIII (1970).

Karcher, Aline. 'L'Assemblée des Notables de Saint-Germain-en-Laye (1583)', *Bibliothèque de l'Ecole des Chartes*, CXIII (1955).

Kingdon, Robert M. *Geneva and the Coming of the Wars of Religion in France, 1555–1563*. Geneva, 1956.

'Problems of Religious Choice for Sixteenth-Century Frenchmen', *Journal of Religious History*, IV (1966).

Geneva and the Consolidation of the French Protestant Movement, 1564–1572. Geneva, 1967.

Kleinclausz, A. et al. *Histoire de Lyon*. Lyon, 1939.

Koch, A. C. F. 'The Reformation at Deventer in 1579–1580: Size and Social Structure of the Catholic Section of the Population during the Religious Peace', *Acta Historiae Neerlandicae*, VI (1973).

Koenigsberger, H. G. 'The Organization of the Revolutionary Parties in France and the Netherlands during the Sixteenth Century', *Journal of Modern History*, XXVII (1955).

Lachiver, Marcel. *La population de Meulan du XVIIe au XIXe siècle (vers 1600–vers 1870): Etude de démographie historique*. Paris, 1969.

Lacombe, Bernard de. *Les débuts des guerres de religion (Orléans, 1559–1564): Cathérine de Médicis entre Guise et Condé*. Paris, 1899.

Lapeyre, Henri. *Une famille de marchands, les Ruiz: Contribution à l'étude du commerce entre la France et l'Espagne au temps de Philippe II*. Paris, 1955.

Laronze, Charles. *Essai sur le régime municipal en Bretagne pendant les guerres de religion*. Paris, 1890.

Latreille, André et al. *Histoire de Lyon et du Lyonnais*. Toulouse, 1975.

Leach, E. R. *Political Systems of Highland Burma: A Study of Kachin Social Structure*. Boston, 1965.

Le Bras, Gabriel. *Etudes de sociologie religieuse*. Paris, 1956.

Lebrun, François. *Les hommes et la mort en Anjou aux 17e et 18e siècles: Essai de démographie et de psychologie historiques*. Paris–The Hague, 1971.

'Démographie et mentalités: Le mouvement des conceptions sous l'ancien régime', *Annales de Démographie Historique* (1974).

et al. *Histoire d'Angers*. Toulouse, 1975.

Léonard, Emile G. *Le Protestant français*. Paris, 1953.

'Les origines de la Réforme et France', *Calvin et la Réforme en France*. 2nd ed. Aix-en-Provence, 1959.

Histoire générale du Protestantisme. Paris, 1961.

Lepelley, Claude. *L'empire romain et le christianisme*. Paris, 1969.

Le Roy Ladurie, Emmanuel. 'Sur Montpellier et sa campagne aux XVIe et XVIIe siècles', *Annales: E.S.C.*, XII (1957).

Les paysans de Languedoc. Paris, 1966.

Le territoire de l'historien. Paris, 1973.

Lestocquoy, Jean. *Histoire de la Picardie et du Boulonnais*. 2nd ed. Paris, 1970.

Lewis, Gwynn. 'The White Terror of 1815 in the Department of the Gard: Counter-Revolution, Continuity and the Individual', *Past and Present*, 58 (1973).

Livet, Georges. *Les guerres de religion*. Paris, 1962.

Mahieu, E. 'Les martyrs montois dans les martyrologes', *Sources de l'histoire religieuse de la Belgique, Moyen Age et Temps modernes*. Louvain, 1968.

Mandrou, Robert. *Introduction à la France Moderne, 1500–1640: Essai de psychologie historique*. 2nd ed. Paris, 1974.

Marchand, Charles. *Le Maréchal François de Scépeaux de Vielleville et ses Mémoires*. Paris, 1893.

Mariéjol, Jean H. *La Réforme et la Ligue*. Vol. 6[1] of Ernest Lavisse, *Histoire de France*. Paris, 1904.

Martin, A. Lynn. *Henry III and the Jesuit Politicians*. Geneva, 1973.

Mastellone, Salvo. *Venalità e machiavellismo in Francia (1572–1610): All'origine della mentalità politica borghese*. Florence, 1972.

Mathorez, J. *Les étrangers en France sous l'Ancien Régime*. 2 vols. Paris, 1919–21.

Maugis, Edouard. *Recherches sur les transformations du régime politique et social de la ville d'Amiens des origines de la commune à la fin du XVIe siècle*. Paris, 1906.

Histoire du parlement de Paris de l'avènement des rois Valois à la mort d'Henri IV. 3 vols. Paris, 1916.

Maury, Alfred. 'La Commune de Paris de 1588', *Revue des Deux Mondes*, XCV (1871).

McGrath, Patrick. *Papists and Puritans under Elizabeth I*. London, 1967.

Merle, Louis. *La métairie et l'évolution agraire de la Gâtine poitevine de la fin du Moyen Age à la Révolution*. Paris, 1958.

Messance, M. *Recherches sur la population des généralités d'Auvergne, de Lyon, de Rouen et de quelques provinces et villes du Royaume*. Paris, 1766.

Meyer, Jean et al. *Histoire de Rennes*. Toulouse, 1972.

Mieck, Ilja. 'Die Bartholomäusnacht als Forschungsproblem: Kritische Bestandaufnahme und Neue Aspekte', *Historische Zeitschrift*, CCXVI (1973).

Moeller, Bernd. *Imperial Cities and the Reformation*, trans. H. C. E. Midelfort and M. U. Edwards, Jr. Philadelphia, 1972.

Mollat, Michel et al. *Histoire de l'Ile-de-France et de Paris*. Toulouse, 1971.

Mols, Roger, *Introduction à la démographie historique des villes d'Europe du XIVe au XVIIIe siècle*. 3 vols. Louvain, 1954–6.

Monter, E. William. *Calvin's Geneva*. New York, 1967.

'The Consistory of Geneva, 1559–1569', *Bibliothèque d'Humanisme et Renaissance*, XXXVIII (1976).

Moreau, Gérard, *Histoire du Protestantisme à Tournai jusqu'à la veille de la Révolution des Pays-Bas*. Paris, 1962.

Mourin, Ernest. *La Réforme et la Ligue en Anjou*. Paris–Angers, 1856.
Mours, Samuel. *Le Protestantisme en Vivarais et en Velay des origines à nos jours*. Valence, 1949
Les églises réformées en France. Paris, 1958.
Le Protestantisme en France au XVIe siècle. Paris, 1959.
Mousnier, Roland. *La vénalité des offices sous Henri IV et Louis XIII*. Rouen, 1945.
L'assassinat d'Henri IV. Paris, 1964.
Olivier-Martin, F. *Histoire du droit français des origines à la Révolution*. Paris, 1948.
Ouvré, Henri, 'Essai sur l'histoire de la Ligue à Poitiers', *Mémoires de la Société des Antiquaires de l'Ouest*. 1854.
Pallier, Denis. *Recherches sur l'imprimerie à Paris pendant la Ligue (1585–1594)*. Geneva, 1975.
Pecquet, Marguerite. 'Des compagnies de Pénitents à la Compagnie du Saint-Sacrement', *XVIIe Siècle*, 69 (1965).
Perouas, Louis. *Le diocèse de La Rochelle de 1648 à 1724: Sociologie et pastorale*. Paris, 1964.
Petit-Dutaillis, Charles. *Les communes françaises: Caractères et évolution des origines au XVIIIe siècle*. Paris, 1947.
Picot, Georges. 'Recherches sur les quarteniers, cinquanteniers et dixainiers de la ville de Paris', *Mémoires de la Société de l'Histoire de Paris et de l'Ile-de-France*, I (1875).
Pineaux, Jacques. *La poésie des Protestants de langue française, du premier synode nationale jusqu'à la proclamation de l'Edit de Nantes (1559–1598)*. Paris, 1971.
Poëte, Marcel. *Une vie de cité: Paris de sa naissance à nos jours*. 3 vols. Paris, 1931.
Porchnev, Boris. *Les soulèvements populaires en France de 1623 à 1648*. Paris, 1963.
Poujol, Jacques. 'De la Confession de Foi de 1559 à la Conjuration d'Amboise', *B.S.H.P.F.*, CXIX (1973).
Pound, J. F. 'An Elizabethan Census of the Poor', *University of Birmingham Historical Journal*, VIII (1962).
'The Social and Trade Structure of Norwich 1525–1575', *Past and Present*, 34 (1966).
Pradel, Charles. 'Un marchand de Paris au seizième siècle (1564–1588)', *Mémoires de l'Académie des Sciences, Inscriptions et Belles-Lettres de Toulouse*, ser. 9, I and II (1889–90).
Prarond, Ernest. *La Ligue à Abbeville, 1576–1594*. 2 vols. Paris, 1873.
Richard, P. *La papauté et la Ligue française: Pierre d'Epinac, Archevêque de Lyon (1573–1599)*. Paris, 1901.
Richard, Willy. *Untersuchungen zur Genesis der reformierten Kirchenterminologie der Westschweiz und Frankreichs mit besonderer Berücksichtigung der Namengebung*. Romanica Helvetica LVII. Bern, 1959.
Richet, Denis. *La France moderne: L'esprit des institutions*. Paris, 1973.
'Aspects socio-culturels des conflits religieux à Paris dans la seconde moitié du XVIe siècle', *Annales: E.S.C.*, XXXII (1977).
Robiquet, Paul. *Paris et la Ligue*. Paris, 1886.
Roelker, Nancy Lyman. 'The Appeal of Calvinism to French Noblewomen in the Sixteenth Century', *Journal of Interdisciplinary History*, II (1972).

Romier, Lucien. *Les origines politiques des guerres de religion*. 2 vols. Paris, 1913–14.
Le royaume de Cathérine de Médicis. 2 vols. Paris, 1922.
La conjuration d'Amboise. Paris, 1923.
Catholiques et Huguenots à la cour de Charles IX. Paris, 1924.

Rosenberg, David. 'Social Experience and Religious Choice: A Case Study, the Protestant Weavers and Woolcombers of Amiens in the Sixteenth Century', unpub. Ph.D. dissertation, Yale University (1978).

Saint-Jacob, P. de. 'Mutations économiques et sociales dans les campagnes bourguignonnes à la fin du XVIe siècle', *Etudes Rurales*, I (1961).

Salmon, J. H. M. 'The Paris Sixteen, 1584–94: The Social Analysis of a Revolutionary Movement', *Journal of Modern History*, XLIV (1972).
Society in Crisis: France in the Sixteenth Century. New York, 1975.

Saulnier, Eugène. *Le rôle politique du Cardinal de Bourbon (Charles X), 1523–1590*. Paris, 1912.

Saulnier, V-L. 'Autour du Colloque de Poissy: les avatars d'une chanson de Saint-Gelais à Ronsard et Théophile', *Bibliothèque d'Humanisme et Renaissance*, XX (1958).

Scribner, R. W. 'Why was there no Reformation in Cologne?', *Bulletin of the Institute of Historical Research*, XLIX (1976).

Seguin, J.-P. *L'information en France avant la périodique*. Paris, 1964.

Shennan, J. H. *Government and Society in France 1461–1661*. London, 1969.

Stone, Lawrence. *The Crisis of the Aristocracy, 1558–1641*. Oxford, 1965.

Thomas, Keith. *Religion and the Decline of Magic*. New York, 1971.

Thompson, James Westfall. *The Wars of Religion in France 1559–1576: The Huguenots, Catherine de Medici and Philip II*. Chicago, 1909.

Toussaert, Jacques. *Le sentiment religieux en Flandre à la fin du Moyen-Age*. Paris, 1963.

Trocmé, Etienne. 'La Rochelle de 1560 à 1628: Tableau d'une société réformée au temps des guerres de religion', unpub. thèse de théologie protestante, Paris (1950).
'L'Eglise Réformée de La Rochelle jusqu'en 1628', *B.S.H.P.F.*, IC (1952).
and Delafosse, Marcel. *Le commerce rochelais de la fin du XVe siècle au début du XVIIe siècle*. Paris, 1952.

Van Doren, Liewain. 'Revolt and Reaction in the City of Romans, Dauphiné, 1579–1580', *The Sixteenth Century Journal*, V (1974).

Van Roey, J. 'De correlatie tussen het sociale-beroepsmilieu en de godsdienstkeuze te Antwerpen op het einde der XVIe eeuw', *Sources de l'histoire religieuse de la Belgique, Moyen Age et Temps modernes*. Louvain, 1968.

Venard, Marc. 'Les confréries de Pénitents au XVIe siècle dans la province ecclésiastique d'Avignon', *Mémoires de l'Académie de Vaucluse*, 6th ser., I (1967).

Vivanti, Corrado. *Lotta politica e pace religiosa in Francia fra Cinque e Seicento*. Turin, 1963.

Vovelle, Michel. 'Analyse spectrale d'un diocèse méridional au XVIIIe siècle: Aix-en-Provence', *Provence Historique*, XXII (1972).

Piété baroque et déchristianisation en Provence au XVIIIe siècle: Les attitudes devant la mort d'après les clauses des testaments. Paris, 1973.

Wolfe, Martin. *The Fiscal System of Renaissance France.* New Haven, 1972.

Wolff, Philippe. *Histoire de Toulouse.* Toulouse, 1961.

Yates, Frances A. 'Dramatic Religious Processions in Paris in the Late Sixteenth Century', *Annales Musicologiques: Moyen Age et Renaissance*, II (1954).

Zeller, Gaston, 'L'Administration monarchique avant les intendants: parlements et gouverneurs', *Revue Historique*, CXCVIII (1947).

Les institutions de la France au XVIe siècle. Paris, 1948.

Index

Index

Index

Index

Index

Index

Index

DUE DATE

201-6503

Print
in